CANADIAN PROFESSIONAL
ENGINEERING
PRACTICE AND ETHICS

10

chen

CANADIAN PROFESSIONAL

ENGINEERING

PRACTICE AND ETHICS

GORDON C. ANDREWS
UNIVERSITY OF WATERLOO

JOHN D. KEMPER
UNIVERSITY OF CALIFORNIA, DAVIS

SAUNDERS COLLEGE, CANADA
A DIVISION OF HOLT, RINEHART AND WINSTON OF CANADA, LIMITED

TORONTO MONTREAL ORLANDO FORT WORTH SAN DIEGO
PHILADELPHIA LONDON SYDNEY TOKYO

Every reasonable effort has been made to acquire permission for copyright
material used in this text, and to acknowledge all such indebtedness
accurately. Any errors and omissions called to the publisher's attention will
be corrected in future printings.

Canadian Cataloguing in Publication Data
  Andrews, G.C. (Gordon Clifford), 1937–
    Canadian professional engineering practice and ethics

  Includes index.
  ISBN 0-03-922875-4

  1. Engineering — Vocational guidance — Canada.
  2. Engineering ethics. I. Kemper, John Dustin.
  II. Title.

  TA157.A53 1992   620'.00971   C91-094680-9

Editorial Director: *Scott Duncan*
Developmental Editor: *Sarah J. Duncan*
Editorial Assistant: *Lee Donald*
Director of Publishing Services: *Steve Lau*
Editorial Manager: *Liz Radojkovic*
Editorial Co-ordinator: *Semareh Al-Hillal*
Production Manager: *Sue-Ann Becker*
Production Assistant: *Sandra Miller*
Copy Editor: *Barbara Czarnecki*
Cover and Interior Design: *Dave Peters*
Typesetting and Assembly: *Bookman Typesetting Co.*
Printing and Binding: *Webcom Limited*

Cover Art: Kell Brothers, lithographers. *Putting Up Side Plates and Top of
Tube*, coloured lithograph. Used with permission of the Canadiana
Department, Royal Ontario Museum, Toronto.

∞ This book was printed in Canada on acid-free paper.

2 3 4 5   00 99 98 97

PREFACE

The goals of this text are to acquaint readers with the structure, practice, and ethics of the engineering profession and to encourage engineers to apply ethical concepts in their professional practice. The text is intended for senior undergraduate engineering students, recent university graduates who are beginning their careers in engineering, practising engineers, and foreign engineers who have immigrated to Canada and wish to practise engineering. The text is directed to engineers in every branch of the profession, practising in any province or territory of Canada, and should be of particular value to persons preparing to write the professional practice examination.

Engineering is a creative profession that played a key role in establishing Canada as a nation. The engineering profession will be even more important to Canada in the future. Canada's riches and political stability should permit the entrepreneurial spirit to flourish, particularly in the next few years as we tap the unknown potential of computer development and applications. Engineers will be among the key participants who generate future prosperity.

Engineers will also be essential in addressing the challenges of international competition and the problems of pollution and waste management, which are already serious threats to the Canadian way of life. As we look further into the twenty-first century, the world problems of overpopulation and shortages of housing, food, and energy will be felt in Canada. Many of these social problems may have engineering solutions, and all of them have ethical implications.

Organization

The text is in four parts.

Introduction – The first two chapters introduce the reader to the engineering profession and to the specific laws that regulate it in Canada. A brief statistical summary shows the distribution and employment of engineers in Canada, and the various provincial and territorial statutes that regulate the engineering profession are reviewed. The standards for admission to the profession are summarized, and the significance of codes of ethics and the definition of professional misconduct are clearly defined. This section concludes with descriptions of the engineer's seal, the iron ring, and the engineering oath. (American practice for regulating the engineering profession is described in a brief appendix, for comparison with Canadian procedures.)

Professional Practice – The second part consists of three chapters that describe the working environment of the engineer in industry, management, and private practice. The text discusses the requirements for entering each sphere of activity, and the typical problems to be encountered. Advice and suggestions are given to avoid some of these problems and to develop a professional approach to engineering practice.

Professional Ethics – The third part deals with professional ethics and consists of seven chapters that outline the basic derivation of ethical theory and codes of ethics, their application to typical ethical problems in industry, management, government, and private practice, and how engineers can best deal with these problems. This section describes extensively the problems associated with product safety, professional misconduct, and the engineer's duty to report (or whistleblowing). The topic of whistleblowing is particularly relevant at this time, since the provincial Associations of Professional Engineers are recognizing the need for an orderly process of reporting unethical behaviour and are accepting a key role in the process. Twenty-five case and historical studies are described in detail.

Maintaining Engineering Competence – The fourth part of the text includes two chapters describing the problem of maintaining continued competence in a rapidly changing world; suggestions for combatting this problem are recommended. Some practical advice is given for engineers contemplating graduate studies, and the importance of engineering societies in communicating new ideas is emphasized. A chapter is devoted to the important topic of choosing and enrolling in an engineering society. In the final chapter, the authors give advice for writing the professional practice examination, which must be passed to gain admission to the profession. Sixty typical examination questions from several provinces are included.

Features

Readers will find this a comprehensive yet readable text that follows a logical sequence in the study of professional engineering practice and ethics. The text is appropriate for individual study, for classroom use, or as a reference for practising engineers. The goals set for the text are achieved through the following features:

- a logical, readable style

- comprehensive coverage of the topic from basic to advanced concepts, suitable for every province and territory in Canada, including comments on some aspects of American practice

- seventeen realistic case studies of ethical problems that ask the reader to suggest the appropriate course of action, followed by the authors' recommended solution for each case

- eight historical studies in which engineering practices that deviated from ethical standards led to disaster or personal tragedy

- sixty brief, typical examination questions, taken from professional practice examinations in several provinces, to assist those readers preparing for examinations

- discussion of professional practice from three perspectives: the engineer as employee, the engineer as manager, and the engineer in private practice

- advice for young engineers to guide their engineering careers

- appropriate excerpts from all of the provincial and territorial statutes that regulate engineering (in appendices), including the codes of ethics and definitions of professional misconduct for all provinces and territories

- extensive reference material (in appendices) concerning guidelines for professional employees, addresses of provincial and territorial Associations of Professional Engineers, and American registration procedures

- topics for further study and discussion, in a standard format, following each chapter

ACKNOWLEDGEMENTS

Professor Kemper and I have received immense help and guidance from many people during the preparation of this manuscript. The task of assembling the joint work into a final manuscript with a Canadian perspective has been my responsibility. I would like to thank all those persons who contributed to making this text a reality, through conversations, provision of materials, or agreement to publish copyrighted articles. Special thanks are due to Scott Duncan of HBJ-Holt Canada, who conceived the project and pushed it through the early stages, and to Sarah Duncan, who is a charming editor with high editorial standards. Grant Boundy, Deputy Registrar of the APEO, and Stephen Jack, Director of Communications for the APEO, graciously co-operated by providing advice and materials, for which I am indebted. Georges Lozano and Wendy Ryan-Bacon of CCPE were very courteous and helpful in response to my inquiries. Colleagues Norman Ball, David Burns, Alan Hale, and Dick van Heeswijk provided encouragement and written material. The contribution of all those who reviewed the manuscript in its various stages is gratefully acknowledged. The reviewers were G.A. Bernard of APEGGA; Wendy Ryan-Bacon of CCPE; Grant Boundy of APEO; E.R. Corneil of Queen's University; Dennis Brooks of APEGGA; John Gartner of Gartner/Lee Limited; C. Peter Jones, formerly of the University of British Columbia; Harold Macklin of LINMAC Inc.; and Gordon Slemon of the University of Toronto. Computer facilities provided by the Manufacturing Research Corporation of Ontario (MRCO) and the National Sciences and Engineering Research Council (NSERC) were invaluable in the preparation of the manuscript. This assistance was important and much appreciated. A very special thanks is due to my secretary, Kathy Roenspiess, who diligently typed (and retyped) the manuscript and contributed many suggestions to improving it. Finally, I would like to thank my graduate students, my wife, Isobelle, and my children, Christopher and Gail Stephanie, for tolerating my reclusive behaviour during the latter stages of this project.

G.C. Andrews
Waterloo, Ontario
December 1991

About the Cover

Our cover features a coloured lithograph depicting the construction of the Victoria Bridge. The bridge spans the St. Lawrence River, and was erected in 1859 as part of the Grand Trunk Railway. The Grand Trunk Railway (GTR) itself was built to provide a main trunk line across the "Province of Canada," and the first leg of track laid was that from Montreal to Toronto. The Victoria Bridge was a key component of the trunk line, and is remembered as one of the most notable engineering feats ever accomplished by the Railway.

The Victoria Bridge is made of tubular wrought iron, and rests on two abutments and twenty-four piers that were designed to resist the crushing ice of the St. Lawrence. The original spans were built from wrought iron rectangular boxes. In the 1890s, however, the GTR began a massive betterment program on its property, and the iron boxes of the Victoria Bridge were replaced by steel trusses. Civil engineer Joseph Hobson also replaced the superstructure with new materials. Amazingly, he accomplished this without interrupting traffic on the bridge.

At the time of Confederation, the Grand Trunk Railway was the largest railway system in the world, maintaining 2055 kilometres of track. However, the Railway ended up a financial disaster and was eventually placed under the management of the Canadian Pacific Railway. No matter the fate of its builders, the Victoria Bridge remains a historic achievement in Canadian engineering.

Publisher's Note to Students and Instructors

This textbook is a key component of your course. If you are the instructor of this course, you undoubtedly considered a number of texts carefully before choosing this as the one that would work best for your students and you. The authors and publishers spent considerable time and money to ensure its high quality, and we appreciate your recognition of this effort and accomplishment. Please note the copyright statement.

If you are a student, we are confident that this text will help you to meet the objectives of your course. It will also become a valuable addition to your personal library.

Since we want to hear what you think about this book, please be sure to send us the stamped reply card at the end of the text. Your input will help us to continue to publish high-quality books for your courses.

C O N T E N T S

CHAPTER 7

Ethical Problems of Engineers in Industry   115

CHAPTER 8

Ethical Problems of Engineers in Management   133

CHAPTER 9

Ethical Problems of Engineers in Private Practice   151

CHAPTER 10

The Engineer's Duty to Society and the Environment   173

CHAPTER 11

Product Safety 211

CHAPTER 12

Disciplinary Powers and Procedures 225

CHAPTER 13

Maintaining Engineering Competence 237

Introduction to the Engineering Profession

The term *engineer* comes from the Latin word *ingenium*, meaning "talent, genius, cleverness, or native ability." The first engineers were soldiers, chosen because of their ingenuity, who were able to devise and operate weapons of war. In time, non-military or "civil" engineers came to supervise the construction of roads, bridges, canals, and irrigation systems. Today the term has become more general, and an engineer is defined as "a person who uses science, mathematics and technology, in a creative way, to satisfy human needs."[1] This definition emphasizes that engineering is the process of putting ideas to practical use, for the common good. An engineer must be a combination of scientist and mathematician, a creative person capable of making decisions and solving problems, and an ethical person, willing to put public welfare ahead of narrow personal gain.

In Canada, the titles "Engineer" and "Professional Engineer" are restricted by law to those persons who have demonstrated their competence and have been licensed in a provincial or territorial Association of Professional Engineers[2] (in Quebec, the Ordre des ingénieurs du Québec). In 1991, there were approximately 140 000 professional engineers licensed in Canada. The regulation of the engineering profession and licensing of engineers are discussed in more detail in Chapter 2.

THE ROLE OF THE ENGINEER

Engineers are primarily concerned with *design and development*, which is the creative process of converting theoretical concepts into useful applications. Engineers may occasionally work alone as consultants or employees, particularly on small projects. However, complex technical projects usually require a team approach, involving persons with widely different abilities, interests, and education who co-operate by contributing a particular expertise to advance the project. Engineers are only one group in the technical spectrum, although they constitute the vital link between theory and application. The full list would include research scientists, engineers, technologists, technicians, and skilled workers. The following capsule descriptions give a rough idea of the typical tasks performed by the different groups in a technical team. (Exceptions to this rough categorization are common, and later in this chapter we will describe a surprisingly wide range of functions that engineers perform.)

Research Scientist – The scientist usually develops ideas that expand the frontiers of knowledge but may not have practical applications for many years. The doctorate is usually the basic educational requirement, although a master's degree is occasionally acceptable. The scientist is rarely required to supervise other technical personnel, except research assistants, and will usually be a member of several learned societies in the particular field of interest.

Typically, the basic task of the scientist is to perform *research* (creating new knowledge), while the basic task of the engineer is to perform *design and development* (creating new things). It is sometimes only the goal of the work, not the actual duties, that differentiates the two. During the 1960s, when the United States was trying to get its space program going, engineers became concerned that every successful rocket firing was hailed as a "scientific achievement" whereas every unsuccessful test was called an "engineering failure." Obviously, the roles of the scientist and the engineer overlap to some degree, and in some projects the boundary may be invisible.

A scientist may be primarily a theoretician (that is, may specialize in creating new theoretical explanations for unexplained phenomena) or primarily an experimentalist. In either event, the final output is usually a report or paper published in a scholarly journal. As soon as the results of a given project are published, the scientist's job is complete with respect to that particular piece of information, and it is the engineer's task to carry the theory through to a useful application.

Engineer – The engineer usually provides the key link between theory and practical applications. The engineer must have a combination of extensive theoretical knowledge, the ability to think creatively, and the knack of obtaining practical results. The bachelor's degree is the basic educational requirement, although the master's degree may be preferred by some employers. In Canada, the engineer is required, by provincial laws, to be a member of the provincial (or territorial) Association of Professional Engineers in order to practise engineering.

Engineers are usually concerned with the creation of devices, systems, and structures for human use. However, it should be noted that the results of an engineer's work may not always be tangible. For example, many engineers are engaged in the management of resources. Engineers are also frequently employed in liaison or consulting capacities in construction, testing, and manufacturing and as agents for government bodies. These engineers are not directly engaged in design, but design is still at the core of their activities. Their role is usually to interpret the design and to see that it is carried out correctly.

Technologist – The technologist usually works under the direction of engineers in applying engineering principles and methods to fairly complex engineering problems. The basic educational requirement is usually graduation from a technology program at a community college, CEGEP (collège d'enseignement général et professionel), or CAAT (college of applied art and technology), although occasionally a technologist may have a bachelor's degree (usually in science, mathematics, or related subjects). The technologist often supervises the work of others and is encouraged to have qualifications that are recognized by a technical society. In some provinces, an association of certified engineering technicians and technologists may confer the designation "Certified Engineering Technologist" (CET). These are voluntary organizations and the title is a beneficial but not essential requirement to work as a technologist.

Technician – The technician usually works under the supervision of an engineer or technologist in the practical aspects of engineering tests and maintenance of equipment. The basic educational requirement is usually graduation from a program at a community college, CEGEP, or CAAT. In some provinces, the title "Certified Engineering Technician" (C. Tech.) may be awarded to qualified technicians, although the title is not essential to work as a technician.

The designations for both technologist and technician are awarded, based on appropriate requirements, by provincial associations of technicians and technologists. In 1991, there were approximately 40 000 certified technicians and technologists in Canada. However, since certification is voluntary, there were probably many more people actually practising as technicians or technologists. The number is estimated to be approximately equal to the number of professional engineers practising in Canada (140 000).

Skilled Worker – The skilled worker usually applies highly developed manual skills to carry out the designs and plans of others. The skilled worker's ability can be learned only at the side of a master artisan; it is the quality of this apprenticeship, not the formal education, that is important. Each type of trade worker (such as an electrician, plumber, carpenter, welder, pattern maker, or machinist) has a different trade guild and certification procedure, which may vary slightly from province to province.

The general categories described above are not, in reality, quite as clearly defined as these rough descriptions might indicate; the boundaries are not and should not be rigid barriers. Transition from one group to another is always possible, although it may not always be easy. Each group in this technical spectrum has a different task, and there are great differences in the skills, knowledge, and training required. In a large project, all five types of technical expertise will be required, although at different times. For a major project to be successfully completed, co-operation is essential between these five groups, and mutual respect for the particular skills and knowledge of each individual creates a positive, productive working environment. Although the task of the engineer is only one phase of a continuous spectrum of technical knowledge, the engineer is usually the key link between theory and practice.

BRANCHES OF ENGINEERING

Over the years, many different branches or disciplines have been established in engineering. The traditional branches are civil, electrical, mechanical, and chemical engineering. Aerospace, industrial, metallurgical, mining, geological, agricultural, and biomedical engineering branches are also recognized by the provincial Associations of Professional Engineering. In addition, since university engineering programs are accredited in Canada on an individual basis, other programs such as computer engineering and systems design are accredited at specific institutions. In the United States, the larger technical base has encouraged even more specific branches to be recognized, as the following partial list shows:

aeronautical and aerospace
  engineering
agricultural engineering
automotive engineering
biomedical engineering
ceramic engineering
chemical engineering
civil engineering
computer engineering
electrical and electronics
  engineering
engineering mechanics
environmental engineering
industrial engineering

manufacturing engineering
marine engineering
materials science and
  engineering
mechanical engineering
mining engineering and
  geological engineering
nuclear engineering
ocean engineering
petroleum engineering
systems engineering
telecommunications
  engineering

The choice of a branch is important and is usually made on entry to university or during the first year of university. Changes from branch to branch are possible, although not common. Since readers of this text are likely to be senior university undergraduates or practising engineers, most will already have chosen a branch, so no detailed discussion of branches is included in this text.

The current distribution of Canadian engineers by branch or discipline is shown in Figure 1-1. The left side of the graph shows the percentage of Canada's engineers who are currently working in that branch. The right side shows the percentage who received their education in that branch. The largest branch is civil engineering, where roughly 19 percent of engineers practise, followed by electrical (13 percent) and mechanical (10 percent). Note that although about 13 percent of Canadian engineers are in petroleum or construction engineering, virtually none of them received undergraduate engineering education in those fields; they have moved from other engineering disciplines. The "other" branches which make up 15 percent of the total in Figure 1-1 include fifteen recognized engineering disciplines with small numbers of graduates, plus fields outside of engineering. (Licensing of graduates from other fields of study is possible through examination programs run by most provincial Associations.)

JOB FUNCTIONS OF PRACTISING ENGINEERS

Although the primary task of the engineer is typically design and development, there are other tasks, jobs, or activities that occupy

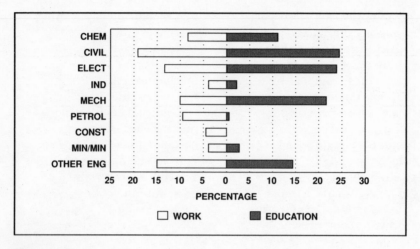

Figure 1-1
Distribution of Canadian Engineers by Branch or Discipline

Source: *Canadian Manpower Inventory Report* (Ottawa: CEMB), March 1987. Reproduced with permission from *The Future of Engineering*, CCPE Task Force Report, July 1988, 30.

engineers and that are included in the broad spectrum of engineering practice. Table 1-1 lists the percentages of professional engineers working in various job functions in Canada. The data are illustrated graphically in Figure 1-2.

The job functions in Table 1-1 and Figure 1-2 are not rigidly defined; some overlap exists from job to job. Typical descriptions for most of these job functions are given in the following paragraphs.

Design and Development

Design is often difficult to distinguish from a related activity: *development*. In practice, the term *development* is likely to refer to the early stages of a project, when various methods through which the project is to be accomplished are analyzed, compared, and tested. *Design* usually refers to the later phases of a project, when the basic method of achievement has been decided and it is now necessary to establish the exact shapes and relationships of the various parts. However, even these distinctions may get mixed up, because real-life projects have a way of getting their phases intertwined, and design and development may be mixed together inextricably.

Table 1-1
Percentage of Engineers by Job Function

Job Function		Percentage of Engineers
Design		20.43
Project Management		16.67
Production		14.58
Research and Development		6.23
Project Planning		4.83
Contruction		4.51
Exploration		1.93
Quality Control		1.42
Other:		
Business Management	10.82	
Administration	5.64	
Marketing	4.36	
Teaching	3.12	
Computers	2.55	
Corporate	2.87	
	Total (other)	29.36
	Total (all)	99.96

Note: Figures do not add up to 100.0% because of rounding.

Source: *The Future of Engineering,* Canadian Council of Professional Engineers (CCPE) Task Force Report, July 1988, 32.

Generally, companies refer to the whole spectrum of their technical activities as *research and development,* usually abbreviated as R&D. In most companies, however, very little research is done, although there are notable exceptions. For the most part, the activities carried out under the heading of R&D are actually those of design and development, particularly in Canada, where more research could (and should) be done.

Research

Research is the process of learning about nature and codifying this knowledge into usable theories. Many scientific fields that were once considered the property of physicists or chemists have become

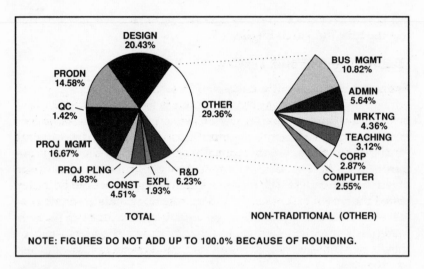

Figure 1-2
Job Functions of Practising Engineers

Source: *Canadian Manpower Inventory Report* (Ottawa: CEMB), March 1987. Reproduced with permission from *The Future of Engineering*, CCPE Task Force Report, July 1988, 32.

primarily the domain of engineers in the last thirty years. These fields, designated as the *engineering sciences* by a committee of the American Society for Engineering Education (ASEE), are mechanics of solids, mechanics of fluids, transfer and rate processes, thermodynamics, electrical sciences, and nature and properties of materials. In Canada, the Canadian Engineering Accreditation Board (CEAB) recently added computer science to this list, thus resolving the debate over whether it is an engineering science or a branch of mathematics. Engineering science seeks new knowledge for the specific purpose of design and development, whereas science in general seeks knowledge without regard to application.

Sometimes the terms *basic research* and *applied research* are used. The former means the search for knowledge for its own sake, and the latter implies that there is a known use for the knowledge being sought. Engineers rarely engage in basic research; if they do, they are more properly looked upon as scientists. But engineers often engage in applied research. In many instances, during the design of new devices or systems, critical scientific data or information may be lacking. A special research program may be needed to get the information. This is clearly applied research, an activity that occurs frequently in engineering. Engineers engaging in such projects often use the title "Research Engineer."

Quality Control and Testing

Engineers are frequently employed in testing or in *quality control*, which can be defined as setting standards for products, processes, or materials, and evaluating performance to see that the standards are being achieved. Some organizations have special departments for these functions, organizationally separate from the design departments. The separation permits test departments to be more objective in their testing procedures than designers would be if they tested their own creations. Test departments usually evaluate prototypes of new designs. They may conduct tests of new parts or materials, or qualification tests of products furnished by others, or they may maintain constant monitoring and inspection of a process or project.

Production and Manufacturing

Before a product can reach the public, it must be manufactured. Many engineers are employed in manufacturing, so many that the field has given rise to a special technical society: the Society of Manufacturing Engineers (SME). The role of the engineer in manufacturing can be quite diverse, although broad distinctions can be made, depending on the engineer's area of responsibility.

Manufacturing engineers are usually responsible for the product, rather than for the production personnel, and are engaged in solving the problems that arise in manufacturing. They are also concerned with developing and improving the production processes themselves, including the tools and machines. Some may be in charge of the inspection process, often called *quality control*, as defined in the previous section.

Closely related to the manufacturing engineer is the *plant engineer*. Whereas the former is concerned with the product and the means of manufacture, the latter is concerned with the buildings and utilities that support the manufacturing process.

Construction

The civil engineering function that is analogous to production and manufacturing is *construction*. Construction engineers may be directly in charge of the construction personnel or may instead have responsibility for the quality of the process. Engineers in charge are usually employees of the construction contractor. If the engineers have responsibility for the quality of construction, instead of being directly in charge, they are usually employees of the consulting engineering firm that designed the structure. Under such circumstances, they are typically civil engineering graduates and carry a title such as "Resident Engineer," meaning they spend all their time on the construction site. Needless to say, construction engineers have to go where the construction is, so they travel a lot.

Marketing and Sales

It is unlikely that most engineers, when starting their engineering studies, ever thought it would lead them into sales activities. Many employers, however, specifically recruit engineering or technology graduates for this purpose. Although many engineers move into straight sales work and thus completely lose contact with engineering, this is not what is generally meant by sales engineering. *Sales engineering* is a field between sales and engineering and occasionally involves engineering design. Such opportunities normally arise in enterprises that manufacture and sell custom-designed systems. In a typical case, a fully operating system put together from off-the-shelf components may be offered in a way that fits the customer's unique requirements. In some instances, it may be necessary to include a special component that has not yet been designed. The sales engineer works with the customer and essentially makes the sale, but also designs the system to meet the customer's needs and, when necessary, works with the home engineering office to develop hitherto non-existent components. Sales engineering is therefore involved as much with technical as with financial aspects.

Consulting

Consulting engineering is the most independent form of engineering, but only a very small percentage of engineers are engaged in consulting. Not every consulting engineer is an individual who offers services to the public for a fee. There are some who work this way, of course, especially among those who are just starting out as consultants. But the consulting engineer is usually not an individual but an organization that hires many engineers, architects, accountants, drafters, clerks, and people of similar skills. Some consulting organizations are very large and hire hundreds of engineers of all kinds: chemical, civil, electrical, mechanical, and nuclear, among others.

Administration and Public Service

Many engineers are involved in administering engineering activities for government agencies at municipal, regional, provincial, or federal levels. These positions normally require a sound knowledge of the agency's engineering tasks, such as highway construction, electrical power generation, or telecommunications, but the engineer's job function may also involve planning, funding, scheduling, regulation, or similar policy-related tasks. The government is, in fact, a major employer of engineers. Engineers working in administration and public service may face special ethical problems that result from political pressure and from decisions concerning the distribution of public resources.

Management

Statistics show that, sooner or later, many engineers go into management. Some engineering graduates are actively interested in management careers; many are sceptical. Nevertheless, management is a major career destination for engineers, whether they plan for it or not.

Teaching

Some engineers become teachers. If one wishes to teach at the community college level, a master's degree and a teaching credential are the usual prerequisites. Professional experience is also highly desirable. A master's degree is usually not adequate in colleges and universities where faculty members are required to maintain active research programs in addition to their teaching. Schools of this type are called *research universities*, and a doctorate is almost universally required for their faculty members. Generally, in such universities, the teaching loads are lighter than in other schools, to allow time for research. Research and graduate studies are usually closely coupled in these institutions, because it is believed that the very best training for graduate students takes place in a research environment.

EMPLOYMENT OF ENGINEERS IN CANADA

The number of professional engineers in Canada has doubled in the last ten years and is still growing. However, there is some doubt that there will be an adequate supply of engineers for the needs of the next decade. Some statistics and projections for engineering employment in Canada are given in the next few paragraphs.

As we would expect, the distribution of professional engineers across Canada is not uniform. Most of them are clustered in the industrially developed areas of Ontario and Quebec, with the next-largest number in the resource-rich area of Alberta. British Columbia has almost the same percentage as the four Atlantic provinces combined: Nova Scotia, New Brunswick, Prince Edward Island, and Newfoundland. The prairie provinces, Saskatchewan and Manitoba, have even fewer engineers, and Yukon and the Northwest Territories have just over one-half of one percent of the nation's engineers. These data are shown in Figure 1-3.

The distribution of employment by job function was described earlier in Figure 1-2. A similar view of employment can be obtained by examining the types of industry that employ engineers. These data are shown in Figure 1-4, which illustrates what percentage of engineers are employed in each major type of industry, regardless of their job function in that industry. The resource industry has the largest number of engineers, followed by public service and consulting. Manufacturing, construction, and other services make up the balance.

These data can also be broken down by region, as shown in Figure 1-5. The patterns are typical of employment in the various regions. Almost half of Alberta's engineers work in the resource sector. In British Columbia and Newfoundland, over 40 percent of engineers work in the technical services (mainly consulting) sector. Ontario

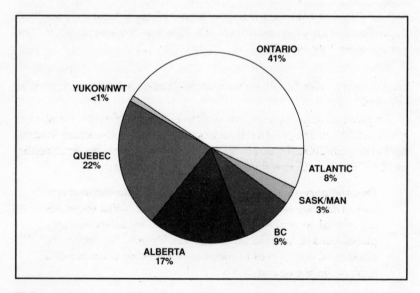

Figure 1-3
Distribution of Professional Engineers in Canada

Source: *Canadian Manpower Inventory Report* (Ottawa: CEMB), March 1987. Reproduced with permission from *The Future of Engineering*, CCPE Task Force Report, July 1988, 28.

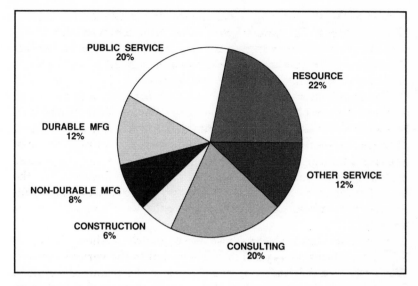

Figure 1-4
Distribution of Engineers by Industry

Source: *Canadian Manpower Inventory Report* (Ottawa: CEMB), March 1987. Reproduced with permission from *The Future of Engineering*, CCPE Task Force Report, July 1988, 28.

and Quebec, with large manufacturing bases, have more balanced profiles.[3]

Employment prospects for engineers have always been very good, and they are predicted to become better in the years leading up to the year 2000. To quote from *The Future of Engineering*, a report by the Canadian Council of Professional Engineers:

> Demand appears to be strong for engineers into the next century. There are two reasons for this: the first is that engineers are crucial to enable Canada to compete in an increasingly global market; and the second is that, despite the above, the number of young people entering engineering is expected to increase only moderately.[4]

This prediction should be viewed in light of the previous employment record for engineers. The unemployment rate for engineers was typically around 1 percent in the years prior to 1982, indicating a very small turnover of professional engineers. In the recession of 1982, unemployment reached a peak of 7000 engineers, or about 6 percent of registered professional engineers. It has gradually de-

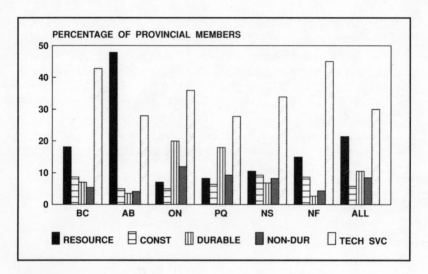

Figure 1-5
Distribution of Engineers by Industry for Selected Provinces

Source: *Canadian Manpower Inventory Report* (Ottawa: CEMB), March 1987. Reproduced with permission from *The Future of Engineering*, CCPE Task Force Report, July 1988, 31.

clined and recently stabilized at about 2 percent, which is a fraction of the unemployment rate for all Canadian workers. It appears that it will return to even lower values in the coming decade.

ENGINEERING AS A PROFESSION

During the debates in the Ontario legislature leading to the passage of the Professional Engineers Act (1968–69), a *profession was* defined as "a self-selected, self-disciplined group of individuals who hold themselves out to the public as possessing a special skill derived from training and education and are prepared to exercise that skill in the interests of others."[5]

This definition is certainly satisfied by the earlier established professions of medicine, law, and theology. When it is applied to engineering, the definition appears to be equally well satisfied: the engineer has skill and knowledge obtained from lengthy education and practical experience and not possessed by the general public, who usually would not be competent to judge accurately the quality of service rendered by the engineer; and each member must, by law, subscribe to a code of ethics established by engineers for the protection of the public. Consequently, in Canada, each province and territory recognizes engineering as a profession and permits engineers to regulate themselves through a provincial or territorial Association of Professional Engineers (or Ordre des ingénieurs du Québec).

However, it might be appropriate to seek a more general meaning of the word, as interpreted by non-engineers. Consider the following definition from *Webster's* dictionary:

> **Profession** ... A calling requiring *specialized knowledge* and often long and *intensive preparation* including instruction in skills and methods as well as in the scientific, historical, or scholarly principles underlying such skills and methods, maintaining by force of *organization* or concerned opinion *high standards* of achievement and conduct, and committing its members to *continued study* and to a kind of work which has for its prime purpose the rendering of a *public service.* [Italics added.][6]

We can see by looking at the italicized items how well engineering fits the definition of a profession. Engineering certainly requires *specialized knowledge* and *intensive preparation,* but the degree of preparation is not quite as great as that in medicine or law, two professions with which engineers frequently compare their own. For many decades, engineering has required four years of university study and two years of professional practice, or a total of six years of preparation beyond high school for entrance into the profession, whereas medicine and law have required from seven to nine years, depending on the program.

There is no doubt that the engineering profession has a very strong *organizational* structure, and that *high standards* are required for admission. Provincial and territorial Associations of Professional Engineers monitor the qualifications of applicants and, through the engineering accreditation board of the Canadian Council of Professional Engineers (CCPE), evaluate and accredit educational programs at all engineering institutions at the university level in Canada. High standards of achievement have therefore been set for admission into the profession and are enforced. The requirements for *continued study,* high standards of conduct, and *public service* are addressed by the codes of ethics that guide the personal conduct of all engineers. Codes of ethics have legal status, since they are established by acts of the legislatures in all provinces. Failure to follow the code of ethics can lead to charges of professional misconduct and disciplinary action for the errant engineer.

Therefore, engineering clearly satisfies the definition of a profession. The difference between engineering and most other professions is the environment in which most engineers practise. In Canada, the majority of engineers are employees of large companies, working in teams on projects. Most other professionals are self-employed and work on a one-to-one basis with clients. The distinction is aptly expressed in the following assessment by a Canadian engineer:

> The hard fact of the matter is that people need physicians to save their lives, lawyers to save their property, and ministers to save their souls. Individuals will probably never have an acute personal need for an engineer. Thus, engineering as a profession will probably never receive the prestige of its sister professions. Although this may be an unhappy comparison, the engineer should take note that physicians and lawyers both feel that the prestige of their professions has never been lower, and they are mightily concerned; yet ... engineers are considered to be sober, competent, dedicated, conservative practitioners, without such devastating problems as embezzlement or absconding members and without the constant references to malpractice and incompetence.[7]

THE PUBLIC IMAGE OF THE ENGINEER

The Problem of Status

Engineers have a high status in the eyes of society. Canadian data are not available, but a 1976 survey conducted in the United States by the Opinion Research Corporation ranked engineers third in prestige behind physicians and scientists. In 1963, they had ranked sixth in a similar survey. The changes between the two surveys can be seen in Table 1-2.

In a 1985 survey, one thousand Americans were asked to rate seventeen different occupations according to their perceptions of honesty and ethical standards in those occupations. The results are compiled in Table 1-3. They indicate that the engineering profession, and engineers themselves, are held in high regard by the general public.

The Problem of Numbers

One of the fundamental facts of life for engineers is that they outnumber every other professional group except teachers. Table

Table 1-2
Ranking of Engineering as a Profession

1963	1976
1. Physician	1. Physician
2. Scientist	2. Scientist
3. Lawyer	**3. Engineer**
4. Architect	4. Minister
5. Minister	5. Architect
6. Engineer	6. Banker
7. Banker	7. Lawyer
8. Accountant	8. Accountant
9. Businessman	9. Businessman

Source: *Science Indicators, 1976* (Washington, DC: National Science Foundation, 1977), 170.

1-4 presents U.S. statistics from 1985 and Canadian figures from 1987.

For a profession that is based upon individual creativity, such numbers may have disturbing implications. Some people doubt that it is possible for engineers to cultivate individuality or to maintain a sense of personal responsibility under these conditions. However, although masses of scientists and engineers are employed by some industries, important challenges are still met on an individual basis. New designs, products, and structures do not spring forth without creative effort at every level. Technical achievements are dependent on professional, competent, creative effort from every member of the engineering team. Although the teams may be larger now than they were in simpler, bygone days, the projects and challenges are even greater, and the incompetent or uncertain team member jeopardizes much larger enterprises. The individual challenge still exists, and maintaining a professional attitude is more important than ever before.

TOPICS FOR STUDY AND DISCUSSION

1. This chapter defines the term "engineer" in a very general way. As will be seen in Chapter 2 and in Appendix A, the term "engineer," meaning

Table 1-3
Ranking of Professions According to Honesty and Ethical Standards

Occupation	Percentage Rating the Occupation as "High" or "Very High" in Honesty and Ethical Standards
1. Clergy	61
2. Medical doctors	48
3. Engineers	**45**
4. Police	37
5. TV reporters	36
6. Bankers	32
7. Newspaper and magazine reporters	27
8. Lawyers	19
9. Business executives	18
10. Local political officeholders	17
11. Building contractors	16
12. Stockbrokers	14
13. Members of Congress	14
14. Real estate agents	13
15. Labour union leaders	13
16. State political officeholders	12
17. Car salespeople	6

Source: *U.S. News and World Report* (December 9, 1985): 53.

"professional engineer," has a legal definition in each province or territory. How many substantially different definitions of "engineer" or "professional engineer" can you find by referring to other dictionaries or encyclopedias? How does the best dictionary definition agree or disagree with the legal definition for your province or territory?

2. Newspaper and magazine writers occasionally refer to "scientific achievement" when things go well but use the label "engineering failure" when problems occur. Examine some recent newspapers and magazines for examples of the use of terms such as "scientific," "engineering," "technological," and "technical." Have the terms been properly used? Have you detected any trends in erroneous usage? If serious

Table 1-4

Comparison of Engineers with Other Professionals

	Canada	U.S.
Occupation	Number in 1987	Number in 1985
Teachers (elementary and secondary schools)	270 000	3 523 000
Accountants	150 000	1 263 000
Engineers	130 000	1 683 000
Teachers (college and university)	58 600	643 000
Physicians	55 300	492 000
Dentists	13 500	131 000

Source: *Statistical Abstract of the United States, 1987* (Washington, DC: U.S. Bureau of the Census), 385; and *Canada Yearbook 1990* (Ottawa: Statistics Canada, 1989).

errors in attribution of credit or blame exist, consider writing a letter to the offending newspaper or magazine to inform them.

3. Do you think the list of engineering sciences given in this chapter is complete? From your own observations or work experience, what additional fields of science should be considered engineering sciences? Discuss the distinction or boundary between engineering and science. Does the role in the design process identify the difference between the scientist and the engineer? What reasons would motivate a person to select a career in one over the other?

4. Examine the course catalogue for your university or college and classify the content of the courses you have taken (or will take). Create a matrix and categorize each course. Each row of the matrix should correspond to one of your courses and each column should correspond to one of the various functions of engineering discussed in this chapter (design and development, research, quality control and testing, production and manufacturing, construction, marketing and sales, consulting, administration and public service, management, teaching). On a percentage basis, rate how each course contributes to preparing you for employment in the various functions that engineers perform. Does your program of courses show a broad coverage or a narrow coverage

of the various functions? Can you draw any trends or conclusions from the pattern that might influence your career plans?

5. Consider each role in the technical spectrum discussed in this chapter (scientist, engineer, technologist, technician, skilled worker). What general characteristics or traits would be helpful for people entering each of these general roles? What general rewards (work environment, prestige, pay, etc.) would generally be associated with each of these roles? Considering your own characteristics and expectations, which of these roles is best for you?

NOTES

1. G.C. Andrews, A.M. Hale, and G.F. Pearce, *Basic Professional Engineering Concepts*, 3rd ed. (Waterloo, Ont.: Sandford Educational Press, 1985), 1.

2. Throughout this text, the term "Association of Professional Engineers," or simply "Association," when capitalized, refers to the legal entity established by statute in the reader's province or territory to regulate the practice of professional engineering. A list of these Associations is given in Appendix B. Similarly, the term "Professional Engineering Act," or simply "Act," when capitalized, refers to the statute itself. A list of the statutes is given in Chapter 2 and excerpts from the statutes are included in Appendix A.

3. Task Force on the Future of Engineering, *The Future of Engineering* (Ottawa: Canadian Council of Professional Engineers, 1988), 29.

4. *The Future of Engineering*, 39.

5. Hon. H.A. MacKenzie, [Opening address for the debate on the Professional Engineers Act, 1968–69], Ontario, Legislature, *Debates*.

6. By permission from *Webster's Third New International Dictionary*, © 1986 by Merriam-Webster Inc., publisher of the Merriam-Webster® dictionaries.

7. J. Carruthers, Director of Communications, Association of Professional Engineers of Ontario, personal communication, June 1977.

CHAPTER 2

Regulation of the Engineering Profession

Most countries in the developed world impose some form of regulation, licensing, or similar government control on the professions. The purpose of this control is to protect the safety of the public, to restrict unqualified persons from practising, and to discipline unscrupulous practitioners. In Canada, the legal right to regulate the professions falls under provincial authority; similarly, in the United States, the states have this regulatory power.

The United States was, in fact, the first country in which the practice of engineering was regulated. Wyoming enacted a law in 1907 as a result of many instances of gross incompetence observed during a major irrigation project.[1] In the years that followed, all the American states and the provinces and territories of Canada enacted licensing laws to control the engineering profession and the title "Professional Engineer." There is a difference between the Canadian and American laws, however. In Canada, the profession is "self-regulating" in that a governing council, most of whom are elected by the members of the provincial Association, approve regulations and by-laws by vote. In the United States, the state governments establish the regulations and license the engineers.

In some countries there is no licensing of engineers and the possession of a degree or membership in a technical society is used as a gauge of the person's competence. In Britain, for example, the term "engineer" is not regulated by law and is often used to mean "mechanic." (The sign "Engineer on Duty" is found outside many garages.) Professional competence is established in Britain by gaining membership in one of the technical societies, which call their members "Chartered Engineers."

PROVINCIAL ACTS

The engineering profession is regulated in each province or territory of Canada by statutes of the provincial legislatures (for the provinces) or legislative councils (for the territories). The names of these statutes are listed below.

- **Alberta:** Engineering Geological and Geophysical Professions Act

- **British Columbia:** Engineers and Geoscientists Act

- **Manitoba:** Engineering Profession Act

- **New Brunswick:** Engineering Profession Act, 1986

- **Newfoundland:** Engineers and Geoscientists Act

- **Northwest Territories:** Engineering, Geological and Geophysical Professions Act

- **Nova Scotia:** Engineering Profession Act

- **Ontario:** Professional Engineers Act, 1984

- **Prince Edward Island:** Engineering Profession Act, 1990

- **Quebec:** Engineers Act (Loi sur les ingénieurs)

- **Saskatchewan:** Engineering Profession Act

- **Yukon Territory:** Engineering Profession Ordinance

Relevant excerpts from these statutes are included in Appendix A for easy reference.

Each of the Acts contains the basic elements of a self-regulating engineering profession. Although there are variations, each Act typically includes:

- the purpose of the Act

- the legal definition of engineering

- the procedure for establishing a provincial or territorial Association of Professional Engineers, and the purpose (or "objects") of the Association

- standards for admission to the Association (or granting of a licence)

- procedures for establishing specific regulations to govern the practice of engineering

- procedures for establishing by-laws to govern the Association's administration and to elect a governing council
- a code of ethics to guide personal actions of the members
- disciplinary procedures

Throughout this textbook, the term "Professional Engineering Act," "provincial Act," or simply "Act" refers to the relevant Act or ordinance above, for the reader's province or territory. Similarly, the term "provincial engineering Association" or simply "Association" refers to the Association of Professional Engineers (or Ordre des ingénieurs) for the reader's province or territory.

LEGAL DEFINITION OF ENGINEERING

Each provincial and territorial Act defines the term "professional engineer" or "the practice of professional engineering." These definitions are important, because they delineate the boundaries between engineering and other professions (such as architecture and town planning) and between engineers and other personnel in the design and development spectrum (such as scientists and technologists). Since the definitions of "professional engineer" and "the practice of professional engineering" vary slightly in each province and territory of Canada, the Canadian Council of Professional Engineers (CCPE) has proposed a simple, national definition. (CCPE is a federation of the twelve provincial and territorial bodies, described in more detail later in this chapter.) CCPE defines "the practice of professional engineering" as:

> any act of planning, designing, composing, evaluating, advising, reporting, directing or supervising, or managing any of the foregoing, that requires the application of engineering principles and that concerns the safeguarding of life, health, property, economic interests, the public welfare or the environment.[2]

The goal of this national definition is to increase the unity of the engineering profession, to permit easier movement of engineers throughout Canada, and to simplify licensing problems. This definition was ratified in November 1990 by CCPE, and it is anticipated that each province and territory will examine its Professional Engineering Act in due course and eventually amend it to agree with the CCPE national definition.

The legal definitions of "engineering" or "the practice of professional engineering" for all the provinces and territories of Canada are included in Appendix A. New Brunswick has the distinction of brevity (29 words), and British Columbia, Quebec, and the North-west Territories share the distinction of length (about 180 words each). No two definitions are identical.

Some provinces (notably British Columbia and Quebec) include a list of types of machinery or structures (such as railways, bridges, highways, and canals) that are within the engineer's area of practice. This makes the definition very clear and specific, but also very long and difficult to read or understand. As time passes, the list will get out of date as some components, such as steam engines, disappear, and new areas, such as engineering software, must be added.

The shorter definitions are easier to understand and remember, but they may contain terms (such as "engineering principles") that are very general and need further interpretation and definition. For example, in the province of Ontario, "the practice of professional engineering" is defined currently as:

> any act of designing, composing, evaluating, advising, report-ing, directing or supervising wherein the safeguarding of life, health, property or the public welfare is concerned and that requires the application of engineering principles, but does not include practising as a natural scientist.[3]

For comparison, we could also examine the definitions of "engi-neer" and "the practice of professional engineering" as defined in the United States. The following definitions are from the Model Law (1986 revision) prepared by the U.S. National Council of Engineer-ing Examiners. The Model Law, like the CCPE definition, serves merely as a guide to lawmaking bodies and has no legal effect unless written into law by state legislatures.

> **Engineer.** The term "Engineer," within the intent of this Act, shall mean a person who is qualified to practice engineering by reason of special knowledge and use of the mathematical, physical, and engineering sciences and the principles and methods of engineering analysis and design, acquired by engi-neering education and experience.

> **Practice of Engineering.** The term "Practice of Engineering," within the intent of this Act, shall mean any service or creative work, the adequate performance of which requires engineering education, training, and experience in the application of special knowledge of the mathematical, physical, and engineering sci-ences to such services or creative work as consultation, inves-tigation, evaluation, planning and design of engineering works and systems, planning the use of land and water, teaching of advanced engineering subjects, engineering surveys, and stud-

ies, and the review of construction for the purpose of assuring compliance with drawings and specifications; any of which embraces such service or work, either public or private, in connection with any utilities, structures, buildings, machines, equipment, processes, work systems, projects and industrial or consumer products or equipment of a mechanical, electrical, hydraulic, pneumatic or thermal nature, insofar as they involve safeguarding life, health or property, and including such other professional services as may be necessary to the planning, progress and completion of any engineering services.[4]

The above definitions, although far from identical, show considerable similarity, so it may not be a large step to a North American definition of engineering, once a national definition has been accepted. However, all of the above definitions use terms such as "engineering principles" that need further explanation. The difference between "engineering" principles and "scientific" or "technological" principles lies in the depth and purpose of the study, since there are similarities to and overlaps with other professional programs. The difference can be explained by referring to the policy statement of the Canadian Engineering Accreditation Board, which is a standing committee of CCPE and has the task of accrediting Canadian engineering programs. One of the key criteria is:

> to identify those programs that develop an individual's ability to use appropriate knowledge and information to convert, utilize and manage resources optimally through effective analysis, interpretation and decision-making. This ability is essential to the design process that characterizes the practice of engineering.[5]

The important words in the above definition are "appropriate knowledge," "manage resources optimally," and "design process." The term "engineering principles" includes mathematics, basic science, and engineering science appropriate to the specific discipline, but these concepts must be applied to the goal of optimal use of resources in the design process. Engineering differs from technology mainly in the depth of study and application of the appropriate subjects. It differs from science mainly in the goal of the study: engineering involves putting scientific phenomena and principles into practical application. This goal is invariable, whether the work involves electrical appliances, bridges, vehicles, chemical fertilizers, networks of roads and streets, or communication systems. In particular, the determination of the "factor of safety" between expected usage and ultimate capacity of the system, device, or structure is the responsibility of the engineer, and it is obtained through study of engineering principles.

PROVINCIAL ASSOCIATIONS OF PROFESSIONAL ENGINEERS

To administer the provincial Act, each province has established a self-governing Association of Professional Engineers. The name of the province is included in the Association name, as can be seen from the list of addresses for the Associations in Appendix B. Quebec has an "Ordre" rather than an Association, and the Associations in Alberta, British Columbia, the Northwest Territories, and Newfoundland include geologists, geophysicists, or geoscientists.

Although attempts to regulate engineering in Canada were begun in the late 1800s, the first Acts were not passed until the 1920s. Early forms of the Acts were "open," in that they protected the title "Professional Engineer," but did not prevent non-members from practising engineering.

Through amendments, each Act is now "closed," and a licence is required to practise engineering in every province and territory. The provincial Professional Engineering Act can be found in any public library, and copies are available from the provincial Associations.

Under the authority of the Act, the Association is delegated the responsibility for administering it. Regulations or by-laws and a code of ethics have been written for each province or territory. In most provinces, the usage is as follows:

- *Regulations* are rules set up to implement or support the Act; they concern topics such as qualifications for admission to the Association and professional conduct.

- *By-laws* are rules set up to administer the Association itself. They concern the methods for electing members to the Association Council, financial statements, committees, and so on.

- The *code of ethics* is a set of rules of personal conduct to guide individual engineers. Every engineer must be familiar with and endeavour to follow this very important document. The code of ethics is a component of the professional practice exam and therefore will be discussed in more detail throughout this text.

Since the regulations, by-laws, and code of ethics are set up under the authority of each Professional Engineers Act, they govern the profession *with the force of law*. Engineers regulate their profession by electing the majority of members to the Association Council (which also contains members appointed by the provincial government) and by confirming (by ballot) the regulations and by-laws passed by the council. For this reason, engineering is called a "self-regulating" profession. Obviously, for this system to work, engineers should be informed when voting on changes to regulations and by-laws, and they must be willing to serve in the elected positions in their Association, particularly at the council level.

ADMISSION TO THE ENGINEERING PROFESSION

Each provincial Association admits applicants to the profession by registering them as members of the Association and granting them licences to practise. The standards for admission are similar in all provinces. An applicant is typically admitted to the profession and awarded a licence if he or she satisfies six conditions.

- Citizenship: citizen of Canada, or with the status of a permanent resident

- Age: minimum age of 18 years, or legal age of majority in some provinces, except Yukon Territory, which has a minimum age of 23 years

- Education: compliance with academic requirements, as discussed below

- Examinations: examinations may be required, as discussed below

- Experience: compliance with experience requirements, as discussed below

- Character: good character, as determined mainly from references[6]

Although these six requirements apply to almost every jurisdiction in Canada, some differences do exist. The following paragraphs give clearer explanations of some of the requirements. Students should check with local associations regarding these requirements, as the admissions process is constantly under review.

Academic Requirements

Academic requirements are usually evaluated by a board of examiners or an academic requirements committee. The most important requirement for admission is the academic accomplishment of the applicant. Graduation from a recognized (CCPE-accredited) program at a Canadian university grants full exemption from the examination program, except for the professional practice exam. (In Quebec, graduation from a Quebec university grants exemption from the professional practice exam as well.)

Degrees in engineering are recognized from many U.S. universities accredited by the U.S. Accreditation Board for Engineering and Technology (ABET). Even for those holding degrees from some of these schools, however, examinations may be required, depending on individual circumstances. Some degrees are not recognized, and such applicants are required to pass a series of examinations confirming the engineering knowledge they have. Applicants must provide documents to substantiate their claims of academic qualifications.

Examinations

Persons without university-level engineering degrees may apply and may be assigned examinations. There are approximately twenty three-hour admissions examinations for each branch of engineering. Applicants may be required to write a subset of the exams to make up deficiencies in their academic qualifications. Permission to enter the examination system varies widely. In British Columbia, it is virtually open, whereas in Quebec, it is fairly tightly controlled. In Ontario, the examination system is open only to those who hold, as a minimum, a three-year engineering technologist diploma from a college of applied arts and technology (CAAT), a technologist-level certificate from the Ontario Association of Certified Engineering Technicians and Technologists (OACETT), or other acceptable education as determined by the Association's academic requirements committee.

Although the examination system provides an alternative route into the profession, the examination system is *not* an educational system. Persons applying for Association examinations present themselves as being qualified and prepared to write and pass the examinations. The Associations do not offer classes, laboratories, or correspondence courses.

The number and type of examinations assigned will depend on the applicant's individual academic achievements to the date of evaluation. The possession of one or more postgraduate degrees beyond the bachelor's degree may be taken into consideration when determining examination assignments. However, postgraduate degrees by themselves are not sufficient if the engineering principles contained in the typical accredited undergraduate engineering program have not been covered.

Professional Practice Examination – Most applicants, regardless of academic qualifications, previous courses taken at university, or membership in other Associations, are required to pass an examination covering topics in professional practice, law, contracts, liability, and ethics. Exceptions are made for persons who transfer from province to province and have written the examination in the previous five years. Quebec does not require its university graduates to sit the exam.

Figure 2-1 shows the typical admissions process for graduates of CCPE-accredited university engineering programs. The process is fairly simple for such graduates, since only one examination is usually required (the professional practice exam, as discussed above). For applicants who are not graduates of accredited programs, a more extensive set of exams may be required.

Experience Requirement

The general experience requirement is two years of direct engineering work after the award of the engineering degree. The experience is usually obtained under the direction of a professional engineer, although, because of the variability of employment opportunities, deviations from this rule are possible. Some provinces require that one year of the experience be obtained in Canada or North America. In general, graduates who continue to a master's or doctorate in

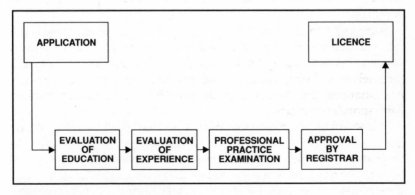

Figure 2-1
The Typical Engineering Admissions Process for Graduates of Accredited University Engineering Programs

engineering are given credit for up to one year's experience upon successful completion of the advanced degree.

Graduates of Foreign Engineering Schools

An applicant who received his or her engineering education from a foreign engineering college or university must provide the provincial or territorial Association with originals (or certified copies) of all transcripts and diplomas. The academic requirements committee (or board of examiners, depending on the province) will assess those documents and determine the admissibility of the applicant. Each case is evaluated individually. However, since foreign universities are not accredited by the Canadian Engineering Accreditation Board, admission is not generally awarded on the sole basis of foreign educational documents; some further evidence of engineering competence is generally required.

Such evidence can be provided in several forms. For example, senior engineers with foreign education may be able to document their actual engineering achievements. Other applicants with a foreign bachelor's degree may validate their training by completing a master's degree (or even a series of advanced undergraduate engineering courses) in an accredited Canadian university. In several provinces, applicants may be required to pass a set of four "confirmatory" examinations in their branch of engineering. The confirmatory examinations are usually set by the Association, and they cover the advanced topics in a small portion of the full engineering program. Readers should contact their provincial or territorial Association for more information on validating credentials.

Applicants from foreign universities should understand that the request for corroborating evidence of academic ability does not imply any lack of respect for the foreign university or for the individual. The Association is required by law to assess the qualifications of applicants and in the absence of an accreditation process for the foreign university, the Association must evaluate other evidence to justify admission.

NON-RESIDENT OR TEMPORARY LICENCES

Most provinces provide two types of engineering licence: full membership for residents of the province, and non-resident or temporary licences. The procedures for obtaining a temporary or non-resident licence vary slightly from province to province. In Ontario, an applicant must provide evidence that he or she is:

- a member of an Association of Professional Engineers in another province or territory with equal admission requirements;

- qualified to work on the specified project and is familiar with the applicable codes, standards, and laws relevant to the project;

- widely recognized in the field of practice of professional engineering relevant to the project; and

- collaborating with a member of the Association in the completion of the project specified for the temporary licence. This last requirement may be waived if the applicant is highly qualified.

LICENSING OF ENGINEERING CORPORATIONS

The licensing of corporations varies from province to province. Controversy has occasionally arisen over the licensing of corporations, since the purpose of licensing is to protect the public against incompetence, negligence, and professional misconduct, and qualities such as competence can be evaluated accurately only for human beings.

In several provinces, the Professional Engineering Act requires every individual or business entity offering professional engineering services to the public to hold a certificate of authorization. To obtain a certificate, an individual must be a member of the Association and have at least five years' engineering experience following graduation. As well, a business entity must designate at least one member associated with the business who assumes responsibility for and supervises the engineering services to be provided to the public.

In Ontario, all holders of a certificate of authorization must carry professional liability insurance or disclose, in writing, to every client that they are not insured. Failure to conform to this regulation is considered professional misconduct.[7]

Engineers who are employees of corporations that have a corporate certificate (or that do not offer engineering services to the public) do not have to apply for individual certificates of authorization. However, if an engineer moonlights, then a certificate may be necessary for the outside assignments.

CONSULTING ENGINEERS

The designation "Consulting Engineer" is not regulated at present in any province but Ontario. It is controlled in Ontario by the regulations under the Professional Engineers Act. To qualify as a consulting engineer, a member:

- must have been continuously engaged for at least two years in private practice;

- must have at least five years of satisfactory experience since becoming a member; and

- must pass (or be exempted from) examinations that may be prescribed by the council.

Since applicants for the designation "Consulting Engineer" must be engaged in private practice and offering their services to the public, they must also be holders of a certificate of authorization in Ontario or associated with a partnership or corporation that is a holder of a certificate.

THE ENGINEER'S SEAL

In every province, the Professional Engineering Act provides for each engineer to have a seal denoting that he or she is licensed. All final drawings, specifications, plans, reports, and other documents involving the practice of professional engineering, when issued in final form for action by others, should bear the signature and seal of the professional engineer who prepared and approved them. This is particularly important for services provided to the general public. The seal has important legal significance, since it implies that the documents have been competently prepared and indicates clearly the person responsible. The seal should not, therefore, be used casually or indiscriminately. In particular, preliminary documents should not be sealed. They should be marked "preliminary" or "not for construction."

The seal denotes that the documents have been *prepared* or *approved* by the person who sealed them. This implies an intimate knowledge and control over the documents or the project to which the documents relate. An engineer who knowingly signs or seals documents that have not been prepared by himself or herself, nor by technical assistants under his or her direct supervision, may be guilty of professional misconduct and may also be liable for fraud or negligence if the misrepresentation results in someone suffering damages.

A fairly common problem involves engineers who are asked to "check" documents, then sign and seal them. This is usually not ethical. The engineer who prepared them or supervised their preparation should seal the documents. If they were prepared by a non-engineer, then perhaps he or she should have been under the supervision of an engineer. The extent of work needed to "check" a document is not clearly defined, and many disciplinary cases have resulted when engineers "checked" and sealed documents that later proved to have serious flaws. This topic is discussed in more detail in Chapter 9.

THE ENGINEERING CODES OF ETHICS

Each provincial Association of Professional Engineers subscribes to a code of ethics, which sets out a standard of conduct that members must follow in the practice of professional engineering. The code of ethics for each province and territory of Canada is included in Appendix A. Each provincial code of ethics defines, in general terms, the duties of the engineer to the public, to the employer (or client), to fellow engineers, to the engineering profession, and to oneself. The major purpose of the code is, of course, to protect the general public from unscrupulous practitioners; however, by instilling public confidence in engineering, the code also raises the esteem of the entire profession.

In most provinces, the code of ethics is specifically mentioned in the Act and therefore has the full force of law. The discussion of the code of ethics as a guide to personal professional conduct is the main topic of the latter half of this text, which describes the evolution and application of codes in detail.

PROFESSIONAL MISCONDUCT

The main purpose of the provincial Associations of Professional Engineers is to protect the public welfare. Therefore, it is occasionally necessary to discipline errant engineers. Under the terms of each provincial Act, the Association is awarded the authority to reprimand, suspend, or expel a member who is incompetent or who is guilty of professional misconduct, which is usually defined as negligence, incompetence, or corruption. These terms, while widely used in common speech, require formal legal definitions to be enforceable, and the Acts and regulations spend many pages defining these terms and giving specific examples of what constitutes professional misconduct.

Each provincial Association, in order to enforce the Act and regulations and to prevent or to discipline misconduct, has staff or council members who receive complaints, prosecute persons practising engineering under false pretenses, and arrange disciplinary hearings for engineers charged with misconduct. Disciplinary decisions are made not by the staff members, however, but by the committee of engineers appointed by the council. Since the council is mainly elected by the engineers of the province, the "self-regulating" aspect of the profession is carried through to disciplinary actions as well. The results of disciplinary hearings are usually published and circulated to all members. (On the disciplinary process, see Chapter 12.)

The most frequently reported complaints concern violations of the code of ethics. In most provinces the code of ethics has been specifically included in the Act and is therefore enforceable under the Act. The terms of the code of ethics are based on common sense, natural justice, and basic ethical concepts. Although everyone should read and understand the code, it is not usually necessary to memorize it; most engineers find that they follow it intuitively and need never fear charges of professional misconduct.

THE IRON RING AND THE ENGINEERING OATH

In addition to the codes of ethics, which, by law, enjoin each engineer to act in an honest, conscientious manner, there is a much older, voluntary oath, written by Rudyard Kipling and first used in 1925, called the Obligation of the Engineer. Those who have taken the oath can usually be identified by the iron ring they wear. The iron ring is awarded during a rather solemn ceremony called the Ritual of the Calling of an Engineer, which is conducted by the Corporation of the Seven Wardens. Although the corporation is not a secret society, it does not seek or require publicity.

The ceremony is generally conducted, at universities that grant engineering degrees, during April or May of each year, and is made known to the graduating students. The ceremony permits non-university engineers to participate, but it is not open to the general public. The iron ring is not an indicator that a degree has been awarded, but it shows that the wearer has participated in the ceremony and has voluntarily agreed to abide by the oath or Obligation of the engineer. The Obligation is fairly brief and directs the engineer to high standards of performance and thought. A more detailed discussion of the engineering oath and the iron ring is included in Appendix C.

CANADIAN COUNCIL OF PROFESSIONAL ENGINEERS (CCPE)

The Canadian Council of Professional Engineers (CCPE) was established in 1936 as a federation of the provincial and territorial Associations that license engineers and oversee the profession across Canada. CCPE, as a federation of Associations, does not have individual members, but every licensed engineer is indirectly a member of CCPE. The role of CCPE is to co-ordinate the engineering profession on a national scale. To achieve this goal, CCPE has three important boards or committees.

Canadian Engineering Accreditation Board (CEAB)

In 1965, the Canadian Council of Professional Engineers established the Canadian Accreditation Board (CAB), now known as the Canadian Engineering Accreditation Board (CEAB). The concept of accreditation was implemented by CCPE to test and evaluate undergraduate engineering degree programs offered at Canadian universities and to award recognition to programs that meet the required standards. With the consent of the engineering Associations, CEAB was empowered to develop minimum criteria for undergraduate engineering degree programs and, through a process of direct investigation, to provide engineering schools with a means to have their programs formally tested against these criteria. The criteria for accreditation are formulated to provide graduates with an education satisfying the academic requirements for professional engineering registration throughout Canada.[8]

An accreditation visit is undertaken at the invitation of a particular engineering school and with the concurrence of the Association for that province. A team of senior engineers is assembled, composed of specialist engineers for the subjects involved and at least one engineer from the provincial Association. Armed with documents including a detailed questionnaire completed by the institution beforehand, the team proceeds to consult with administrators, faculty, students, and department personnel.

The team examines the academic and professional quality of faculty, adequacy of laboratories, equipment, computer facilities, and so forth. They also evaluate the quality of the students' work on the basis of face-to-face interviews with senior students, assessment of recent examination papers, laboratory work, reports and theses, records, models or equipment constructed by students, and other evidence of the scope of their education.

Furthermore, the team performs a qualitative analysis of the curriculum content to ensure that it meets the minimum criteria. Finally, the team reports its findings to CEAB, which then makes an accreditation decision. It may grant (or extend) accreditation of a program for a period of up to six years, or it may deny accreditation altogether.

CEAB publishes an annual listing of the accreditation history of all programs that are presently (or have ever been) accredited.

Canadian Engineering Human Resources Board (CEHRB)

Since 1972, the Canadian Engineering Human Resources Board (formerly the Canadian Engineering Manpower Board) has been a window on the engineering profession, providing detailed information about the supply and demand for Canadian engineers to business, government, and educational institutions. CEHRB is a standing committee of the Canadian Council of Professional Engineers. Its mandate is to collect and maintain data relating to the engineering profession in Canada. It does this through surveys and studies and through its engineering human resources database.

In addition to these sources of information, CEHRB's close links to government, industry, and educational institutions afford it an excellent source of information on trends that affect the engineering labour market and the profession in general. CEHRB makes this information available to its members through its reports, a newsletter, and a specialized information service.

Canadian Engineering Qualifications Board (CEQB)

The Canadian Engineering Qualifications Board (CEQB) was established fairly recently and deals with qualifications for entering the engineering profession. The board's work is of particular importance for evaluating credentials of candidates who have studied abroad. The committee is also in the process of preparing CCPE guidelines for admission to the practice of engineering in Canada.

SUMMARY

Figure 2-2 illustrates how the engineer interacts with the various organizations mentioned in this chapter. The licensed engineer is a member of a provincial Association and is usually a member of at least one engineering society. All provincial Associations are federated members of CCPE. The members of the Association elect the council, who appoint the staff.

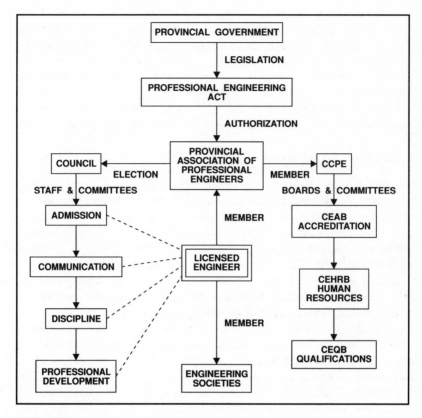

Figure 2-2
The Relationship of the Licensed Engineer to the Many Organizations Mentioned in This Chapter

TOPICS FOR STUDY AND DISCUSSION

1. Should the "professional" person be more concerned about the welfare of the general public than the "average" person? Should persons in positions of great trust, whose actions could cause great harm to the general public, be required to obey a higher code of ethics than the average person? How does your answer apply to engineering?

2. The definitions of "engineering" and "engineering practice" vary from province to province (to territory), as described in this chapter and in Appendix A. Consult Appendix A and review the definitions for your province or territory. Do they agree with the CCPE definition and the U.S. Model Law definitions given in this chapter? Can you think of any

activities that are clearly engineering activities but that would *not* be covered by the definition for your province or territory? From the various definitions available in this text, select the one you consider to be most accurate and explain why.

3. Most professions in Canada have a two-pronged structure in which one organization regulates the members of the profession, and an independent organization works on behalf of the members, by setting fees and organizing pension plans and the like. A good example is law: the Law Society regulates members and the Bar Association works on their behalf. Similarly in medicine, the College of Physicians and Surgeons regulates the profession, and the Medical Association works on behalf of the members. In engineering, a similar two-pronged structure does not exist. In some provinces, the provincial Association is empowered to act on behalf of engineers, and in some provinces the Association is not legally permitted to act on behalf of engineers as directly as the Bar Association and Medical Association can. Discuss the advantages and disadvantages of the two-pronged structure. Should it be implemented in engineering?

NOTES

1. Hon. H.A. MacKenzie, [Opening address for the debate on the Professional Engineers Act, 1968–69], Ontario, Legislature, *Debates*.

2. "CCPE Set to Ratify National P.Eng. Definition," *Engineering Dimensions* 11, no. 5 (September/October 1990): 21.

3. Professional Engineers Act, *Statutes of Ontario* 1984, c. 13.

4. *Model Law* (Clemson, SC: National Council of Engineering Examiners, 1986), 15. Excerpts reproduced with permission.

5. Canadian Engineering Accreditation Board, *1988/1989 Annual Report* (Ottawa: Canadian Council of Professional Engineers, 1989), 13–15.

6. Association of Professional Engineers of Ontario, *General Information: Licensing Requirements* (Toronto: APEO, 1990).

7. Association of Professional Engineers of Ontario, *Guideline to Professional Practice* (Toronto: APEO, 1990).

8. CEAB, *Annual Report*; and C. Ella, "Ensuring Quality Engineering Programs: The Canadian Engineering Accreditation Board," *Engineering Dimensions* 11, no. 3 (May/June 1990), 40–41.

CHAPTER 3

Engineering Employment

The majority of engineers in Canada are employees of corporations or private companies. The qualifications for professional licensing presently include two years of satisfactory engineering experience under the guidance of a senior engineer, and this experience is generally obtained as an engineering employee. This chapter traces the path of recent university graduates through their first employment as engineers (or "engineers in training") and describes the characteristic challenges, benefits, and disadvantages they are likely to encounter.

MAKING THE TRANSITION

The transition from university to the workplace is sometimes called "entering the real world." This terminology irritates some recent graduates who recall that their workload as students was very "real." But whether real or unreal, a full-time engineering job is certainly very different from being a student.

One of the major differences reported by new graduates as they enter full-time jobs is that their personal time management usually becomes more critical. When they were students, many courses and activities were rigidly scheduled. On the job, it is important to control one's time commitments, and it is not always possible to focus on one assignment at a time. Another difference is that university courses are rather short and end at a predictable point. On the job, a given project may take a long time, perhaps a year or more, and have important future implications. A project may go on to production, construction, or fabrication, yielding profit for the company and recognition for those involved.

In many companies, a new engineer is assigned to a training program, but in some organizations the new engineer may merely be handed an orientation manual and a set of equipment specifications. One new engineer at Digital Equipment reported that this happened to her, but things stayed that way for only two days: "The first guy I was introduced to brought a design problem over to my desk and said, 'Here, see if you can do this.' I worked out an answer, and we went over it." This pulled her directly into the design activity of a major new computer system. As time passed, she was delighted that her ideas found their way into a new product. She said: "The feeling was *Wow!* It's mine and it's on the market!" After three years her responsibilities had expanded and her salary had grown by nearly 50 percent. She also reported that her working day typically extended from 8 A.M. to 6 P.M. and that she occasionally worked 80 hours a week when a project deadline approached.[1]

Another new graduate, a civil engineer, kept a diary of his first few weeks on the job. During his first week, he was given the usual mountain of personnel forms to fill out, then was given some specifications to read and some drawings to check and was asked to inspect a recently completed security fence. He was surprised that he received remarkably little supervision. During the next three weeks he got deeper into the paperwork and found himself getting involved in meetings with suppliers, subcontractors, and the structural engineer. He wrote in his diary: "Feel more like a clerk than an engineer. ... It is hard not to become discouraged when you feel underemployed."

In his fifth week, he found it necessary to make a presentation before a group of people, and he wrote: "I've learned the hard way that whenever you identify a problem you had better have some recommendations on how to resolve it." In his sixth week he recorded a sense of surprise at how much time he was spending on the telephone, and in the seventh he was even more surprised to find that he was helping to make decisions on architectural features like roofing, tile, glass, wall coverings, and paint colours. In week nine, he did some design on a roof support structure and noted that he was asked to do things like this because he was "fresh out of school and up to date." As the months passed, he was given greater responsibility, and soon he was writing major contracts, doing construction reviews, and managing subcontractors.[2]

Two other engineers, one of them experienced and the other a recent graduate, offer several suggestions for a new engineer during the first few weeks on the job.

- Act like a pro. Dress neatly and appropriately.

- Be alert. Stay loose. Keep cool but don't freeze.

- Finish an assignment before you attempt to present it.

- Be careful. Check your work.

- Accept tough assignments. Seek out the complicated and unusual jobs.

- Learn to describe what you are doing in simple, concise terms. Buy a dictionary. Learn to spell.

- Select active and competent engineers as role models.[3]

A study in 1987 of 200 professionals at seven U.S. companies showed that the following qualities were strongly apparent in the individuals identified by their managements as above-average achievers.

- They were better at picking up clues regarding others' reactions.

- They listened well and questioned skilfully.

- They could deal with objections and encouraged positive responses.

- They gathered more information before presenting ideas.

- They recognized when to go through channels and when not to, whom to inform, and whom to check with.[4]

In a nutshell, recent university graduates entering their first full-time engineering job must recognize that a period of adjustment is required. The older employees may be as apprehensive as the new employees during the adjustment phase. The new employee should recognize that having a friendly attitude, behaving courteously, and making minor allowances for personality traits can sometimes reap big dividends by making the workplace friendlier and making supporters and allies out of colleagues who might otherwise be polite but aloof.

TRAINING PROGRAMS

Although almost every company claims to have a training program, the term is used loosely and may mean full-time study leading to an advanced degree, or it may mean on-the-job training, wherein the new employee is put directly to work and the supervisor provides instruction as the need arises.

The U.S. National Industrial Conference Board has identified some differences between formal and on-the-job programs. Formal training may last one, two, or even three years. Time is spent in several different departments, mostly observing. Written reports and examinations are included. The emphasis usually is on preparation for management. On-the-job training programs are generally shorter than formal programs. The training usually focusses more on a particular job, at the expense of a broader orientation, and involves actual work participation.[5]

Interestingly, on-the-job training is more popular than formal training among recent graduates. One explanation offered for the greater popularity is that the new graduate, saturated with formal classroom education, is eager to get started in practical work.

A recent study carried out in Canada reveals that formal training in Canada lags behind that provided in other countries.

> While reliable comparative statistics on training investment are notoriously hard to come by, most evidence indicates that spending on training by Canadian industry is considerably lower than comparable spending in other countries. Preliminary data from the 1987 Statistics Canada Survey of Human Resource Development and Training shows that employers in Canada spent about $1.4 billion — less than .3 percent of Gross Domestic Product — on formal training that year.[a] This represents a little over $100 per worker employed. A number of studies in the U.S. estimate formal industry training expenditures at levels more than *twice* the Canadian effort.[b] For example, the American Society of Training and Development estimated national average per employee training expenditures in industry at U.S. $238 in 1984.[6]

Clearly the training programs for Canadian industries require improvement if Canada is to compete in the new global economy. This applies to all new technical employees, from the apprentice to the engineer.

JOB FAMILIARIZATION METHODS

Edgar H. Schein, professor of industrial management at the Massachusetts Institute of Technology in the 1960s, listed the following "induction strategies" or familiarization methods used by organizations to acquaint new employees with their engineering duties.

1. Sink or Swim – The new graduate is simply given a project and is judged by the outcome. If given little information for guidance, the newcomer is partially judged by how good a job is done in self-structuring the assignment. This requires the new employee to take vaguely stated objectives and translate them into specific tasks that can be dealt with one by one.

2. The "Upending" Experience – The intent of this strategy is to jar the new employee loose from the presumed impracticalities acquired in college and to confront the trainee with the "realities" of industrial life. In one approach of this nature reported by Schein, each new engineer is given a special electrical circuit, which violates several theoretical assumptions, to analyze. When the new engineer reports that the circuit will not work, it is demonstrated that it not only does work but has been in commercial use by the company for several years. Chastened, the engineer is then asked to find out *why* it works. When this proves impossible, depression sets in, and the newcomer is then considered ready to tackle a real assignment.

3. Training While Working – This is the typical on-the-job induction program. The new person is given an assignment commensurate with his or her experience level and carries it out under the close guidance of a supervisor.

4. Working While Training – The new person is considered to belong to a formal training program but is given small projects involving real work. Rotation through several different departments may occur during the course of the program. It is sometimes difficult to decide whether the programs of this type should be classified as on-the-job or formal.

5. Full-time Training – These programs clearly belong in the formal category. They usually involve classwork and rotational assignments that call for the trainee to observe the work being done by others; direct participation is minimal. Schein observed that some trainees criticize such observational activities as mostly meaningless or "Mickey Mouse."

6. Integrative Strategies – In an approach of this type, an attempt is made to adjust to the different needs of different trainees. In one such program, the new employees are given regular job assignments for a year and then sent to a summer-long, full-time university training program. A key feature of the initial assignments is that the supervisors have been specially selected and trained to be sensitive to the problems of new people. Some of these programs lead to advanced degrees.[7]

Of the six strategies recorded by Schein, the first two seem to show little appreciation for the proper objective of any inductive strategy, which is to turn a new engineer into a productive employee as soon as possible. Schein argued that initial assignments should give the employee as much responsibility as possible, for the sake of the individual and the organization. Admittedly, there is a risk that the new person could fail an important assignment. However, there is much to gain by using people at their highest potential and much to lose by using them at their lowest.

One important purpose of a formal training program is to help a new graduate find a "best fit" in a company. Often, a best fit may be a job quite different from what the graduate was aiming for. A typical program of this sort rotates the new employee through several different jobs, each one averaging six months' duration, looking for that best fit.

TYPICAL COMPANY ORGANIZATION

An important task of a new employee is to learn how the company is organized. With this knowledge, the employee is better able to assist in achieving the company's goals, to anticipate problems, and to recommend improvements. If we consider the most typical case, a company involved primarily in design and development (possibly with some research activity also), three basic types of organization can be delineated: the project structure, the functional structure, and the hybrid structure.

The *project structure* (Figure 3-1) corresponds in form to that of the decentralized corporation. Each subgroup of the department is responsible for a complete project (or projects) and contains within itself all the functional specialties necessary to complete its projects. The major advantage of such a structure is that the boundaries of responsibility are crystal clear; the major disadvantage is that functions are duplicated among groups.

The *functional structure* (Figure 3-2) is highly centralized. A department is split into its functional specialties, and the functional subgroups operate on all projects passing through the department. One company might separate electronic design and mechanical engineering design. Another company might separate the functions into aerodynamics, stress analysis, weights, materials, and test groups. Obviously, the kind of grouping depends upon the branch of industry in which the company operates. The major advantage of the functional structure is that a greater technical competence can be achieved in the various engineering specialties than under the project structure. (It is more likely that the company will possess true expertise in material science, for example, if a group can focus all of its attention on this activity rather than spreading its expertise among many project groups.) The principal disadvantage of a func-

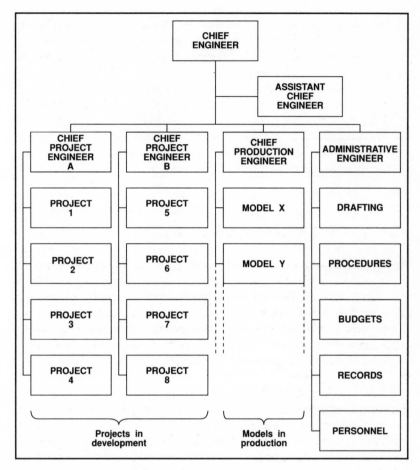

Figure 3-1
Example of Project Organizational Form

tional structure is that it is difficult to pinpoint responsibility, and certain important matters may get overlooked.

The *hybrid structure* combines the foregoing two forms and is characteristic of large companies. Functional groups exist, but each project is under the supervision of a project manager who shepherds it through the various functional activities. Those who choose the hybrid structures generally do so in the hope that they will obtain the advantages of both the project form and the functional form.

One further important aspect of a company's organization is whether it is relatively "closed" or relatively "open." A *closed system* typically exhibits a strong adherence to the usual organizational

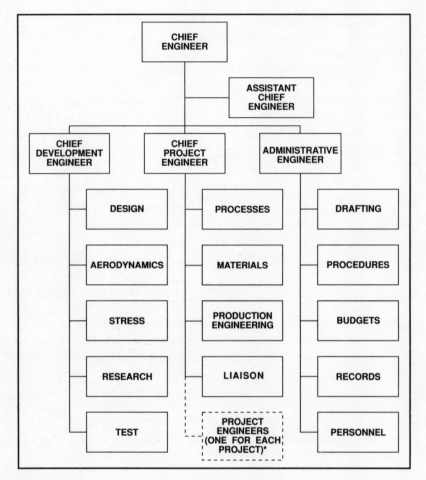

Figure 3-2
Example of Functional Organizational Form

*If there are no project engineers (block in dotted outline), the organizational form is known as "functional." If there is a project engineer for each project, the organizational form is known as "hybrid."

rules, with authority flowing from the top down along the lines of the organization chart, and accountability for results flowing in the opposite direction. Great emphasis is placed on productivity, on enforcement of budgets and schedules, and on going through proper channels. Even though such practices seem properly efficient and businesslike, some unexpected by-products can occur, such as high dependency (of individuals upon superiors), low autonomy, low opportunity for interaction, and low individual influence potential.

In the *open system*, greater emphasis is placed upon the autonomy of individuals, and less reliance is given to achieving results by means of administrative control. It might be said that the open system emphasizes subject matter, while the closed system emphasizes the methods by which the subject matter is to be handled. In a closed system, new jobs tend to be adapted to the organizational structure, while in an open system the structure is adapted to the jobs.

Not surprisingly, the open system usually results in higher individual satisfaction, less conflict, higher group performance, and greater individual opportunity.

A 1982 book that gave strong support to open organizational systems was *In Search of Excellence: Lessons from America's Best-Run Companies*, by T.J. Peters and R.H. Waterman, Jr.[8] It has been called the best-selling management book of all time. Peters and Waterman spent three years conducting in-depth studies of 62 major American corporations that had shown long-term success, as measured by such factors as equity growth and return on investment. They found that the "excellent" companies had in common a number of organizational precepts, mostly unwritten. Among these were a bias for action, an emphasis on autonomy and entrepreneurship, a willingness to take risks, an obsession with the importance of people as a key to productivity, and a constant pressure to maintain simple organizational forms. These elements are exactly what is meant by an "open" organizational form.

Although a new employee may find it difficult to understand the complete organizational structure of a new company, and even more difficult or impossible to influence it, the knowledge will yield dividends to the person who makes the effort.

PROBLEMS OF PROFESSIONALS

Some serious attempts have been made to identify and analyze the kinds of problems that are commonly experienced by young professionals. In his book *Characteristics of Engineers and Scientists*, Lee Danielson reported the results of interviews with 367 American engineers and scientists, conducted by the Bureau of Industrial Relations at the University of Michigan. Danielson found the following to be the most frequently mentioned problem areas of young professionals, in order of their frequency of mention:

1. Adjusting to company practices
2. Advancement slow or uncertain
3. Accepting routine jobs
4. Learning what is expected
5. Finding one's own niche
6. Unrealistic ambitions
7. Lack of initiative
8. Gaining social acceptance
9. Lack of specialized courses
10. Lack of recognition[9]

Obviously, the first problem could be alleviated (or even eliminated) by company training programs. Problems 4, 5, and 8 will diminish with the passage of time, as the new employee adjusts to the company (and vice-versa). The remaining items are probably the most important ones on the list and are also the most difficult to deal with constructively.

Young engineers are often simultaneously criticized for not being ambitious enough (problem 7) and for being too ambitious (problem 6). Great things are expected of them because of their education; at the same time, they are told that they do not know enough to handle anything important and are given routine tasks. To achieve the desired amount of humility and yet avoid torpidity is a considerable challenge for the young engineer. One writer warns against "producing the apathetic, uncreative, passive kind of employee whom most organizations seem to welcome at the outset but regret being saddled with at a later time."[10]

Enthusiasm is one of the most valuable assets a young engineer possesses. Yet it is this very enthusiasm that might sometimes be interpreted as overaggressiveness or unrealistic expectations. If consistently rebuffed, enthusiasm can easily degenerate to a permanently low level. This would be a tragedy, because enthusiasm is too precious to be smothered — and lost — in this fashion. One of the best ways to move out of routine assignments is to handle each of them with as much skill, dispatch, and enthusiasm as one possesses. There are few better ways, if any, in which to come to the attention of management and move into more challenging tasks.

The problem of slow promotions is another matter. Probably no one is ever promoted as fast as hoped for. Moreover, most young people have heard the adage that "the squeaky wheel gets the grease," and they test its truth in practice. But management is generally unimpressed by any agitation for promotion unless it is coupled with proven ability and achievement. The best advice to a new engineer in a position of slow promotion is to devote time to improving technical knowledge, developing management and people skills, and letting one's ability speak for itself. Intelligent employers recognize the value of promoting capable people.

CONSTRUCTIVE ACTION BY EMPLOYERS

Once the individual engineer has adjusted to industry and demonstrated professional attitudes of patience, enthusiasm, diligence, alertness, and thoroughness, the next moves are up to the employer. The engineer's responsibility is to do a good job of engineering; management's responsibility is to do everything possible to help the engineer do that job.

One constructive point upon which everyone appears to agree (at least in principle) is that good communication must be maintained between engineering and management. This means that engineers must be supplied with information concerning company objectives, particularly those that affect engineering projects. There is a natural limit to the degree to which such a program can be pursued, however. Much information about company objectives may also be precisely the kind of information that will aid and comfort the competition if it should come into their hands. Management can hardly be blamed if it tends to hold back such sensitive information, particularly from new employees, since it knows full well that engineers do quit the organization from time to time, and sometimes join competitors. Hence, the goal of complete communication is never achieved, although with honest effort it can be approached.

Another important problem area is that of salaries, reviews, and promotion. It is generally agreed that salaries should reflect the contributions made by the engineers. This is by no means an easy task, and many companies do a less than adequate job in this area. In one survey involving 350 American engineers and engineering managers, 88 percent of the engineers thought it was imperative for their companies to establish salary progressions that reflect engineers' contributions; when asked if their companies realistically followed such a policy, only 23 percent answered in the affirmative.[11]

Good facilities and support personnel are also emphasized in virtually every list of recommendations. This includes such things as secretarial and clerical support, provision of technicians, equipment, computers, and telephones, and reasonably private quarters. The day of the giant bullpens, with engineers stacked at desks ranged row on row, is nearly gone. Most companies have gone to considerable trouble and expense to provide semi-private quarters for engineers, with perhaps two or three persons per office.

A survey of engineers and engineering managers in 1987 sought to find out just what it is that motivates engineers and what is most important to them. The engineers in the survey made the following choices; in each case the percentage of the respondents making that choice is shown. (The respondents were asked to make choices between contrasting pairs.)

- Interesting work was more important than prestige and recognition (100 percent).

- Technical tasks were more important than managerial tasks (87 percent).

- Diversified work was more important than concentrating on a single project (80 percent).

- Work on one's own ideas was more important than knowing what is expected (76 percent).

- Sense of individual accomplishment was more important than good supervisor and associates (68 percent).

- Working in a group was more important than working alone (67 percent).

- Good salary was more important than recognition for work well done (64 percent).

- Opportunity for advancement was more important than job security (61 percent).[12]

PROFESSIONAL EMPLOYMENT GUIDELINES

An important U.S. document that is equally relevant in Canada is the Guidelines to Professional Employment for Engineers and Scientists, developed by the National Society of Professional Engineers. The Guidelines are discussed in more detail in Chapter 7 and are printed in their entirety in Appendix F. The emergence of these guidelines was a major event in the history of the engineering profession in the United States and recognized that most engineers are employees of someone else and that the usual codes of ethics apply primarily to engineers in private practice and sometimes are not very helpful to engineers in industry, government, and education.

The Guidelines contain far more injunctions for employers than for employees. In brief, the employee is expected to be loyal to the employer's objectives, safeguard the public welfare, avoid conflicts of interest, and pursue professional development. The employer is expected to keep professional employees informed of the organization's objectives and policies, establish equitable compensation plans, minimize new hirings during layoffs, provide for early vesting of pension rights, assist in professional development programs, provide timely notice in the event of termination, and assist in relocation efforts following termination. The Guidelines are not legally binding, but they have had a constructive impact upon employee-employer relationships.

The Guidelines were first published in 1973. In 1981, the American Association of Engineering Societies made a survey to see how well the Guidelines had been incorporated into industry employment practices. The survey showed that the large majority of the responding companies conformed to most of the Guidelines. However, there were some important areas in which the respondents lagged behind the Guidelines. The responses to the survey are shown in Table 3-1.

Table 3-1

Survey of Employment Practices in 92 Companies in the United States

The survey made the following request of the companies: "Please indicate whether or not the following are part of the employment agreement between your company and its professional employees."

	Yes	No
Position and title	85	7
Salary	85	7
Extra compensation arrangements		
Bonuses	35	53
Pay for extra time over extended period	53	38
Compensation for inventions or patents	32	57
Relocation financial assistance	81	10
Profit-sharing	28	61
Description of responsibilities	78	14
Confidentiality clause	68	21
Patent arrangements	70	20
Limitations on future employment by competitors	20	66
List of benefits	84	8

(continued)

Table 3-1 *(continued)*

	Yes	No
Professional Development		
Is each position classified by level within overall salary structure clearly defined and accurately categorized by title?	79	13
For those who do not choose the management route, is provision made for comparable advancement?	79	12
Is provision made for accelerated promotion and extra compensation for superior performance and/or special accomplishments?	81 / 83	10 / 3
Are formal performance reviews conducted?	90	1
Is continuing education encouraged?	89	0
Is it supported financially?	34	56
Is time off normally granted for daytime courses?	90	2
Is participation in professional society activities encouraged?	73	17
Is professional society activity subsidized?		
Are employees encouraged to publish technical material that doesn't fall within proprietary limits?	73	15
Is legal defence provided for any suits or claims against present or former employees in connection with their authorized activities on behalf of your company?	76	2
Is there any policy in your company that would require a professional employee to join a labour organization as a condition for employment?	1	91
Termination and Transfer		
Is the employee informed of the specific reasons for termination of employment?	92	0
If termination is without cause, compensation recommended by the AAES *Guidelines* is equal to one month of pay plus one week of pay for each year of service. Does your company pay:		
That amount?	24	50
More than that amount?	16	41

Note: Where number of responses fails to add to 92, it is because some companies did not answer the question.

Source: *Survey of Employment Practices Among Employers of Engineers—1981* (New York: American Association of Engineering Societies, 1982). Reproduced with permission.

TOPICS FOR STUDY AND DISCUSSION

1. Consider two companies with which you are familiar (for example, a company for which you have worked and a company for which you might like to work), and compare them using the information in this chapter. For example, which form of company organization most clearly represents each company's structure? What form of training program is usually offered to recent engineering graduates? How do the companies compare in terms of the characteristics listed in the section "Constructive Action by Employers"? Does the comparison show one company to be a more attractive employer than the other?

2. Make a list, in priority order, of those things that you believe are important to you in professional employment, such as salary, location, potential for advancement, and type of work. Then, assuming you are an employer, make a similar list, putting down those things that the employer is likely to be seeking from you as a new employee. Compare the two lists. What differences do you see? How would these differences influence your behaviour in a job interview if you were: (a) the applicant, or (b) the interviewer?

3. The Guidelines to Professional Employment for Engineers and Scientists mentioned in this chapter are included in Appendix F. These Guidelines state, "The professional employee should be loyal to the employer." Elsewhere they say, "The professional employee should have due regard for the health, safety, and welfare of the public." Consider some situations in which these guidelines could come into conflict, and state what you believe to be the proper course of action for the professional employee in each situation. (Such conflicts are discussed in more detail later in this text.)

4. An issue that occasionally causes controversy is the payment of overtime to engineers. Should engineers be paid overtime, or should engineers expect to work some additional time because of the professional nature of their work, which permits them, in most cases, to set their own priorities and work schedules? If overtime should be paid, under what circumstances should it be monitored? Should engineers punch a time clock or should their attendance be checked by supervisors? Should a bonus take the place of an overtime payment? Would it make any difference if the company had a flex-time system, in which personnel have much more latitude in the times that they arrive and leave?

5. Another controversial issue in engineering employment is the formation of engineering unions. From your knowledge of unions (and from any other sources, if you wish), write a list of good effects and bad

effects of the unionization of engineers. Using your own beliefs and values, decide for yourself whether a union would be good or bad for you. After you have come to a conclusion, read Chapter 7, which refers briefly to the unionization dilemma. Does this discussion support your conclusion?

NOTES

1. M. Everett, "What It's Like to Work at Digital," *Graduating Engineer* (December 1986): 35–37.

2. T. Towle, "The Diary of a New Engineer," *Graduating Engineer* (January 1987): 75–77.

3. C. Lucas and D. Grauvogl, "The Early Days: Tips for the Entry Level Engineer," *Civil Engineering* (December 1984): 44–46.

4. "Managing Technology," IEEE *Spectrum* (November 1987): 20.

5. S. Habbe, *College Graduates Assess Their Company Training*, Personnel Policy Study no. 188 (New York: National Industrial Conference Board, 1963), 45–46.

6. Premier's Council of Ontario, *People and Skills in the New Global Economy* (Toronto: Queen's Printer, 1990), 91–92. © Reproduced with permission from the Queen's Printer for Ontario.

6a. Employment and Immigration Canada, *Success in the Works: A Profile of Canada's Engineering Workforce*, Ottawa, 1989.

6b. Commission on Workforce Quality and Labour Market Efficiency, *Investing in People*, 1989. (See especially papers 7a, 7b, and 7c on private sector training in Volume 1 of Background Papers.)

7. Edgar H. Schein, "How to Break In the College Graduate," *Harvard Business Review* (November-December 1964): 68–76.

8. T.J. Peters and R.H. Waterman, Jr., *In Search of Excellence: Lessons from America's Best-Run Companies* (New York: Warner, 1982).

9. L.E. Danielson, *Characteristics of Engineers and Scientists* (Ann Arbor: University of Michigan, 1960), 55–78.

10. Schein, "College Graduate."

11. *Engineering Professionalism in Industry* (Washington, DC: The Professional Engineers Conference Board of Industry, 1960), 35–37.

12. E. Raudsepp, "What Motivates Today's Engineers?" *Machine Design* (January 21, 1988): 84–87.

CHAPTER 4

Engineers in Management

Some people believe that management represents a natural path of advancement, but engineers frequently are not convinced. Their view is that if they had wanted to aim for management, they would have gone to business school, not engineering school. This chapter does not try to persuade readers one way or the other. However, since so many engineers *do* eventually go into management (perhaps as many as two-thirds), it seems desirable for engineers to be well informed on the topic.

WHAT DO MANAGERS REALLY DO?

There is a simple answer to the question of what managers do. They manage money, materials, and people to meet corporate objectives. During the office day, however, the manager is seldom alone. There are many meetings as well as informal interactions with associates, because the manager, as an executive, is primarily concerned with people. The single most distinctive characteristic of an executive's job is getting numbers of people moving in the same direction.

The chairman of the board of an American engine company graphically described the multiple pressures that operate on an executive:

> To illustrate, let us suppose we can see inside the head of the president of a large manufacturing organization. His company employs 20,000 persons and operates half a dozen plants. It distributes its products in every state and in many foreign countries, and — most frightening of all — it has competitors.
>
> Now let us suppose that these competitors are extremely vigorous, and that our president knows that to maintain his share of the market and to make earnings which will please his directors, he must accomplish the following very quickly: design and perfect a brand-new and more advanced line of products; tool up these products in such a way as to permit higher

quality and lower costs than his competitors; purchase new machinery; arrange major additional long-term financing. At the same time his corporation's labor contract is up for negotiation, and this must be rewritten in such a way as to obtain good employee response and yet make no more concessions than do his competitors. Sales coverage of all customers has to be intensified, and sales costs reduced. Every one of these objectives must be accomplished simultaneously, and ahead of similar efforts on the part of his competitors — or the future of his company is in great danger. Every head of a corporation lives every day with the awareness that it is quite possible to go broke. At the same time he lives with the awareness that he cannot personally accomplish a single one of these vital objectives. The actual work will have to be accomplished by numerous individuals, with some actually unknown to him, most of them many layers removed from his direct influence in the organization.[1]

The second most characteristic aspect of a manager's job is decision making. As we will show later, the engineer is a decision maker, too, and by virtue of this function is also a manager; however, the effects of decisions made by a person in management are more immediately apparent than the effects of those made by an engineer. The effects of an engineer's decisions may ultimately be far-reaching, but they are usually subtle. This is not the case with the executive, who may be acutely aware that a decision today to cut back production means that hundreds of people will be out of work tomorrow.

Making decisions is a lonely privilege. Inevitably there is a time in the career of every person who follows the management route when the realization comes that there is no one to turn to for help in making a decision. Before this point, there was always a boss who could provide advice. But for the manager it soon becomes apparent, with a shock, that the boss cannot help. There are many possible reasons why this might be so. The boss may be too far away, may not have the special background necessary to understand the situation, or may not have the necessary time. Even more troubling, the manager may fear that the boss will not *take* the time. Finally, it may simply be that the boss has delegated major responsibilities to the manager and *expects* decisions to be made. This is complicated by the fact that one of the hardest decisions to make is the decision of what to take to the boss and what to determine for oneself.

In the effort to ease this loneliness, executives may turn to committees to help them make decisions. It may even be possible for executives to bury the responsibility for their decisions in the anonymity of committee action. But this is feasible only to a limited degree. Even if a decision has been made by a committee, the ultimate responsibility for a bad decision will probably come to rest upon the individual executive who originally had the responsibility for acting. Knowing this, most executives use a committee in two major capacities: as a sounding board to enlarge their own perceptions of the problem, and as a means to involve their associates and subordinates in the decision-making process and thus to approach unity of purpose as nearly as is possible. Following a committee meeting during which the problem has been thoroughly aired, the executive then makes the final decision.

LEVELS OF MANAGEMENT

Management authority and responsibility vary considerably, depending upon the level. A list of some management levels, together with typical titles of those in each category follows:

- Executive: chairman of the board, president, vice-president (of manufacturing, of engineering, of marketing, of finance, and so forth), general manager, treasurer, controller

- Manager: plant manager, chief engineer, director of engineering, general sales manager, personnel manager

- Superintendent: chief project engineer, chief industrial engineer, group head, regional sales manager, assembly-line superintendent

- Supervisor: project engineer, office manager

In *The Executive Life*, the editors of *Fortune* list the five characteristic functions of an *executive* as setting policy, making major decisions, co-ordinating, organizing, and delegating responsibility. The term "top management" is frequently used to identify this level.

According to *Fortune*, a person at the *manager* level does not set policy but interprets and carries out policies formulated by others. Such an individual may have the authority to make decisions of considerable importance—for instance, approval of union contracts—but makes these decisions within the limits set by top-executive policy.

A *superintendent* differs from a manager primarily in the magnitude of the decisions to be made and from the category below by virtue of functioning as a supervisor of supervisors. The term "middle management" generally encompasses the two categories of manager and superintendent.

A *supervisor* enforces rules, sees that quotas are met, administers personnel matters, and in other ways operates within fairly narrow and well-defined limits. Usually the term "first-line supervisor" is employed to describe these activities; this phrase signifies that the people being supervised are the productive workers themselves.[2]

Generally, when people state a desire to "go into management," they mean being an executive or a manager; the positions of supervisor and superintendent are likely to be regarded as way stations on the road to ambition's fulfilment. Most of the discussion below is relevant to these two higher categories, since these are the levels where money, prestige, and influence (attractions) as well as stress and loss of personal freedom (drawbacks) are most in evidence.

ATTRACTIONS TO MANAGEMENT CAREERS

Everybody knows that executives make plenty of money. Probably the only question that remains to be answered is the personal one: "How much am *I* likely to make?" It is interesting that the salaries of the top moneymakers are public knowledge. Some make millions of dollars a year. But there are only a handful of such people; very few aspiring managers—even ambitious ones—really expect to make that much. It is more probable that they are thinking of jobs in the $100 000-plus category.

According to *The Executive Life*, there seems to be some kind of unwritten formula for determining executive salaries. If the number one person gets $100 000, then the next one is likely to be paid $75 000. There are no hard and fast rules, and company size is an important deciding factor. In an extremely large company like General Motors, there would be many levels, including several jobs in the $800 000-plus category. However, General Motors can hardly be considered a typical corporation.

A good deal of salary compression has occurred in recent decades. A national survey of engineers' salaries in 1988 showed that supervisors had salaries overlapping executives' salaries to some extent. The survey also showed that supervisors' salaries averaged about 25 percent more than non-supervisors salaries.[3]

Challenge and Creativity

After the basic human wants — food, shelter, and security — have been satisfied, people look around for new worlds to conquer. If there are no natural obstacles to be overcome, they will invent some.

Thus people compete in business, climb mountains, engage in sports, and write books; many undertake difficult educational programs that go far beyond what would be necessary solely for economic survival.

All these things are manifestations of challenge, which in itself is one of the most compelling urges that propel people into management careers. It is the excitement and exhilaration of the game itself that some enjoy. A high level of energy and drive are universally recognized as essential ingredients for management success. A person who does not have this high level of drive but who aspires to a management career has already made an important mistake.

When an executive speaks of the job as being creative, this is not just giving idle play to a fashionable word: the statement is sincere. Executives enjoy seeing programs that they originated take shape and prosper, accompanied by organizational flowering and growth. Nor should it be doubted that many are motivated by a genuine desire to give service. Almost all human beings wish to feel their existence has meaning and value to the rest of the world, and managers are no exception.

Management as Leadership

Complex organizations staffed with motivated professionals need leaders first and managers second. Good leaders are not only born; they can also be created through an individual commitment to developing the skills necessary. Fundamental to the process is the knowledge that to lead others you must first manage yourself. This idea is clearly expressed in an article by John Farrow, reproduced in full from *Engineering Dimensions*, with permission.

> The following advertisement was published in the *Wall Street Journal* by United Technologies Corporation:
> People don't want to be managed. They want to be led. Whoever heard of a world manager? World leader, yes. Educational leader. Political leader. Scout leader. Community leader. Labour leader. Business leader. They lead, they don't manage. The carrot always wins over the stick. Ask your horse. You can *lead* your horse to water, but you can't *manage* him to drink. If you want to manage somebody, manage yourself. Do that well and you'll be ready to stop managing and start leading.
> People today are better educated and have different expectations from those of 20 years ago. Professionals, including engineers, are one of the groups leading this change towards a different management style. They seek involvement and par-

ticipation at the work place. Their managers must be leaders; in fact, most working enterprises acknowledge the need for better leadership at all levels.

Leaders are not just born; they can also be created. If you can manage yourself, and develop your skills, you have the discipline needed to lead others.

Philosophy of Leadership

For some, the word "leadership" implies that one person is a dictator who makes all the decisions and does all the work of leading others. However, in groups with more than two or three members, there are usually too many factors for one person to do everything. A good leader works as a senior partner with other members of the group to achieve the task, build the team and meet individual needs. From moment to moment, the leadership of the group can shift from one member to another, depending on the circumstances.

The leader must also recognize that most groups have three categories of need. Leadership functions, therefore, break down into three groups: task needs, group maintenance needs and individual needs. The leader must not only recognize these different categories of need, but must also understand that others will share the job of satisfying these needs. Leadership itself must be a team effort.

There are six key leadership requirements: *vision, planning, communicating, monitoring, organizing, and role modelling.*

Vision

Having a vision is the basis for all leadership. It is a big task in leading big organizations, but it is also necessary for smaller groups, because it involves bringing to life objectives that can be understood in personal terms. We often create a vision to help ourselves achieve a desired goal. Athletes trying to achieve peak performance at a prescribed moment use this technique a great deal. For Muhammad Ali, it was "to float like a butterfly, sting like a bee." My guess is that his coach coined this phrase to help Ali focus more closely on his performance in the boxing ring.

Individuals within organizations need visions as well. In the early days of Polaroid, Edwin Land inspired his team with the vision that they could "achieve the impossible." This compelling vision led to achievements for Polaroid that other organizations thought unrealizable.

However, these corporate visions are not easily created. They often require much thought, study, trial and error. Effective visions for organizations are not the product of semi-mystical revelations, but the result of hard work — by the leaders. Furthermore, a good vision is not simply offered once and then allowed to fade away. It must be repeated often so it becomes part of the organization's culture and is reinforced through the decision-making process. It must also be re-evaluated often against changing circumstances and, if necessary, updated.

A vision often starts with the leader, but must then be "owned" by the whole organization. To achieve this, a leader must explain the vision, what is involved, and why it exists. The vision must also be related to individual roles, and hence must be broken down into tasks individuals can relate to.

Planning

Planning involves bridging the gap between where you and the organization are today and where you and the organization want to be at some point in the future. Planning is a response to the group's need to determine how the task will be achieved. This, in turn, leads to such questions as: "Who does what?" and "When does it have to be done?" A leader without a plan is unlikely to be effective.

The development of a plan is not always as easy as it seems. Good planning is usually, but not necessarily, participatory. An effective plan development process ensures that a broad range of people have a common understanding of the objectives. It involves examining alternatives, in order to select the best solution. Finally, it involves a detailed description of tasks that will become the responsibility of small groups or individuals.

Vision is what; planning is how, who and when.

Communicating

Good leaders communicate their visions, in a way that many can relate to. When they are communicating specific planned activities, they must conduct detailed briefings which are precise and clear. Good communication requires:

- *Preparation.* Create a structure that people can remember and into which they can fit details.
- *Clarity.* Think through potential difficulties and ensure that complexities are made sufficiently simple to be understood.
- *Energy.* Ensure that the message demands attention and is easy to remember and pass on.

- *Sincerity*. Communicate what you believe and what can, in turn, be trusted.
- *Follow-up*. Has the message been received? Follow-up can be done through question periods and/or careful observation. If the message hasn't been fully understood, try again.

Monitor, Evaluate, Control

These three functions conform to what some used to see as "management." Each of these steps is closely linked with the others.

Monitoring involves checking progress against the plan. Groups must be sensitive to the need for this to ensure that the task is realized. A leader is often responsible for monitoring, but it is a task that is readily delegated. For example, monitoring the financial performance of many companies is often the primary responsibility of the vice president, finance. However, deciding *what* needs to be monitored is a more critical decision, and usually involves leadership.

Similarly, *evaluating* the results of the monitoring to determine what it means can be simple or complex, and again, is usually a leadership responsibility. Ideally, a group that is experienced, skilled and able to determine the appropriate action will respond well to the majority of situations. However, for the group to demonstrate this ability, the circumstances must have been anticipated and responsive action decided upon in advance. This, in turn, requires planning and training.

Controlling usually involves some type of intervention. In most cases, teams should be self-controlling; however, one of the roles a leader may assume is that of ensuring that this self-controlling mechanism is working effectively, and of taking responsibility for intervention when it is not.

Engineers are usually familiar with these process control skills because they apply to production equipment. The process of intervening in groups is much more difficult and requires that the basic technical approaches to monitoring and controlling be supplemented by people-management skills. The type of intervention required will depend on the circumstances. Hence, from a management perspective, the key is to match the type of intervention to the needs of the group or individuals being managed.

Organizing

To achieve anything, some structure must be imposed, especially if the group is large and the task is complex. The structure may be permanent, but could be temporary if the group is responsible for a single task. In organizing, three principles are especially useful:

1. Smaller work groups tend to be more effective than larger ones.
2. The capability of the leaders of the sub-groups should be considered when sizing groups.
3. Creating additional levels in the organization is costly and often slows communication.

How you decide to structure a group is dependent on both the task and the people. It is not a science, but an art; therefore, if what exists now isn't working, change it — but make the changes in consultation with those concerned with an eye to minimizing short-term disruption.

Role Modelling

A good example is the most powerful individual communication and leadership tool. One key role for the leader is to represent, time and again, what he or she wants the organization to be. The larger the organization, the more important it is for the leader to play a symbolic role which can be consistently interpreted by a large number of people. However, leaders faced with the complexity of larger organizations must be prepared for greater difficulty in being consistent and meaningful models.

Trustworthiness is perhaps the most effective example. In any organization, many different individuals must learn to trust each other. Trust within a group is something that the leader can strongly influence, especially by exemplifying openness and consistency. Being a model in this regard is vital for a good leader.

Conclusion

Leaders are born less often than they are created. This creation comes, in part, from circumstances and from individual commitment to developing the requisite skills.[4]

ACADEMIC REQUIREMENTS FOR MANAGERS

Engineers appear to make good managers; for example, a 1986 survey showed that one-third of the 50 largest corporations in the world are run by CEOs (chief executive officers) who have engineering backgrounds. This does not necessarily mean that they were promoted through the engineering departments, but it does mean that they received their basic degrees in engineering. Simultaneously, the percentage of CEOS with financial backgrounds appears to be diminishing. In 1985, 44 percent of the newly appointed CEOS had technical or operations backgrounds, and only 12 percent of them had financial backgrounds.[5]

One of the reasons for the popularity of engineering as a background is the training in solving problems that engineers receive in university; this skill is obviously a useful one to managers. But another reason is the growing technical complexity of industry. As *Management Practice Quarterly* says: "U.S. business is responding to some of the bitter lessons of globalized competition, where pragmatic nuts-and-bolts skills may be more critical than abstract managerial skills." In spite of these favourable views, there are still plenty of critics of engineers as managers. They lack organizational and political instincts, say some, and often have no sense of finance.[6]

University students interested in management careers sometimes decide that the best thing is to get a bachelor's degree in engineering, followed by a master's degree in business administration (MBA). An MBA program certainly does contain the kinds of organizational financial material that managers need, but there is also a danger if one acquires an MBA before seeking first-time employment. The danger exists partly because the number of people earning MBAS has become quite large (more than 50 000 a year in the United States in the 1980s) and because they may never get the engineering experience needed to register as a professional engineer, but also because people with such academic credentials often turn prospective employers off by their attitude. The attitude stems, according to *Time* magazine, from their belief that they are destined to take command of the organizations they join. Said *Time*, "A growing number of corporate managers look on them as arrogant amateurs, trained only in figures and lacking experience." They are seen as too expensive, too aggressive, and lacking in loyalty.[7]

Nevertheless, the skills learned through an MBA program are important for management. A 1980 study of 12 000 top executives, done by the University of Michigan, showed that 30 percent of them had MBAS — up from only 10 percent fifteen years earlier.[8] The best advice for aspiring managers seems to be that they do need to acquire these skills; but if they do so through an MBA program, aspirants should be aware of the pitfalls cited above.

Persons with technical backgrounds have a strong edge when it comes to managing high-tech companies. Also, managers of such firms are likely to earn more than their counterparts in other industries. Northeastern University, in Boston, made a survey in 1987 of

35 top American executives in the fields of manufacturing, high-tech, insurance, banking, and utilities. The average salaries for the executives in high-tech or manufacturing companies were roughly double those in banking or utilities. Of those in the manufacturing area, 23 percent had engineering backgrounds; in the high-tech areas, 60 percent had engineering backgrounds.[9] A 1984 study of 25 leading Japanese manufacturing companies showed that two-thirds of their top executives had degrees in engineering or science.[10]

Another graduate program that is accessible to engineers with management aspirations is the master's program in industrial engineering, management sciences, or engineering management offered by a number of universities in the United States and Canada. The prospective master's student is usually expected to have a bachelor's degree in engineering and will study a combination of management and technical courses. Typical courses are organizational theory, marketing management, production management, human relations, accounting, engineering law, project management, value analysis, computer science, and operations research. Most often, graduates from these programs obtain their first jobs in production, industrial engineering, or marketing.[11]

PERSONAL CHARACTERISTICS OF MANAGERS

The earlier sections of this chapter defined the management task, but did not set out the personal characteristics required to be an effective manager or executive. As an aid to the engineer who aspires to management and the executive suite, the following checklist of personal characteristics may be useful. The engineering manager should have:

1. A willingness to place the company first.

2. A high degree of aggressiveness and drive, including a willingness to work long hours.

3. An ability to manage people.

4. A strong desire for personal status and economic gain.

5. A desire to be in control.

6. A high degree of tolerance for frustration and disappointment.

7. Persistent optimism. No matter how bleak things look, the ideal management aspirant always has a constructive program on tap. The cynic is unpopular in management.

8. The ability to *finish* a job as well as to initiate it. Actually, this characteristic is in demand at all times and places and not just for management positions. It is among the rarest of the world's commodities, and its absence is seldom detected by people who do not have it.

9. Good judgement and logical thinking ability. These qualities are sometimes known simply as intelligence. In a complicated situation, the manager must be able to sort things out into their proper relationships and to dig beneath surface irrelevancies to get at the heart of issues. This having been accomplished, it is necessary to forecast the future and be right most of the time.

10. The ability to communicate, not only in writing but, above all, orally.

Surveys show that the maturity that comes with age is also a factor in becoming a manager. The U.S. National Engineers Register for 1973 shows the division of responsibility as a function of age, as shown in Table 4-1. Thus, by age 35, more than half the engineers surveyed could be considered managers, and by age 45 over two-thirds of them could be so classed. It is likely that the distribution has changed little since 1973.

Table 4-1

Engineers' Management Responsibility as a Function of Age

	Age		
	30–35 (%)	40–45 (%)	50–55 (%)
General management	4	12	15
Manager of major division	12	24	27
Project supervisor	25	24	20
Unit supervisor	16	12	9
Indirect supervisor	21	16	16
No supervisory responsibility	22	12	13
Total	100	100	100

Source: *The Engineer as a Manager* (New York: Engineering Manpower Commission of the American Association of Engineering Societies, Washington, D.C., September 1973). Reproduced with permission.

DEVELOPING NEW PRODUCTS

This section deals with one of the most difficult problems facing management: how one goes about developing successful new products. Today it is well known that any successful product has only a limited life. Booz, Allen, and Hamilton, a major consulting firm, claims that when a product reaches its peak in sales volume, it has already started its downhill slide in profits.[12] In the current world, a continuing stream of new products is absolutely essential to the well-being of a business.

Top management usually takes the viewpoint that one of its most important functions is to foster, analyze, and develop new product ideas. Hence, there is a tendency to keep the new-product function in the highest echelons of management. If the new products in question are mostly extensions of the present product line, these responsibilities may be entrusted to the marketing vice-president. However, if the new-product investigations reach into areas that are completely unexplored, such responsibilities are more likely given to a new-products department, sometimes directly attached to the president's office.

Generally, the functions of a new-products department are to:

1. Generate new ideas

2. Seek, analyze, and screen ideas from all sources

3. Co-ordinate market needs with research and development ideas

4. Conduct pilot tests of new products under market conditions

Of these four functions, the most useful and important is probably the second, since new ideas may come from many sources. Most companies rely on their research and development departments to generate new ideas (function 1), but other sources may be equally prolific. Other possible sources of new ideas are unused patents, government, and top management itself.

A veritable avalanche of new patents is issued every year; very few of these patents see commercial use because patent owners may find themselves unable to press ahead with commercial development. As a result, many patents are available for licence or sale. In addition, an examination of issued patents may generate entirely new product ideas. If one wished to find a route to the largest number of creative minds in this country, the trail of issued patents would surely be the best starting place.

Supplying goods needed by the government is big business. Many companies have offices in Ottawa and Washington whose purpose is to maintain constant contact with government agencies in order to ascertain their needs and to anticipate trends.

In some organizations, particularly those that were founded by creative technical people, a major source of new ideas continues to be top management. It is interesting to note how many companies were literally started in garages with only a few technical people making things go. Hewlett-Packard, one of today's giants, was started in a garage with $5000 in capital; a more recent example is Apple Computer.[13]

Whatever their source, after a group of ideas has been collected, they must be carefully screened (function 2). Out of this group, an average of only 1 in 58 actually becomes a successful product, according to Booz, Allen, and Hamilton.

Ideas that survive the screening step are analyzed on a return-on-investment basis. At this point, an estimate of the future market must be made; usually this estimate is coupled with a market survey. However, the information acquired through a market survey must be examined with an experienced and sceptical eye. Many companies have been seriously misled by accepting survey results at face value. One incident, reported by a vice-president of Westinghouse, concerns portable televisions. When portable TVs were first being considered, two electronics manufacturers conducted surveys on their market potential and both received negative reports. One company abandoned the idea, the other went ahead. Today, of course, portable television sets are a major product.[14] The point of the story is that the wants of today (which are mostly what a market survey will reveal) may be quite different from the wants of tomorrow.

Many products fail because of insufficient field testing under actual market conditions (function 4). The customer can be relied upon to find all sorts of defects in the product that have somehow not shown up during in-plant testing. Efficiently conducted, field testing can show whether the wants of the marketplace have been correctly identified, *before* costly and nearly irrevocable steps have been taken toward mass production and distribution.

Return-on-Investment Analysis

Before a project goes very far, someone must take a hard look at the future and try to decide if the proposed product has any chance of yielding a profit. In order to do this, two things are necessary: somebody must devise a reasonably clear configuration of the proposed product, so that production costs can be estimated; and somebody must predict the anticipated annual sales.

Table 4-2 shows a typical return-on-investment analysis for a consumer product that will sell for $300. For this product, it is estimated that $1 000 000 will be required for development and another $1 000 000 for plant expansion, tooling, and distribution start-up (including sales training costs, service training costs, and the expense of staffing new offices). Such a capital investment is by no means unusual; in fact, the usual tendency is to underestimate the amount of capital required.

In the analysis shown, it is assumed that the third year after introduction of the product represents what will be a steady-state condition and that the return of 27 percent per year will continue henceforth. (Return on investment is calculated by dividing the gross annual return by the total capital investment, in this case $820 000/$3 080 000 \cong 0.27.) At this rate, the company's investment would be recovered by the fifth year. However, such an assumption might be naive. For one thing, the competition cannot be expected to stand still during this five-year period, and there is a high likelihood that additional R&D investments will be required during the five years to keep ahead of the competition. Furthermore, if the sales estimates are optimistic, as often seems to be the case, or the manufacturing cost estimate turns out to be too low, the whole proposition could become unattractive.

An interesting outline of some of the problems involved in creating new products was provided by a vice-president of research and development for a large American company. He said that a product in his field may take as long as seven or eight years from research discovery to commercial success, and that the decision on a new product will prove to have been justified:

- *if* it can be achieved technically in the laboratory;

- *if* it can be reproduced on a factory scale;

- *if* after four years of research, the board of directors will approve the appropriation to build the plant;

- *if* rejects and costs are reasonably low in factory production;

- *if* consumers will buy the predicted volume of the product in six years;

- *if* consumers will pay enough for the product to provide a satisfactory gross profit; and

- *if* all this comes to pass before a competitor markets a similar product.[15]

Table 4-2

Sample of a Return-on-Investment Analysis for a Consumer Product

	First Year	Second Year	Third Year
Initial investment (R&D, plant expansion, tooling, and so forth)	$2 000 000		
Number of units required for sales inventory	4 000	8 000	12 000
Dollars tied up in inventory, at factory value	($150 × 4 000) = $600 000	($100 × 8 000) = $800 000	($90 × 12 000) = $1 080 000
Total capital investment	$2 600 000	$2 800 000	$3 080 000
Annual sales (number of units)	3 600	7 200	12 000
Manufacturing cost, per unit	$150	$100	$90
Selling price, per unit	$300	$300	$300
Selling expense (at 37.5%)	$112	$112	$112
General and administrative expense (at 10%)	$30	$30	$30
Net return, per unit	$8	$58	$68
Gross annual return	$29 000	$420 000	$820 000
Annual return on investment (%)	1	15	27

DRAWBACKS IN MANAGEMENT CAREERS

In any discussion of management careers, it is important to point out that there may be negative factors or "drawbacks," although many people in management may find these factors minor or a "fair price" to pay for the benefits. A decision concerning the direction of a person's career is, after all, a personal one and is made according to each person's own value judgements about all the advantages and disadvantages of a given set of alternatives.

Loss of Personal Freedom

One infringement on a manager's freedom concerns the right to select social companions as one pleases. Some managers make it a rule never to socialize with other company people, for fear that such an arrangement may someday prove embarrassing. Conversely, others feel *compelled* to socialize with company people, especially if the company is in a small town. Both conditions are a curtailment of freedom.

The young executive may find that much socializing is in the form of company obligations. For example, entertaining out-of-town VIPs may be required, and the question may arise as to what all this has to do with the job. Nevertheless, it must be recognized that many executives enjoy this part of their work. While some regard it as a curtailment of freedom, others look upon it as a kind of fringe benefit.

Of a more serious nature is the demand of practically all companies that an executive give total allegiance to the organization. One student of management behaviour stated that to get to the top one must put on a pair of blinders and shut out everything except business. In other words, the corporation must become one's life.[16]

Suppression of Emotion: Stress

The executive with ulcers is a standard fixture in the popular image of the modern business world. Like all stereotypes, this one is often false; nevertheless, many managers do experience physical disorders that have their origin in emotional stress. It is pressure, of course, that causes this situation; but what causes the pressure?

In some instances, pressure has been used by the higher-ups as a conscious management tool to maintain an atmosphere of urgency and to make sure everyone is working at maximum output. Managers who object to the nervous strain are almost sure to hear the admonition "If you can't stand the heat, get out of the kitchen." Hence, any adverse feelings may be forced under wraps. The result is more stress.

There are many other well-known sources of stress, such as anxiety concerning job security, slowness of promotion, and intense competition with rivals. Not so well known, but probably one of the biggest ulcer-producers, is the requirement that the ideal executive always present a calm, self-assured façade. Even though, internally, the executive may be as much assailed by feelings of weakness and self-doubt as anyone, these can never be allowed to show.

Experts at the Yale Labor and Management Center, who have been very active in research on managers and management characteristics, offer the following as some of the important qualities of the executive.

1. Has high tolerance for frustration
2. Permits criticism without feeling personally threatened
3. Engages in continual self-examination
4. Is a strong, cool competitor
5. Expresses hostility tactfully
6. Accepts both victories and setbacks with controlled emotions[17]

After studiously suppressing emotions, as implied by these characteristics, the executive is then surprised when they flare up in the form of a physical disorder.

Promotion to a position of increased responsibility often brings on a state of mind *Fortune* calls "promotion neurosis," in which the subject experiences great anxiety and emotional conflict. The most common sufferer from this neurosis, says *Fortune*, is the engineer or scientist who has been forced into an administrative job. *Fortune* quotes a psychologist who says that engineers in management have "a very real tendency to regard people (especially subordinates) as complicated machines which are different from tools primarily in two ways—they are harder to renovate and more costly to oil."[18]

Family Impact

The demand that the executive put the job before everything else means one's family life is often a casualty. Naturally, it must be recognized that not all people assign the same values to the same things. Many will accept the intrusion on family life that frequently goes with being an executive and never feel they have missed anything.

One of the things young people very quickly learn is that corporations generally expect instant mobility in their management hopefuls. If one is in Calgary and the company offers a transfer to Ottawa (presumably a promotion), it usually expects a "yes" answer with little hesitation. If the offer is declined, then the next person on the list will be chosen, and it can be assumed that one's own climb up the promotion ladder may be slower. Most companies consider mobility important.

Obviously, a person's spouse will have a great deal to say about such matters. In many families, both husband and wife hold jobs, and an instant move for one may not be easy to arrange. Understandably, family relations could become strained under such circumstances unless both spouses are thoroughly committed to the same objectives.

A considerable amount of investigation has been conducted regarding the impact of a management career upon family life, based upon actual experiences of both men and women managers. One major study involved interviews with 30 male managers who worked for a very large American corporation. Their wives were also interviewed. Most of the managers were in sales, but some were in personnel, production, and research. A pronounced feature of the lives of nearly all of the managers was that they had moved frequently. In general, the men looked upon these moves positively, because they were invariably associated with promotions. But the author of the study, Diane Margolis, reported: "For the man it is a reward. For the woman and the children it is a penalty. ... He gets higher status; they lose home and community."[19]

Another problem with moving is the impact on family finances that results from moving from an inexpensive part of the country to a major city such as Toronto or Vancouver, where housing prices have escalated dramatically in recent years. Although some companies have enlightened policies for helping the employee to sell a house conveniently, there is always a risk of serious financial loss when promoted to a job in a big city.

Because of the problems with frequent moves, executives appear increasingly reluctant to move if it means disrupting their families. It has been estimated that half the executives who are asked to move each year would now decline to do so, compared with only 10 percent in 1971.[20]

Many books have been published on the particular problems of women executives. In 1982, a conference on "The Woman in Management" was held at Cornell University, bringing together women executives to share their experiences. One of them said:

> Women have to deal with an environment where women in management may or may not be something new. You are moved to a new office; the men there may be older than you are and they may not be terribly excited at the prospect of reporting to you. They may never like you but if they are tuned in, they will realize that you can offer them opportunities that they would not have if you were not their supervisor.[21]

Many professional women are members of dual-career couples, and these pose a special problem if a move to a new location comes up, because some choices have to be made. Either one of the partners has to do a lot of commuting, or jobs for both have to be found at the new location, or one of them has to quit working. More and more, the second choice — jobs for both at the new location — is becoming possible. Companies in many cases are beginning to accept such conditions as a part of doing business, and some have joined in networks to find jobs for the spouses — sometimes wives, sometimes husbands — of the persons being moved.

If a dual-career couple decides to have a family, then the expense of child care can enter the picture. Some employers have sponsored child-care facilities for their employees, but finding reliable, high-quality child care remains a problem. Even when the problems are solved, one woman executive says:

> It is a pressure-cooker existence. It means sixteen hours of a fast-paced, nonstop schedule for the mother; a few hours more or less, depending on his evening schedule, for the father. Their life is all work and family. There is barely time to sit down, never mind time for friends or personal hobbies.[22]

Nevertheless, the concluding consensus at the Cornell conference was:

> Women managers [were advised] to get the very most out of their jobs that they could and to fight for promotion to higher-paying posts. Top jobs are few and far between but they are so much fun to do that getting them and keeping them is worth the struggle.[23]

Underscoring this point of view is the advice given by David Dougherty in his book *From Technical Professional to Corporate Manager* — advice that is applicable to both men and women: "With each step you will enter a more select group of individuals, who do things right most of the time. The individuals in the higher groups are more confident, more enthusiastic, and more fun to work with."[24]

A Conflict of Moralities

A serious potential difficulty in a management career arises in the sphere of moral action. The problem comes into being because some companies demand that their managers follow a policy of seeking only the good of the company, to the exclusion of other considerations. A three-year study conducted at the University of California, Los Angeles, on executives and how they get ahead showed that some executives were not sure the usual moral standards observed by most people in their personal lives are applicable to business.[25]

Such a policy can lead to serious problems. When the policy expresses itself in the form of trusts and cartels, society reacts by passing antitrust laws. When the policy results in the exploitation of workers, labour reacts by forming unions. When it expresses itself in the form of cheap, unsafe equipment, government agencies step in with restrictive laws.

In price-fixing suits against the U.S. electrical industry in 1961, the presiding judge described the individual defendants as "torn between conscience and an approved corporate policy. ... [They are examples of] the company man, the conformist, who goes along with his superiors and finds balm for his conscience in additional comforts and the security of his place in the corporate setup." It was shown that, within the organizations, managers who believed in obeying the law were sidetracked from promotions; their respect for ethical behaviour was mocked as "religious." One of the defendants stated: "I was to replace a man who took a strictly religious view of it; who, because he had signed this slip of paper wouldn't contact competitors or talk to them — even when they came to his home." He added, "I was glad to get the promotion. I had no objections."

Fortune commented on these law suits: "No thoughtful person could have left that courtroom untroubled by the problems of corporate power and corporate ethics. ... Big Business ... establishes the kind of competition that is typical of our system and sets the moral tone of the marketplace."[26]

In a 1977 *Harvard Business Review* survey, the respondents indicated that they felt a considerable degree of personal concern because of conflicts between company interests and personal ethics. However, the concerns were not the same ones that had been expressed in similar surveys taken in the 1960s. For example, price fixing was less of an issue than it had been earlier, and concern over honesty in communication and over bribes and kickbacks headed the list of worries. For example, a vice-president of engineering in one company stated that he was worried about misrepresentation of products, while another was concerned about deliberate understating of delivery times in order to get contracts. Nevertheless, in spite of these concerns, 98 percent of the respondents expressed agreement with the statement "In the long run, sound ethics is good business."[27]

A bit of homely advice — advice that runs counter to the impressions gained from TV — is to practise scrupulous honesty and to become known for keeping your word:

> The moment you're guilty of any dishonesty, no matter how slight—whenever you take anything at all for your own personal use without paying for it, no matter how small—you've weakened your moral authority over your subordinates. Your

employees will criticize, ridicule, despise you. You'll never be able to regain their complete respect.[28]

Some final advice is offered for any engineer, management bound or not. It is important to attend professional conferences at every opportunity, because that way you learn not only what is going on in your field but also what is happening at other companies. Another piece of good advice is to keep up with what is happening in your *own* company by reading its annual reports.

TOPICS FOR STUDY AND DISCUSSION

1. An argument could be presented that engineering *is* management, because it is decision-oriented. However, not everyone agrees with this conclusion, and some have argued the opposite view. For the purpose of this exercise, adopt the contrary view — that engineering is *not* management — and write out a statement refuting the position of the authors. Which argument do you believe to be closer to the truth? Do you believe an engineer's performance on the job might be influenced by whether that engineer holds to one view or the other?

2. Most engineers eventually have to decide whether they want to move into management or stay in purely technical work. Make a list for yourself of the pros and cons of each alternative.

3. In Chapter 3, two kinds of organizational systems were described: "closed" and "open." Write down what you consider to be the good and bad points of each system, and try to formulate a set of reasons why you might prefer to work under one system rather than the other. Would your answer be different if you were evaluating the organizational system from the viewpoint of management rather than as an employee?

4. Visualize yourself some twenty years in the future: you are now the chief engineer of a medium-sized manufacturing company, employing about 50 to 100 engineers. Decide for yourself what kind of product your company is manufacturing, picking something with which you have some familiarity. Now, assuming you are going to organize into a functional structure like that described in Chapter 3, decide what functions need to be represented in your engineering department. Describe how the development of new products would occur, with the follow-on activities of product design and testing, given your functional structure.

5. In the return-on-investment analysis shown in Table 4-2, what happens if the manufacturing cost can never be brought below $110? How many

years would it then take to recover the total capital investment? What if sales cannot be increased beyond the level of 3600 units per year? What if the analysis proceeds as shown for the first three years, but the annual sales in the fourth year are 7200 and in the fifth and succeeding years are back to 3600 because of the introduction of similar products by competitors?

NOTES

1. J.I. Miller, "The Dilemma of the Corporation Man," *Fortune* (August 1959): 103. © 1959 Time Inc. All rights reserved.

2. Editors of *Fortune, The Executive Life* (Garden City, NY: Doubleday, 1956).

3. *Professional Income of Engineers: 1988*, (Washington, DC: Engineering Manpower Commission, 1988).

4. J. Farrow, "Getting Rid of Management," *Engineering Dimensions* 10, no. 5 (September/October 1989): 22–24. Reproduced in full with permission.

5. A. Chapple, "Engineers as CEOs: Those on Top Show the Field Begets Managers," *Engineering Times* (June 1988): 1ff.

6. Cited in Chapple, "Engineers as CEOs."

7. "The Money Chase," *Time* (May 4, 1981): 58–69.

8. Cited in "The Money Chase."

9. P.T. Crotty, "Riding on the Fast Track," *Management World* (March/April 1988): 22–23.

10. "America's New Commitment to Manufacturing Education," *American Machinist* (June 1985): 105–20.

11. D.L. Babcock, "BS and MS Programs in Engineering Management," *Engineering Education* (November 1973): 101–108; D.B. Smith, "Graduate Engineering Management with Flexible Options," *Engineering Education* (November 1973): 108ff; M. Everett, "The EM Route to Management," *Graduating Engineer* (March 1987): 21–23.

12. *Management of New Products* (New York: Booz, Allen, and Hamilton, 1964), p. 6.

13. Adapted, by permission of the Publisher, from "Supplementary Opportunities for Innovation," by Wade Worth, from *Developing a Product*

Strategy, E. Marting, ed., © 1959 AMACOM, a division of American Management Association, New York. All rights reserved.

14. Worth, "Supplementary Opportunities."

15. Worth, "Supplementary Opportunities."

16. B.G. Davis, "Executivism: How to Climb the Executive Ladder," *Mechanical Engineering* (July 1964): 22–25.

17. C. Argyris, "Some Characteristics of Successful Executives," *Personnel Journal* (June 1953): 50–55.

18. *The Executive Life*, 87.

19. D.R. Margolis, *The Managers: Corporate Life in America* (New York: William Morrow, 1979).

20. J.D. Arnold, *Shooting the Executive Rapids* (New York: McGraw-Hill, 1981).

21. J. Farley, ed., *The Woman in Management: Career and Family Issues* (Ithaca, NY: ILR Press, 1983).

22. Farley, *Woman in Management*.

23. Farley, *Woman in Management*.

24. D.E. Dougherty, *From Technical Professional to Corporate Manager* (New York: Wiley, 1984).

25. R.M. Powell, "How Men Get Ahead," *Nation's Business* (March 1964): 58.

26. R.A. Smith, "The Incredible Electrical Conspiracy," *Fortune* (April 1961): 132ff.

27. S.N. Brenner and E.A. Molander, "Is the Ethics of Business Changing?" *Harvard Business Review* (January-February 1977): 57–71.

28. J.K. Van Fleet, *The 22 Biggest Mistakes Managers Make and How to Correct Them* (West Nyack, NY: Parker, 1973).

Engineers in Private Practice

Engineers who offer their services to the general public, whether as individuals, in partnership, or as principal officers of corporations, are said to be in *private practice*. The work of professional engineers in private practice can be varied and challenging, particularly if new clients with new problems are continually being served. However, the additional responsibilities associated with providing engineering services to the general public tend to balance the benefits. An engineer in private practice is subject to increased legal responsibilities and the need to administer a professional practice while seeking out new clients and projects. In 1989, the Association of Consulting Engineers of Canada (ACEC) had 800 consulting engineering firms (sole proprietorships, partnerships, and corporations) on its membership list. In that same year, the total number of licensed professional engineers in Canada was approximately 135 000. Even though many engineers in private practice are *not* members of ACEC, these numbers seem to indicate that a minority of licensed engineers are in private practice. The numbers are similar in the United States.

CONSULTING ENGINEERS

Engineers in private practice are frequently called "consulting engineers." However, although all consulting engineers are in private practice, not all engineers in private practice are consulting engineers. In the province of Ontario the title "Consulting Engineer" (or any variation with the same meaning) is regulated under the Professional Engineers Act and may not be used without authorization from the provincial Association. Although this regulation is unique to Ontario, the requirement was generated by a desire to protect the general public and may be of interest to all readers, whether residents in Ontario or elsewhere.

To be designated a consulting engineer in Ontario, a licensed professional engineer must satisfy several additional requirements.

- Authorization: Permission from the provincial Association must be obtained to engage in private practice, as indicated by a certificate of authorization.[1]

- Experience: Consulting engineers must have five years' experience in addition to that required for registration; at least two years of the experience must be in private practice.

- Professional Liability Insurance: Proof of liability insurance must be filed with the provincial Association, although permission to offer services to the public without liability insurance may be awarded, provided that all clients are informed in writing of this fact.

Provincial Consulting Engineering Associations

In eight Canadian provinces (and Yukon Territory) organizations devoted to assisting consulting engineers have been set up. The names of these organizations are listed below; the current addresses can be obtained by consulting the directories of the cities indicated.

- Consulting Engineers of Alberta (Edmonton)

- Consulting Engineers of British Columbia (Vancouver)

- Association of Consulting Engineers of Manitoba (Winnipeg)

- Consulting Engineers of New Brunswick (Moncton)

- Nova Scotia Consulting Engineers Association (Halifax)

- Consulting Engineers of Ontario (Toronto)

- Association des ingénieurs-conseils du Québec (Montreal)

- Association of Consulting Engineers of Saskatchewan (Regina)

- Consulting Engineers of Yukon (Whitehorse)

The goals of the organizations are to promote in various ways the interests of the consulting engineers who form their memberships.

- Publications: Each organization publishes a directory of its members and of services provided by the members. The directories are available in most public libraries. Other publications, on selecting a consulting engineer and on various aspects of professional practice, are also available.

- Communication: The organizations communicate with their members on issues that affect the profession. They also provide a central source of information on consulting engineers for the public, industry, and government.

- Advocacy: The organizations make representations to municipal, regional, and provincial governments on behalf of members, when requested, or when an issue affects consulting engineers as a body.

Association of Consulting Engineers of Canada (ACEC)

Membership in one of the provincial consulting engineering organizations includes membership in the Association of Consulting Engineers of Canada (ACEC). Membership is voluntary and is limited to companies primarily engaged in providing consulting engineering services directly to the public. ACEC is a national Canadian non-profit organization founded in 1925 with the goal of promoting satisfactory business relations between its member firms and their clients and fostering the exchange of professional, management, and business information. When necessary, ACEC acts to safeguard the interests of consulting engineers, to improve the high professional standards in consulting, and to provide liaison with the federal government.[2] The American counterpart of ACEC is the American Consulting Engineers Council (ACEC also).

International Federation of Consulting Engineers (FIDIC)

Both the ACECs (Canadian and American) are member associations of the International Federation of Consulting Engineers (FIDIC), founded in 1913, which is made up of the national consulting engineers' associations of more than 50 countries.[3] Member associations must comply with FIDIC's code on professional status, independence, and competence. FIDIC publishes an international directory and works on behalf of consulting engineers at the international level.

SERVICES PROVIDED BY
CONSULTING ENGINEERS

Although the largest single group of consulting engineers is in civil engineering, the range of engineering services provided by consultants is very broad. The need to attract clients stimulates consulting engineering companies to expand their capabilities to suit the demands of the engineering marketplace. Consulting activity is a good example of free enterprise in the provision of engineering services.

A client may need consulting advice on almost any topic and at any stage of a project. The capabilities of consulting firms reflect this wide range. Typical functions of a consulting engineer could be in any of the following six categories.

- Engineering Advice: Advice may be needed on specific projects or problems or on a continuing basis, in areas of design, development, inspection, testing, quality control, management, and so forth.

- Expert Witness: A consultant may be needed to provide engineering opinions or advice to a court, commission, board, hearing, or similar government or judicial body.

- Feasibility Studies: Consultants are particularly useful in preliminary stages of a project when feasibility, economic or financial justification, cost estimates, and completion dates are being determined. The advice of the consultant could decide whether the project goes ahead or is cancelled. It is clearly not advisable to make commitments to hire personnel before the project's feasibility and justification are proven. The use of consultants is therefore convenient and prudent.

- Detail Design: Consulting engineers have the expertise to carry out detail design, including the preparation of drawings, specifications, and contract documents.

- Specialized Design: Custom design and development is available, particularly for manufacturing machinery, mining, and other specialized areas. Consulting engineers may work independently or in conjunction with the client's staff. Assistance may be needed to develop inventions or to prepare patents.

- Project Management: Supervision of part (or all) of a project is commonly carried out by consulting engineers. This could include the design, manufacturing, construction, or assembly phase of the project, or the initial start-up (called *commissioning*) of a large plant.

In sum, consulting engineers can be found performing any task that requires professional engineering knowledge on behalf of a client who lacks the personnel or expertise to conduct the work.

THE CONTRACTING PROCEDURE

When a consulting engineer is needed to carry out a project, the client is faced with the problem of choosing an individual or firm that can provide the best service for the specific project. Procuring engineering services is not the same as purchasing material or taking bids for construction, where the goal is to obtain the best price or the lowest bid. Although this is not illegal or unethical, and provincial Associations cannot and would not prevent such a process, it is preferable to separate the technical aspects of a project from the negotiation of a fee. Guidelines for the contracting process are available from the provincial Associations, the provincial consulting organizations, ACEC, and FIDIC. The process recommended by ACEC is reproduced below.

Step 1 – Select a Long List of Possible Consultants

A *"long list"* of qualified consulting engineering firms can be developed from contacts with other owners who have undertaken similar projects or from published rosters such as the Director of Member Firms of the Association of Consulting Engineers of Canada.

Each firm should be requested to provide a general statement of qualifications and a listing of relevant project experience. The request must be accompanied by a brief description of the assignment, together with an outline of the scope of services required.

Once such "pre-qualification" documents have been received, they may be judged on the following, but not exclusive, criteria:

- Staff qualifications and experience
- Experience on similar projects
- Current workload
- Ability to mobilize staff and equipment and to initiate and complete the project within a realistic schedule
- Available computing and drafting facilities
- Consultant's familiarity with local codes, procedures, etc.

Given the data received, a *"short list"* of, normally, not more than three to five firms may be selected and requested to submit proposals.

Step 2 – Request for Proposals

The Request for Proposal (or RFP) is a comprehensive document outlining in detail the requirements of the project, the expected scope of services and the time frame in which the assignment is to be completed. It also requests the consultant to provide a statement of the methodology and approach to the specific task, details on the organization of the project team along with the experience records of the individual team members assigned to the project, a detailed project schedule including the mobilization phase, evidence of the consultant's familiarity with the local conditions and a statement of the management mechanisms that will be set in place to ensure proper control and reporting procedures.

However the RFP ought not to request that a consulting engineer quote a fee for services. Price competition sets the consulting engineer and his client in an adversarial role. Price, and not the task at hand, becomes the central focus. Rather, best value should be the guiding principle. Furthermore, if consulting engineers are forced to bid against each other, the result will ultimately be to the detriment of the owners, as the consultant responds to lower fees by rendering diminished services, by spending less time on the project, by assigning less qualified personnel and by omitting to consider alternative design approaches. Such minimal engineering often leads to greater construction and material expenditures and to higher life cycle costs for the facility.

Step 3 – Rank the Proposals

Once the proposals have been submitted at a date and time specified beforehand, the owner ranks the documents on the basis of their technical and managerial quality. This may be achieved using a point system, weighted for each aspect of the proposal; the task may be assigned either to an internal or to an external adjudication committee.

Step 4 – Negotiate a Contract

The highest ranked consulting firm should be invited to negotiate a contract. Such negotiations should first establish the exact scope of work as this item may require modification in light of the submitted proposal. Thereafter, a fee that is acceptable to both parties should be negotiated. This is done on the basis recommended in provincial fee schedules or prevailing rates.

If agreement cannot be reached, the negotiations should be terminated. A similar interview should then be commenced with the second ranked consultant and, if necessary, with the third ranked consultant, and so on.

The result of such a process will be the matching of the best qualified consulting engineer to a mutually acceptable price. Standard forms of agreement such as those published by the ACEC may be used along with legal advice to provide the basis for a contract.[4]

COMPENSATION FOR CONSULTING ENGINEERS

In the past, the consulting engineer's fee was often calculated as a percentage of the final construction cost, but there now appears to be a trend away from this method. One of the arguments against this historical practice is that it penalizes the engineer for creating an economical design, instead of producing a reward, as it should. The following are a few of the methods currently employed for establishing the consultant's fee.

Lump Sum: when the services to be performed are known with considerable precision, it may be possible to agree upon a fixed sum as the engineer's compensation. The obvious disadvantage is that the consultant may incur a serious loss if the job has been underestimated.

Payroll Cost Times a Multiplier: Under this method, the client essentially pays the engineering costs as they occur, including a sufficient amount to cover overhead and profit.

Per Diem: If the job is a short one, a fixed daily rate may be charged; this is known as a *per diem* arrangement. Direct out-of-pocket expenses, such as travel costs, are reimbursed in addition to the per diem payments.[5]

Many kinds of consulting engineering services do not involve construction. For example, some consulting concerns make a business of performing product-development services for clients. Often firms of this type place their own personnel, upon request, within a client's firm to work side by side with the client's engineers. In this fashion the client can absorb unexpected peak workloads without hiring and training people who may become surplus when the peak has passed. Consulting companies of this type usually charge a fixed rate per hour per person employed on the project for as long as the client employs their services. The rates are set high enough to enable the consulting company to recover all costs, including overhead, and to provide it with a profit.

LEGAL RESPONSIBILITIES AND LIABILITY INSURANCE

In the course of carrying out a contract, an engineer can sometimes acquire unexpected and unwanted legal obligations. For example, *supervision* and *inspection,* two words frequently used in engineering contracts, sometimes cause trouble.

Many contracts in the past have used the statement "The Engineer (or Architect) shall have general supervision and direction of the work." In some court decisions, it has been held that the design professionals (a term embracing both engineers and architects) were responsible for defective construction techniques in cases where they undertook the responsibility of supervising.[6]

The word *inspection* has caused trouble because it has sometimes been interpreted to mean exhaustive and continuous inspection of all details of the construction. Most often, this has not been the type of function the engineer had in mind when it was agreed that "inspection of the work" would be involved. More likely, some kind of educated spot-checking was envisioned; hence, the word *observation* has been proposed as a substitute that more accurately describes the service intended. If actual detailed inspection is desired, then professional groups recommend that the contract provide for a full-time project representative whose task is to perform detailed and continuous inspections.

Special legal hazards are involved in the use of new materials or equipment. Courts have generally held that the engineer or architect is obliged to conduct tests of the new material or to have reliable information concerning the results of tests conducted by others. Sole reliance upon manufacturers' sales literature and specifications has been held to be insufficient. The question of the obligations of the design professional in the use of new materials remains a tricky legal matter.

Any one of the legal hazards involved in offering consulting services could be financially catastrophic for the consultant. Because of this, professional groups recommend that architects and engineers maintain professional liability insurance, often known as *errors and omissions insurance*. Furthermore, the written language of the contract may be insufficient to protect the engineer if services are embarked upon in an area beyond the scope of the contract. One expert says, "Having once moved into that area [an engineer] may be charged with the responsibility for all the functions involved, such as failure to exercise reasonable care in performing the services or failing to do what one experienced in the field would do in the exercise of reasonable care."[7]

In the 1980s, the cost of professional liability insurance increased so rapidly in the United States that some consulting firms decided to go without it. In 1987, about 23 percent of the members of the American Consulting Engineers Council reported that they carried no liability coverage. For small organizations (one to five persons) the proportion was 41 percent without coverage.[8] For some kinds of work, such as hazardous waste reduction, engineers claim that liability insurance is almost impossible to obtain.[9] According to some, liability insurance is the most disruptive problem facing engineers. One writer has complained, "What you see today is the engineer brought in as one of 15 people in the lawsuit because his name is on the building, or on the drawings, or in the phone book. ... The chance of being sued is not a function of committing sins or errors; it's a function of how much money, or how big an insurance policy you have."[10]

In Canada, similar problems were experienced. In Ontario, for example, when the new Professional Engineers Act was promulgated in 1984, engineers providing services directly to the public were required to have a certificate of authorization and a minimum of $250 000 in liability insurance (or to be employees of a company with both of these). However, the major insurance companies were unable to provide this insurance, at reasonable cost, to the large number of engineers and firms who applied. Because of the confusion over a requirement that could not reasonably be satisfied, the Association obtained permission from the Attorney General of Ontario to postpone the requirement. The regulations were later amended to permit engineers in private practice to advise their clients in writing that they are practising without liability insurance, before entering into an agreement to provide professional engineering services.[11] Statistics reported by the Association of Professional Engineers of Ontario in 1990 showed that of 2389 holders of certificates of authorization, 1027 were insured in accordance with the regulations, 186 were insured in equivalent ways, 60 were exempted as practising in a field for which insurers will not provide coverage (for example, environmental and nuclear projects), and 1116 elected to disclose to clients that they do not have professional liability insurance.[12] Consequently, whether by choice or by exemption, roughly 49 percent of holders of certificates of authorization were offering professional engineering advice to the Ontario public in 1990 without liability insurance.

BECOMING A CONSULTING ENGINEER

A person beginning consulting work is much more likely to fail because of lack of business ability than because of a a lack of technical ability. Virtually all consultants warn the prospective newcomer about "that depressing first year." Some even declare that the lean period is apt to be three years instead of one.[13]

Some of the things the beginning consultant may neglect are such ordinary business matters as accounting, collections, overhead, taxes, and insurance. *Overhead,* for example, includes many items often overlooked. Vacations, sick leaves, insurance, and social-insurance taxes may add from 10 to 15 percent to the direct costs of operating the practice. Rent, supplies, telephone service, and secretarial service may come to as much as 30 or 40 percent of the direct costs. If there are more than six or eight employees, additional supervision may be required; this may add another 15 percent. Finally, there is the often belatedly recognized factor of non-productive time, which may add another 10 percent. Thus, the direct engineering costs may have to be increased by as much as 65 to 80 percent of the original estimate, with no allowance made as yet for profit.[14]

Even a determination to work extra hours cannot compensate for a lack of good business ability and adequate financial reserves, because extra hours and consulting work appear to go hand in hand as the normal situation. One consultant writes: "If you object to working long hours and if you intend to dismiss all the business problems from your mind when you leave the office, don't try to be a consulting engineer, for the problems will be with you 24 hours a day."[15]

These are one writer's recommended minimum requirements and personal characteristics for those who would like to enter private practice.

1. Appropriate education, including humanities
2. Engineering registration
3. Confidence in one's professional ability
4. Broad prior experience in the responsible discharge of engineering work
5. Business acumen
6. Financial reserves to last at least one year (some say two to three years)
7. Ability to get along with people, especially clients and employees
8. A reputation for keeping your word
9. Good health and a willingness to work hard[16]

The basic problem of the new consultant is simple: to acquire that first project, it is necessary to demonstrate a minimum level of competence by pointing to projects that have been completed in the past. Given such circumstances, getting that first job can be understandably difficult. Yet every consultant in business today has had to get past this barrier.

Some consultants have made their start by quitting their jobs and taking one or more of their former employers' clients with them. However, such a practice is unethical and usually illegal. Other aspirants have associated themselves with an established consultant as a junior partner. This is certainly ethical but offers a difficulty in that the senior partner has to be convinced there is something to gain by taking on a new partner.

Consultants who are already in the business sometimes complain about the difficulty they have in hiring new engineers, because the expectations held by new graduates are often unrealistically high and starting salaries are substantially lower than those offered by high-tech firms. Says one: "Young people who want to get into the … industry must be willing to start with a lower salary and pay their dues. The good news is that within five or ten years the successful design professionals will be earning more than their high-tech counterparts, who will be locked into more rigid salary structures and won't be appreciated for developing the managerial and sales skills so highly valued by design firms."[17]

Although there are risks and problems, there is a possibility of proportionate rewards. Canada needs people with entrepreneurial ability to stimulate the generation of jobs, services, and material wealth. If you decide to enter private practice, good luck!

TOPICS FOR STUDY AND DISCUSSION

1. Compare the list of personal characteristics in this chapter under the heading "Becoming a Consulting Engineer" with the characteristics of a manager listed in Chapter 4 under the heading "Personal Characteristics of Managers." In many ways, these characteristics are similar, since both of these engineering careers require leadership. However, in some ways, the requirements are different. Read both sections and find at least three ways in which the requirements or characteristics are different. Compare your own qualifications and characteristics with those given. Do you see a pattern that suggests which of these career paths may be suited to you?

2. Consider the list of nine personal characteristics in this chapter under the heading "Becoming a Consulting Engineer." Rate your own ability under these nine headings on a scale of zero to 10. (Ten means absolute confidence, five means reasonable certainty, and zero means there is serious doubt.) Total your scores to get a rating out of 90. Give yourself an additional five points for each further qualification listed below:

- You have published three or more technical papers.
- You have already been involved in consulting.
- You have a master's degree.
- You have contacts with five or more local companies who might need your services.
- You have previous experience making group presentations and writing technical proposals.
- You enjoy making important (and expensive) decisions under pressure.

Total your rating; it should not exceed 120 points. If your rating is 90 points or more, and you have been scrupulously honest in your personal assessments, then you may be ready to enter the field of consulting. If your rating is less than 80 points, then you clearly need more experience.

3. Imagine that you have decided to enter private practice and you are trying to become better known in your local area, so that you can attract more clients and contracts. Advertising is a sensitive issue, since it must be consistent with the codes of ethics. Read the section in Chapter 9 on "Advertising" and then devise at least five methods for becoming better known as a competent, ethical, professional engineer that are clearly consistent with Chapter 9 and your provincial or territorial code of ethics.

4. Architects and engineers frequently work for the same firm, doing work that overlaps somewhat. Architects are supposed to design structures for attractive appearances and to provide building arrangements that fulfil certain functions. Yet, in carrying out these responsibilities, they often get into such matters as spacing of columns, which are structural in nature. Similarly, in providing for structural integrity, engineers may impose constraints on shape and function, which are the architects' realm. As a consequence, relationships between these two professional groups have sometimes been strained, particularly over the issue of whether an engineer or an architect is to be in charge of the project. Consider both sides of this issue and prepare an argument for whichever side you choose: should an engineer or an architect be the ultimate boss? Does it make any difference whether the project is a factory, an apartment building, a downtown office building, or a bridge? Consult the Act from your province or territory (some Acts do define the architect/engineer boundary) and see if it agrees with your point of view.

NOTES

1. Professional Engineers Act, 1984, *Statutes of Ontario* 1984, c. 13, as amended.

2. Association of Consulting Engineers of Canada, *Directory of Member Firms* (Ottawa: ACEC, 1990).

3. International Federation of Consulting Engineers, *International Directory of Consulting Engineers* (The Hague: FIDIC, 1990).

4. ACEC, *Directory*, viii–x. Reproduced with permission of the Association of Consulting Engineers of Canada.

5. ACEC, *Directory*, viii–x.

6. J.R. Clark, *Concerning Some Legal Responsibilities in the Practice of Architecture and Engineering* (Washington, DC: American Institute of Architects, 1961).

7. Clark, *Legal Responsibilities.*

8. "Consulting Eng'rs Bemoan Liability Costs, Suits," *Engineering Times* (April 1988): 8.

9. R.T. Cosby, "Professional Liability — Are You Protected?" *Consulting/Specifying Engineer* (April 1987): 104–108.

10. Clark, *Legal Responsibilities.*

11. Ontario Regulation 538/84, s. 88, made under the Professional Engineers Act, 1984, *Statutes of Ontario* 1984, c. 13, as amended.

12. C.C. Hart, "Professional Liability Insurance: Some Interesting Statistics," *Gazette* (Association of Professional Engineers of Ontario) 10, no. 3 (May/June 1990): 2.

13. J.S. Ward, "Starting Your Own Consulting Practice," *Civil Engineering* (January 1965): 53–55.

14. A.J. Ryan, "Operating Your Practice," *American Engineer* (November 1955).

15. J.B. McGaughy, "So You Want to Open a Consulting Office — By Way of Qualifications," *American Engineer* (October 1955).

16. D.G. Sunar, *Getting Started as a Consulting Engineer* (San Carlos, CA: Professional Publications, 1986).

17. M.C. Zweig, "New Grads Need Realism," *A/E Job Mart* (October 1988): 1.

Principles of Engineering Ethics

Ethical problems occur often in engineering. An engineer may have to choose between risking the health of workers on a project and stopping the project to install safety equipment, thereby causing delays and increasing costs for the engineer's clients or employers. At what point does the severity of the risk and potential harm to the workers overcome the real loss to the client or employer that will result if the engineer stops the project to install safety equipment? In another instance, an engineer in a position of authority may have to decide whether a small gift is an innocent kindness or a serious attempt at bribery. As we shall see in subsequent chapters, many issues in engineering practice give rise to ethical problems, and it is useful to have a methodical approach for solving these problems.

To develop a method for solving ethical problems, let us first examine solution methods for *technical* problems. An engineer faced with a technical problem will generate one or more possible solutions and then analyze these solutions using axioms, theorems, and laws of mathematics, science, and engineering that are known to be tested and true. It is therefore reassuring to know, when faced with an ethical problem, that there is a similar set of ethical theories that have been developed over the centuries. These ethical theories are the basis for the laws, regulations, and codes of ethics that guide the engineer in ethical decision making.

When an engineer is faced with a technical problem, there is usually more than one solution, and the goal is to select the best or "optimum" solution. Similarly, in dealing with ethical problems, there may be several possible solutions, and the goal is to determine the best solution from the ethical standpoint. This is not always easy, since ethical theories sometimes generate contradictions when applied. Alternative solutions frequently require diametrically opposite actions that are totally incompatible. This leads to a moral dilemma, which may require breaking one ethical code to satisfy another.

An example from daily life is easy to provide. We are all taught to be truthful and not to tell lies. However, if we hear gossip that would be hurtful to friends, relatives, or co-workers, we might alter the information to spare their feelings. We would argue that a greater good is served by lying or denying the truth than by following precisely the ethical precept "Do not tell lies." When solving ethical problems in engineering, it is almost always necessary to evaluate several competing theories before making a decision; moral dilemmas will frequently result, and the best course of action must then be chosen.

In the next few paragraphs, we will examine four important ethical theories that have evolved over the centuries and develop a methodical approach to solving ethical problems.

ETHICS AND PHILOSOPHY

Ethics may be defined as the study of right and wrong (or good and bad) actions or behaviour. Ethics is one of the five subdivisions of philosophy; the other four are logic, aesthetics, politics, and metaphysics. More precisely, ethics involves defining, analyzing, evaluating, and resolving moral problems and developing moral criteria to guide human behaviour. Ethics has been a vital field of study since the dawn of civilization and has had a written history for more than 2500 years. In fact, many ethical concepts that we commonly apply today are older than the basic concepts of engineering analysis (calculus, dynamics, stress analysis, etc.), which trace their origins to the seventeenth century.

Philosophy involves the examination of questions that are very fundamental, questions such as "What is truth?" "How do we define justice?" "What constitutes beauty?" Truth, justice, and beauty are concepts that we use every day. We cannot, in fact, recall when we first learned their meanings. It is therefore shocking to find that we cannot easily define these basic terms that we have used all our lives. The desire to define these important but basic concepts is one of the fundamental motivations of philosophy.

In ethics, the goal is to differentiate between good and bad, between right and wrong. Therefore, the key question is "What is good?" Again we find it is difficult to define the basic term "good." Attempts to define goodness usually result in circular arguments or in definitions that describe the effects (or the lack) of goodness. For example, if goodness were to be defined as that property of an object, person, or act that creates pleasant, positive, or useful results, most persons would probably agree. However, this is not a precise definition, since the terms "pleasant," "positive," and "useful" depend on subjective evaluations that vary from individual to individual. Therefore, this definition is not fully satisfactory as a basis for the application of ethics. However, even if we cannot precisely define goodness, we must agree on some working definition if we are to apply criteria to differentiate it from its opposite, and the above definition is suggested as a starting point.

FOUR ETHICAL THEORIES

Many prominent philosophers have devoted their lives to the development of ethical theories, and a complete discussion of their thoughts would fill a thousand textbooks. It is presumptuous to think that this wealth of philosophical thought could be condensed into this single chapter. However, some review of ethical theories is essential to understand the origin of codes of ethics and also to deal with cases that "fall through the cracks": cases that cause ethical problems but are not clearly addressed by the codes of ethics. This brief summary is merely an introduction, but it should be adequate to illustrate the basic concepts; perhaps it may inspire readers to investigate the subject more profoundly.

There are at least four moral theories or moral maxims that have evolved over the centuries and are relevant to the application of ethics in engineering. Each theory, when it was proposed, was considered by its originators to be the basis for all ethical thought. All of the theories have stood the test of time and are useful aids to decision making. Although the theories may appear to differ significantly, and none of them is clearly universally superior to the others, it is nevertheless startling to see how much they agree when applied to common ethical problems. The four theories are listed and described in detail on the next few pages. Each theory is identified by the name of its best-known proponent, although many earlier philosophers contributed to the formulation of the theories and many contemporary philosophers have suggested modifications to improve the theories.

- Mill's utilitarianism

- Kant's formalism, or duty ethics

- Locke's rights ethics

- Aristotle's virtue ethics

Mill's Utilitarianism

This theory was set out most clearly by John Stuart Mill (1806–73). It states that the best choice in a moral dilemma is that which produces the maximum benefit for the greatest number of people. The utilitarian theory is probably the most common justification for ethical decisions in engineering, or indeed in modern society. Democratic government itself can be justified on utilitarian grounds, since it permits the maximum good (control over government) for the maximum number of people (the majority of voters). Although dictatorships or absolute monarchies may be more efficient, more convenient, or more stable, citizens who have lived in a truly democratic society would tolerate no other form of government.

The difficulty of applying the utilitarian principle lies in making a quantitative calculation of the "maximum benefit." Mill proposed that the intensity and duration of a benefit or pleasure (or avoidance of pain) and the number of people affected should be the three key factors. For example, in automobile seat-belt legislation, an inconvenience is applied to all automobile drivers and passengers, whereas the benefit (avoiding injuries or death) accrues to only a few people, but the duration and intensity of the pain one might suffer in a car accident more than outweigh the inconvenience of requiring all persons in automobiles to wear protective seat belts.

In evaluating benefits, it is important that certain principles should apply. The benefit to oneself must not be given any greater value or importance than the same benefit to any other individual. Benefits should, of course, be calculated without regard to discrimination on the basis of the nationality, creed, colour, race, language, or gender of the persons involved, and no preference should be given to any particular group. Moreover, the equality of distribution of the benefit is important when choosing a course of action on a utilitarian basis: an equal distribution of benefits is preferable to an unequal distribution. That is, the best course of action in an ethical dilemma is the choice that produces the maximum benefit for the greatest number of people, with the benefit most equally divided among those people.

The utilitarian theory is consistent with the concept of democracy, is easily understood, and, for simple cases, is easy to apply. For example, income tax is easily justified by utilitarian theory: a modest hardship (paying tax) is imposed equally on all residents (as a percentage of income), while yielding an immense benefit to those who need the roads, hospitals, schools, and other infrastructure of our society, which are built mainly with tax funds. Although we may, from time to time, disagree with details of the taxation system (who should get tax exemptions, what priorities should be used in tax expenditures, etc.), the practice is rarely challenged as unethical.

Kant's Formalism, or Duty Ethics

Duty ethics, or formalism, was put forward by Immanuel Kant (1724–1804), who proposed that each person has a fundamental duty to act in a correct ethical manner. He evolved his theory from the belief (or observation) that each person's conscience imposes an absolute, "categorical" imperative (or unconditional command) on that person to follow those courses of action that would be acceptable as universal principles for everyone to follow. For example, every person has a duty not to tell lies, because if lie-telling were to be done by everyone, then no promises could be trusted and our social fabric would be at risk of unravelling.

Kant believed that the most basic good was "good will," or the active seeking to follow the categorical imperative of one's conscience. This is in marked contrast to Mill, who believed that universal happiness was the ultimate good. In Kant's philosophy, happiness is the result of good will: the desire and intention to do one's duty. Kant emphasized that it is the *intention* to do one's duty that is significant, not the actual results or consequences. One should always do one's duty, even if the consequences, in the short run, are unpleasant, since this strengthens one's will. For example, even white lies should not be tolerated, since they weaken the resolve to follow one's conscience. Therefore, in solving a moral dilemma, the formalist theory states that one has a duty to follow rules that are generated from the conscience (the "categorical imperative"), and if the person strives to develop a good will, then happiness will be the result.

Examples of moral rules that result from applying this universal concept are easy to generate, and, not surprisingly, our happiness would certainly improve if everyone followed these rules. Examples are: "Be honest," "Be fair," "Do not hurt others," "Keep your promises," and "Obey the law." Kant also stated that a consequence of following the categorical imperative is an increased respect for humanity. Life should always be treated as an end or goal, but never as a means of achieving some other goal. Consequently, any engineering activity that endangers life by water or air pollution (regardless of the purpose or cause of the pollution) would be condemned as unethical. In Kant's philosophy, every engineer or engineering manager has an individual duty to prevent harm to human life and to consider the welfare of society to be paramount.

Kant's formalism therefore stresses the importance of following universal rules, the importance of humanity, and the significance of the intention of an act or rule, rather than the actual outcome in a specific case. The most significant problem with applying formalism is Kant's concept that duties based on the categorical imperative *never* have exceptions. We can all imagine cases where rules conflict, resulting in moral dilemmas. Which rule we will follow requires deeper insight, and other moral theories are useful aids to moral choice.

Locke's Rights Ethics

The rights-based ethical theory comes mainly from the work of John Locke (1632–1704). It proposes that everyone has rights that arise from one's very existence as a human being. The right to life and the right to the maximum possible individual liberty and human dignity are fundamental, and other rights arise as a consequence. The rights of the individual must be recognized by others, who have a duty not to infringe on these rights. This is in contrast to duty-based ethical theory, which states that duty is fundamental; in the rights-based theory, duties are a consequence of personal rights.

The writings of Locke had a significant effect on political thought in Britain in the 1690s and also influenced the French and American revolutions. Basic human rights are embedded in Canadian law through the Canadian Charter of Rights and Freedoms. The Charter recognizes that everyone has:

- fundamental freedom of conscience, religion, thought, belief, opinion and expression, peaceful assembly, and association;

- legal rights to life, liberty, and security of the person and the right not to be deprived of these rights except in accordance with principles of fundamental justice; and

- equality rights before and under the law and the right to equal benefit and protection of the law.

In evaluating ethical choices in engineering problems, it is important to recognize that individuals have these basic rights, which should not be infringed upon. However, this list does not contain every right that should exist, only the fundamental rights that have been hammered out in the Houses of Parliament and in the courts of law over the last few centuries. There are, of course, more specific rights that stem from this theory. For example, everyone has the right to a working environment that is free of sexual harassment or racial discrimination, and the employer has a duty to provide it. In specific cases, more rights may be derived, using the respect for human dignity and individual liberty as the basis.

The rights-based ethical theory does have flaws and limits, however. For example, consider the earlier example of income tax: a few people, even today, challenge the concept of income tax, claiming that it infringes on individual rights to retain one's property. Clearly the rights-based argument conflicts with the utilitarian argument, leading to a moral dilemma, which has been resolved in favour of utilitarianism. Therefore, rights-based ethics has an important place in evaluating ethical problems and resolving moral dilemmas, but it is not sufficient by itself to deal with every case.

Aristotle's Virtue Ethics

One of the earliest and most durable ethical theories was proposed by the ancient Greek philosopher Aristotle (384–322 B.C.), who observed that the goodness of an act, object, or person depends on its function or goal. For example, a good chair is comfortable; a good knife cuts well. Similarly, happiness or goodness will result for humans if they can allow their specifically human qualities to function fully. The one quality of humans that all other animals lack is the power of thought; therefore, Aristotle stated that true happiness would be achieved by developing qualities of character through thought, reason, deduction, and logic. Aristotle called these qualities of character "virtues" and visualized every virtue as a compromise between two extremes or vices. His guide to achieving virtue was to select the "golden mean" between the extremes of excess and deficiency. For example, modesty is the golden mean between the excess of vanity and the deficiency of humility; courage is the golden mean between foolhardiness and cowardice; generosity is the golden mean between wastefulness and stinginess, and so forth.

Aristotle's concept of virtue as the golden mean can be applied to resolving moral problems by examining the extremes of excess or deficiency and seeking the compromise, "happy medium," or golden mean between the extremes.

AGREEMENT AND CONTRADICTION IN MORAL THEORIES

These four moral theories have survived the tests of centuries and can be considered true. However, while each is true for a wide range of applications, none of the theories is universally true or clearly superior to the other theories in every instance. Philosophers strive to find the single principle upon which all ethical thought is founded, but no single unifying concept has yet emerged. Each moral theory has a distinctive contribution; in some areas of ethical thought, they are in complete agreement. Occasionally, however, the moral theories are in contradiction.

As an example of agreement between the theories, let us consider the Golden Rule: "Do unto others as you would have others do unto you." The Golden Rule is a clear statement of Kant's formalism: it imposes a duty on the individual to hold human life as a goal, rather than as a means to a goal. On the other hand, it could be considered a utilitarian principle, since it imposes an inconvenience on an individual while benefiting everyone with whom that person comes into contact. The proponents of rights-based ethics would agree with the Golden Rule but would claim that the duty of the individual to act fairly comes from the rights of others to be treated fairly. Finally, the concept of fairness embodied in the rule would be recognized as a virtue by Aristotle. The four moral theories are therefore in agreement that the Golden Rule is a good maxim to guide human behaviour, as we should expect.

Similarly, if we were to examine almost any of the basic precepts of most religions, we would find that each one would be supported by all four moral theories. Consider, for example, the Ten Commandments from the Book of Exodus, which are part of the ethical basis of Judaeo-Christian religions. Each of the commandments clearly imposes a duty on the individual while granting rights to others, requiring behaviour that would be virtuous, and creating a stable environment that would yield the maximum of benefit for all concerned.

However, although the moral theories show remarkable agreement on general principles, they occasionally give conflicting or contradictory guidance when applied to specific cases. Consider, for example, the case of engineers Smith and Jones, who are both employed in the design of the control system for an electrical power generating plant. If Jones has definite knowledge that Smith has an addiction to alcohol or drugs that is seriously affecting Smith's mental stability and technical judgement, what is Jones's proper course of action? The duty-based theory would state that Jones has a duty to the employer and should report Smith to management for reassignment or disciplinary action. The rights-based theory would state that Smith's health is a private matter; Smith has a right to privacy and Jones has no right to investigate it or discuss it with others. Clearly these two theories give contradictory guidance.

When there is conflict or contradiction between two moral theories, it is helpful to examine all four theories to see if there is a majority of agreement favouring a particular course of action. In the case of Smith and Jones, the contradiction between the duty-based theory and the rights-based theory can be resolved by considering the utilitarian and virtue-based theories. The degree of danger to others and the degree of incapacitation resulting from Smith's drug or alcohol addiction are important factors that must be considered. The seriousness of the addiction and the possibilities of recovery with and without intervention should also be considered. The utilitarian theory would then state that the risk of harm to others must be balanced against the harm that will be done to Smith if Jones invades Smith's privacy by exposing the addiction. The decision depends on the degree or intensity of several factors, and therefore a decision could be made with knowledge of the specific case. If the virtue-based theory were applied to this case, similar knowledge would be required; the golden mean between the excess of harmful intervention and the deficiency of inaction would depend on a balance between factors specific to the individual case. However, since this information would be known by Jones, an informed ethical decision could be made.

When applying all four theories to the case does not resolve the dilemma, then the moral theory that is considered most appropriate must be selected and followed. This step requires a value judgement that may vary from person to person and is therefore not an *absolute* rule — one that always yields the same answer. Nevertheless, if the decision has been made in an orderly fashion, is consistent with at least one recognized moral theory, and has not been made lightly or wantonly, then the person who has made the decision will have a clear conscience. These ideas are expanded into a decision-making strategy later in this chapter.

A word of caution is in order here: we should always be alert to avoid subconscious bias when selecting a course of action that benefits oneself at a cost to someone else. A decision that renders a benefit to oneself raises a "conflict of interest"; professional engineers encounter this situation frequently. To avoid subconscious bias, it is sometimes essential to have an ethical decision verified by someone who does not have a conflict of interest. In important cases where life, safety, security, or personal reputation is at stake, a decision not only must be ethical but also must be seen by others to be ethical.

The statements of the four moral theories and indications of where they may be in conflict are summarized in Table 6-1.

Table 6-1
A Summary of Four Ethical Codes

Mill's Utilitarianism
Statement: An action is morally correct if it produces the greatest benefit for the greatest number of persons. The duration, intensity, and equality of distribution of the benefits should be considered.

Conflict. A conflict of interest may arise when evaluating the benefits. It is important that a personal benefit must be counted as equal to a similar benefit to someone else.

Kant's Duty-Based Ethics
Statement: Each person has a duty to follow those courses of action that would be acceptable as universal principles for everyone to follow.

Conflict: Conflicts arise when following a universal principle may cause harm. For example, telling a "white" lie is not acceptable, even if the truth causes harm.

Locke's Rights-Based Ethics
Statement: All persons are free and equal and each has a right to life, health, liberty, possessions, and the product of his or her labour.

Conflict: It is occasionally difficult to determine when one person's rights infringe on another person's rights.

Aristotle's Virtue-Based Ethics
Statement: Happiness is to be achieved by developing "virtues" or qualities of character, through deduction and reason. An act is good if it is in accordance with reason. This usually means a course of action that is the golden mean between extremes of excess and deficiency.

Conflict: The definition of "virtue" is occasionally vague and difficult to apply in specific cases. However, the concept of seeking a "golden mean" between two extremes is frequently useful in ethics.

CODES OF ETHICS AS GUIDES TO CONDUCT

In order to put ethics into practice, most people need clearer day-to-day guidance than is provided by general philosophical principles. Therefore, customs, conventions, laws, and ordinances have developed over the centuries that are consistent with the ethical theories but give more specific guidance. For example, criminal and civil law are probably the most important guides to ethical or moral conduct. Throughout the world there is remarkably close agreement in these laws, in spite of the different political systems, cultural influences, and moral attitudes that exist in different countries. The similarity is closest in the criminal law: every country forbids theft, perjury, assault, and murder, although punishment may vary from country to country. The similarities are understandable; the laws are merely formal statements of the ethical theories discussed earlier in this chapter, and the theories are generally in full agreement where basic standards of conduct are concerned.

In engineering, the legislatures of all the provinces in Canada have passed acts to regulate professional engineering. Under the authority of these acts or laws, provincial Associations of Professional Engineers have been established and empowered to write and enforce regulations, by-laws, and codes of ethics, which prescribe acceptable conduct for professional engineers. Infringements can lead to penalties enforced by the provincial justice system or by the Association, as described in Chapter 12.

The codes of ethics for all provinces and territories are contained in Appendix A. They give specific rules to guide the conduct of the engineer. The codes usually include statements of general principles, followed by instructions for specific conduct, and they emphasize the duties that an engineer has to society, to employers, to clients, to colleagues, to subordinates, to the engineering profession, and to oneself. Although the various codes express these duties slightly differently, their intent and result is very similar. The following paragraphs summarize the content common to each of the provincial and territorial engineering codes of ethics.

Duty to Society – Engineers are required to consider their duty to the public, or society in general, as most important. This is consistent with the utilitarian concept that authority has been given to engineers under the provincial Act to use the title "Professional Engineer," to define standards of admission, and to regulate professional behaviour. The purpose of awarding this authority is to create a greater benefit for society in general: protecting the average person from physical or financial harm by ensuring that professional engineers are competent, reliable, professional, and ethical. Engineers have a particular duty to protect the safety, health, and welfare of society, if these are affected by the engineer's work.

Duty to Employers – Engineers have a duty to an employer to act fairly and loyally, and to keep the employer's business confidential. Engineers also have an obligation to disclose any conflict of interest that may arise, in which engineers may benefit by harming the employer's business.

Duty to Clients – Engineers in private practice are employed by clients, and therefore have the same obligation to a client as employed engineers have to their employer. Since the contract with a client is usually shorter than the typical employment contract, there are special concerns to avoid conflicts of interest and to co-operate with other personnel involved in the project.

Duty to Colleagues – Engineers have a duty to act with courtesy and good will toward colleagues. This is a simple statement of the Golden Rule, supported by all four ethical theories. This duty benefits the persons involved, their clients or employers, and the engineering profession in general. Clearly, a person who is awarded a professional status should act "professionally" and should not permit personal or unrelated problems to intrude into the professional relationship. Most codes also advise that it is unethical to review the work of a fellow engineer without the engineer's knowledge.

Duty to Employees and Subordinates – Engineers have a duty to recognize the rights of others, particularly if they are employees or subordinates, who are obligated to work with them by contracts of employment.

Duty to the Engineering Profession – Engineers have a duty to maintain the dignity and prestige of the engineering profession and not to bring the profession into disrepute by scandalous, dishonourable, or disgraceful conduct.

Duty to Oneself – Finally, engineers must ensure that their duties to others are balanced by their own rights. Engineers must insist on adequate payment, a satisfactory work environment, and the rights awarded to us all through the Charter of Rights and Freedoms. Engineers also have a duty to strive for excellence and to maintain competence in the rapidly changing technical world.

Readers should turn to Appendix A and review the code of ethics for your province or territory. The seven sets of duties will be evident.

COMPARISON OF CODES OF ETHICS

In addition to the seven general duties just listed, individual provinces may have additional requirements in their engineering code of ethics. A brief overview of the differences in the codes follows.

Alberta – The Alberta code entreats engineers to serve in public affairs when their professional knowledge may be of benefit to the public, to demonstrate understanding for members in training under their supervision, to have proper regard for the physical environment and to advise the provincial registrar of any practice by other members of the Association that is contrary to the code of ethics.

British Columbia – The British Columbia code gives both general principles and specific actions. It is one of the most comprehensive codes, with over 40 clauses or subclauses describing ethical conduct. Some clauses are not typically found in the other codes, such as guidelines on advertising, the duty to dissociate from public discussions on technical matters if facts are distorted, the duty not to sell goods to a public body of which the engineer is a member, the duty not to accept engagements on a contingent-fee basis, and the duty to advise the registrar of unethical, illegal, or unfair practices of other members.

Manitoba – The Manitoba code specifically states that breaches of the code may be considered unprofessional conduct and subject to disciplinary action under the Act. The code includes a duty to the state, as well as to the public, to "maintain its integrity and law," and a duty to "contractual parties" to act with fairness and honesty and to make every reasonable effort to complete work in accordance with the contract. The Manitoba code also requires members to inform the registrar of the Association of colleagues engaging in unethical, illegal, or unfair practices.

New Brunswick – The New Brunswick code includes clauses prohibiting the use of free engineering designs from suppliers in return for specifying their products, requiring members to provide opportunities for professional development for engineers in their employ, and advising on the proper standards for professional advertising.

Newfoundland – The Newfoundland code is arranged in three sections, which specify the duties of the professional engineer or geoscientist to the public, to the client or employer, and to the profession. The code is brief (21 clauses) and clear.

Northwest Territories – The code for the Northwest Territories is virtually identical to the Alberta code of ethics.

Nova Scotia – The Nova Scotia code is fairly brief (28 clauses) and contains clauses typical of the other Acts, except for an admonition to refrain from conduct contrary to the public good, even if directed by the employer to act in such a manner, and a complementary instruction to employers not to direct employees to perform acts that are unprofessional or contrary to the public good.

Ontario – The Ontario code of ethics is different from those in other provinces, because it is specifically *not* enforceable under the Act. A separate regulation defining "professional misconduct" contains many of the clauses that appear in the codes of other provinces. One clause that appears to be unique to Ontario defines "permitting, counselling or assisting a person who is not a practitioner to engage in ... engineering" as a form of professional misconduct. Two clauses in the code of ethics that are also unique to Ontario (but not enforceable under the Act) require an engineer to display his or her licence at the place of business and require moonlighting engineers to inform their clients that they are employed and to state any limitations on service that may result from this status.

Prince Edward Island – The code of ethics for Prince Edward Island is relatively brief (24 clauses) and clear. All of its clauses are similar to clauses in other codes.

Quebec – The Quebec code of ethics is one of the longest (50 clauses) and is arranged slightly differently than those of the other provinces. However, the basic clauses mentioned above are all represented in the code, and additional clauses are included. These clauses include engineers' duties to show reasonable availability and diligence, to serve on committees of the Ordre unless they have exceptional grounds for refusing, and to refrain from communicating with any persons who have lodged a complaint against them. In addition, one section of the code describes criteria for setting fair and reasonable fees for service.

Saskatchewan – The Saskatchewan code (30 clauses) has two clauses not common to other codes. Engineers are required to constantly strive to improve their knowledge and experience by keeping abreast of new techniques and development. Also, engineers must not offer services for a fee without first notifying the council of the Association and receiving permission to do so.

Yukon Territory – The code of ethics for Yukon Territory is similar to the code for Saskatchewan, with the exception of three or four clauses. For example, the Yukon code does not contain the Saskatchewan clause requiring council's permission to offer services for a fee.

The above overview shows that the codes for each province or territory are very similar, although they are not identical. They are useful guides to personal conduct. Adherence to the provincial code of ethics is not voluntary, nor is it a lofty ideal that "would be nice but not essential" to achieve. In each province, the code of ethics (or an equivalent definition of professional misconduct) is legally enforceable through the Act or through regulations or by-laws made under the authority of the Act. Clear violations can be the basis for disciplinary action resulting in reprimands, suspension, or expulsion from the profession, as described in Chapter 12. Fortunately, behaviour that is consistent with the basic ethical theories is rarely in conflict with the code of ethics.

In addition to the provincial and territorial codes, most engineering societies have developed codes of ethics. Three of these are included in Appendix E for comparison. The code promulgated by the U.S. National Society of Professional Engineers is very similar to the provincial codes and has been endorsed by many engineering societies. Since engineering societies do not have the regulatory power of provincial and territorial Associations, serious infractions of the society codes are punished by expulsion from the society.

A STRATEGY FOR SOLVING COMPLEX ETHICAL PROBLEMS

Most of the ethical problems that arise in everyday life are clear and simple and are solved by intuitive use of the ethical theories. Complex ethical problems can be much more challenging; intuitive methods usually do not work and many people are in a quandary trying to decide where to start and how to proceed to a logical solution. Engineers should have an advantage in resolving ethical dilemmas, since problem-solving and decision-making techniques are a routine part of engineering. This section illustrates the similarity between ethical problem solving and engineering design methods. Although the formal strategy set out here would rarely be needed, it is reassuring to know that it exists and can be applied to complex cases.

The Engineering Design Process

The design for a new machine, structure, or electronic device does not spring fully developed into the minds of the designers. Rather, it is the result of a series of steps requiring inspiration and deduction in the right order at the right time, which are well known to effective designers. The design process usually begins with a vaguely perceived need or problem and ends with the manufacture of the device or structure that satisfies the need. Similarly, the solution to an ethical problem can be developed by following a comparable series of steps. The typical steps or phases in the design process are:

1. Recognizing that a problem or need exists

2. Gathering information and defining the problem to be solved or goal to be achieved

3. Generating alternative solutions or methods to achieve the goal (synthesis)

4. Evaluating benefits and costs of alternate solutions (analysis)

5. Decision making and optimization

6. Implementing the best solution

The design process begins by recognizing a need in the marketplace, the community, the factory, the machine shop, etc. For example, people living in the suburbs may want to travel to work in the city conveniently and believe that they need a new freeway or superhighway. Once the need is perceived, the precise problem must be explored in depth before committing resources to a single course of action. In our example, we must find out whether the travelling public really needs a new highway; would a new subway or bus line be more effective? It is important to gather data and define the problem precisely before committing resources to designing the highway. When the need is investigated, it may be concluded that a new subway is the most desirable goal. The detail design work would then begin with that goal in mind, and alternative routes for the subway would be drawn up. Alternative sources for materials and alternative methods to make or buy trains and passenger cars would be considered. Each alternative would then be analyzed to obtain the cost estimates for acquiring property and constructing the line. Each route would be analyzed for safety, convenience to riders, and inconvenience to neighbouring residents. Finally the optimum (or best) solution, which gives the maximum benefit at minimum cost, would be selected. The design would then be implemented; materials would be ordered; construction would start.

Applying the Design Process to Ethical Problems

The design process described above is really a simple, straightforward, problem-solving technique. We can develop a strategy for ethical problem solving based on this design process.

Recognizing the Need or Problem – Ethical problems may be poorly defined and difficult to recognize, particularly in the early stages. For example, a manufacturing process once thought to be harmless may be suspected over a period of years to be the cause of cancer or toxicity in the workplace. Recognizing that a problem exists is an important first step.

Gathering Information and Defining the Problem – As a general rule, it is advisable to act on an ethical problem quickly and decisively, but it is equally important to have all the facts. Premature action will almost always offend someone and may create an even more serious problem. When the information has been collected and examined, the proper course of action may be quite different than what one initially perceived.

When the problem is clearly defined, the proper course of action is usually perfectly clear. The necessary action may be dictated by law, codes of ethics, or ethical theory, and one can skip directly to the implementation step. However, in some cases there may be conflicts that lead to a moral dilemma. For example, the code of ethics may give conflicting directions. In these cases, some inspiration is required, as explained in the next step.

Generating Alternative Solutions ("Synthesis") – When a moral dilemma results, in which the engineer must choose between two courses of action, each of which is undesirable, then the engineer should strive to generate a new, positive, desirable course of action. This phase of the solution procedure requires creative thought and therefore is usually difficult. The new course of action may be a compromise, or a modification of one alternative to eliminate its negative aspects. For example, consider the case of an engineer who receives a small cash gift and is uncertain whether the gift is a favour to cover incidental expenses or a bribe. This creates a dilemma; if the gift is a well-intended favour, then returning it would offend the donor. On the other hand, if it is a bribe, then keeping it would incur an obligation. In this case, a creative compromise might be to use the cash for a charitable purpose (preferably in the name of the donor), thus avoiding offence without incurring an obligation. Other courses of action may exist, and some ingenuity is needed. Many of the creative methods used to generate alternatives in technical problems (such as brainstorming) can also be applied to generating alternatives in ethical problems.

Evaluating Alternatives ("Analysis") – When two or more conflicting courses of action exist, they must be analyzed to see what consequences are likely to result, before a decision can be made. The analysis involves examining the results of each of the possible courses of action. What benefits accrue? For whom? What hardships are involved? Are the benefits and hardships equally distributed?

Decision Making and Optimization – If the previous steps have been thoroughly followed, decision making is simple and involves comparing the consequences of each course of action with the code of ethics or moral theories discussed earlier, and selecting the best course of action. If no solution appears to be acceptable, it may be necessary to go back to step 2 and verify that the problem has been properly defined.

In making decisions, a decision chart is sometimes useful to summarize the courses of action and their consequences. A decision chart is merely a matrix showing the various courses of action and the outcomes or consequences for the persons concerned. The decision chart is particularly useful when numerical costs and benefits can be calculated, or when numerical probabilities for good and bad events are known. The decision chart is then transformed into a type of balance sheet, with a numerical sum for each course of action.

For example, consider the simple case mentioned earlier, in which an engineer supervising a construction project has received a small cash gift from a contractor. Rather than keeping the gift or returning it, the engineer might generate an innovative third course of action: the cash gift could be used to install a temporary pop cooler on the work site that would benefit all the workers and indirectly aid the project.

The decision chart illustrating the various choices and outcomes is shown in Table 6–2. The outcomes are the sums in the bottom row. The first two courses of action generate a negative sum; the third choice is the only positive course of action. In this simple example, the decision chart merely illustrates what we already knew: the best course of action is to use the gift for the benefit of the workers. The example illustrates the method but is too simple to show its full value. The true usefulness of the decision chart lies in its ability to separate the courses of action and to identify the consequences of each possible course of action. The chart may stimulate the need to generate new courses of action, to review the information provided, or to restate the goal, so that an optimum course of action can be found.

In some cases it may appear that a solution cannot be achieved; the arguments for conflicting alternatives may be so equally balanced that no choice of action is clearly superior. In this case, the engineer should pose the following questions:

- Is the problem clearly stated?

- Has all the necessary information been obtained?

- Have I sought advice from the persons concerned?

- Is there an alternative or compromise solution that has been overlooked?

Table 6-2

Typical Decision Chart

Persons Affected	Possible Courses of Action		
	Keep the Gift	Return the Gift	Use the Gift for Workers
Donor	No offence to donor (0)	Result may offend donor (–1)	No offence to donor (0)
Engineer	Result may incur an obligation (–1)	No obligation (0)	Project benefits (+1)
Sum	–1	–1	+1

- Have all the consequences of each alternative choice been fully evaluated?

- Do I have a personal benefit or conflict of interest that is affecting my judgement?

If the above questions can be answered correctly and there is still no optimum course of action, then it would be advisable to select the course of action that does not yield a benefit to the person making the decision. If the choices are equally balanced, and the possibility of personal benefit exists, then this choice will ensure that the decision is *seen* to be morally right.

If there is no personal benefit involved, then the moral theory that is considered most appropriate must be selected and followed. Although this involves a personal value judgement, the person making the decision will have a clear conscience.

Implementation – The implementation of the decision is the final step. Although the appropriate action will vary from case to case, it is usually advisable to act speedily and unequivocally when ethical decisions are needed, particularly if health, safety, or reputation is at stake.

This strategy is a rather formal process that would be followed in detail only for very complex cases, or cases in which a written report is to be prepared describing the justification for a specific decision. However, this strategy may be a useful source of inspiration when people trying to solve simpler problems become stuck. In these circumstances, it is reassuring to know that many of the well-known methods of engineering — problem solving, generating creative ideas, and decision making — can be applied to ethical problems as well. Engineers, in fact, should be much better prepared than the average person to resolve complex ethical problems, as a result of their design education and problem-solving experience.

TOPICS FOR STUDY AND DISCUSSION

1. Examine the code of ethics for your province or territory in Appendix A. Does it include all seven of the basic duties described in this chapter?

2. Examine the code of ethics for your province or territory to see if it contains clauses that require engineers to:

- advertise in a dignified, professional manner;
- report infractions of the code of ethics to the registrar of the Association;
- consider the difficulty of the task and the degree of responsibility in setting fees;
- refuse to pay commissions or reduce fees in order to obtain engineering work.

3. At least one of the provincial codes of ethics requires engineers to encourage employees "to attend and present papers at professional and technical meetings." Which provincial code is it?

4. Compare the NSPE code in Appendix E with the provincial codes in Appendix A. There is a similarity between the NSPE code and one of the provincial codes, particularly in the latter clauses. Which provincial code bears the greatest similarity to the NSPE code?

5. The codes of ethics for IEEE and ASME, two of the largest engineering societies in the world, are included in Appendix E. These codes are very brief. Compare these codes with the code of ethics for your province or territory. Do all three codes cover the seven basic duties described in this chapter? Since the code of ethics is a guide to personal conduct, is it preferable, in your opinion, to have a brief code that can be easily remembered or a more comprehensive code that gives more specific guidance? Examine the codes of ethics in Appendices A and E and find the longest and the shortest.

6. Write a brief statement of your philosophy as to the purpose of human life. Is it to maximize economic gain? Is it to survive? Is it to maximize individual pleasure? If so, what kind of pleasure? Is it to ensure the survival of the species? Is it to ensure a balanced natural ecosystem on Earth? Perhaps it is something other than any of these. How does your philosophy agree with the code of ethics for your province or territory?

7. At the beginning of this chapter, it was stated that basic concepts like truth, justice, beauty, and goodness are very difficult to define. Is it possible to define *any* of these terms objectively, without using subjective opinions, so that your definition would be true for all cultures, for all time? Consult textbooks on philosophy in order to prepare your answer, and don't be disappointed if you are unable to make completely objective definitions of these well-known terms.

8. The six-step strategy for solving complex ethical problems discussed in this chapter is similar to the design process. This strategy may appear to be too formal and structured for enthusiastic engineers who want to dive into a problem and get a fast solution. For these engineers,

there is another process, usually distributed in bumper-sticker form, which outlines the following six phases of the design process:

1. Initial enthusiasm
2. Unco-ordinated hard work
3. Gradual disillusionment
4. Evidence of chaos
5. Punishment of the participants
6. Bestowing of honour on the uninvolved

This process is easier to apply, but less likely to achieve a useful solution. Comment on these two six-step problem-solving methods. Is it really necessary to have a methodical process? Derive a method or mnemonic for remembering the six-step solution process described in this chapter. Are any of the six steps unnecessary? Have any important steps been omitted?

NOTES

The following sources were consulted in the preparation of this chapter and are recommended for additional reading:

P.L. Alger, N.A. Christensen, and S.P. Olmsted, *Ethical Problems in Engineering* (New York: John Wiley & Sons, 1965).

M.I. Mantell, *Ethics and Professionalism in Engineering* (New York: Macmillan; Toronto: Collier-Macmillan Canada, 1964).

M.W. Martin and R. Schinzinger, *Ethics in Engineering*, 2nd ed. (New York: McGraw-Hill, 1989).

C. Morrison and P. Hughes, *Professional Engineering Practice: Ethical Aspects* (Toronto: McGraw-Hill Ryerson, 1988).

J.T. Stevenson, *Engineering Ethics: Practices and Principles* (Toronto: Canadian Scholars' Press, 1987).

CHAPTER 7

Ethical Problems of Engineers in Industry

Engineers in industry are mainly employees and are occasionally subjected to pressures that constrain their ability to act professionally. A frequent source of pressure is the employer. However, other influences also may affect the engineer's ability to act professionally: conflicts of interest, employer/employee negotiation procedures, trade secrets, and confidentiality are issues that the employee engineer will encounter at some time in a professional career.

In this chapter, we attempt to define the limits of the employer's authority and of the engineer's obligation, and to examine the miscellaneous factors that affect employee engineers in industry.

EMPLOYER AUTHORITY AND EMPLOYEE DUTIES

When an engineer accepts an offer of employment, a contract is created in which the engineer, as an employee, agrees to use his or her ability to achieve the employer's legitimate goals. The employer has a duty under the same contract to treat the engineer in a professional manner but also clearly acquires the authority to direct the engineer. The need for authority is obvious, particularly in large organizations, where lack of direction could lead to chaos and bankruptcy. The employer has "management authority" to direct the resources of the company, whereas the engineer has "technical authority" to exercise the special knowledge and skill acquired through university education and practical engineering experience. In a well-run organization, the distinction between management and technical authority will be well defined; the individuals involved will show mutual respect and will co-operate to achieve the goals of the employer.

In many corporations, engineers will be responsible for evaluating the technical feasibility of various courses of action, but the management of the corporation will have the authority to decide which course will be followed. In general, the process works well and benefits the engineer, the managers, the shareholders, and society in general.

However, over the length of a professional career, an engineer may be directed to do something that, in the opinion of the engineer, is morally wrong. For example, an engineer may be asked to alter calculations to show that a gear train has a slightly greater factor of safety against overload, so that it meets the specifications requested by a client or customer. An engineer may be asked to direct the disposal of industrial waste water that is suspected to contain low levels of toxic chemicals. There are many well-publicized cases where the pressure on management to show a profit was converted into pressure on an engineer to act unethically. Although the problem does not occur frequently, it does exist and usually results in ethical dilemmas. At what point does the engineer's duty to follow one's conscience exceed the obligation to the employer? To resolve an ethical dilemma, the procedure stated in the previous chapter should be followed. A useful distinction can be drawn between the following categories or degrees of moral conflict.

Illegal Acts – An engineer may be asked to perform an act that the engineer considers unethical and that is also clearly contrary to the law. The law may be a criminal law, a civil or business law, a regulation made under the authority of an act (such as an environmental regulation), or an infringement of trademark, copyright, or industrial design legislation. In a case such as this, the engineer should advise the employer that the action is illegal and should resist any direction to break the law; the employer clearly does not have the authority to direct the engineer to break the law.

Acts Contrary to the Code of Ethics – An engineer may be asked to perform an act that, while not clearly illegal, is a breach of the code of ethics of the provincial Association. In this case, the engineer should advise the employer of the appropriate section of the code of ethics and should decline to take any action on the employer's request. If the employer is not an engineer, he or she may not be sufficiently familiar with the code of ethics and its legal significance. If the employer *is* an engineer, then he or she is equally bound to follow the code. In either case, the employee engineer has a legal basis for insisting on ethical behaviour; an employer cannot direct the engineer to take action that is clearly in violation of the code of ethics.

Acts Contrary to the Conscience of the Engineer – An engineer may be asked to perform an act that, while not illegal nor clearly a violation of the code of ethics, nevertheless contravenes the engineer's conscience or moral code. These are, of course, the most difficult cases. For situations such as this, the methodical procedure described in the previous chapter should be most useful. The engineer must gather all the relevant information and define the ethical problem as clearly as possible. In precisely what way does the required action offend the engineer's conscience? The employee must attempt to see the problem from the employer's viewpoint. Alternative courses of action must be generated and examined in light of the basic ethical theories discussed earlier, and the optimum course of action should be selected. In these problems, the personal consequences to the engineer must, of course, be considered. Refusal to follow an employer's directive may result in disciplinary action or dismissal, if the employer cannot be convinced otherwise. The possibility and consequences of dismissal and the remedies for wrongful dismissal should be considered by the engineer.

PROFESSIONAL EMPLOYEE GUIDELINES

In 1973, the U.S. National Society of Professional Engineers (NSPE) developed a set of Guidelines to Professional Employment for Engineers and Scientists. The factor that stimulated their development was the U.S. government's cutback on aerospace expenditures in the late 1960s, including the cancellation of the proposed supersonic transport aircraft (SST). Many American scientists and engineers were unemployed and suffered severe financial hardship in the years following the cutbacks.

The NSPE Guidelines are very similar, in many respects, to the codes of ethics adopted by Canadian Professional Engineering Associations and U.S. technical societies. The Guidelines have, in fact, been adopted by at least 26 U.S. or international technical societies. However, unlike the codes of ethics established by provincial Professional Engineering Associations under the authority of acts of provincial legislatures, the Guidelines do not have any legally binding authority, in either the United States or Canada. Nevertheless, they establish ethical practices for employment of engineers (and scientists) that are consistent with, but much more specific than, the provincial codes of ethics. A copy of the Guidelines is included as Appendix F of this text.

As described in Chapter 3, the emergence of these guidelines is a major event in the history of the engineering profession and recognizes that, first, most engineers are employees of someone else and, second, the usual codes of ethics apply primarily to engineers in private practice and sometimes are not very helpful to engineers in industry, government, and education.

The NSPE Guidelines contain far more injunctions for employers than for employees. In brief, the employee is expected to be loyal to the employer's objectives, safeguard the public welfare, avoid conflicts of interest, and pursue professional development programs. The employer is expected to keep professional employees informed of the organization's objectives and policies, establish equitable compensation plans, minimize new hiring during layoffs, provide for early vesting of pension rights, assist in professional development programs, provide timely notice in the event of termination, and assist in relocation efforts following termination.

The Guidelines are not legally binding, but they have had a constructive impact upon employee-employer relationships. Certain items in them are clues to some of the problems that in the 1970s beset aerospace engineers who suddenly found themselves out of work. For example, the emphasis upon early vesting of pension rights reflects the fact that many persons found, after several years of service with employers, that they had acquired little or no right to the contributions made by the employers to the employee's future pension funds. Many — perhaps most — pension plans provide that the employees' rights to employers' contributions become vested only after many years of service. Thus, an employee who changes jobs every few years could easily reach retirement age with no pension except what the government might provide.

A related concern is reflected in the Guidelines' reference to limiting new hiring during periods of layoffs. This guideline was stimulated by the realization on the part of some engineers that the companies that had just laid them off were continuing to hire brand-new engineering graduates. The companies explained that they had new needs that could not be met by the persons who had been let go, but the newly unemployed engineers were more likely to believe that their former employers were trying to save money by hiring less expensive people. Some companies replied by saying that the desire to save money could not be a correct explanation, because new graduates could hardly be considered cheap, were certainly expensive to recruit, and generally could not be very productive for a year or two anyway.

The NSPE Guidelines are useful information for employee engineers and give direction on cases that are more specific than the provincial codes of ethics. Although the Guidelines do not have the legal authority of the codes of ethics, they are consistent with the codes and form an excellent basis for ethical decision making.

PROFESSIONAL ENGINEERS AND LABOUR UNIONS

Engineers have a right to fairness in negotiating pay scales and conditions of employment. The NSPE Guidelines outline basic conditions of employment and also specify that clear policies should exist for negotiating pay raises, for evaluating personal performance, and for advancing within the company. Occasionally, employers will fail to provide these basic conditions, and the engineer is usually faced with the dilemma of resigning or taking collective action against the employer. This creates a moral dilemma, since the employee engineer has an obligation to the employer but also has an obligation to himself or herself, and to the engineering profession as a whole, not to accept unprofessional working conditions or inadequate pay.

It has been well established, in both Canada and the United States, that engineers are entitled to take collective action and even to form or join unions, if desired. Each province has a labour board and a labour relations act that can provide advice and assist engineers who are contemplating collective action. Engineers who are part of the company management are not permitted to organize collectively, since it would be illogical to do so. However, employee engineers are under no such prohibition.

As a general policy, engineers should try to resolve problems with employers through negotiated contracts that do not involve formal unionization for the simple reason that it usually will be less work. Requesting the provincial labour board to create a formal union will require the employer to negotiate in good faith but will also create a lot of formal procedures and bureaucratic overhead. On the other hand, in every province, labour legislation guarantees the rights of employees to form unions and to negotiate in good faith with employers, and this is a very effective procedure when every other route is closed.

Although employee engineers are free to join existing labour unions within their company or industry, it is usually advisable to form a collective group composed entirely of engineers, if possible. This guarantees that the goals of the group will always be consistent with the wishes of the engineers. Otherwise, there is a risk that the engineers will be a minority in the union and may be obliged to support labour action that is not in their best interests.

When the question of unionization is discussed by engineers, it is frequently an emotional and intemperate debate. Engineers are professional people and deserve professional employment. However, in the modern world, the majority of engineers are also employees, and when policies for negotiating pay or other terms and conditions of employment do not exist, they are entitled to take the same collective action as other employees. The need to resort to collective action does not generally indicate a failure of the engineer to act ethically; it shows a failure of the employer to act professionally by establishing fair policies and negotiating procedures within the company.

The Canadian Society of Professional Engineers (CSPE) has been formed with the goal of establishing a professional group, modelled on medical associations and bar associations, that works collectively for professionals while not incurring the problems usually associated with unions. CSPE is active mainly in Ontario.

UNETHICAL MANAGERS

In very rare instances, the management of a company may appear to be unethical. An engineer who finds evidence of dishonesty, fraud, misrepresentation, pollution, or similar unethical acts should take immediate action to inform management of the problem and suggest remedial action. A dilemma arises for the engineer if the management is unresponsive to arguments based on ethics. This puts the engineer's duty to the employer in direct conflict with the duty to the public welfare, which should be considered paramount, as all codes of ethics clearly state.

The engineer must therefore make a serious assessment of the situation and balance the seriousness of the risk to public welfare against the likelihood of overcoming management resistance to remedial action. The engineer should act quickly on the problem, since delay may be interpreted by management as agreeing to or condoning the unethical action. The engineer would then risk involvement and possible loss of professional reputation. The engineer is generally faced with three possible courses of action.

First, the engineer could continue to work for the company while trying to correct company policy. This is probably the friendliest action and would be possible if the dishonest actions are minor, and if management is open to improvement and change. In most cases, this is the effective and preferred choice.

Second, the engineer could continue to work for the company while alerting external regulatory agencies that the company is acting dishonestly. This is commonly called whistleblowing, and it is an unpleasant and usually unfriendly act. However, in rare cases, where the engineer has full knowledge (preferably documented) of a clear and serious hazard to the public, where supervisors and management have refused to take action to correct the problem, and where attempts to correct the situation have failed, then whistle-blowing may be the last resort. However, it should be noted that this course of action is not recommended until all other possible courses of action have been exhausted. Whistleblowing and the problems associated with it are discussed in Chapter 10.

Third, the engineer could resign in protest. This course of action may be necessary in serious cases where complicity may be suspected if the engineer remains with the company. In this case, the engineer should consult a lawyer before resigning. There may be grounds for considering such a forced resignation as equivalent to wrongful dismissal.

▼ ▼ ▼

INTRODUCTION TO CASE STUDIES

In Chapters 7, 8, and 9, seventeen case studies have been presented, in which the reader is presented with a moral dilemma stemming from an engineering problem and asked to make a decision that can be substantiated using a code of ethics or basic ethical concepts. By their nature, case studies are slightly artificial, the information is restricted to a brief summary, the opportunity to gather more information is not available, and the opportunity to propose creative alternatives is therefore limited. Nevertheless, case studies are useful exercises in ethical decision making, regardless of their shortcomings.

All of these case studies used are based on real cases (or reports of real cases), but names and some details have been changed to provide complete anonymity. Any similarity to real persons in comparable situations is entirely coincidental.

▼ ▼ ▼

CASE STUDY 7.1—ACCEPTING A JOB OFFER

Statement of the Problem

During a period of economic recession, an electrical engineering student, Joan Furlong, is nearing graduation and seeks a permanent position with an electronics company in digital circuit design and analysis. She is interviewed by several electronics and power companies. Her résumé clearly states her qualifications, job objective, and interests, which are mainly in digital circuit design. As her graduation day approaches, she receives an offer from the Algonquin Power Company to work on scheduling of maintenance activities at their substations. The salary is good, so she writes immediately and accepts. About two weeks later, she receives a letter from Ace Microelectronics, offering her a position on a new project in digital circuit design; the salary is approximately equal to the Algonquin offer, although the employment may end when the project ends. She is uncertain what to do, as she realizes that she sincerely wants to work in digital circuit design and not in scheduling of maintenance activities. She identifies three possible courses of action.

First, she could write to Algonquin Power, tell them that her plans have changed, and apologize for the inconvenience. She is aware of the code of ethics of her provincial Association, but she is not yet a member of the Association and does not feel bound to follow the code. Although she is a student member of the Institute of Electrical and Electronics Engineers (IEEE), the IEEE code does not appear to have any clause that pertains to this particular case.

Second, she could write to Algonquin Power, as above, but offer to reimburse them for the recruitment expenses that they have paid on her behalf.

Third, she could write to Ace Microelectronics and advise them that she has unfortunately already accepted an offer from Algonquin Power but might be in a position to join them on a later project, in a few years' time, when her obligation to Algonquin Power is satisfied.

Question

Which of the above three alternatives is best, from the ethical viewpoint?

Authors' Recommended Solution

This problem is not clearly defined in codes of ethics, although almost every code states that an engineer has an obligation to act with "good faith" or "good will" toward clients, employees, and employers.

The first course of action is clearly unethical. Furlong *does* have an obligation to Algonquin Power, which cannot be erased with a simple apology. The power company has probably sent rejection letters to the other applicants for the position and may stand to lose more than just the recruitment cost if its maintenance program is delayed. (The seriousness of a failure to recruit personnel is rarely appreciated by personnel outside the company.) The argument that Furlong is not bound by the Association's code of ethics is spurious, legalistic, and unacceptable as a justification for her actions.

On the surface, the third course of action might seem to be the most ethical: Furlong made a promise to Algonquin Power, and she has a duty to fulfil it. However, it is clear that the job is not in the area that she wanted, and she chose it mainly for security. Consequently, although she may grow to enjoy her job, the probability is that she will not enjoy it, will regret the missed opportunity, will not be as productive an employee as the company would want, and may leave in a few years. This course of action is ethically correct, but is not ideal.

The second course of action is the mean, or compromise, between the evils of the other two courses of action. It is possible that Algonquin Power may request the return of expenses paid during the recruitment, but that would be a small price to pay for realigning her career path to suit her goals. This choice acknowledges her ethical duty, maximizes the benefits, and tries to ensure that the person who benefits most from this course of action (Furlong) alleviates at least part of the losses incurred by Algonquin Power.

▼ ▼ ▼

CASE STUDY 7.2—SLOW PROMOTION AND JOB DISSATISFACTION

Statement of the Problem

John Smith is a licensed professional engineer in the jigs and fixtures group of the Dominion Press and Stamping Company, which is a fairly large, privately owned manufacturing company. He was first hired by Dominion during his final summer at university. They offered him a part-time job during his final year of university and a permanent position after graduation. Smith learned a great deal of useful information during his first year of permanent employment, which was almost entirely devoted to training. He was sent away on a two-month computer course and then given on-the-job familiarization with each of the three divisions of the company (design, manufacturing, and sales) during the rest of his first year. He elected to stay in the design division and has worked there productively for three years.

Unfortunately, he now feels that he has reached a dead end. He has mastered all the skills necessary to carry out his present job, but he sees that further promotions are blocked by colleagues with more seniority. Moreover, the design job has become routine, and his request to transfer to the manufacturing division was denied because there was "no opening" and because he was considered "too valuable" in his present job. He feels very guilty about resigning to apply for a job in another company, since he is sincerely grateful for the experience he has obtained over the past four years with Dominion, has an excellent working relationship with his co-workers, and knows the company will have trouble replacing him. He also feels it may be unethical to change jobs now that he has been fully trained and is of maximum benefit to the company. On the other hand, he is aware of several vacant positions with rival manufacturing companies.

Question

Is it ethical for Smith to seek employment elsewhere?

Authors' Recommended Solution

This problem occurs fairly often among engineers in their first full-time job in industry. Training periods for junior engineers may take one or two years, and then, when the engineer is finally a productive member of the company, he or she wants to move on to greener pastures. A dilemma arises, since the employee clearly has an obligation yet also has the right to seek advancement in his or her career, commensurate with talent, effort, and education. This problem cannot easily be resolved by examining the provincial code of ethics, since the code stipulates that engineers must act with "fairness and loyalty" to employers, but precisely what is "fair" in this instance requires further discussion.

When an employee accepts a training benefit, an implied contract is created. A company invests in a new engineer during the training period, and that investment is returned during the period of useful employment that follows. The cost and extent of the training period is therefore a factor in determining how much useful employment would be a "fair" return. Using this concept of return on investment, it seems that we can reduce an ethical decision to a simple computation. However, it is not easy to determine how much expense was actually incurred during the training period. Did the engineer receive full wages? Did he or she carry out useful duties while being trained? Was the company reimbursed for training or for work done during training? What obligation does a company have to carry out technical training? The calculation may be rather approximate and subjective, but the concept of fairness hinges on showing that the obligation incurred by training has been satisfied by adequate useful service.

In the case of Smith, common sense would dictate that if most of his first year was training, then he would be obligated to remain for at least an equal one-year period. However, a company would usually expect to amortize the initial training over more than one year. As a comparison, most military postings are four years long, the average term of a member of Parliament is four years, and in the United States presidential terms are four years. Each of these jobs would include some initial familiarization or training.

When the initial training is particularly lengthy or expensive, then the company should stipulate, in the contract of employment, what time period would be expected to amortize the cost. For example, university students who want to become engineering officers in the Canadian Forces may receive full room, board, and tuition expenses during their university education; however, in return they must usually sign employment contracts for a minimum of five years' service after graduation.

Therefore, since Smith has completed three years of satisfactory service after the initial year of training, and no minimum period was specified in his contract, he has probably satisfied any indebtedness he might have incurred. If he is unable to advance or transfer within the company, then he should feel no guilt about moving on to a job with another company that has more challenge and interest for him.

▼ ▼ ▼

CASE STUDY 7.3—PART-TIME EMPLOYMENT (OR MOONLIGHTING)

Statement of the Problem

Philip Fortescue is a licensed professional engineer who has worked for Federal Structural Design for ten years. Unfortunately, for reasons that are not clear (to either Fortescue or his employer), the company has not had many large contracts, and Fortescue's salary is very low. His pay raises have rarely exceeded cost-of-living increases over the ten years of his employment. As a result, he has been forced to take on extra employment in his spare time, and he secretly brings the work to his office in the evening, where he uses the CAD (computer-aided design) system on the computer. He is careful to ensure that the paper, pens, and photocopying are paid out of his own pocket, and he argues that the computer would be sitting idle in the evening anyway, so his employer is suffering no loss. In fact, he argues that his evening work benefits the employer, since it permits him to continue to work for Federal Structural Design, in spite of his low salary.

Question

Is it ethical for Fortescue to carry on his part-time employment in this manner?

Authors' Recommended Solution

The question of an engineer accepting part-time employment (or moonlighting, as it is commonly called) occurs frequently, and guidelines have evolved over the years. In general, it is not unethical for an employee to work for more than one employer, although it requires determination and stamina.

However, as every code of ethics indicates, the employee engineer must show fairness and loyalty to the employer. This means that the part-time employer should not compete for the full-time employer's contracts, that the time and effort spent should not reduce the employee's efficiency during the usual workday, and that the employer must be fully informed in order to verify the situation.

It is clear that Fortescue is not acting ethically in this case, since he has not informed his employer of his part-time employment. Therefore it cannot be verified whether his part-time work competes or conflicts with his full-time job. The fact that an engineer would remain with an employer for ten years with no promotion or significant increase in salary is curious and implies that there are other unstated factors that influence this case. It is not clear whether the engineer is exploiting the employer's facilities and contacts to generate a large part-time income, or whether the employer is exploiting the engineer by forcing him to carry two jobs to survive financially. However, the engineer's secrecy about his part-time employment is clearly unethical.

▼ ▼ ▼

CASE STUDY 7.4—ENGINEERS AS MEMBERS OF LABOUR UNIONS

Statement of the Problem

Jeanne Giroux is a licensed professional engineer working for Acme Automotive Manufacturing, a small-to-medium-size company that makes parts for cars and trucks. She works in the design engineering office (four engineers, six designers) and supervises modifications to parts, including stress analysis, detail drawing, and prototype testing — a wide range of duties. In her job, she has frequent contact with the machinists and other tradespeople in the manufacturing plant and observes that the shop union is very effective in negotiating terms and conditions of employment. The union steward informs her that the employer is required, by law, to bargain in good faith with the union and that there are procedures for mediation and arbitration in case of stalemates in the negotiations.

In contrast, the design and engineering staff have had very low pay raises in recent years, are limited to short vacations, and are required to work overtime (and occasional Saturdays) without additional pay when there is a crisis. Although all four of the company's engineers are licensed, the provincial Association of Professional Engineers cannot assist them in negotiating with the employer. The Association has, however, provided them with a survey of engineering salaries. Giroux notes that the mean salary for the four staff engineers is 20 percent below the median salary for the appropriate group in the survey. The company administration manual does not mention procedures for staff pay raises. As a comparison, the sales staff in the company (none of whom are engineers) are paid partly on a commission basis and always receive higher pay than the engineers.

Giroux has been assured by the union steward that the design and engineering staff could be included in the bargaining group if at least six of the ten employees sign application forms. Giroux believes that all ten would probably join, if asked.

Question

Is it ethical for engineers to join a labour union?

Authors' Recommended Solution

Yes, it is ethical and legal for engineers to join labour unions, provided that the engineers do not exert managerial control in the company. From the details of the case above, it would appear that the design engineering staff are not considered part of management. However, although it may be ethical and legal to join the union, it may not be appropriate; labour relations acts in some provinces specifically permit professional engineers to form a bargaining unit composed entirely of professional engineers, unless the majority of engineers wish to be included in a bargaining unit with other employees. Moreover, it is not essential to have the support of an established union to form a bargaining unit. This can be done directly through the labour board of the provincial government (in most provinces). A majority of members of the bargaining group may request certification of the group as a bargaining unit. The elected representatives then negotiate contracts for the entire group.

However, for small groups, such as described in this case, it might be more appropriate to make management aware of their dissatisfaction and of the routes open to resolve the problem, and to suggest the negotiation of individual contracts, a collective contract, or a salary negotiation procedure for the design engineering staff. If the employer is unco-operative, it would be advisable to obtain legal advice when negotiating.

▼ ▼ ▼

CASE STUDY 7.5—FALSE OR MISLEADING ENGINEERING DATA IN ADVERTISING

Statement of the Problem

Audrey Adams is a licensed mechanical engineer with marine experience, working for a manufacturer of fibreglass pleasure boats. She has conducted buoyancy tests on all the boats manufactured by the company and has rated the hull capacity of each according to the procedure specified by Transport Canada. She observes in the company's sales literature that a boat hull rated for a maximum of five persons is consistently shown in photographs with six persons on board. The sales literature appears to be otherwise correct. Adams is aware that the boat would be safe in still water with six persons, but could be flooded and sink in rough water. Adams believes the sales literature is misleading and possibly hazardous.

Question

In this case, it appears that the data developed by the engineer have been misrepresented, distorted, or portrayed incorrectly by the sales literature. What action should the engineer take?

Authors' Recommended Solution

The code of ethics for every provincial Association and technical society states that the welfare of the general public must be considered most important in a case like this. There is a potential hazard to the public, and the engineer has an ethical duty to take action to reduce or eliminate this hazard.

Adams's first step should be to inform the engineering manager about the problem. This would typically be done in an internal memorandum describing the errors in the sales literature. If the errors are simple errors or oversights by the sales personnel, then they will be easy to rectify. Most companies are honest and would take immediate action to correct the sales literature by issuing new data to customers. The problem would then be quickly remedied.

In a rare instance, the management of the company may be dishonest. For example, if Adams, while investigating the problem, should discover that test results had been altered or that the manufactured boats were being sold with incorrect capacities stamped on the serial nameplates, then the problem would be much more serious. In this case, the management of the company would be guilty of misrepresentation, which could be a criminal act. If a serious failure should occur (such as sinking of an overloaded pleasure boat with a loss of life), the erroneous literature and incorrect capacities would become public knowledge, and the engineer could be the subject of investigation for possible unethical acts, incompetence, or collusion with management in the misrepresentation.

Therefore, if an engineer recognizes that she or he is working for a dishonest company, a decision must be made quickly to dissociate oneself from any unethical activity, to work for change within the company, and, in extremely rare cases, to act as a whistleblower or to resign in protest. Fortunately, extreme action is rarely necessary.

▼ ▼ ▼

CASE STUDY 7.6—DISCLOSING PROPRIETARY INFORMATION

Statement of the Problem

This incident allegedly has occurred in the aircraft industry. An aeronautical research engineer from Company A conducted tests of a certain aircraft tail assembly configuration in his company's wind tunnel and knew that devastating vibrations could occur in the configuration under certain circumstances, leading to destruction of the aircraft. Later, at a professional meeting, Company A's engineer hears an engineer from Company B, a competitor, describe a tail assembly configuration for one of Company B's new aircraft that runs the risk of producing the same destructive vibrations that Company A's engineer discovered in his tests. Presumably there is an obligation, as a matter of both morals and law, to maintain company confidentiality regarding Company A's proprietary knowledge. On the other hand, engineers have a duty to safeguard public safety and welfare. If the engineer from Company A remains silent, Company B might not discover the destructive vibrations until a dreadful crash occurs, killing many people.

Question

What would you do if you were the engineer from Company A?

Authors' Recommended Solution

On the one hand, you have an obligation under the code of ethics to your employer to maintain the confidentiality of proprietary information. Your company paid a lot of money to test the tail assembly, and it would not be fair to your employer to turn this information over to Company B. Moreover, if Company B is as diligent in its testing and analysis as Company A, then they will discover the vibration problem in due course, and you need take no action.

On the other hand, you also have an obligation under the code of ethics to consider the welfare of society as paramount and to report a condition such as this, which endangers public safety. If Company B should fail to discover the design flaw and the aircraft later crashes as a result of this problem, your lack of adherence to the code of ethics will be painfully clear.

Therefore, you have an ethical dilemma with two undesirable courses of action. In this case, the duty to society must prevail over the loss of advantage, and Company B should be informed of the potential problem. You would, of course, notify your employer before contacting Company B. You should also keep in mind the objective of this exchange of information. It would be unethical to convey the information in a way that harmed the reputation of Company B. However, it is *not* your duty to release detailed data or to save money for your competitor. Your goal is merely to ensure that public safety is not endangered by Company B's defective design. Therefore, in consultation with your employer, you would determine what minimum information would achieve this purpose, and convey it in a direct and unambiguous way.

TOPICS FOR STUDY AND DISCUSSION

1. Consider the circumstances of Case Study 7.6, in which it has been recommended that Company A inform Company B that its aircraft tail assembly design has serious vibration problems. If the vibration was *not* dangerous to passenger safety but merely increased fuel consumption and created noise in the cabin, would Company A still be ethically bound to inform Company B? Explain your answer in a sentence or two.

2. The engineer who accepts an offer of employment creates a contract in which the engineer agrees to use his or her ability to achieve the employer's legitimate goals. Consider the case where you have been hired to design electrical or mechanical components of manufacturing machinery. During a recession, the employer decides to diversify into new areas to attract more business. What would your position be, both ethically and personally, if the employer asked you to participate in the design of:

    -   bottling equipment for the beer and liquor industry
    -   manufacturing equipment for the tobacco and cigarette industry
    -   medical equipment to make abortions safer and more convenient
    -   pill-making machines for the birth-control or pharmaceutical industries
    -   security locks for the prison system
    -   equipment for nuclear power plants

3. As an employee of a large Canadian manufacturing corporation, you have been assigned as assistant to the chief engineer on a six-person team that is to establish a branch plant in an underdeveloped country. Your task is to supervise the installation and commissioning of the manufacturing equipment. The local people who will be running the

equipment are rural people with little or no education. As soon as you arrive on the site and familiarize yourself with the plan, which is well under way, you realize that the manufacturing line to be installed was removed from service in Canada because it created toxic waste. The waste must be disposed of by special incineration equipment that does not exist in this foreign country. Although the manufacturing line would not be permitted in Canada, the underdeveloped country does not have pollution control laws that would prevent its installation and operation. You have some concerns about this project and discuss them with the chief engineer. He is sympathetic but points out that the manufacturing line ran in Canada for over ten years before pollution laws stopped it, and no deaths were attributed to it. Moreover, the local people will be much better off when the line is running and there is useful employment for all concerned.

What guidance does your provincial code of ethics give on this problem? (See Appendix A.) Does the code apply to activities conducted in a foreign country? What alternative courses of action are open to you? Which course is the best from the ethical standpoint?

4. Assume that you are working as a professional engineer in a small consulting company that gives the employee engineers considerable latitude in scheduling of tasks, meeting deadlines, and reporting expenses. You are approached by the company president, who states that your professional attitude and attention to high standards have been recognized by the senior management. The president also expresses concern about the lax attitudes of your colleagues, who appear to be abusing the freedom awarded to them. Would it be ethical for the president to offer, and for you to accept:

   • a secret assignment to monitor the behaviour of your colleagues and your immediate superior and report back to him?
   • a promotion to head engineer to replace your immediate superior, on the basis that the head engineer is not competent as a manager and should be replaced?

CHAPTER 8

Ethical Problems of Engineers in Management

Engineers in management positions are also employees and may experience some or all of the ethical dilemmas discussed in the previous chapter. Managers, however, control the resources of the corporation to a much greater degree than their subordinates, and ethical problems may arise from the potential conflict of interest that accompanies increased authority. Managers are in a position to hire, fire, delegate, and direct other employees and to control the use of the corporation's resources. Conflicts of interest that benefit the manager may occur. Managers may also negotiate and make agreements with other businesses, and the potential for unethical practices exists in these dealings as well.

Specific problems will vary from company to company and may differ according to whether the company is an industrial manufacturer, a consulting engineering firm, or a municipal, regional, provincial, territorial, or federal government. The engineering management must be alert to the potential for conflict of interest and must avoid involvement, or even the possible appearance of involvement, in such conflicts.

ADHERENCE TO THE PROVINCIAL ACT

One of the most obvious responsibilities of the professional engineer in a management position is to ensure that the Professional Engineering Act is being obeyed within the manager's area of responsibility. The two most common infringements of the Act in most provinces are the use of unlicensed personnel to carry out the work of professional engineers and the misuse of engineering titles.

The use of unlicensed personnel is by far the more serious infringement, since it has the potential for harm to the client, the employer, or the general public. If personnel are carrying out professional engineering work, as defined in the Professional Engineering Act for that province or territory, the work must be done by, or under the direct supervision of, a professional engineer. If this is not the case, the situation must be rectified. This sort of problem is not uncommon in many smaller industries in Canada, usually through ignorance of the law. If a manager tries to restrict a practice that may have endured for years, hard feelings and antagonism are likely to result. The manager must risk offending the employee in order to obey the Act. A certain amount of diplomacy may be required, depending on the circumstances of the case and the flagrancy of the violation. In cases where the employee would be eligible for a licence, the appropriate action is to insist on proper registration. When this is not possible, the employee must be put under the supervision of a professional engineer, perhaps the manager, in order to continue to perform useful but now regulated work.

The misuse of engineering titles is usually less serious. Many companies have positions with the word "engineer" or "engineering" in the title, such as a "design engineer" who is really a designer, or an "engineering manager" who is really a manager, giving the erroneous impression that the person holding the position is a licensed professional engineer. If the tasks performed do not require a licence, the title must be changed to eliminate the ambiguity. Again, this is a situation where tact and diplomacy may be needed to alter practices that may go back many years. It may take some creative thinking to identify new job titles that are elegant and accurate but do not contravene the Act.

In both of the above cases, the action is quite clear. It is not only unethical and unprofessional to continue such practices, it is illegal; these practices are contrary to the Professional Engineers Act in every province and territory.

REVIEWING WORK AND EVALUATING COMPETENCE

Engineers, whether employees or managers, are required by law to practise only within their limits of competence. Engineers should not undertake, and managers should not assign, work that is not within the competence of the engineer. In some cases, preparation or review may be needed to gain (or regain) the needed competence. In these cases, the question of fairness to the employer may be raised. An extensive period of education at the employer's expense to gain competence in a specific field is not uncommon, but the expense to the employer should be approved before a commitment is made.

Work Review for Accuracy

Most engineers have their work routinely reviewed by a second engineer for accuracy. In some industries, particularly aircraft, aerospace, and nuclear power industries, where errors could be extremely costly and could have serious liability implications, the review of calculations is a common, expected procedure. In these industries, an important decision should never be made on the basis of a single engineer's unchecked calculations. These reviews are always carried out with the knowledge of the person who did the original work, and the purpose of the review is always to guarantee safety, improve quality, or reduce liability.

Work Review to Assess Competence

It is common practice to evaluate the performance of all employees on a regular basis, and the engineering manager is generally responsible for this evaluation. It may be necessary to review an engineer's work to evaluate competence at other times as well. However, a manager should never ask a professional engineer to review the work of another engineer without the knowledge of the engineer who prepared the work. This precept is included in most codes of ethics, is simple common courtesy, and should apply to any professional employee. Since the work of a professional, by definition, requires specialized knowledge, additional information, data, or explanations might be required. A professional reputation is a valuable asset, requiring years of study and experience to build up. The review of any professional's work must not be done in a careless or cavalier way that could inadvertently damage one's professional reputation. A secret review is like a trial in absentia, and this is generally contrary to our system of natural justice. Consequently, although reviews of an engineer's work for accuracy or competence are common and do not require the *permission* of the engineer, such reviews must not be done without *informing* the engineer. Engineering managers should be particularly sensitive to the need for this common courtesy.

DISCRIMINATION IN ENGINEERING EMPLOYMENT

Since the engineering manager plays a key role in hiring, evaluating performance, and dismissing engineers, the manager is in the front line of the battle against discrimination in engineering. Discrimination should not be a problem in Canada; the Charter of Rights and Freedoms prohibits discrimination on the basis of race, national or ethnic origin, colour, religion, sex, age, or mental or physical disability. Although progress in overcoming discrimination is evident, there still is a serious underrepresentation of certain groups in engineering, such as women, native peoples, people with disabilities, and other visible minorities. The problem is particularly obvious where women are concerned, since they are a majority in the general population but are definitely a minority in the engineering profession.

Until the 1970s the number of women who entered the engineering profession was minuscule. The numbers have gradually risen over the last two decades, and women made up approximately 11 percent of the enrolment in engineering schools across Canada in 1987, although they still made up less than 2 percent of the number of licensed engineers in Canada.[1] By comparison, female enrolment in U.S. engineering schools was 16 percent in 1987.[2]

In the 1950s and earlier, this low participation rate used to be explained (if it was considered at all) as a lack of interest or a lack of aptitude in engineering on the part of women. However, those who have examined this question believe that gender discrimination is part of the answer. Following graduation, women start at about the same salary level as do men, but some surveys have shown that salary disparities develop after a few years. For example, an American survey conducted by the Institute of Electrical and Electronics Engineers in 1984 showed that female electrical engineers between the ages of 20 and 29 earned about 13 percent less than their male counterparts.[3] Other studies showed a tendency for male evaluators to judge male applicants as more acceptable for hiring, more highly qualified with respect to potential, and more suitable for promotion.[4] One study has shown that male faculty members are often likely to perceive female students as less capable and less professionally committed than male students.[5] Although accurate data are not readily available, similar problems are believed to exist for the minority groups mentioned above.

The laws are now quite clear: Discrimination is not only unethical, it is illegal. Managers, in particular, must keep this in mind when hiring and promoting engineers. Women and minority groups have a legal right to be treated fairly; although they would not expect preference over their colleagues, artificial obstacles must not be created for them.

SPECIAL PROBLEMS RELATED TO COMPUTERS

In the last twenty years, computers have invaded every engineering office. Drawing tables have been pushed out of the way to make room for computer-aided design (CAD) systems, and storage files for drawings have been replaced by magnetic tape and computer disk files. It is hard to remember (or to imagine) what engineering was like before the computer revolution. Almost every engineering office has equipment and programs for CAD, automated drafting, computer-aided analysis, spreadsheets, and word processors. The next decade will see the introduction of expert systems and artificial intelligence, so the use of computers will continue to grow.

These new facilities create additional responsibilities and problems for the engineering manager, such as security, back-up, infringement of copyright, and the possibility of engineering errors caused by flaws or bugs in the computer programs.

Computer Security and Back-up

Computer equipment (hardware) and computer programs (software), including stored data, represent a large financial investment; in a small engineering office, they may be one of the major assets of the practice. It is the responsibility of the manager to be alert to any risks, problems, or damage that could occur to this investment. Maintaining the equipment and providing for alternate facilities in the event of failures are the most obvious responsibilities. The manager should have a disaster plan for the possibility, however remote, of complete malfunction or destruction of the computers and for possible corruption or loss of the programs and data. The simplest protection is to have key data and programs duplicated on back-up disks or tapes and stored in a safe, secure location. Many textbooks are available to provide further advice on this subject.

Program Copyright Protection

One of the most frequently encountered conflicts of interest that arise today in engineering concerns protection of program copyright for engineering software. Violation of copyright is so easily done that the practice, whether through ignorance or by intent, is widespread.

The purchase of a computer program permits use of the program but does not include the right to duplicate the program (except for back-up). Some programs are leased (particularly large programs) and may include a monitor program that checks the date given by the computer and disables the program if the lease has expired and no extension is indicated (usually in the form of a secret password provided by the leasing supplier). It is contrary to the Copyright Act to duplicate programs for personal use or to disable the password protection on leased programs. This may create an ethical dilemma for an engineering manager, since unauthorized use of programs duplicated elsewhere or unauthorized use of leased programs (and many similar practices) may be illegal or unethical, but they certainly improve the efficiency and productivity of the office. This dilemma has only one solution: the unethical practices must not be allowed, and it is the responsibility of the engineering manager to protect the copyright of software. This issue has been clarified in the Ontario Guidelines to Professional Practice. Two circumstances arise in which it is not an infringement of copyright to make duplicate copies of programs.

> The first exception provides that it shall not be infringement for a person in a lawful possession of a copy of a computer program to modify, adapt, or convert a reproduction of the copy into another program to suit needs, provided that:
>
> i)   the modified program is *essential* for the compatibility of the computer program with a particular computer;
> ii) the modified program is used only for the person's own needs;
> iii) not more than one modified copy is used by the person at any given time, and;
> iv) the modified copy is destroyed when the person ceases to be entitled to possession of the copy (i.e. upon expiry of a software licence).
>
> The second exception provides that a person who is in *lawful possession* of a copy of a computer program or of a modified reproduction of a program may make a single backup copy of the program, provided that the backup copy is destroyed when the person ceases to be the owner of the copy of the computer program.
>
> The intention of these exceptions is to give the authorized user of software a limited right to change the software to ensure compatibility of the software with the authorized user's computer system, and to allow for the protection and security of the original program.[6]

Liability for Errors in Computer Programs

Computer programs, even those that are widely distributed and highly regarded, can occasionally have hidden flaws or bugs that cause incorrect calculations. The question of liability arises if the errors should result in an incorrect engineering decision. Disclaimers on the documentation for computer programs usually state quite clearly that, in the event of malfunction, the liability of the seller of the computer program is limited to the cost of the program. The Ontario Guideline for the Development and Use of Computer Programs by Professional Engineers is much more specific. It states clearly that the engineer is responsible for errors of this sort. The engineer must ensure that he or she is competent to deal with the subject matter and must validate the program as follows.

> The engineer must ascertain that the program is relevant, accurate and correctly used for each application. To do this, the engineer should:
>
> a) determine the exact nature of assistance the program provides the engineer;
> b) identify the theory on which a program is based;
> c) determine the limitations, assumptions, etc., that are included in both the theory and the program;
> d) check the validity of the program for the intended applications;
> e) make sure the program is correctly used;
> f) verify that the results are correct for each application.[7]

So proper practice requires the engineer to make extensive independent checks to evaluate the program before using the results in a design situation. It is the manager's responsibility to ensure that this is done by the engineers under his or her direction.

HIRING AND DISMISSAL

The engineering manager usually hires and dismisses engineering staff, when required. The engineering manager should therefore be aware of these aspects of hiring and dismissal.

Employment Contracts and Policies

The best method for employing professional engineers is through clear-cut employment contracts. These contracts eliminate uncertainty by specifying the duration (either fixed-length or indefinite); the remuneration and how it will increase with time and duties; vacation entitlement and statutory holidays; what would constitute just cause for termination; and terms and amounts of severance pay and other payments. When a company has too many employees for each engineer to have a personal contract, then the company must have clear policies that deal with these issues. The NSPE Guidelines to Professional Employment (in Appendix F) give a good explanation of the topics that should be included in the company policies for the benefit of the professional employees.

Terminating Employment for Just Cause

A manager must take responsibility for terminating or discharging employees when their services are no longer required. Such terminations must be in accordance with the employment contract or published company policies. In addition, employees may be discharged for *just cause*, which is defined below.

> Those matters which would allow an employer to terminate an employee, without notice or severance pay, are as follows:
>
> (1) serious misconduct;
> (2) habitual neglect of duty;
> (3) serious incompetence, not just management dissatisfaction with performance;
> (4) conduct incompatible with his or her duties or prejudicial to the company's business;
> (5) wilful disobedience to a lawful and reasonable order of a superior in a matter of substance;
> (6) theft, fraud or dishonesty;
> (7) continual insolence and insubordination;
> (8) excessive absenteeism despite corrective counselling;
> (9) permanent illness; and
> (10) inadequate job performance over an extended period as a result of drug or alcohol abuse and failure to accept or respond to the company's attempt to rehabilitate.
>
> If one of these elements of misconduct exists, and is ascertained even after the employee has been discharged, the company can rely on that misconduct and not pay the employee any severance allowance.[8]

Wrongful Dismissal

When an employee without an employment contract is dismissed, and the reason does not constitute just cause, as described above, then there is a risk of *wrongful dismissal*. These cases may have to be resolved in a court of law and legal advice is extremely useful, for both the employee and the manager.

In a comprehensive article on wrongful dismissal, lawyer Howard Levitt described six situations that could also be considered wrongful dismissal, even though the employee is not technically dismissed. These are forced resignation, demotion, a downward change in reporting function, a unilateral change in responsibilities, a forced transfer, and serious misconduct of the employer toward the employee.[9]

In summary, it is important for a manager to be alert to the myriad of difficulties and complications that are associated with supervising the work of other human beings. The manager needs leadership ability, sensitivity, and a professional attitude. A knowledge of the law or access to legal advice is also beneficial and, when needed, should be obtained *before* taking hard decisions, not after the fact.

▼ ▼ ▼

CASE STUDY 8.1—THE UNLICENSED ENGINEER

Statement of Problem

Assume that you are the manager of the engineering design department for a fairly large consulting engineering firm. As part of your job, you hire and dismiss department staff members, including engineers, designers, CAD operators, and secretarial workers. Six months ago, you hired Jorges Xavier, who had recently moved to your area from another province. During the employment interview, you emphasized that it was essential that he be licensed, and the letter of appointment sent to him stipulated that he was being hired as a "Professional Engineer." After he started work, you had a sign placed on his door and business cards printed, both of which had the designation "P.Eng." after his name.

You are startled to receive a complaint from a client who claims that Xavier is not a licensed professional engineer. The client is furious that you and your company would send unqualified people to work on his project. You contact the provincial Association of Professional Engineers and they confirm that Xavier has *not* been awarded a licence. Now *you* are furious.

Question

Who is responsible for this problem? Can you fire Xavier for just cause? Would it make any difference if:

- *Xavier is licensed in another province but has neglected to apply for a transfer of licence?*
- *Xavier has applied to transfer his licence, but it is still being processed by the provincial Association?*
- *Xavier has never been licensed in any province?*

Authors' Recommended Solution

It is not presently possible in all cases to transfer a licence from one province to another. However, a person who has been licensed in one province will generally be accepted as qualified for licensing in another province, and although additional requirements (such as a professional practice examination) may be required, they can generally be satisfied fairly easily in a matter of months. This case involves the code of ethics and a more fundamental problem: a breach of the Professional Engineers Act.

There can be little doubt that Xavier is guilty of practising professional engineering without a licence. He has used the business cards that clearly say "P.Eng." without protest or correction, and he is not licensed in the province where he is working. Consequently, he is responsible to the provincial Association for any infraction of the Act, although the fact that you, as manager, had the business cards prepared could be considered a mitigating factor. You will be guilty of a breach of the code of ethics if you permit Xavier to continue practising engineering.

It is essential to determine what work Xavier has done for the client. If Xavier has been in a junior or training position during his first six months with the firm and his work has been supervised by another engineer, as would usually be the case, there is no problem. There has been no risk to the client or the public, and no damage has occurred.

However, it would probably be advisable to discuss the case with a lawyer if Xavier has been involved in making independent decisions on engineering projects, since the engineering firm would undoubtedly be liable for any problems that arise from those decisions. In any discussion of liability, it would probably be made clear that it was your responsibility, as manager, to verify the qualifications of your subordinates.

The appropriateness of dismissal and the basis for it are slightly different, depending on which of the three possible situations applies. If Xavier has failed to apply for a licence in six months of employment but has a valid licence from another province, then it could be argued that this constitutes either "serious misconduct" or "habitual neglect of duty," which are both recognized as breaches of the code of ethics and just cause for dismissal.

If Xavier has applied for a licence but it has merely been delayed, and he has a valid licence from another province, then he has probably complied with your requirements, and dismissal would probably be unjust. If Xavier has never been licensed in another province, then he has been dishonest in his employment interview with you, and such fundamental dishonesty would be just cause for dismissal.

Xavier clearly contravened the Act when he used the designation "P.Eng." while not licensed. However, you, as manager, must bear much of the responsibility for any embarrassment or liability that the firm suffers because of Xavier's lack of a licence. Although you stated the requirements for a licence clearly, you did not follow up on the request to verify that it had been issued. A company involved in offering services to the public has a duty to verify that its engineers keep their licences up to date.

Xavier is of course at fault for using the designation "P.Eng." and he may also be subject to a charge under the Act, as discussed above, particularly if he does not have a valid licence from another province.

▼ ▼ ▼

CASE STUDY 8.2—DISMISSAL OF OFFENSIVE ENGINEER

Statement of the Problem

You are a licensed professional engineer employed as manager of an engineering department with ten employee engineers and eighteen designers and draftspersons. You are summoned to the office of the vice-president of development, your direct superior, who instructs you to fire one of your engineers, who disgraced himself by talking in a loud, vicious, and offensive way to the vice-president the previous week at a company picnic, an event that you witnessed.

You point out to the vice-president that the engineer's work has always been satisfactory. The vice-president states that the engineer's behaviour was offensive and insubordinate, and insubordination is grounds for dismissal. He hints that he would interpret your failure to co-operate as insubordination, also.

Question

You know that the incident has gravely offended the vice-president and has created some awkwardness in the department, which you believe would be eliminated if the engineer was fired. And you think the vice-president will jeopardize your salary increase and possibly your job if you don't co-operate. What should you do and how should you do it?

Authors' Recommended Solution

This problem is typical of the pressure applied to middle-level managers. The first step is to get the facts and to define the problem: Was the behaviour of the engineer just cause for dismissal? Since your action could result in a wrongful dismissal, it is a very serious matter and also involves issues of law. However, you must make a decision quickly, and you probably will not have the luxury of discussing the case with a lawyer or labour consultant. Since you witnessed the incident and did not initiate the dismissal action, you evidently did not consider it a serious case of insubordination. Moreover, for the engineer's behaviour to be considered sufficiently scandalous to justify dismissal, there must be a record of continual insolence and insubordination or wilful disobedience on a matter of substance, not merely an altercation at a social event. There does not appear to be sufficient basis to justify dismissal of the engineer, and under the code of ethics, you have a duty to the employee as well as to the employer.

Therefore, the ethical issue is quite clear: The engineer's behaviour does *not* constitute just cause. Although it might solve some of your immediate problems, it would be unethical and unwise to dismiss him. A reprimand to the engineer might, however, be appropriate, but the best action would probably be to do nothing more. If the vice-president was speaking in a moment of anger, he may later realize the error and be relieved that you did not follow his instructions. However, should he later approach you and insist that you follow his instructions, you should ask to have the order in writing. In your reply to the written order, you would decline to carry out his instructions, justify your decision, and mention the reprimand that you have given the engineer. This would probably end the matter. However, should it be pursued further, the written record would be essential to show senior management that you were protecting the company against a legal case for wrongful dismissal. The documents might also be useful as the basis for a complaint of unethical conduct against the vice-president or as evidence in your own suit for wrongful dismissal, however unlikely that may be.

▼ ▼ ▼

CASE STUDY 8.3—CONFLICT OF INTEREST

Statement of the Problem

You are an engineering manager in a fairly large company, and you have been asked to sit on a ten-member standards committee, which sets performance and safety specifications for the automotive equipment that your company manufactures. The committee comprises three industry representatives such as yourself, three government representatives, and three engineering professors, and it is chaired by a representative from an engineering society associated with the automotive industry.

One of the other industry representatives has proposed a revision to the specification for a component that you manufacture. The change will make a fairly modest improvement in quality but will require specialized manufacturing expertise and equipment. During the meeting on the specification, you realize that the revision, if approved, will be very beneficial to your company, since you have the necessary expertise, but it will create hardships for some of your competitors.

You believe that the person proposing the revision would also benefit in a similar way. You are uncertain whether you should draw these points to the attention of the committee. You did not propose this revision, but it does improve the quality of the product, and any benefit that your company receives would come strictly by chance.

Question

Do you have an ethical obligation to inform the committee that your company may benefit from this revision? Do you have an obligation to point out that the person proposing the revision may also stand to benefit?

Authors' Recommended Solution

This is a clear conflict of interest, and you must disclose it to the committee. The code of ethics states that the engineer must put the welfare of society above narrow personal interest. In fact, the main function of a standards committee is to serve the public welfare, not the parochial interests of its members. The committee may nevertheless decide, after discussion, in favour of the revision. Although it would probably be acceptable for you to express an opinion on the revision, once the conflict has been disclosed, it would be inappropriate for you to participate in a formal vote, particularly if there is controversy over the revision.

You do not have an obligation to speak about the member who is proposing the revision, unless you believe that there is deliberate fraud, which does not appear to be the case. In fact, your disclosure of a conflict would place an expectation on the other industry representatives to declare their positions.

Conflicts of interest are common in such committees, for the simple reason that the best-informed people are those involved in the design and manufacture of the components concerned. However, this makes it particularly important to be alert to unfair and unethical advantages that may result from such positions of trust.

▼ ▼ ▼

CASE STUDY 8.4—ERRORS IN PLANS AND SPECIFICATIONS

Statement of the Problem

You are the engineering manager for the Acme Assembly company, which designs, fabricates, and assembles machinery. You have received a contract to construct twenty gearboxes that have been designed by Delta Designs, a company that is occasionally a competitor. However, Delta is extremely busy and does not have the capacity for this work at the present time.

One of your engineers notices that the sizes of shafts and gears on the drawings appear to be rather small for the torque and power ratings of the gearboxes, and rough calculations seem to confirm that assessment. You call the chief engineer at Delta Designs, and he states that he is too busy to double-check the drawings. He has full confidence in his designers and says you should get on with the job. He also points out that you are employed in this contract as fabricator, not as designer, and should not be reviewing his work.

Question

Do you have an ethical obligation to pursue this apparent discrepancy further? Would it make any difference if failure of the gearboxes could result in injury or death, rather than mere financial loss?

Authors' Recommended Solution

Under the code of ethics, an engineer has an obligation to a client to ensure that the client is fully aware of the consequences of failing to follow the engineer's advice. In this case, a single telephone call probably would not be deemed to satisfy this requirement, either ethically or legally. You should follow up the telephone call with a letter describing your concerns and request written instructions to proceed.

If the chief engineer at Delta Designs then instructs you in writing to proceed with the fabrication, you would do so, unless you consider the flaws in the design to be obvious and serious. This might indicate a problem of incompetence, negligence, or fraud on the part of the chief engineer at Delta Designs. In this case, it would be appropriate to ask your provincial Association to investigate or mediate.

The possibility of injury or death in the case of failure is important, because it makes the potential danger much greater, and failure to guard the safety of the public would surely be considered professional misconduct on your part. It is irrelevant that the chief engineer complains about others reviewing his work; you have not tried to injure his reputation. In fact, through your diligence, you have sought to protect him.

▼ ▼ ▼

CASE STUDY 8.5—MANIPULATION OF DATA

Statement of the Problem

You are a professional geologist responsible for all exploration and ore assays in a mine. You report directly to the chief executive officer (CEO) of the mine, who is an accountant by training. You have just finished evaluating initial ore assays for a newly opened part of the mine, and they show much lower ore content than hoped or expected. The CEO is very disappointed at the news, even though you reassure him that the results are preliminary and that more thorough results will be available in a week or so. The CEO had hoped to present good news about the exploration to shareholders at a meeting to be held in the next few days.

The CEO asks you to keep the poor results confidential and not to report or discuss them until after the shareholders' meeting, even with people within the company.

Question

Is it ethical to keep this information confidential from the shareholders, who are the owners of the company?

Authors' Recommended Solution

In the mining, oil, and gas industries, geological data are extremely sensitive information and can be the sole basis for major decisions. The financial welfare of the company may depend on keeping such data confidential. In this case, you have initial results and they have been classed as preliminary. The release of preliminary data showing low ore content could provoke a loss of confidence in the company. Therefore, providing that there is no concern of fraudulent intent, it would be ethical to keep these reports confidential until definite results are known with certainty.

TOPICS FOR STUDY AND DISCUSSION

1. John Jones is a professional engineer who is assistant engineering manager of the engineering department for a fairly large Canadian city. He has been assigned to supervise the construction of a new sewage treatment plant, since he participated in designing the plant. The contract for construction has been awarded (after a competitive bidding process) to the Zenith Construction Company. About ten days before construction is to begin, he finds a gift-wrapped case of rye whisky on his doorstep (approximate value: $300). A card attached to the box says: "To an esteemed colleague. We look forward to a long and professional relationship — Zenith Construction." Is it ethical for Jones to accept this gift? Justify your answer using your provincial code of ethics.

2. You are a manager of a new project, and one of your first responsibilities is to make a realistic estimate of the time the project will take and the cost that will ensue. You come up with very high estimates, so high that you fear the project may be discontinued. Some older engineers on the project say that many earlier projects would have been cancelled if the true extent of their final costs had been known early in the game. However, no one can ever be really sure of what something is going to cost; after all, these are only *estimates*. In the earlier projects, a very optimistic face was put on the cost estimates and, even though the final costs exceeded the estimates, the projects were successful.

   The older engineers urge you to reduce your estimates so the project will not be cancelled. But you have put a lot of careful work into your estimates and believe your figures are as correct as any estimate of the future can ever be. Therefore, if you reduce the estimates, you know you will be lying. Furthermore, you know your own reputation in the company will be flawed if it becomes apparent that you shaved your estimates. However, you fear that some of the people in your project team may be laid off if your project is cancelled. You are caught in a dilemma and, as a manager, you must decide one way or the other. Explain how you would try to solve this ethical dilemma. Summarize the process and your decision. For assistance, review Chapter 6.

3. René Brown is a professional engineer who has recently been appointed president of a large dredging company. He is approached by senior executives of three competing dredging companies and asked to co-operate in bidding on dredging contracts put out by the federal government. If he submits high bids on the next three contracts, then the other companies will submit high bids on the fourth contract and he will be assured of getting it. This proposal sounds good to Brown, since he will be able to plan more effectively if he is assured of receiving the fourth contract. Is it ethical for Brown to agree to this suggestion? If not, what action should be taken? If Brown agrees to this suggestion, does he run any greater risk than the other executives, assuming that only Brown is a professional engineer?

NOTES

1. *The Future of Engineering,* Canadian Council of Professional Engineers (CCPE) Task Force Report, July 1988, p. 36.

2. *Engineering and Technology Enrolments, 1978–1987* (Washington, DC: Engineering Manpower Commission).

3. "Women EEs Reported to Earn $2600 Less Than Male Peers," *The Institute* (Institute of Electrical and Electronics Engineers), (March 1984): 1.

4. B. Rosen and T.H. Jardee, "Influence of Sex Role Stereotypes on Personnel Decisions," *Journal of Applied Psychology* (February 1974): 9–14; B. Rosen and T.H. Jardee, "Sex Stereotyping in the Executive Suite," *Harvard Business Review* (March–April 1974): 45–58; B. Rosen and T.H. Jardee, "Effect of Applicant's Sex and Difficulty of Job on Evaluations of Candidates for Managerial Position," *Journal of Applied Psychology* (August 1974): 511–12.

5. R.M. Hall and B.R. Sandler, "Women Winners," in *Project on the Status and Education of Women* (Washington, DC: Association of American Colleges, 1982).

6. Association of Professional Engineers of Ontario, *Guideline to Professional Practice* (Toronto: APEO, 1990), 8. Reproduced with permission of APEO.

7. Association of Professional Engineers of Ontario, *Guideline for the Development and Use of Computer Programming by Professional Engineers* (Toronto: APEO, 1987), 3. Reproduced with permission of APEO.

8. H.A. Levitt, *The Law of Dismissal in Canada*, as quoted in *CSPEAKER*, Canadian Society of Professional Engineers (CSPE) (September 1981): 1–4.

9. Levitt, *Law of Dismissal*.

Ethical Problems of Engineers in Private Practice

In addition to those difficulties described in the previous two chapters, the engineer in private practice may face ethical problems that involve clients and contracts. The contract negotiation procedure described in Chapter 5 is not always strictly followed by the corporations and government agencies that award engineering contracts, and engineers may face an ethical dilemma: Should they adopt unethical practices to obtain contracts, even though the contracts themselves are competently and conscientiously carried out, or should they refuse to become ensnared in unethical practices and run the risk of financial loss or hardship to themselves and their employees?

It is not hard to find spectacular examples of unethical methods. In the mid-1970s, the vice-president of the United States resigned because of his involvement in a kickback scheme for engineering contracts.[1] In Canada at about the same time, there was a national scandal concerning price fixing in dredging contracts; and, as this chapter is being written, allegations are in the news concerning the involvement of a Canadian senator in the awarding of a million-dollar government contract for computer software.

However, it is not our purpose to dwell on past iniquities nor to cause embarrassment to those alleged to be acting unethically; our purpose is to alert the engineer to the possibility of unethical practices and to urge the adoption of fair, legal, and ethical methods. In this chapter, we will examine some of the ethical implications of obtaining and carrying out engineering contracts.

ADVERTISING FOR ENGINEERING WORK

An engineer in private practice may not be known to the many corporations seeking engineering services and may feel the need to advertise. This brings up a thorny issue that has plagued all the professions in North America. Every province has some restrictions, usually in the code of ethics or in practice guidelines, on advertising of engineering services. The purpose of the restrictions is to ensure fairness and honesty in competitive evaluation of professional qualifications and experience.

Advertising fills our newspapers, magazines, radio programs, and television screens, and it seems obviously demeaning and unprofessional to have engineering services promoted in the same way as soap powder or chewing gum. However, advertising that communicates facts and data about the availability, experience, and areas of expertise of an engineer in private practice would be fair and unobjectionable. In the past, the "calling card" or "business card" form of advertising was the only acceptable advertising method, and the back pages of many engineering publications continue to be filled with these advertisements. In recent years the restrictions have eased slightly, but many rules still apply.

Most codes of ethics state that the engineer "shall not advertise his or her professional services in self-laudatory language or in any other manner derogatory to the dignity of the profession." Alberta and the Northwest Territories require engineers to advertise through "factual representation without exaggeration"; Saskatchewan and Yukon state that an engineer shall "not advertise in a misleading manner or in a manner injurious to the dignity of the profession." Quebec and Ontario do not mention advertising in their codes of ethics, but each has a regulation under the Act that gives specific instructions. In Quebec, Regulation 10 under the Act gives very precise rules concerning the information that may be conveyed on business cards, stationery, newspapers, magazines, directories, and signs on work premises, offices, and vehicles. The instructions are clear and comprehensive.

In Ontario, Regulation 538/84, section 89 made under the authority of the provincial Act expressly forbids the use of the engineer's seal or the Association's seal in any form of advertising, including business cards and letterheads. The seal has a legal significance (explained later in this chapter) that is totally incompatible with advertising. On the other hand, the Association's "badge," an attractive and decorative logo that includes the Association's name and motto, *may* be used on business cards and letterheads, but only to signify membership in the Association. The Association's general guidelines are given below.

Advertising may be considered inappropriate if it:

i) claims a greater degree or extent of responsibility for a specified project or projects than is the fact;

ii) fails to give appropriate indications of cooperation by associated firms or individuals involved in specified project(s);

iii) implies, by word or picture, engineering responsibility for proprietary product or equipment design;

iv) denigrates or belittles another professional's projects, firms or individuals;

v) exaggerates claims as to the performance of the project or;

vi) illustrates portions of the project for which the advertiser has no responsibility, without appropriate disclaimer, thus implying greater responsibility than is factual.[2]

In general, advertising that is factual and truthful and that communicates information about an engineer in private practice concerning qualifications, experience, location, or availability, in a dignified manner, is acceptable.

ENGINEERING COMPETENCE

Engineering competence gained through education or experience is an important and valuable asset. The client is, in fact, paying for that competence when the engineer is hired to work on the client's project. An engineer who accepts an assignment that is beyond his or her level of competence is guilty of unethical conduct and could be guilty of unprofessional conduct or incompetence, which could be the basis for disciplinary action.

This does not mean that an engineer must be a world-class expert in every phase of a proposed project before accepting it. However, the engineer must be sufficiently familiar with the subject matter to know that he or she can become competent through study or research in a reasonable period of time or that a colleague or consultant can be hired without delaying the project or incurring unnecessary expense. The essential criterion is that the client's project must not be put at risk because of the engineer's lack of competence.

Each engineer must be the monitor of his or her level of competence. This means making use of opportunities to expand one's knowledge and experience and maintaining one's engineering competence, as discussed in more detail in Chapter 13. It also means being realistic about evaluating one's own abilities, a difficult task at the best of times. However, no one knows the limits of one's knowledge better than oneself.

USE OF THE ENGINEER'S SEAL

Each provincial Act provides for engineers to obtain and use a seal of a specific design for that province. The seal is usually an inked rubber stamp indicating that the person named on the stamp is licensed in that province or territory.

As mentioned in Chapter 2, all final drawings, specifications, plans, reports, and other documents involving the practice of professional engineering, when issued in final form for action by others, should bear the signature and seal of the professional engineer who prepared and approved them. This is particularly important for services provided to the general public. The seal has legal significance, since it denotes that the documents have been *prepared* or *approved* by the person who sealed them. This implies an intimate knowledge of and control over the documents or the project to which the documents relate. An engineer who knowingly signs or seals documents that have not been prepared by the engineer or under the engineer's direct supervision may be guilty of professional misconduct and may also be liable for fraud or negligence if the misrepresentation results in someone suffering damages.

Preparation and Approval

If one engineer has prepared a document or drawing and another engineer must approve it, then *both* seals should appear on it whenever possible. If for any reason this is not possible or expected, then only the approving engineer should seal it, indicating that he or she takes the responsibility for the document or drawing.

Preliminary Documents

Preliminary documents, drawings, or specifications are usually not sealed but are clearly marked "preliminary" or "not for construction." Only the final drawings are sealed. Similarly, an engineer should not seal a document that has no engineering content.

Occasionally, to satisfy the requirements of a regulatory agency, a preliminary document may need to be sealed. In this case, the comment "preliminary" or "not for construction" should be included prominently.

Reports

Individual pages of a report or drawings included in a report need not be sealed providing that the report as a whole has been signed, sealed, and dated.

Sealing of Detail Drawings

The engineer generally has responsibility for a project as a whole, and the engineer's seal must appear on the major reports, specifications, or drawings that describe the project. Usually it is not expected that the engineer should seal every detail drawing, although the drawings must be prepared under the engineer's control and supervision and the engineer assumes responsibility for them, whether sealed or not. The process for the special case of structural steel is described in the Ontario *Guideline to Professional Practice:*

> In the case of structural steel, it is the practice that the steel supplier provide shop drawings for review by the structural engineer. The steel supplier has selected standard connections from the handbook published by the Canadian Institute of Steel Construction in accordance with the moments and forces given by the engineer for each connection. The selection of "standard connections" is not considered the practice of professional engineering and such shop drawings need not be sealed. Shop drawings depicting special connections do require sealing.
>
> Some design engineers require a seal on all shop drawings and erection diagrams. This is their prerogative. Alternatively, a letter signed by a professional engineer stating that the shop drawings have been prepared under his or her supervision may be acceptable.[3]

Sealing of Masters and Prints

The master drawings must of course be complete and unambiguous, since they are usually the major reference for describing the concepts and the details of the structure, machine, process, or whatever is being designed. It is important that an engineer in private practice have an effective procedure for controlling the issuing of preliminary and final drawings, so that security and confidentiality of the client are protected and so that no confusion arises. The appropriate time to seal a drawing is when it is approved and released for fabrication or construction. Modifications to final drawings must be rigidly controlled and documented. This control is aided by sealing only prints and not the master. In this way, the prints can be checked for modifications when sealed.

Sealing of "Soft" Drawings

Computer-aided design has simplified the easy, rapid production of drawings, but it has resulted in problems of control over modifications. Erroneous data or unauthorized modifications are usually difficult to detect. Although the development of electronic seals and signatures may evolve over time, it is important for an engineer in private practice to implement controls within the firm to prevent unauthorized copying or modifications to computer files. Until standards and procedures develop, it is recommended that final drawings in computer file form be protected by password or by storing them on magnetic media in secure locations and that seals be applied only to prints made from these files. The prints or hard copies of the files would then be the master document. Copies of the engineer's seal generally should *not* be reproduced on the computer file, since this is equivalent to losing secure control of the seal.

CONFIDENTIALITY AND CONFLICT OF INTEREST

The engineer has a clear obligation to keep the affairs of the client confidential. This obligation is described in the code of ethics or regulations of every provincial or territorial Association, in either a direct or an indirect form, and it should not need to be included in a contract to be understood. The engineer and client must be free to discuss every aspect of a project, and this is possible only if there is a clear obligation to keep the discussions confidential. The engineer should not disclose the client's affairs to any third party unless authorized to do so by the client or compelled to do so by law, as may occur in court proceedings or under regulations or acts such as environmental protection acts. This may cause some concern when accepting a new client who is a competitor of a former client. An engineer in private practice should not accept a contract that requires disclosure of a previous client's affairs, whether technical, business, or personal. This is particularly applicable to proprietary information or trade secrets, whose disclosure could cause financial loss.

Conflicts of interest may occasionally occur during an engineer's work on a project. For example, an engineer may have an interest in a company that provides goods or services to the client, or an engineer may be tempted to recommend an engineering decision that will reduce the workload of the engineer. In every instance of conflict (or potential conflict) of interest, the engineer must make a full disclosure to the client of any personal interest, whatever that may be. The client is then able to make a fully informed choice.

A client who learns after the fact that an engineer benefited personally and secretly from a decision that was ostensibly based on technical factors would be justified in contacting the provincial Association to lodge a complaint of professional misconduct.

REVIEWING THE WORK OF ANOTHER ENGINEER

The sensitive problem of reviewing the work of another engineer was discussed in an earlier chapter with respect to an employee. The question of review is equally delicate when engineers are in private practice. In all instances, the welfare of the client or the general public must come before the personal wishes of the engineer. Moreover, it must be emphasized that an engineer should be *informed* when his or her work is to be reviewed, but it is *not* necessary to seek or obtain the engineer's permission for the review. The Ontario *Guideline to Professional Practice* summarizes the situation as follows:

> The Code of Ethics permits an engineer to be engaged to review the work of another professional engineer when the connection of that engineer with the project has been terminated. Before undertaking the review, the reviewer should know how the information will be used. Even when satisfied that the connection between the parties has been terminated, the reviewer should, with the agreement of the client, inform the other engineer that a review is contemplated. The reviewer should recognize that the client has the right to withhold approval to inform the engineer. However, the reviewer should satisfy himself or herself that the reasons for the owner's decision are valid before proceeding with the review.
>
> If a client asks an engineer to review the work of another engineer who is still engaged on a project either through an employment contract or an agreement to provide professional services, the reviewer should only undertake the assignment with the knowledge of the other engineer. Failure to notify the engineer under this circumstance constitutes a breach of the Code of Ethics. On the other hand, should a second engineer be engaged by another person (say, a building department) to provide professional engineering services on the same project, he or she would have no obligation to advise the original client of the commission.
>
> Senior engineers are often asked to review a design prepared by another engineer. (Most engineers are expected to have their work routinely reviewed as part of an ongoing quality control and professional development process.) If the reviewer finds

design changes are necessary, the reviewer should inform the design engineer of these findings and the reasons for the recommended changes. During the design stage, the engineer and the reviewer (who is in this case the client's agent) may agree on changes to the engineer's proposal. However, the design engineer must not agree to any change or alternative suggested by the reviewer which could result in an unworkable installation or be in conflict with the relevant codes, or create a risk of damage or injury....

Once the review has been completed, there is no obligation or right for the reviewer to disclose his or her findings to the other engineer. In fact, in most cases disclosure of the findings would not be permitted by the client. The contractual obligation of the reviewer is to the client. However, the reviewer should seek approval of the client to inform the engineer of the general nature of the findings, and if appropriate, should try to resolve any technical differences.[4]

CHECKING DESIGN CALCULATIONS

A client may request that an engineer submit calculations that were done to support a recommendation. This amounts to a review of the engineer's work, but obviously it is done with full knowledge and co-operation of the engineer. The client has an ethical right to review these calculations and to make a copy for a permanent record. However, the time necessary to prepare the calculations in a format understandable to the client should be included as part of the contracted service.

Occasionally the computation techniques or the data on which the computation is made may be proprietary and the engineer may not wish to divulge them. In this case, the conditions for viewing the calculations should be negotiated beforehand and the extent of disclosure should be understood in advance. The usual procedure is to provide the proprietary data to the client with the clear understanding that they will be kept confidential.

COMPETITIVE BIDDING FOR SERVICES

A detailed procedure for selecting an engineer in private practice was given in Chapter 5. The procedure involves three stages and separates the process of selecting the best-qualified engineer (or firm) from the process of negotiating the fees. This prevents many of the problems that arise when engineers are selected on a competitive basis by lowest bid.

However, it should be stressed that seeking professional services by lowest bid is not illegal or unethical, and no one should be dissuaded from the procedure by the misguided belief that competition is harmful. Quite the opposite; ingenuity thrives through healthy competition. However, there is a danger in competitive bidding, as explained in the Ontario *Guideline to Professional Practice*: "With professional services there are ultimately only two elements which a client is retaining, i.e. the engineer's knowledge and time. Shortchanging on a professional engineering fee will result in the substitution of less skilled engineers or less time put into the assignment, thus potentially shortchanging the project."[5]

However, some competitive activities in obtaining contracts are considered to be unfair and therefore unethical. For example, any agreement to pay a kickback, gift, commission, or consideration, either openly or secretly, would be considered an unfair and unethical method of obtaining contracts. Many codes also describe supplanting a colleague as unethical, where *supplanting* is defined as intervening in the client/engineer relationship of a colleague and, through inducements or persuasion, convincing the client to fire the engineer and hire the intruding engineer.

NEGLIGENCE AND CIVIL LIABILITY

The engineer in private practice generally has two sources of concern that can give rise to civil liability: breach of contract and negligence. Both of these are usually inadvertent events and are to be distinguished from professional misconduct and incompetence, which are discussed in Chapter 12. A *breach of contract* is failure to complete the obligations specified in a contract, whereas *negligence* is failure to exercise due care in the performance of engineering. Although it is possible to obtain protection for breach of contract by incorporating a practice, and protection against negligence by purchasing liability insurance, it is not possible to avoid disciplinary action for negligence, incompetence, or professional misconduct. The Ontario *Guideline to Professional Practice* summarizes the situation as follows:

> An individual engineer can protect personal assets against an action for damages for *breach of contract* by incorporating the practice. After incorporation, it is the company that is the contracting party and not the individual. As far as protection from liability for *negligence* there is nothing available

to an engineer other than careful, thorough engineering and insurance.[6]

ACEC CODE OF CONSULTING ENGINEERING PRACTICE

The Association of Consulting Engineers of Canada (ACEC) has a code of practice that applies to member firms of ACEC and requires them to fulfil their duties with honesty, justice, and courtesy toward the public as a whole, clients, other consulting engineers, and employees.

ACEC Code of Consulting Engineering Practice

Members of the Association of Consulting Engineers of Canada shall fulfil their duties with honesty, justice and courtesy towards Society, Clients, other Consulting Engineers and Employees.

Society

Members shall practice their profession with concern for the social and economic well-being of Society.

Members shall conform with all applicable laws, by-laws and regulations.

Members shall satisfy themselves that their designs and recommendations are safe and sound and, if their engineering judgment is overruled, shall report the possible consequences to clients, owners and, if necessary, the appropriate public authorities.

Members expressing engineering opinions to the public shall do so in complete, objective, truthful and accurate manner.

Members should participate in civic affairs and work for the benefit of their community and should encourage their employees to do likewise.

Clients

Members shall discharge their professional responsibilities with integrity and complete loyalty to the terms of their assignments.

Members shall accept only those assignments for which they are competent or for which they associate with other competent experts.

Members shall disclose any conflicts of interest to their clients.

Members shall respect the confidentiality of all information obtained from their clients.

Members shall obtain remuneration for their professional services solely through fees commensurate with the services rendered.

Other Consulting Engineers

Members shall relate to other consulting engineers with integrity, and in a manner that will enhance the professional stature of consulting engineering.

Members shall respect the clientele of other consulting engineers and shall not attempt to supplant them when definite steps have been taken towards their employment.

Members shall compete fairly with their fellow consulting engineers, offering professional services on the basis of qualifications and experience.

Members engaged by a client to review the work of another consulting engineer, shall inform that engineer of their commission, and shall avoid statements which may maliciously impugn the reputation or business of the engineer.

Employees

Members shall treat their employees with integrity, provide for their proper compensation and require that they conform to high ethical standards in their work.

Members shall encourage their employees to enhance their professional qualifications and development.

Members shall not request their employees to take responsibility for work for which they are not qualified.[7]

FIDIC PROFESSIONAL CODE AND GUIDELINES ON CONDUCT

The International Federation of Consulting Engineers (FIDIC) has adopted a Professional Code and Guidelines on Conduct for individual members and member firms of consulting engineers. The Professional Code discusses the definition of a consulting engineer, professional status, and independence of advice, judgement, and decisions from undue influence and competence. These points have all been discussed earlier in this text, and the FIDIC Professional Code appears to be in complete agreement with the ACEC code of practice and other codes of ethics discussed in this textbook. The FIDIC Guidelines on Conduct concern special advice for consulting engineers in private practice.

FIDIC Guidelines on Conduct

Taking Over Work of Another Consulting Engineer for the Same Client

No member of a member association of FIDIC shall attempt, directly or indirectly, to supplant another consulting engineer, nor shall he review or take over work of another consulting engineer for the same client until he has either obtained the consent of such consulting engineer or has been formally notified by the client that the connection of such consulting engineer with the work has been terminated.

Consulting Work in Foreign Territories

It is unethical for members of member associations to seek or accept appointment for professional consulting work on terms or under conditions which conflict with those laid down by the national association of the country in which the work is to be executed. Members are bound by their own association's rules where there is no FIDIC member association.

Personal Advertising

Corporate advertising, when recommended as necessary in the best interest of the profession, may be supplemented by individual advertising in appropriate cases as judged by the national association concerned. Any brochure or other form of advertisement must be dignified and factual. To ensure this, the material should comply with the criteria established by the association to which the individual member belongs.

Competitive Bidding

It is not in the interest of the client or of the profession that consulting engineers should seek or accept appointment under any system of competitive bidding for professional services. Selection of a consulting engineer for appointment should be made on consideration of competence and availability, leaving the negotiation of fees and costs to be settled only with the engineer selected.

Payment of Commissions to Influence the Acquisition of Assignments

In some countries it may be necessary for consulting engineers to make use of local agents when negotiating contracts. Indeed, some governmental procurement procedures may require this.

Such agents should only be reimbursed for the time spent and material service which they render, but contingent percentage fees may be paid where such fees are in accordance with usual professional practice in that location. Agents shall not be officials or employees of the client. Agents should be advised that no payments are to be made by them to officials in the employment of the client nor to any one else for the purpose of influencing the selection of the consulting engineer.

FIDIC reaffirms its policy in regard to selection procedures based upon ability and experience and considers any attempt to impose influence as the result of payment of a commission to be in conflict with the principles of the consulting profession.

Environment

It is recommended that members of FIDIC member associations, when appointed by any client, whether public or private, for any project that might have an effect, directly or indirectly, upon the human and natural environment, consider it a professional duty to discuss with their client the consequence of such effects, whether or not their client has included this aspect in the consultants' terms of reference. FIDIC has issued a policy statement on the environment. A copy is contained in *About FIDIC*.[8]

▼ ▼ ▼

CASE STUDY 9.1—APPROVAL OF ENGINEERING PLANS BY TOWN COUNCIL

Statement of the Problem

Edward Smith is a consulting engineer in a small town. He has been elected to sit on the town council as a councillor, a part-time job that he does mainly as a form of public service. Smith has also been hired by a developer to draw up plans for the street layout and water and sewage facilities for a new residential subdivision in the town. The developer's submission to town council includes Smith's drawings and specifications. Later, in a town council meeting, Smith votes to approve the subdivision. During the discussion, Smith does not publicly state his relationship with the developer, nor does he conceal it. His signature and seal are on some of the plans submitted to council; everyone knows that he is the only engineer in town who does this type of work, and he is certain that they would prefer to see local people hired for this project.

Question

In voting to approve this project, has Smith acted unethically?

Authors' Recommended Solution

This situation sometimes occurs in small towns with few engineers, where a conflict of interest cannot be avoided. Engineers certainly should not be disqualified from projects because they are performing a public service as members of town councils. However, in this case, it is not enough that "everyone knows" that Smith has a business relationship with the developer. Smith had a serious conflict of interest when he voted to approve plans that he himself prepared. He should have made a clear, unequivocal statement of his involvement in the project and his relationship with the developer, then withdrawn from the debate and abstained from the vote. By participating in a formal vote without declaring the conflict of interest, Smith has exposed himself to the possibility of a complaint to the provincial Association and possible disciplinary action.

▼ ▼ ▼

CASE STUDY 9.2—ADVERTISING PRODUCTS AND ENGINEERING SERVICES

Statement of the Problem

Alonzo Firenze is a consulting engineer to the Acme Amphibious Transporter Company, which manufactures small amphibious recreational vehicles with a moulded plastic hull. Each vehicle is driven by eight low-pressure balloon tires and can manoeuvre quickly and safely on land and water. In preparing a television campaign to increase the sales of the vehicle, the television producer suggests that Firenze should appear on camera and endorse the safety aspects of the vehicle, as a professional engineer and safety expert. The television producer points out that Firenze has conducted extensive tests, studies, and surveys on the vehicle and can speak with authority. In addition, Firenze is very photogenic and would like the exposure to the general public.

Question

Would it be unethical for Firenze to appear in the television commercial and make a statement endorsing the recreational vehicle?

Authors' Recommended Solution

Although participation in a television news or documentary program on vehicle safety would be considered a suitable professional activity (and perhaps more engineers should be seen in these roles), endorsing a product in a television commercial would be seen to be unprofessional, would lower the public esteem for the engineering profession, and would therefore be unethical. The key distinction is that the purpose of a commercial is to increase sales, and it is a sad commentary on the television industry that commercial advertisements have a rather sordid history of half-truths and appeals to emotion rather than logic. Moreover, an engineer who publicly praises a product manufactured by a corporation that employs him clearly has a conflict of interest, and the endorsement would lack the expected professional detachment.

A second point at issue is Firenze's interest in appearing because of the personal exposure he will receive. This is not the proper format for advertising professional services. Moreover, although Firenze is willing to participate and is convinced of the safety of the product, how would he respond in future in different circumstances? For example, what response would he give if the employer expected his endorsement as part of the employment contract, but Firenze was not confident of the product's safety? This illustrates the risk: the profession and Firenze's reputation could both suffer by subordinating professional standards to the pressures of the marketplace.

▼ ▼ ▼

CASE STUDY 9.3—CONTINGENCY FEE ARRANGEMENTS

Statement of the Problem

As an engineer in private practice, you are considering whether to offer your services on a contingency basis, an arrangement in which you would be paid a percentage of some outcome.

Two clients wish to retain you. Client A wants to retain you to act as an expert witness in a lawsuit against a third party. The lawsuit, if successful, should result in the award of a very large sum as a settlement. Client B has shown a hesitant interest in retaining you to recommend changes to the energy usage in a manufacturing process. After an initial study of the problem, you believe that the energy savings could be immense. You believe Client B would be more responsive if fees were contingent on the savings.

Question

Would it be ethical to offer your services on a contingency basis to either of these clients, with the understanding that you would be paid a percentage of the legal settlement (Client A) or a percentage of the value of the energy savings (Client B)?

Authors' Recommended Solution

These two cases seem similar but are distinctly different.

An expert witness is permitted to express opinions, whereas a "non-expert" witness must confine his or her testimony to known facts; therefore, an engineer testifying as an expert witness must have an impartial attitude toward the outcome of a case. However, as a recipient of a percentage of the potential settlement, you would have a conflict of interest and your testimony would be suspect. Therefore, it would be unethical to accept this case on a contingency basis. You should bill Client A for time and expenses (or on a flat-rate basis), so that the reimbursement is independent of the outcome of the case.

The case of Client B is somewhat different, since there is no need for impartiality. In fact, your bias toward reducing energy consumption could be very beneficial to the client. Also, you have a duty to yourself and to your colleagues to charge an adequate fee. From your study, you evidently believe this fee will be adequate. Therefore, the proposal to base the fee on a contingency is not unethical. However, a word of warning is appropriate, since there might be a perception of unethical behaviour unless the results can be measured accurately and impartially and can be achieved without degrading the client's product or facilities. Therefore, although this method of setting a fee is not unethical, it has some risks associated with it. You would be well-advised to use one of the more common billing methods (as described in Chapter 5), unless the client expresses a preference for the contingency method and the savings can be clearly and unequivocally measured. A word of warning to engineers in British Columbia: the code of ethics in that province specifically forbids contingent fee arrangements that depend on a "finding of economic feasibility," such as this case describes.

▼ ▼ ▼

CASE STUDY 9.4—ADHERENCE TO PLANS AND CONTROL OF SEALED DRAWINGS

Statement of the Problem

A professional engineer in private practice is engaged by a building contractor to prepare drawings for the forms and scaffolding needed to construct a reinforced concrete bridge. The forms and scaffolding must sustain the weight of about 1400 tonnes of concrete until the concrete is cured. The engineer prepares the drawings and signs and seals the original, which he gives to the contractor. The contractor later engages the engineer to inspect the completed structure; the engineer finds many obvious deviations from the plans. It is not obvious whether the structure is safe or unsafe.

Question

The contractor has stated that time is of the essence, and concrete is to be poured in the next 48 hours. The engineer feels an obligation to the contractor because of their previous professional relationship and hopes that it will continue. What should the engineer do?

Authors' Recommended Solution

There are two issues at stake here. When the engineer passed the sealed original drawings to the contractor, control was lost. Changes could have been made to the original that, if unsafe, could have created problems for the engineer. As a general rule, only prints should be signed and sealed; modifications will then be evident. In this case, apparently no harm resulted. However, the contractor did not construct the forms and scaffolds according to the plans, and the engineer is now faced with the unpleasant task of informing the contractor that the changes to the plans must be evaluated to ensure that they are safe. This will undoubtedly require some calculations, and perhaps a second inspection. The engineer should notify the contractor in writing that concrete must not be poured until the review and reinspection is complete and that the changes could constitute a hazard to workers and the general public. The strength analysis should be carried out as quickly as possible, but if the 48-hour deadline cannot be met, then the project must not proceed until all safety concerns have been satisfied. It is perhaps useful to point out that the contractor could have consulted the engineer about the changes earlier in the construction, and the delay might have been avoided.

▼ ▼ ▼

CASE STUDY 9.5—FEE REDUCTION FOR SIMILAR WORK

Statement of the Problem

Susan Johnson is a professional engineer in private practice. She is hired by Client A to design a small explosion-proof building for storage of flammable paints, chemicals, and explosives. The work is carried out in her design office, and copies of the plans are provided to her client. After construction is complete, she is approached by Client B, who has seen the building and has a similar requirement. Client B suggests that the fee should be substantially reduced since the design is already finished and only minor changes would be required.

Question

Would it be ethical for Johnson to reduce her fees as suggested? Would it be good business practice?

Authors' Recommended Solution

The establishment of fair and reasonable fees depends on five factors:
- time required
- level of knowledge and qualifications required
- difficulty and scope of the assignment
- speed with which the work must be accomplished
- responsibility that the engineer must assume

Although successful completion of a similar project will reduce the time required to complete the new project, this is a benefit to the client as well as to the engineer. The level of knowledge and qualifications and, most important, the responsibility that the engineer must assume are unchanged. The client benefits by receiving a design that is likely more dependable and easier to construct. Therefore, it would be unfair to Johnson, unethical, and poor business practice to accept a substantial reduction in fee for providing the drawings for this structure.

▼ ▼ ▼

CASE STUDY 9.6—ALLEGED COLLUSION IN FEE SETTING

Statement of the Problem

A large corporation wants to expand its manufacturing facilities and interviews three consulting engineering firms to design and supervise the construction of the new plant. Each consulting engineering firm states in its proposal that fees would follow the schedule proposed by the provincial Association. Later, the corporation decides that it could reduce the cost of the project by conducting some initial studies in-house and by providing engineers to assist in supervising the construction of the plant. The corporation asks each consulting firm to quote how much its consulting fees would be reduced if the corporation provides this assistance.

The three consulting firms meet, discuss the corporation's request, and then submit the same amount as a fee reduction. The corporation complains to the provincial Association that the engineers are colluding in their bids and that this is unethical, if not illegal, conduct.

Question

Is it unethical for the three consulting firms to agree on the fee reduction to be allowed for the assistance?

Authors' Recommended Solution

The contracting procedure recommended by the Association of Consulting Engineers of Canada (ACEC) for engaging consulting engineers is fairly well established, as described in Chapter 5. The procedure provides for competition on the basis of qualifications, experience, scheduling, and service but discourages competition based on price alone. Although competitive bidding is not illegal or unethical, corporations must make the basis for selection clear when the request for proposal is issued.

In this case, the corporation appears to have been following the ACEC procedure in the early stages, and the engineers responded appropriately. It appears that the corporation misunderstood the procedure. Price competition is not part of the ACEC contracting procedure, although fee negotiation is appropriate once a consulting firm has been selected. In any case, the co-operative action by the firms is not unethical. At no time was it made clear that the corporation wanted competition on a fee basis, and the complaint after the fact appears to reveal a misunderstanding on the part of the corporation.

TOPICS FOR STUDY AND DISCUSSION

1. You are a consulting engineer in a partnership arrangement. Your partner suggests that your business cards and stationery should contain some discreet advertising and suggests that the following should be printed on them:

   - a stylish logo
   - your engineering seal, reduced in size to fit
   - the slogan "The best in the business!"

   Which of these advertising components would conform to the constraints on advertising defined in your provincial or territorial code of ethics (or provincial advertising regulation)?

2. You have been hired as a machine design consultant to a soap manufacturer to suggest methods of speeding up a liquid detergent production line. During your work you have access to confidential company documents and observe that the company is adding very small quantities of a known carcinogen (cancer-causing substance) to the detergent but is not listing it as an ingredient. You know that the substance has been banned. This confidential information is totally irrelevant to the job you were hired to perform, and you discovered it entirely by chance. Do you have any obligation to act on this information? If so, what action would you take?

3. A rural town in a resort area has been instructed by the provincial government that it must replace an old wooden bridge for safety reasons. The town council hires a consulting engineer, Ali, to design a concrete bridge to replace the unsafe wooden structure. Because of poor soil conditions, pilings are required, and the resulting design will clearly be very expensive to construct. One of the town councillors discusses the matter with a neighbour, Baker, who is also a consulting engineer and has a summer cottage in the town. Baker suggests that a culvert might serve the same purpose and would be much cheaper than the bridge, in view of the soil problems. Since Ali is a concrete specialist and is not capable of carrying out the redesign for the steel culvert, he is paid for his work on the concrete bridge design and replaced by consulting engineer Gambon, who designs a large culvert structure. The culvert is subsequently constructed at a fraction of the predicted cost of the concrete bridge. Ali is disappointed that the concrete bridge did not proceed (and fees for supervising the construction therefore

were not paid). Ali alleges that there was unethical conduct by Baker or Gambon (or both). In this example, were the actions of any of the engineers unethical? Would the replacement of Ali by Gambon be considered "supplanting" as defined in this chapter?

NOTES

1. B.J. Lewis, "The Story Behind the Recent National Scandals Involving Engineers," *Engineering Issues* (April 1977): 91–98. Reprinted in J.H. Schaub and K. Pavlovic, eds. *Engineering Professionalism and Ethics* (New York: John Wiley & Sons, 1983), 237–43.

2. Association of Professional Engineers of Ontario, *Guideline to Professional Practice* (Toronto: APEO, March 1990), 8. Excerpt reproduced with permission.

3. APEO, *Professional Practice*, 7. Excerpt reproduced with permission.

4. APEO, *Professional Practice*, 4. Excerpt reproduced with permission.

5. APEO, *Professional Practice*, 5. Excerpt reproduced with permission.

6. APEO, *Professional Practice*, 8. Excerpt reproduced with permission.

7. Association of Consulting Engineers of Canada, *Directory of Member Firms* (Ottawa: ACEC, 1990/91), xxvii. Reproduced with permission.

8. International Federation of Consulting Engineers, *International Directory of Consulting Engineering, 1991–92* (The Hague), 8. Reproduced with permission.

The Engineer's Duty to Society and the Environment

Each of the many engineering codes of ethics discussed in earlier chapters contains a clause requiring engineers to consider their duty to society to be paramount. However, the codes also stipulate duties to clients, employers, colleagues, and employees. At what point does the duty to society exceed the duty to others, if their activities appear to be in serious conflict with the good of society? For example, the engineer is, on the one hand, obligated not to disclose confidential information concerning the client or employer. On the other hand, the engineer must report to the appropriate authority any situation that the engineer believes may endanger the health or safety of the public. Failure to report a hazardous situation is considered professional misconduct in every province and territory of Canada.

Reporting a client or employer for unsafe, unethical, or illegal activities is called whistleblowing. Provincial Associations of Professional Engineers have always been available to mediate in concerns over unsafe, unethical, or illegal practices, and in recent years some Associations have made the reporting process more formal.[1] A survey of 100 Ontario engineers attending a seminar on whistleblowing in 1985 revealed that about 40 percent had seen practices that justified reporting the client or employer, but most had not "blown the whistle." Peter Osmond, the registrar of the Association of Professional Engineers of Ontario, says the Association receives "an average of one whistleblowing inquiry per month, but few are true whistleblowing situations. Most are really complaints of misconduct or incompetence. ... Some are false alarms." In Osmond's first five years as registrar, he dealt with four genuine whistleblowing cases.[2] The whistleblowing dilemma does exist, but is relatively rare.

In this chapter we examine the topic of environmental hazards, the engineer's duty to society, and the appropriate action that an engineer should take in those rare instances where the duty to society takes precedence over obligations to clients, employers, and colleagues.

RECOGNIZING AND REDUCING ENVIRONMENTAL HAZARDS

There can be little doubt that engineering, science, and technology have brought immense benefit to humanity. It is said that medicine has given people health, the humanities have given people pleasure, and engineering and technology have given people the time to enjoy both. In particular, the development of agricultural tools and disease-resistant plants has freed us from the uncertainty and hard labour of agricultural production and increased the sustainable population of the world. More goods and services are available to more people with less human effort than ever before. Most people have a range of activities open to them for personal fulfilment that would have been absolutely incredible only a generation or two ago. Moreover, since we are now in the midst of a computer revolution, this beneficial trend is likely to continue. Development and industrialization have, in general, been good for society.

However, this development has not been completely beneficial; there have been some problems in the process of industrialization. The two most obvious of these are the proliferation of hazards resulting from human activity and the degradation of the environment.

Because of the wider use of manufactured goods and the heavier use of public facilities, some risks to the public have actually increased. Even "safe" structures, highways, automobiles, aircraft, and appliances pose a risk of death or injury, simply because we use them more commonly and widely than previous generations. In addition, the manufacture of toxic chemicals (such as herbicides and pesticides), the generation of power by nuclear energy, and similar hazardous processes were unknown 50 years ago. Engineers must be alert to these hazards and should reduce or eliminate them, where possible.

The lifestyle of industrialized nations requires high energy usage. The consumption of fossil fuels and the careless disposal of waste products have caused a gradual deterioration in the environment.

The deterioration is evident in increased water pollution, acid rain, the greenhouse effect (global warming), and the increasing problem of waste disposal, to mention only a few of the most obvious aspects.

These are some of the well-known Canadian environmental tragedies of recent years:

> The 1970s was a period of awakening to the reality of the costly effects of pollution resulting from industrial by-products. This recognition was based on scientific investigations and frightening, sometimes painful, experience. For example, in northern Ontario hundreds of residents along the English-Wabigoon river system lost their jobs as commercial fishermen, their community stability and their expectation of a long and healthy life because of invisible, poisonous mercury in the fish. The mercury was dumped as waste material by a local paper mill before 1970, but will remain a danger in the water and fish for another century. In New Brunswick, although several children have died, residents continue to be exposed to aerial spraying with a pesticide designed to kill forest insects and protect the forest industry. At Port Hope, Ontario, thousands of tonnes of slightly radioactive wastes, dumped years earlier, were removed from beneath houses, schools and stores to lessen the danger of cancer developing among citizens. In Toronto, public clinics are held to test the blood of residents of some neighbourhoods for low levels of lead dust from nearby factories, which could lead to nervous disorders and learning disabilities. ...
>
> In 1981, Canadian scientists discovered, for the first time, very small amounts of one of the most deadly man-made chemicals, Dioxin TCDD 2, 3, 7-8, in the Great Lakes. Dioxin is a by-product of agricultural chemical production and the degradation of industrial wastes. As little as a droplet of the pure chemical is deadly in thousands of litres of water. Researchers are only beginning to consider the problems which would be involved in the protection and purification of Great Lakes water for human consumption if Dioxin concentrations increase.[3]

Since this is a critically important issue, and is so greatly influenced by ethical actions of all Canadians, the following paragraphs contain a brief overview of some common but serious environmental challenges, problems, and hazards. Engineers must be alert to these problems and must work to stop and reverse the trend toward environmental degradation.

Waste Disposal

The most common activity that causes degradation of the environment is the indiscriminate disposal of wastes — whether solid, liquid, or gaseous — as a by-product of manufacturing, processing, or construction activities. The control of this waste disposal is usually within the authority and responsibility of an engineer.

Waste disposal from industrial and domestic sources is approaching a crisis in many parts of Canada. Some small towns have dumps, which are a source of disease, a fire hazard, and a danger to groundwater. Dumps are gradually being replaced by closely monitored landfills, but some major cities are unable to find locations for landfills so they can dispose of their wastes.

With the advent of environmental protection legislation in many provinces and the introduction of recycling programs, a measure of control is being gained over the disposal of solid waste, but some liquid wastes, particularly toxic or hazardous chemicals, are still being illegally dumped because of the shortage of proper incineration and disposal areas. Hazardous liquid waste can pose a serious threat to health if it leaks out of a dumpsite into the underground water table.

The solution to this problem requires both technical ability and political awareness. Needless to say, professional engineers have a duty to assist in this area by attempting to reduce the amount of solid, liquid, or gaseous waste being created and, even more important, by ensuring that toxic or hazardous wastes are safely recycled or legally discarded.

Air Pollution

There are many components to air pollution, but the most publicized are sulphur oxides and nitrogen oxides. Sulphur oxides arise principally from the burning of fossil fuels, such as coal and petroleum, although many other kinds of industrial activity also produce them. SO_2 is a gas that reacts with oxygen in the atmosphere to form SO_3, which then combines immediately with water to yield sulphuric acid in the form of droplets. The highest SO_2 values have been reported in the northeastern region of North America and in Europe, where large quantities of high-sulphur fossil fuels have been burned. For most large cities, the pollution from SO_2 has improved in recent years, mostly because of the shift from high-sulphur coal to low-sulphur natural gas.

Sulphur oxides are detrimental to plant life, with severe plant damage observed miles downwind from certain smelting operations. They produce corrosion in metals, discolouration of fabrics, and deterioration of building materials. A combination of sulphur oxides and particulates seems to be especially damaging to human health, partly because of the action of small particles in conveying sulphuric acid into the lungs and partly because of the chemical role of particulates in converting SO_2 to sulphuric acid. Dramatic episodes involving high mortality have occurred in which sulphur oxides and particulates have figured prominently.

Even in the absence of sulphur, combustion of fossil fuels causes serious air pollution in urban atmospheres. Exhaust gases usually contain unburned hydrocarbons (HC), carbon monoxide (CO), nitrogen oxides (NO_x), and the normal combustion products, such as CO_2 and water. In the atmosphere, many of these products react chemically to produce new contaminants. These processes are stimulated by sunlight, and the products are thus termed generally *photochemical oxidants.* Two of the principal photochemical oxidants are ozone and peroxyacetyl nitrate (PAN). Ozone is also continually being created in the atmosphere by natural processes, but not to a degree great enough to constitute a pollution hazard. This type of polluted air is often referred to as photochemical smog. All large cities in the world are afflicted with smog. The worst case of smog in Canada occurred in southern Ontario in 1962 and lasted five days. It was called the "Grey Cup smog" because the Grey Cup football game was postponed that year because of poor visibility.[4]

Nitrogen oxides, collectively called NO_x, are also a problem in air pollution. There are several known oxides of nitrogen, but the important ones from the standpoint of air pollution are nitric oxide (NO) and nitrogen dioxide (NO_2). NO_x is a product of almost any combustion process that uses air, since nitrogen is the chief component of air. To a great degree, the formation of NO_x is the result of high combustion temperatures. The principal sources are motor vehicles, which account for as much as 50 to 60 percent of NO_x in the atmosphere in industrialized urban areas.

The nitrogen oxides participate actively in photochemical reactions with hydrocarbons, thus helping to produce photochemical smog. NO_2 plays a double role in air pollution, both as a component in the formation of photochemical smog and as a toxicant in its own right. NO is much less toxic than NO_2, but NO is readily converted into NO_2 in the atmosphere by reaction with oxygen, and in the presence of water, it becomes nitric acid.

The harmful effects of air pollution on humans and animals include serious lung disorders, reduced oxygen in the blood, eye and skin irritation, and damage to internal organs.[5] Damage to paints, automobiles, and buildings is mainly the result of acid rain, which is discussed in detail below.

Most provinces and the federal government have clean air acts that specify emission standards and ambient air quality standards. Air pollution control is mainly a provincial responsibility, although the federal government regulates trains, ships, and gasoline.[6] These government regulations must, of course, be followed, and reducing emissions of SO_x and NO_x should be a prime objective in engineering operations where possible.

Acid Rain

In the 1980s, the problem of acid rain captured the attention of the nation. Both sulphur and nitrogen oxides are implicated, because they form sulphuric and nitric acids in the atmosphere and cause rainfall to become more acidic than otherwise would be the case. Neutral water ideally has a pH of 7.0, but "normal" rainfall in remote areas that are unpolluted has a pH of about 5.0 because of the presence of small amounts of acid of natural origin. The acid rain problem arises because the rainfall in many areas of Canada and the northeastern United States has pH values lower than this, ranging down as low as 4.0. Since these same areas lie downwind from the states that produce most of the sulphur and nitrogen oxides, the downwind people obviously feel that the upwind people should take corrective action, which is costly. In 1981, sulphur oxide emissions were estimated at 24 million tonnes in the United States and 4.8 million tonnes in Canada.[7] Most of these emissions come from thermal electric-power plants and non-ferrous smelters.

When acid rain falls to earth, it harms fish life, trees, farms, buildings, automobiles, and human health. Aquatic life begins to be affected when the pH falls below 5.0, and most fish are killed when a pH of 4.5 is reached.[8] The result is hundreds of lakes (in north-eastern North America and Scandinavia) that are devoid of fish, and thousands of lakes that are threatened.[9] Human health is also threatened, because the acidity leaches aluminum and heavy metals out of the soil and concentrates them in drinking water.

Acid rain is an international problem, with pollutants flowing both ways over the border, although the heavier flow is from the United States into Canada, because of the greater industrial activity in the United States. The federal governments have established agreements to control acid rain, but engineers (particularly those in the power generation and smelting industries) must monitor this problem and work to alleviate it where possible. Although the remedy will be costly, a 1981 study shows that, in addition to the benefit of a cleaner environment, the economic benefits are about equal to the cost of the controls.[10]

Water Pollution

Some rivers are less polluted now than they were in the nineteenth century. In that era, there was a serious water pollution crisis. For example, in the mid-nineteenth century, 20 000 people in London were killed by cholera in what has been called the greatest pollution disaster in the Western world.[11] Typhoid and cholera epidemics were widespread, stemming from water contaminated by sewage.

Water pollution may result from at least six sources:

- disease-causing bacteria

- organic waste decaying in the water, reducing the dissolved oxygen content

- fertilizers that stimulate plant growth and also depress oxygen levels

- toxic materials, such as heavy metals and chlorinated hydrocarbons (DDT, PCB)

- acidification

- waste heat, which can also reduce dissolved oxygen levels.[12]

Cholera and typhoid are virtually unknown in Canada today as a result of sewage treatment plants and the use of chlorine to kill bacteria in drinking water. Nevertheless, a comprehensive survey of American rivers in the early 1980s showed that there were more losses than gains in overall water quality. Widespread improvements had occurred in fecal bacteria and lead concentrations, but deterioration had taken place with respect to nitrate, sodium, chloride, arsenic, and cadmium. It was believed that the nitrate came mostly from the enormous increase in fertilizer use that had occurred during the previous decade and that the sodium and chloride came from the even greater increase in the use of salt on highways in winter. The arsenic and cadmium apparently came from fossil-fuel combustion products and primary metals manufacturing.[13] The increased presence of nitrate and sodium in the surface waters was especially troubling, because these come mostly from "non-point sources" (meaning from all over the place) instead of from "point sources" like sewage treatment plants, power plants, and factories. Many strategies have been developed to deal with point sources, but reducing pollution from non-point sources will require new approaches.

It is not commonly realized that agriculture is one of the biggest polluters and one of the biggest users of water. As water passes across farmland, it picks up dissolved salts, fertilizers, nitrogen from animal manure, and pesticide residues. When it drains off the land, the pollutants it carries wind up in our surface waters. Nutrients such as nitrogen and phosphorus promote the growth of algae. The algae then consume the dissolved oxygen in the water, rendering it unlivable for most other aquatic life.[14]

One success story has been that of Lake Erie. In the 1970s, there were many news reports that Lake Erie was "dead" because of heavy algae growth and serious declines in the fish populations. It was not dead, of course, and in fact has been slowly recovering as a result of water pollution control programs. Full recovery will be in the distant future, however, if it can be achieved at all.

Every summer, many beaches in Canada are closed to swimmers because of high bacteria counts in the water. This is a scandal for a country that boasts the largest endowment of fresh water in the world. Efforts to control pollution are being introduced at all levels of government. It is the task of the professional engineer to assist this effort to get the problem of water pollution under control.

The Greenhouse Effect and Ozone Depletion

Since the end of the nineteenth century, the amount of CO_2 in the atmosphere has increased by about 23 percent, to 340 parts per million. The increase is attributed to two factors: the burning of fossil fuels and deforestation in the tropics. Carbon dioxide is vital to the Earth's heat balance, because it causes the trapping of a certain amount of heat in the atmosphere, creating a greenhouse effect. If there were substantially less CO_2 in the atmosphere, so little heat would be retained that the surface of the Earth would be coated with ice. But if the amount of CO_2 were to double, the Earth's average temperature might increase by 3 or 4°C, with uncertain but probably harmful consequences. The time it will take to double the CO_2 is dependent upon the rate at which we burn fossil fuel, but estimates have ranged from 88 to 220 years.[15] The global warming of the twentieth century, and especially of the 1980s, has caused some people to declare that the greenhouse effect is already upon us. They may well be correct, but short-term temperature variations cannot be relied upon as proof.

The aspect of the greenhouse effect that has attracted the most attention is the rise in sea level. The rise of 15 cm in this century has already caused some beaches on the Atlantic coast to erode at the rate of 0.9 to 1.5 m per year.[16] It has been predicted that the sea level in the next 100 years could rise another 8 to 25 cm if the average global temperature increases by 1.5 to 5.4°C, mostly because of the melting of glaciers. The huge glaciers in Antarctica, which make up 85 percent of the total ice on Earth, are not involved in this calculation, because it is believed that they are currently subtracting water from the Earth's oceans and thus might remain in balance.[17] The Arctic ice cap is not involved at all, since it is largely floating; its melting would not substantially change the overall sea level.

A somewhat more worrisome scenario emerges from the computerized climate models that have been developed. Some of them have suggested that a global warming would drastically shift existing climatic patterns. The overall hydrological cycle might be intensified, with higher temperatures and greater rainfall at northern latitudes; simultaneously, rainfall at middle latitudes might decrease. Although Canada might prosper, the wheat fields of the United States might turn into dust bowls. Those who work with the climate models hasten to remind everyone that their models are not yet very good. Overall warming is something we can predict with reasonable confidence, but its accompanying regional effects are uncertain. The Earth's atmosphere and oceans are so complex in their behaviour that the current models are not able to give reliable regional projections. For example, when the models are run with known historical data, they give widely divergent results from what actually took place.

Carbon dioxide is not the only greenhouse gas.[18] Others are methane (CH_4), nitrogen dioxide (NO_2), ozone (O_3), the chlorofluorocarbons ($CFCl_3$ and CF_2Cl_2, called the CFCs), and various synthetic chemicals. The CFCs are believed to be destroying the ozone layer in the stratosphere, and they are much more potent greenhouse gases than CO_2. One molecule of the CFCs has the same greenhouse effect as 10 000 molecules of CO_2. The role of CFCs in depleting the ozone layer has been fairly well established. Ozone in the stratosphere helps to screen out damaging ultraviolet rays. (Ozone at ground level is a pollutant and irritant.) The CFCs combine with ozone and create gaps in the stratospheric ozone layer. Major international strategies are being developed to phase out the use of CFCs, which not only will help the stratospheric ozone but will also help lessen the greenhouse effect.

What should we do about all this? There is the possibility, of course, that any greenhouse warming will be completely overshadowed by normal variations in the Earth's climate. Such variations have occurred many times in the past. Nevertheless, unnecessary burning of fossil fuels should, of course, be discouraged. And the indiscriminate dispersal of CFCs is much more serious. Since CFCs (in the form of freon) have been used in refrigerating systems for decades, there is a lot of it around. Refrigeration lines containing freon should never be voided into the atmosphere.

Energy Shortages and Nuclear Power

During the 1970s there were two oil shortages, which caused long line-ups at gasoline stations. By the 1980s there was an oil glut. Gasoline became cheaper, and we lost interest in energy conservation. But as the last decade of the twentieth century came on, analysts warned that a new energy crisis was impending.[19]

The depletion of fossil fuels is envisioned in the near future; the world's oil reserves are predicted to be 90 percent depleted by the year 2020, although coal reserves will last another three or four centuries.[20] None of the alternative sources (solar, wind, wave, and geothermal) have made more than a minor addition to the global energy supply. Nuclear fission and nuclear fusion (should it ever be developed) appear to be essential if we are to maintain our present standard of living and extend it to the citizens of the developing nations.[21]

Atomic Energy of Canada Ltd., designers of the CANDU heavy-water nuclear reactor, argue that the CANDU is safer and more reliable than the American light-water reactors, since it is fuelled by natural uranium and moderated by heavy water. The CANDU consistently wins international honours for technical excellence.[22]

The alternative to nuclear energy is coal-fired power generation, with its associated problems of air pollution. In the aftermath of the Three Mile Island and Chernobyl disasters, a bitter argument has developed over whether coal power or nuclear power is more dangerous. One writer has asserted that their dangers are similar, even if one accepts the high estimate of 39 000 future cancer deaths from Chernobyl. He estimates that the death toll from the use of coal in the USSR is between 5000 and 50 000 a year. Many of these deaths occur in mining and transporting coal, because the use of coal requires the handling of 100 times as much material as does the use of uranium for an equivalent energy output. In the United States, 100 or more coal miners die each year, and nearly 600 of the 1900 deaths in railroad accidents each year are the result of the shipping of coal. But the big killer is air pollution, although it is impossible to say with certainty that any given death is specifically caused by coal burning. Nevertheless, it has been estimated that 50 000 people each year in the United States experience early deaths because of air pollution, mostly coming from coal. It is by extrapolation to similar populations and similar pollution conditions that the estimate of 5000 to 50 000 early deaths from coal burning in the USSR is derived.[23]

Another major issue with nuclear power is the long-term disposal of highly radioactive wastes. It will be necessary to keep the wastes out of circulation for thousands of years because of the extremely long half-lives of some of the elements, such as plutonium. At present, the plan is to store such wastes in stable geological underground layers from which water has been absent for millions of years. As with most matters having to do with nuclear energy, the disposal of wastes is surrounded by bitter debate. One of the issues has to do with the level of certainty regarding the future. The supporters of nuclear energy admit that no absolute guarantee can be made that the wastes will remain out of human contact for thousands of years into the future. However, they say that the risk of future exposure is very small. The opponents of nuclear energy, on the other hand, have insisted on a guaranteed method for keeping nuclear wastes permanently out of contact. Since they readily agree that no such guarantee can be made, they say that this is reason enough to phase nuclear energy out of existence.

The debate will not be resolved in this textbook; however, the issue illustrates the seriousness and importance of conserving energy, increasing efficiency, and avoiding waste. The energy problems of the twenty-first century will be upon us much too soon, and some hard decisions will have to be made. These decisions must not be made in a moral vacuum; ethical reasons must prevail.

EVALUATING RISKS TO SOCIETY

The question may fairly be asked "What is best for society? Who should take the benefits of new developments and the hazards that accompany them?" The answer has usually been formulated using the utilitarian principle of creating the maximum good for the maximum number of people. In a recent report on risk management in the IEEE *Spectrum* the following observation was made:

> In any applied technology that touches human lives, the decision to accept some level of risk as inevitable calls on subjective judgment about the worth of those lives. The classic, if callous, tradeoff is a cost/benefit analysis of the expense of installing safety systems versus the value of the lives they may save and the political effectiveness of the move. At times the monetary

value of a human life is even assigned actuarially, up front, from insurance tables; sometimes it can only be inferred after the fact, from legal settlements for damages claimed.[24]

As a general rule, the good of society is determined on a utilitarian basis, weighing the benefits against the disadvantages. When the benefits accrue to a large population, when the risks are very small, and when the potential damage is not life-threatening, then the good of society is served by encouraging the project to continue. This is true for the vast majority of engineering projects.

In projects where moderate risks exist, the safety of the public can usually be guaranteed simply by using established methods and accepted factors of safety. For a new, untested process, however, such as a chemical plant or nuclear facility, the potential for disaster must be rigidly controlled, and a "cradle-to-grave" systems approach is needed to ensure that all hazards are considered. The designers must foresee the problems of decommissioning and disposal of the plant, which may be 50 years in the future, as well as the immediate problems of design and construction. The operating hazards must also be considered and controlled. In these cases, sophisticated studies such as failure modes and effects analysis, event tree analysis, and fault tree analysis would be required. The designers must examine every conceivable mode of failure, evaluate the probability of it occurring, and devise a remedy for combatting harmful results.

In summary, the utilitarian theory states that the good of society would be served when the benefits of a project can be conclusively proved to exceed the costs of the project, including the cost of failure (probability of failure × cost of damage), and when the benefits and risks accrue to the same sector of the population.

A DISSENTING VIEW OF THE ENGINEER'S DUTY TO SOCIETY

Professional engineers have an obligation to the general public, or society. This is confirmed in the first or second clause of *every* code of ethics: engineers must consider their duty to society to be paramount, or most important. This clause seems clear and unequivocal. However, one well-known expert on engineering ethics, Samuel Florman, disagrees with this clause as a general guide because it does not have a precise meaning.

> If this appeal to conscience were to be followed literally, chaos would ensue. Ties of loyalty and discipline would dissolve, and

organizations would shatter. Blowing the whistle on one's supervisors would become the norm, instead of a last and desper-
ate resort. It is unthinkable that each engineer determine to his
own satisfaction what criteria of safety, for example, should be
observed in each problem he encounters. Any product can be
made safer at greater cost, but absolute freedom from risk is an
illusion. Thus, acceptable standards must be specifically established by code, by regulation, or by law, or where these do not
exist, by management decision based upon standards of legal
liability. Public-safety policies are determined by legislators,
bureaucrats, judges, and juries, in response to facts presented
by expert advisers. Many of our legal procedures seem dis-
agreeable, particularly when lives are valued in dollars, but
since an approximation of the public will does appear to prevail, I cannot think of a better way to proceed. ...

The regulations need not all be legislated, but they must be
formally codified. If we are now discovering that there are tens
of thousands of potentially dangerous substances in our midst,
then they must be tested, the often-confusing results debated,
and decisions made by democratically designated authorities
— decisions that will be challenged and revised again and
again. ...

This is an excruciatingly laborious business, but it cannot be
avoided by appealing to the good instincts of engineers. If the
multitude of new regulations and clumsy bureaucracies has
made life difficult for corporate executives, the solution is not
in promising to be good and eliminating the controls, but rather
in consolidating the controls themselves and making them
rational. The world's technological problems cannot even be
formulated, much less solved, in terms of ethical rhetoric: especially in engineering, good intentions are a poor substitute
for good sense, talent, and hard work.[25]

The comments by Florman are thought-provoking and refresh-
ing. However, the test comes when we observe that there are at
present many areas where the regulations and standards are well
known, yet companies still choose to ignore them because of the
costs involved or the loss of profit that could result. The development of more regulations will not change the attitudes of unethical
people, and the professional engineer will still encounter cases
where the public good must be weighed against the benefit of client
and employer.

In spite of the apparent contradiction, both of the above approaches to the problem are correct. The statement in the code of

ethics is an ideal and a guide to personal behaviour; the regulations and standards proposed by Florman are a method of making that ideal more easily attainable.

WHISTLEBLOWING: THE ENGINEER'S DUTY TO REPORT

A good definition of a whistleblower is given in a recent article: "Whistleblowers are people (usually employees) who believe an organization is engaged in unsafe, unethical or illegal practices and go public with their charge, having tried with no success to have the situation corrected through internal channels."[26]

Two important points distinguish a whistleblower from a troublemaker: the motive of the engineer involved and the methods used to achieve the goal of protecting the public. As an APEO Guideline states:

> An engineer must act out of a sense of duty, with full knowledge of the effect of [proposed] actions, and accept responsibility for his [or her] judgment. For this reason any process which involves "leaking" information anonymously is discouraged. There is a basic difference between "leaking" information and "responsible disclosure". The former is essentially furtive, and selfish, with an apparent objective of revenge or embarrassment; the latter is open, personal, conducted with the interest of the public in mind and obviously requires that engineers *put their names on the action and sometimes their jobs on the line.* [Italics in original.][27]

A whistleblower must also be aware that the process may involve public exposure and scrutiny of the engineer and may place his or her career in jeopardy. Therefore, whistleblowing is not an act that should be entered into casually, unknowingly, or wantonly. The provincial Association should be contacted and their reporting process should be followed.

THE REPORTING PROCESS

Provincial Associations of Professional Engineers have frequently taken on the role of mediators or conciliators to help engineers who perceive their clients or employers to be behaving unethically. The Association can serve a useful role by assisting the engineer to define the ethical issues involved, to assess the issues and advise the engineer, to communicate the concerns to the client or employer in an unbiased way, and generally to help resolve the issue as informally as possible. The following discussion of "Reporting Unprofessional Practice" is from the *Manual of Professional Practice Under the Code of Ethics*, published by the Association of Professional Engineers, Geologists and Geophysicists of Alberta (APEGGA).

> Professional engineers, geologists and geophysicists shall advise the Registrar of any practice by a member of the Association that they believe to be contrary to this Code of Ethics.
>
> [This rule is accompanied in the *Manual* by the following commentary:]
>
> Through informal contact, normal working relationships, or special circumstances such as design reviews, one professional may develop the opinion that the work of another professional is deficient. The inadequacies may arise from unskilled practice and/or unprofessional conduct.
>
> While it is not the role of the first professional to conduct a disciplinary investigation, he or she should be certain there is sufficient substance to warrant a serious allegation against a colleague. A professional should carefully consider the necessity and merits for disciplinary action for minor unprofessional inadequacies where protection of the public is not involved. But if it is decided to proceed, as a general rule, the first professional should discuss the situation with the second professional to clarify the facts and check for extenuating circumstances.
>
> Ignoring unprofessional practices, either for expediency or sympathy, may indirectly endanger the public and certainly circumvents the responsibility of self-regulation that has been granted to the profession. Intentionally refraining from reporting substantive breaches of the Code of Ethics on the part of another member of APEGGA therefore constitutes unprofessional conduct.
>
> If the immediate physical safety of the public is in jeopardy, speedy notification of the owner, operator or appropriate regulatory authorities is the immediate duty of the professional. So that a full investigation may either substantiate or dismiss the concern, notification to the Registrar is the professional's next duty. Prompt notification is necessary to prevent potential harm to the public through the continuation of unacceptable engineering, geological or geophysical practices. Professionals have a responsibility to be aware of hazards to society created by their profession, and also have a responsibility to report unethical practice so it may be dealt with through the disciplinary process.[28]

A similar idea is included in almost every code of ethics. The Association of Professional Engineers of Ontario has defined the procedure for reporting even more clearly in a recent publication, *A Professional Engineer's Duty to Report: Responsible Disclosure of Conditions Affecting Public Safety*.

Reporting Process

Engineers are encouraged to raise their concerns internally with their employers or clients in an open and forthright manner *before* reporting the situation to the APEO. Although there may be situations where this is not possible, engineers should attempt to resolve problems themselves *as the first step in the process*.

1. If resolution as above is not possible, engineers may report situations in writing or by telephone to the Office of the Registrar of APEO. In reporting the situation to the APEO, engineers must be prepared to identify themselves and be prepared to stand openly behind their judgments if it becomes necessary.

2. The Office of the Registrar will expect the reporting party to provide the following information:
   a) the name of the engineer who is reporting the situation;
   b) the name(s) of the engineer's client/employer to whom the situation has been reported;
   c) a clear, detailed statement of the engineer's concerns, supported by evidence and the probable consequences if remedial action is not taken.

3. The Office of the Registrar will treat all information including the reporting engineer's name, as being confidential to the fullest extent possible.

4. The Office of the Registrar will confirm the factual nature of the situation and, where the reporting engineer has already contacted the client/employer, obtain an explanation of the situation from the client/employer's point of view.

5. Where the Office of the Registrar has reason to believe that a situation does exist which may endanger the safety or welfare of the public, the Office of the Registrar will take one or more of the following actions:

a) report the situation to the appropriate municipal, provincial and/or federal authorities;

b) where necessary, review the situation with one or
more independent engineers, to obtain advice as to the
potential danger to public safety or welfare and the
remedial action to be taken;

c) request the client/employer to take steps necessary to
avoid danger to the public safety or welfare;

d) take such other action as deemed appropriate under
the circumstances;

e) follow up on the action taken by all parties to confirm
that the problem has been resolved.

6. Wherever possible the Office of the Registrar shall maintain accurate records of all communications with the reporting engineer, any authorities involved and the cli-
ent/employer.

In Summary

The Office of the Registrar will co-operate with any engineer
who reports a situation that the engineer believes may endanger the safety or welfare of the public. Wherever possible, the
confidentiality of reporting engineers and the information they
disclose will be maintained. The Office of the Registrar will
emphasize in all dealings with the engineer's client/employer
and the public the engineer's duty to report under the Act and
Regulations, and will provide the reporting engineer with an
endorsement of the performance of his/her duty, provided that
the Registrar has determined that the engineer has acted properly or in good faith.[29]

Engineers are, to a very great degree, the caretakers of the environment, whether or not they want the role, since they design the
industrial plants upon which we depend, the structures in which we
live, the machinery that lightens our workload, and the infrastructure of water, gas, and electric supply and sewage disposal that are
critically important to our quality of life. Occasionally, it may be
necessary to take extreme actions.

In reviewing the reporting processes developed by the Alberta
and Ontario Associations, several comments and concerns come to
mind.

• Informal Resolution: It is extremely important that the engineer
strive to resolve problems informally and internally in an open,

professional manner. In the vast majority of cases, clear communication is all that is required. The use of formal reporting
procedures must be a last resort.

- Confidentiality: Even if it should be necessary to report an
  individual, either colleague or employer, the report should be
  made to the appropriate regulating body and not to the news
  media. The goal is to remedy a problem, not to embarrass an
  individual. Although full publicity may at some point be necessary, it is not the first step in reporting.

- Retaliation: In extreme cases, where it has been necessary to
  report an unethical, illegal, or unsafe act to public authorities,
  an employer may attempt to retaliate by firing the engineer.
  Persons in such positions should know that their actions would
  not constitute just cause for firing, as explained in Chapter 8,
  and an engineer in such circumstances could file a suit to recover lost wages and costs.

INTRODUCTION TO HISTORICAL STUDIES

The seven historical case studies that follow are actual histories of
ethical conflicts in which the good of society was at stake. Each case
has unique characteristics and shows a wide range of results. The
cases describe events that took place in the United States and the
Soviet Union, and they are all well known. In fact, these conflicts,
most of which occurred during the 1970s, spurred the development
and review of codes of ethics and generated much discussion about
ethics in general and whistleblowing in particular. The lessons that
these cases teach are still valid today, in Canada and elsewhere.

▼ ▼ ▼

HISTORICAL STUDY 10.1—WHISTLEBLOWING:
THE BAY AREA RAPID TRANSIT (BART) CASE

In 1975 a lawsuit was filed in Oakland, California, by three engineers
who had been fired by Bay Area Rapid Transit (BART). These engineers, all of whom were involved in the design of the computers that
were to control BART, a new, modern transit system, had called
attention to practices by BART that they believed would jeopardize
public safety. They were suing BART for damages and to get their jobs
back. The Institute of Electrical and Electronics Engineers (IEEE) filed
an *amicus curiae* ("friend of the court") brief in the case. The IEEE
called the court's attention to the codes of ethics adopted by the

various engineering societies, particularly to the provision that says that engineers must hold their duty to public safety and welfare as paramount and should

> not complete, sign, or seal plans and/or specifications that are not of a design safe to the public health and welfare and in conformity with accepted engineering standards. If the client or employer insists on such unprofessional conduct, [the engineer] shall notify the proper authorities and withdraw from further service on the project.[30]

What the IEEE asked the court to do, in its *amicus curiae* brief, was to rule "that an engineer is obligated to protect the public safety, that an engineer's contract of employment includes as a matter of law, an implied term that such engineer will protect the public safety, and that a discharge of an engineer solely or in substantial part because he acted to protect the public safety constitutes a breach of such implied term."[31]

Such a ruling by the court would have created a powerful precedent governing future relations between engineers and their employers. The ruling — even if the judge had been inclined to make it — never appeared, because the three engineers settled their case out of court.

▼ ▼ ▼

HISTORICAL STUDY 10.2—CONFLICT OF INTEREST: THE HYDROLEVEL CASE

Ethical problems can arise in subtle ways to surprise the unwary. The American Society of Mechanical Engineers (ASME) received just such an unpleasant surprise in 1975, when it found itself the target of a lawsuit for unethical behaviour, conflict of interest, and restraint of trade.

The case — known as the Hydrolevel Case — involved the administration of ASME's boiler and pressure vessel code. ASME is very proud of its record in administering safety codes, and the one on pressure vessels is its crown jewel. Before the society established the code, boiler explosions were common and had caused the loss of many lives. A steamboat explosion in 1865 had killed 1450 Union soldiers, and in 1894, at Shamokin, Pennsylvania, the simultaneous explosion of 27 boilers had levelled the town and killed thousands of people. By 1910, boiler explosions were occurring at the rate of 1400 a year.[32] Frequently explosions occurred because the water in the boiler was allowed to reach too low a level, so the code called for the use of a fuel cut-off device, which would act whenever the water level became too low.

Hydrolevel, Inc., manufactured an innovative cut-off device. The nature of the innovative design required inclusion of a time-delay so that premature cut-off would not occur during momentary surges. One of Hydrolevel's competitors, McDonnell & Miller (M&M), wrote a letter to ASME, asking if the time-delay feature met the provisions of the code. The letter was routinely referred to the appropriate ASME subcommittee for answer. The chairman of the subcommittee wrote a reply that implied that Hydrolevel's time-delay feature might not comply with the code, and M&M used this reply in a sales campaign to discourage potential customers from using the Hydrolevel device. However, as it developed, the chairman of the subcommittee — the one who drafted the letter — was associated with M&M. It also turned out that Hydrolevel's device, under a different interpretation of its operation, might actually meet the code. ASME found itself in court.

Many professional societies operate standards-setting programs, and these are typically implemented by volunteers who come from the very industries that are being regulated. Countless professional engineers have served in such roles and are justifiably proud of the public service they have provided, usually without remuneration. However, in the Hydrolevel suit, it was charged that under such conditions industrial organizations can easily rig the standards process to prevent the entry of new competitors.

In addition to suing ASME, Hydrolevel also sued M&M. In 1978, M&M settled out of court for $725,000. However, ASME refused to settle, believing that it was innocent of the charges. Its defence was that it was being tried for a conspiracy of which it had no knowledge, in which it played no conscious part, and in which it did not stand to gain financially.

ASME lost, appealed its case all the way to the United States Supreme Court, and lost again. In 1983, after eight years of litigation, it paid $4.75 million to Hydrolevel. Hydrolevel had argued that "corporations, unlike human participants, can harbor no intent and can perform no acts, except through their agents." The Supreme Court agreed and in its decision said: "ASME wields great power in the nation's economy. ... When it cloaks its subcommittee officials with the authority of its reputation, ASME permits those agents to affect the destinies of businesses and thus gives them power to frustrate competition in the marketplace."

Standards-setting organizations like ASME, the court added, are potentially rife with anticompetitive activity, since they are composed of, or associated with, members of the industries being regulated. ASME had been lax in providing procedures that would guard against such abuses and would have to pay the price, partly as a warning to others. ASME paid the price and set up new procedures. Now, in addition to other safeguarding procedures, at least five persons must review all statements regarding the code before release.[33]

▼ ▼ ▼

HISTORICAL STUDY 10.3—FAILURE TO REPORT: KICKBACKS TO COUNTY ENGINEER

Allan Kammerer was 32 years old and a principal in a struggling young consulting firm. One day he was visited by the county engineer, who came to discuss the possibility of Kammerer's firm doing highway work for the county. A condition, Kammerer learned, was that 25 percent of the project's cost would have to be kicked back to the county engineer. Kammerer paid, and paid again — a total of $100 000 over four years. His justification to himself was that the work was needed to keep his new firm's head above water and that he had a responsibility to his employees. Besides, he was made to understand that this was "the way things were done in the real world."

An investigation of the county's public works activities by the Attorney General caused Kammerer's records to be subpoenaed, along with those of all others doing business with the county. Before the subpoena arrived, Kammerer was urged to destroy the evidence of his dealings with the county, but he refused to do so. Instead, he became a witness against the county engineer, who was convicted on five counts of extortion, sentenced to five years in prison, and fined $10 000. As for Kammerer, he entered seven years of hell.

Kammerer's offer to serve as a witness was rewarded by immunity from prosecution, but this did not shield him from civil suit. His liability, under the rule of treble damages, could have come to $250 000, but his case never came to trial. Then he faced hearings before the state Department of Transportation concerning whether he possessed the "requisite moral character" to do state work. Apparently, the hearing officers were impressed by Kammerer's behaviour after the kickbacks were discovered, because he was cleared for eligibility to receive future work. After that, he underwent hearings by the American Society of Civil Engineers (ASCE) to determine whether he should be expelled from membership. In addition, he had to face family, friends, and colleagues in the relentless glare of public exposure in the media. He had been active in many civic and fraternal organizations in addition to being an elder in his church. During all this, his firm shrank from 30 employees to four.

The ASCE, instead of expelling Kammerer, suspended him for a year, evidently swayed by his remorse and his willingness to co-operate with the authorities. Seven years after the case came unravelled, Kammerer's firm was finally showing prospects of going into the black and was back up to thirteen employees.[34]

▼ ▼ ▼

HISTORICAL STUDY 10.4—FAILURE TO REPORT: THE *CHALLENGER* DISASTER

On January 28, 1986, the space shuttle *Challenger* blew up, killing seven people and putting the United States space program into deep freeze. After exhaustive investigations of the accident, it was finally decided that it was caused by hot gases blowing past one of the seals in the rocket boosters. It was concluded that the seal had been unable to do its job properly because of the unusually low temperature in Florida on the day of the launch — about –8°C. Claims were made that the management of Morton Thiokol, the manufacturer of the boosters, had engineering information that cast doubt on the seals but decided to launch anyway.

The primary source of detailed information was Roger M. Boisjoly, who was an engineer with Morton Thiokol at the time and who was directly responsible for the seals in question. Here is a summary of Boisjoly's version of the events.[35]

Following a shuttle launch a year earlier, Boisjoly had noticed, in a post-flight examination of the boosters, that hot combustion gases had apparently blown past the primary seal in one of the booster joints, although the gases had been stopped by a secondary seal. (Each joint was provided with two seals because the booster sections could distort under pressure; if distortion occurred and the primary seal failed to hold, the secondary seal would maintain joint integrity.) The ambient temperature at the time of that launch had been in the –8 to –5°C range for several days prior to launch and was 15 to 18°C at launch time. It was calculated that the seal itself was at a temperature of about 12°C.

Laboratory simulations of these conditions were set up by Morton Thiokol but were not conclusive. At 10°C, if the seals were compressed 1.02 mm and then separated 0.76 mm, there was loss of seal contact for more than 10 minutes. (The 0.76 mm separation was to simulate the effect of booster-section distortion under pressure.) If the seals were compressed 1.02 mm and then separated 0.26 mm, the seals successfully maintained contact. In another test the seals maintained their integrity down to 1°C, but this test fixture was rigid and did not simulate the effects of distortion.

Boisjoly wrote memos and reports to document his concern about the problem with the seals. He recommended the formation of a special team to work on the sealing problem, to consist of three engineers and four technicians. Approximately six months before the accident occurred, in a memo to Morton Thiokol's vice-president of engineering, he said:

> It is my honest and very real fear that if we do not take imme-diate action to dedicate a team to solve the problem, with the field joint having the number one priority, then we stand in jeopardy of losing a flight along with all the launch pad fa-cilities.

The night before the disaster, a teleconference was held between Morton Thiokol and NASA personnel. The overnight low temperature in Florida was predicted to be –8°C. Boisjoly presented his calcula-tions, which showed a predicted seal-ring temperature of –3 to –2°C under those conditions. He urgently recommended that no launch take place unless the temperature were 12°C or higher. Management — placing its reliance on the laboratory test that showed that the seal had retained its integrity down to 1°C (but without providing for distortion) and on its belief that if the primary seal did not hold, then the secondary one would—ordered that the launch proceed. The next day, 73 seconds after launch, *Challenger* blew up.

Boisjoly was appointed to the failure investigation team and was placed in charge of the redesign of the seal. During subsequent hearings before a presidential commission, he freely volunteered information and handed over packets of his internal company cor-respondence, contrary to instructions from Morton Thiokol's attor-ney. Boisjoly says that his actions incurred strong company disap-proval and that he was subsequently isolated from any contact with NASA and from the main redesign activity of the seals. Feeling that the environment at Morton Thiokol had turned hostile, he resigned in July 1986. The company gave him six months of extended sick leave and after that placed him on two years of long-term disability at 60 percent salary. Boisjoly then filed a $1-billion lawsuit against Morton Thiokol and a $10-million lawsuit against NASA for his lost salary and ruined career.

Boisjoly places the blame for the accident on a subtle shift in philosophy in the space shuttle program. In prior time, Boisjoly said, it was necessary to prove that conditions were *safe* before a go-ahead would be given for launch. In the case of *Challenger*, he said, the burden had shifted so that it was now considered necessary to prove that conditions were *not safe* before a launch would be cancelled.

▼ ▼ ▼

HISTORICAL STUDY 10.5—WHISTLEBLOWING: THE GOODRICH BRAKE CASE

A celebrated case of whistleblowing involved alleged falsification of data by B.F. Goodrich Co. in the design of a wheel brake for the A7D light attack aircraft. The case is especially noteworthy because it appeared as the lead chapter in a book entitled *In the Name of Profit*, published by Doubleday & Co. The book presented a number of cases in which corporations purportedly placed their allegiance to profit ahead of their responsibility to society. The chapter involving the B.F. Goodrich brake was entitled "Why Should My Conscience Bother Me?" and was written by one of the participants in the incident, Kermit Vandivier. Subsequently, the case was included in several texts on engineering ethics, which gave it special prominence.[36]

We will start with Vandivier's account of what occurred.

In 1967, B.F. Goodrich received a contract to supply wheels and brakes for the A7D. The prime contractor was Ling-Temco-Vought (LTV). Goodrich is a major supplier of aircraft wheel brakes and was very anxious that the brake be successful. A part of Goodrich's proposal that made the brake attractive was that it had only four disks instead of the usual five. This made it very compact and light — premium advantages for a military aircraft brake. It also meant that the development program would be very demanding and fraught with risk.

A young engineer one and a half years out of college, Searle Lawson, was assigned to have test models of the brake constructed and to run the tests that would be necessary to qualify the brake for service. Vandivier, a technical writer, was assigned to prepare the qualification report.

During the tests, the brake temperatures often reached 1100°C, causing the linings to fail. When Lawson reported this, he was told that success would simply be a matter of finding the right lining material. He was directed to continue testing.

After nearly a year, the brake was still a failure, in spite of the fact that irregular procedures had been used in an effort to get the brake to qualify, such as dismantling the brake between simulated stops to repair warpage, using fans to cool the brakes, and making deliberate miscalculations to indicate lower braking pressures than were actually applied. Both Vandivier and Lawson complained to their superiors about these irregularities but were told to continue with the tests. Nothing about all this was communicated to LTV, according to Vandivier.

After thirteen failed qualification tests, the word came down from above that, on the fourteenth attempt, "it's going to qualify." Following the fourteenth test, a formal qualification report was issued by Goodrich that certified that the brake had qualified. Vandivier asserted that this report contained nearly 200 pages of graphics and other displays, nearly all of which he had falsified. His motive, he said, was fear for his job and the welfare of his family if he refused to co-operate.

During the flight tests that followed, difficulties developed with the brake. On one occasion the brake plates welded themselves together, causing the plane to skid. Upon receiving this news, Vandivier went to the FBI and told them his story, to be followed by Lawson a few days later. Subsequently, both Vandivier and Lawson resigned. (Vandivier, incidentally, became a newspaper reporter, and Lawson went to work for LTV.)

At about the same time that Vandivier and Lawson resigned, Goodrich withdrew the four-disk brake and substituted a five-disk brake at its expense.

This accounting of events would be enough to shock almost anyone, and United States Senator William Proxmire was shocked enough when he heard of the case that he requested the General Accounting Office (GAO) to investigate. Senator Proxmire also subsequently conducted hearings before the Subcommittee on Economy in Government, of which he was chairman. Vandivier and Lawson both testified at this hearing, as did representatives of Goodrich.

The GAO sent a team to the Goodrich plant who spent a week going over the raw test data and examining the procedures that had been employed. The GAO report, in brief, said the following:

- In some instances, Goodrich's test procedures did not appear to comply with specification requirements.

- Some discrepancies in the data had occurred that "might be considered significant."

- Opinions differed as to the degree of danger to the pilot that might have been caused; no significant aircraft damage had been reported because of the brake.

- Goodrich had replaced the four-disk brake with a five-disk brake at no additional cost to the government. No schedule delays had been caused.

- The procedures used by both the prime contractor (LTV) and the Department of Defense had been inadequate to protect the interests of the government.

- The Air Force had protected the interests of the government by withholding approval of the qualification report.

During the hearings before Senator Proxmire's committee, representatives from Goodrich made the following statements in reply to the allegations that had been made by Vandivier:

- Goodrich was the manufacturer of the brakes for the Boeing 707, 720, 727, Lockheed L-1011, C-5A, General Dynamics F-111, North American XB-70, and many other civilian and military aircraft. It was a leading manufacturer of brakes and could have no possible incentive to falsify information or produce a defective brake.

- A total of 267 test flights had taken place. In two of the flights a problem developed with the four-disk brake, in which the brake plates "fused slightly" (Goodrich's words) at low speeds. Following the test flights Goodrich conducted further tests at its factory, employing the full brake system (including the hydraulic system and antiskid mechanism, which were not made by Goodrich), instead of just the brake alone. From these tests, Goodrich concluded that the four-disk brake was not going to work and substituted the five-disk brake.

- There were indeed some deviations from the specifications. For example, some of the stop times were longer than allowed by the specifications. These deviations had been discussed with and approved by LTV, and LTV had notified the Air Force, contrary to Vandivier's assertion that LTV had been kept in the dark. Vandivier simply had not known what was going on.

- It was true that "rolling stops" had been employed, which was contrary to the specifications. The Air Force itself had established such a precedent when testing brakes at Wright Field. This variation had been discussed with LTV in advance and approved by them.

- Test data had not been changed or falsified, but in evaluating the data, the project design engineer had arrived at judgements regarding the validity of the data.

- Some of the discrepancies noted by GAO came about because certain data points were recorded by two different methods: one set of data was visually recorded, whereas the other was recorded by computer. If the data points differed, the computer-recorded points were used. This had caused some revisions in the report.

- In one case, in which the test brake had been disassembled and a spacer plate replaced by a pressure plate, this was done so that adjusters could be installed and the correct pressures could be applied.

- Some of the pressure values had been changed because the use of adjusters during some of the stops had caused incorrect values to be recorded. These values had to be revised to compensate for the adjuster pressures and thus show the correct values.

- In another case, some of the temperature figures had to be revised because the thermocouple leads had become interchanged on the slipring.

So there we have it. A situation that, when presented from one point of view, looked like a shocking case of corruption instead turned into a confusing set of complexities. If Goodrich did something wrong, it probably was to deviate from the specifications, but here it apparently had the willing co-operation of LTV and the Air Force. Clearly, Goodrich, in its proposal for a four-disk brake, had moved right to the edge of technical feasibility and was trying very hard to produce a technological breakthrough. In this it failed, and it had to fall back on the proven technology of the five-disk brake.

Perhaps the most we can learn from the case is that there are always two sides to every story. In fact, it may sometimes be difficult to figure out who the "good guys" are. Vandivier and Lawson certainly felt that they had done the right thing in taking their information to the FBI, and indeed they had done exactly what they were supposed to do, according to the duty spelled out in codes of ethics, that engineers "shall notify the proper authorities and withdraw from further service on the project."

But, if we can believe the testimony of the Goodrich officials, Vandivier and Lawson had only a part of the story. It is clear that the lodging of a charge of wrongdoing against other persons carries with it an enormous responsibility, because those other persons have rights too.

▼ ▼ ▼

HISTORICAL STUDY 10.6—FAILURE TO REPORT: THE DC-10 CASE

A prime example of a case in which a danger was clearly perceived but the whistle was *not* blown is that of the DC-10. On March 3, 1974, nine minutes after a DC-10 took off from Paris, a cargo door blew open. The resulting decompression of the cargo compartment caused the cabin floor to collapse. In the DC-10, the control systems are routed through the floor (instead of through the ceiling, as in the 747), so when the floor collapsed, control of the ailerons and rudder was lost. The plane crashed, killing all aboard. [37]

The case revolves around the design of the cargo door latches. In 1968, McDonnell Douglas, the manufacturer of the DC-10, gave a subcontract to Convair Division of General Dynamics to perform the detail design of the fuselage of the DC-10, including its cargo doors. (Such arrangements are common in the aircraft industry, whereby one manufacturer subcontracts portions of the design to others.) Initially, the specifications required the use of hydraulic actuators to drive the cargo latches, but later Douglas told Convair that electric actuators were to be used instead, since they were lighter.

The distinction between hydraulic actuators and electric actuators is important to the case. If, for some reason, the latches failed to seat properly, a fairly moderate degree of internal fuselage pressure would force a hydraulic latch to open. Such a sequence of events, if it occurred, would take place at fairly low altitude and pressure differential, and the resulting decompression would not be disastrous. The aircraft could land safely. But with electric latches, if they did not fully seat, the cargo doors would probably be forced open at a time when a much higher pressure differential had developed, so that the resulting decompression would be catastrophic. In the year prior to the certification of the DC-10 for service, there had been five instances in which cargo doors on DC-8s and DC-9s had blown open during flight. Because the DC-8s and DC-9s were equipped with hydraulic actuators, the accidental openings occurred under moderate pressure differentials, and the planes landed safely.

During the design of the fuselage, Douglas asked Convair to prepare a failure mode and effects analysis (FMEA) for the cargo door system. In the FMEA, Convair pointed out that little reliance could be placed on the use of warning lights to indicate the presence of an improperly latched cargo door, because the warning lights themselves were subject to malfunction. Even less reliance could be placed upon the alertness of ground crews to check such things as fully closed latches, because any such procedure was too much subject to human error. Beyond this, the FMEA described a number of scenarios of events that could produce a hazard to life. One of these scenarios involved a failure of the latch to seat properly, leading to an explosive decompression of the cargo hold and producing collapse of the cabin floor and loss of control of the aircraft.

In 1970, during the ground tests of the first DC-10, the aircraft was being subjected to pressurization tests when a cargo door suddenly blew open. The accident was blamed on the failure of a mechanic to close the door properly. But even before the accident Douglas had decided that further safeguards were needed to prevent the possibility of such an accident. A hand-driven locking handle was provided, together with a small door near the locking handle. The door was supposed to stand open until the locking handle was operated. A member of the ground crew would look through the door to be sure that the locking pins had fully seated; then the door would be closed. However, there was no necessary connection between the two. If the locking handle failed to seat properly, the door could still be closed. Thus, the DC-10 system depended upon a member of the ground crew to understand and follow the correct steps.

The DC-10 was certified for use in 1971. In 1972, a cargo door blew out on a DC-10 over Windsor, Ontario, and part of the cabin floor collapsed. Miraculously, the pilot was able to land the aircraft safely.

But now the United States Federal Aviation Administration (FAA) was officially in the picture. FAA personnel prepared a draft of an "airworthiness directive," which would have ordered Douglas to take certain actions before the DC-10 could resume operation. But the airworthiness directive was not issued. Instead, an informal agreement (referred to later as the "gentlemen's agreement") was worked out between Douglas and the head of the FAA, detailing certain steps that Douglas would take to correct the situation. (These steps apparently included the provision of small inspection windows, deeper latch engagement, and stiffer latch linkages.) The aircraft that crashed near Paris did not receive these modifications, even though the inspectors responsible for the aircraft had certified that the modifications had been done. A further relevant factor is that the instructions printed on the aircraft were in English. The ground crew member who was responsible for cargo door closure knew several languages, but English was not one of them.

Shortly after the Windsor blowout, Convair's director of product engineering wrote a memo to his superiors that declared that the safety of the cargo door latching system had been progressively degraded since the inception of the program. After the first blowout (the one that occurred during ground testing), Convair had discussed possible corrective action with Douglas, including the possibility of providing "blowout panels" in the cabin floor. If the cargo area suddenly lost pressure, these panels would be blown out, but the cabin floor would not collapse. Instead of that alternative, however, Douglas had opted for the small doors that would provide visual observation of the manual latching system. The memo also suggested strengthening the cabin floor so that it could resist a sudden decompression, but this would add 1400 kg in mass — a serious matter for an aircraft.

The memo contained this paragraph:

> My only criticism of Douglas in this regard is that once this inherent weakness was demonstrated by the July 1970 test failure [the ground test], they did not take immediate steps to correct it. It seems to me inevitable that, in the twenty years ahead of us, DC-10 cargo doors will come open and I would expect this to usually result in the loss of the airplane.

Convair management responded to the memo essentially as follows:

- Exception to Douglas's design philosophy had not been registered by Convair at the beginning of the program. By not taking exception, Convair in effect had agreed that a proper design philosophy was the design of a safe cargo door latching system, in lieu of designing a stronger floor or providing blowout panels.

- A design philosophy involving a safe latching system would satisfy FAA safety requirements.

- Douglas had unilaterally redesigned the cargo door latch system and had previously rejected the proposal of blowout panels.

- Convair management had been informally advised that Douglas was making corrections to the latching system and was reconsidering the provision of blowout panels.

As a result of the above, Convair management made no formal communication to Douglas. Their justification was that the arguments advanced in the memo were already well known to Douglas, and it was not likely that any additional actions would be produced beyond those that they understood were already taking place. In addition, an adversarial relationship between Douglas and Convair had developed, in which Douglas was seeking to shift the costs of redesign to Convair. It was feared that if Convair now questioned a design philosophy with which it had originally concurred, Douglas would use this as a further pretext for shifting all the costs of redesign to Convair.[38]

The case makes sorry reading. There certainly were opportunities to provide a safe locking system. For example, when the inspection door was provided to go with the manual latching system, it could have also been provided with an absolute interlock, which would have prevented the closing of the door unless the locking pins were fully seated. Probably the saddest feature of the story is that the FAA failed so badly in its role of safety watchdog.

From the viewpoint of design engineers, the case has value not only because it underscores the responsibility for safety borne by engineers but because it introduces the idea of "design philosophies" and what those philosophies might mean with respect to safety. Also, the case brings home a point of view that many people overlook: a safety system that depends upon human beings to execute a series of actions, such as making visual checks to see if latches are fully seated, is almost guaranteed to fail sometime. Safety needs to be designed into the system itself.

▼ ▼ ▼

HISTORICAL STUDY 10.7—NUCLEAR SAFETY: THREE MILE ISLAND AND CHERNOBYL

One of the major sources of public concern over engineering and technology involves the generation of electric power by nuclear fission, even though American and British studies show that power generation by coal is 250 times more hazardous, and oil is 180 times more hazardous than nuclear power. Only natural gas poses fewer hazards to workers and the general population.[39] There were, in fact, some serious radiation releases in the early days of Canadian nuclear power development; however, the record of nuclear power generation was comparatively spotless until the reactor accident at Three Mile Island in Pennsylvania in 1979. There have been very few deaths in North America attributable directly to power reactor accidents. However, the accident at Three Mile Island and the later accident at Chernobyl in the Soviet Union in 1986 caused serious public concern and set back development of nuclear power for at least a decade. The heightened caution may be the only benefit to come out of these tragedies.

The Three Mile Island accident began when a routine maintenance operation caused a blockage in one of the main feedwater lines. This caused the reactor to trip, and within eight seconds it had shut itself down. That would have been the end of the event, except for the fact that a pressure relief valve stuck open, allowing radioactive water to escape from the system for more than two hours — leaving the reactor core partially uncooled — before the problem was correctly diagnosed and fixed.[40] By the time the event was over, more than a third of the reactor core had melted and fallen to the bottom of the reactor vessel.[41]

The Three Mile Island event was the worst possible nuclear accident come true: the core had melted. In the scenario for a core-melt accident, the molten mass is supposed to burn its way through the bottom of the reactor vessel, then burn through the thick concrete lining at the bottom of the containment shell, and finally penetrate the groundwater table. In a cynical version of this event, the molten mass continues to eat its way through the interior of the Earth until it emerges in China, thus giving the scenario the name "the China Syndrome." Humour aside, the accident was frightening in its possible consequences, because eventually the containment shell would be breached and massive amounts of radiation could have spread across the countryside.

However, in the case of Three Mile Island, except for the fact that the core did indeed melt, none of the scenario took place. The molten mass did not even penetrate the shell of the reactor vessel but instead acted as an insulating layer as it cooled. The amount of radiation that escaped into the environment turned out to be negligible. Although experts had predicted that an enormous amount of radio-iodine would be released in gaseous form, very little radio-iodine escaped. Instead, it was converted into an iodine that readily dissolved in water and thus remained inside the reactor containment shell.[42] Virtually all the other radioactive materials also remained inside the containment shell, except for inert gases like krypton and xenon, which pose little hazard. It is believed that the person who received the worst exposure from the accident was a man working on an island nearby in the Susquehanna River, who received an estimated exposure of 40 millirems. (Natural background radiation causes an average annual dose of about 100 millirems for each person in North America.)[43]

The Three Mile Island accident may not have been a catastrophe for the public, but it was for the utility that owned it. The plant was a total loss. Furthermore, just the obligatory clean-up of the radioactive materials cost nearly $1 billion. It is small wonder that utilities began to retreat from nuclear power and in some cases abandoned plants that were nearly finished. In 1984, the Public Service Company of Indiana announced cancellation of work on a huge plant that was half completed; cost: $2.5 billion. Cincinnati Gas & Electric stopped construction on its Zimmer nuclear plant, 97 percent complete, and announced that it would be converted to coal; cost to date: $1.7 billion. About nuclear plants, one utilities executive said, "They are just too expensive for a company like us to construct any more." Another said, "Don't build nuclear plants in America. You subject yourself to financial risk and public abuse."[44]

The Chernobyl accident in 1986 scared almost everyone in the northern hemisphere, and with good cause. Not only did the core melt, but the graphite blocks used for moderation caught fire and burned fiercely for days, spreading radioactivity around the world. (Canadian nuclear power plants use heavy water, not graphite, for moderation.) The Chernobyl accident occurred during the supposedly routine low-power test. To prevent the reactor from automatically shutting itself off, the automatic trip safety system was disconnected. Much publicity has been given to the improper procedures used by the reactor operators, which contributed to the accident, but the real problem lay with the design. At low power levels, the Chernobyl-type reactor is inherently unstable, because it has what is called a "positive void coefficient." In broad terms, this means that as the available water in the core decreases (i.e., when steam bubbles form), the reactivity *increases*. In a light-water reactor (LWR), just the opposite happens. As steam bubbles form, or if the water decreases for any other reason, the reactivity goes down, not up. Thus an LWR is inherently stable. (Almost all commercial power reactors in the United States are LWRs.) The Canadian CANDU reactor is even safer; the presence of heavy water is needed for the fission to proceed. Loss of the heavy water would cause the fission process to stop automatically.[45]

At Chernobyl, the operators apparently thought they could manage the reactivity of the plant by manipulating the controls. But the instability of the reactor at low power was so extreme that there was no chance of doing so. When the accident began, the plant was being run at about 6 percent of its full power rating. As the operators started the planned test, the power level began to rise. Because of the positive void coefficient, the rise became exponential. Within 2.5 seconds the power level had gone from 6 percent to 120 percent of full load. In just 1.5 seconds more, it was 100 times the normal full load. It exploded.[46]

Thirty-one people died in the Chernobyl accident. Twenty-nine of them were firemen and two were reactor operators. Of the latter two, one was on top of the reactor when it exploded and was killed instantly; the other ran into the reactor building trying to find out what happened. About 200 people were exposed to high levels of radiation and developed acute radiation sickness. Some of them will die early deaths as a result of their exposure. About 7 million curies of iodine-131 and 2.4 million curies of cesium-137 were released. The smoke plume carried these high into the atmosphere and around the world. By contrast, about 15 curies of iodine-131 and essentially no cesium were released by the Three Mile Island accident.[47]

At first, it was the release of radio-iodine at Chernobyl that dominated the concern of public health officials, because of the way in which iodine enters the food chain. But iodine-131 has only an eight-day half-life, and it later became apparent that the radio-cesium was more threatening than the iodine, partly because its half-life is 30 years. One year after the accident, a report by the U.S. Department of Energy (DOE) estimated that the number of cancer deaths among the exposed worldwide population might be 14 000 to 39 000 greater than would normally occur. The "normal" number of cancer deaths among the same population is expected to be 630 million, so the estimated increase in deaths because of Chernobyl lies between 0.002 and 0.006 percent. The authors of the DOE report warned that, because of the uncertainty in the statistical methods being used, they could not rule out the possibility that the future cancer increase might actually be zero. But even if the highest number of estimated future deaths occurs, the authors of the report said it will be impossible ever to identify them as such, among the 630 million "normal" cancer deaths.[48]

A further problem, said the report, is that our current knowledge of radiation cancer risks is based upon high doses, usually delivered at high rates. However, there seems to be substantial amelioration of latent health effects for those exposed to *low* doses, based upon animal experiments. Thus, they said, the actual health effects of Chernobyl might turn out to be two to ten times less severe than those given in their report.[49]

The possibility of a high death toll from a major accident must remain a serious concern. We should not acquire a false sense of security from the fact that the toll at Chernobyl was as low as it was, even though the accident in other ways was extremely severe.

TOPICS FOR STUDY AND DISCUSSION

1. You have graduated from university and have been working for three years as a plant design and maintenance engineer for a pulp and paper company in northern Canada. The company is a wholly owned subsidiary of a large multinational conglomerate. When you received your P.Eng. licence, you were promoted to chief plant engineer, and now you work directly for the plant manager, Smith, who reports to the head office, which is not in Canada. The company employs about 150 persons, which is most of the adult population of the nearby village, either directly as employees or indirectly as woodcutters.

    In the course of your work, you have become aware, because of your knowledge of the processes used by the plant, that the effluent from the plant contains a very high concentration of a mercury compound that could be dangerous. In fact, since the plant has been discharging this material for 25 years, the river is thoroughly unfit for drinking or swimming downstream from the plant, and you suspect that the curious illness reported in a native Indian village about 60 km downstream is really Minamata disease, which is caused by mercury contamination. The classic symptoms are loss of co-ordination, spastic muscle movement, and eventually death. You suspect that the fish in the river are contaminated with the mercury and have spread the contamination to all the downstream lakes. To remedy this problem involves drastic changes to the plant and would cost at least $1 million. At present, no one knows of the suspected problem except you and your boss, Smith. You have discussed this problem at length with Smith, who is not an engineer, and he has confided that the head office considers the plant to be only marginally profitable, so an expenditure of this magnitude is simply not possible. The head office, he says, would close down the plant, causing massive unemployment in the area, and would probably cause the workers from the village to abandon their homes to seek work elsewhere, since the alternative would be severe poverty. What should you do?

2. Between 40 000 and 50 000 people are killed every year in car accidents in North America, yet people throughout the world show every sign that they consider the benefits of the car to be worth the risks, in spite of the dreadful annual carnage. In the case of nuclear power, fewer than ten people have been killed in North America by reactor accidents, yet many people are frightened of nuclear power, knowing that a major reactor accident could kill thousands. Many people die every year in the process of producing food (farming is dangerous), and thousands of coal miners have been killed so far in the twentieth century. In each case cited there are benefits, but there are also terrible

risks involving the deaths of many. Discuss these issues. Are we entitled, as a matter of moral behaviour, to accept benefits, if the benefits entail risks to others? Using the concepts of this chapter and Chapter 6, state, on one or two pages, an ethical guideline for deciding when construction of a dangerous facility such as a nuclear power plant or production of a dangerous chemical such as a pesticide is morally justified. Include financial, engineering, or political arguments in your answer, as well as ethical concepts.

NOTES

1. Association of Professional Engineers, Geologists and Geophysicists of Alberta, *Manual of Professional Practice Under the Code of Ethics* (Edmonton: APEGGA, 1990); Association of Professional Engineers of Ontario, *A Professional Engineer's Duty to Report: Responsible Disclosure of Conditions Affecting Public Safety* (Toronto: APEO, 1991).

2. C. Mucklestone, "The Engineer as Public Defender," *Engineering Dimensions* 11, no. 2 (March/April 1990): 29.

3. *The Canadian Encyclopedia*, 1st ed., s.v. "pollution."

4. *The Canadian Encyclopedia*, 1st ed., s.v. "air pollution."

5. *Canadian Encyclopedia*, "air pollution."

6. *Canadian Encyclopedia*, "air pollution."

7. *Canadian Encyclopedia*, 1st ed., s.v. "acid rain."

8. *Canadian Encyclopedia*, "acid rain."

9. *Canadian Encyclopedia*, "acid rain."

10. *Canadian Encyclopedia*, "acid rain."

11. D.E. Carr, *Death of the Sweet Waters* (New York: Berkley, 1971), 41.

12. *The Canadian Encyclopedia*, 1st ed., s.v. "water pollution."

13. R.A. Smith, R.B. Alexander, and M.G. Wolman, "Water-Quality Trends in the Nation's Rivers," *Science* (27 March 1987): 1607–15.

14. "Rescuing a Protein Factory," *Time* (23 July 1984): 84–85.

15. P.H. Abelson, "Carbon Dioxide Emissions," *Science* (25 November 1983).

16. "The Politics of Climate," *EPRI Journal* (June 1988): 4–15.

17. M.F. Meier, "Contributions of Small Glaciers to Global Sea Level," *Science* (21 December 1984): 1418–21; *Carbon Dioxide and Climate: A Second Assessment* (Washington, DC: National Academy Press, 1982).

18. V. Ramanathan, "The Greenhouse Theory of Climate Change: A Test by an Inadvertent Global Experiment," *Science* (15 April 1988): 293–99.

19. "Back to the Energy Crisis," *Science* (6 February 1987): 626–27; R.L. Hirsch, "Impending United States Energy Crisis," *Science* (20 March 1987): 1467–73; I.V. Borg and C.K. Briggs, *U.S. Energy Flow: 1987* (Livermore, CA: Lawrence Livermore National Laboratory, University of California, 1988).

20. E. Titterton, "Nuclear Energy: An Overview," in H.D. Sharma, ed., *Energy Alternatives: Benefits and Risks* (Waterloo, Ont.: University of Waterloo Press, 1990), 146.

21. Titterton, "Nuclear Energy."

22. *The Canadian Encyclopedia*, 1st ed., s.v. "nuclear safety."

23. "Letters: Chernobyl Public Health Effects," *Science* (2 October 1987): 10–11.

24. T.E. Bell, "Managing Risk in Large Complex Systems," IEEE *Spectrum* 26, no. 6 (June 1989): 22.

25. S.C. Florman, "Moral Blueprints," *Harper's Magazine* (October 1978). Copyright © 1978 by *Harper's Magazine*. All rights reserved. Reprinted by special permission.

26. Mucklestone, "Public Defender."

27. APEO, *Duty to Report*. Excerpt reproduced with permission.

28. APEGGA, *Manual of Professional Practice*, 38. Excerpt reproduced with permission.

29. APEO, *Duty to Report*. Excerpt reproduced with permission.

30. National Society of Professional Engineers, *Code of Ethics for Engineers* (Alexandria, VA: NSPE, 1987).

31. R.J. Baum, ed., *Ethical Problems in Engineering*, 2nd ed. (Troy, NY: Center for the Study of the Human Dimensions of Science and Technology, Rensselaer Polytechnic Institute, 1980) vol. 2: *Cases*, 88–91.

32. A. Nesmith, "A Long, Arduous March Toward Standardization," *Smithsonian Magazine* (March 1985): 176ff.

33. C.W. Beardsley, "The Hydrolevel Case: A Retrospective," *Mechanical Engineering* (June 1984): 66–73.

34. *Civil Engineering* (January 1978): 54–55.

35. R.M. Boisjoly, "Ethical Decisions: Morton Thiokol and the Space Shuttle Challenger Disaster" (Paper presented at the ASME Winter Annual Meeting, Boston, December 13–18, 1987); S. Jaeger, "Failures in Ethics Doomed Challenger, Says Engineer," *Engineering Times* (September 1987): 12.

36. J.H. Schaub and K. Pavlovic, eds., *Engineering Professionalism and Ethics* (New York: John Wiley & Sons, 1983), 350–72; Baum, *Ethical Problems in Engineering*, vol. 2, 136–54; R.L. Heilbroner et al., *In the Name of Profit* (Garden City, NY: Doubleday, 1972).

37. Baum, *Ethical Problems in Engineering*, vol. 2, 175–85; Schaub and Pavlovic, *Engineering Professionalism and Ethics*, 388–401.

38. Baum, *Ethical Problems*; Schaub and Pavlovic, *Engineering Professionalism*.

39. *The Canadian Encyclopedia*, 1st ed., s.v. "nuclear safety."

40. "Prelude: The Accident at Three Mile Island," *EPRI Journal* (June 1980): 7–13.

41. W. Booth, "Postmortem on Three Mile Island," *Science* (4 December 1987): 1342–45.

42. C. Norman, "Assessing the Effects of a Nuclear Accident," *Science* (5 April 1985): 31–33.

43. "Assessment: The Impact and Influence of TMI," *EPRI Journal* (June 1980): 25–33.

44. "Pulling the Nuclear Plug," *Time* (13 February 1984): 34–41.

45. *The Canadian Encyclopedia*, 1st ed., s.v. "nuclear power plants."

46. J.F. Ahearne, "Nuclear Power after Chernobyl," *Science* (8 May 1987): 673–79.

47. A.P. Malinauskas et al., "Calamity at Chernobyl," *Mechanical Engineering* (February 1987): 50–53. E. Marshall, "Recalculating the Cost of Chernobyl," *Science* (8 May 1987): 658–59.

48. Marshall, "Cost of Chernobyl."

49. M. Goldman, "Chernobyl: A Radiobiological Perspective," *Science* (30 October 1987): 622–23.

Product Safety

Not too many years ago, the doctrine of *caveat emptor* prevailed in seller-buyer relationships. *Caveat emptor* means "Let the buyer beware." In other words, once you bought something, you were stuck, whether the object was defective or not. Today matters have shifted so far the other way that some have said the doctrine has now become "Let the *seller* beware."

The issue that concerns us in this chapter does not have to do with whether the product does or does not function as intended. We have come to expect proper function as a matter of course: a washing machine should be capable of getting clothes clean; a refrigerator should be capable of keeping food cold. Such matters come under the doctrine of *implied warranty*, to which we will refer only briefly. Our major concern is with the doctrine of *strict liability*, which covers product defects and consumer safety.

D.L. Marston, in his text *Law for Professional Engineers*, states:

> In products liability cases in the United States, a manufacturer may be strictly liable for any damage that results from the use of his product, even though the manufacturer was not negligent in producing it. Canadian products liability law has not yet adopted this "strict liability" concept, but the law appears to be developing in that direction.[1]

This chapter deals mainly with strict liability and examples are therefore drawn entirely from American experience.

Engineers obviously have a great deal to do with product safety; the engineer's responsibility for public safety is part of every engineering code of ethics. What is not so evident is that the engineer's responsibility to the public for safety coincides with a responsibility to protect the engineer's employer. Up to the present time, legal suits involving product liability have been brought not against product designers (unless they were negligent, of course) but against manufacturers and sellers. Some of these have been enormously costly, so an action by an engineer to protect the public is at the same time an action to protect the engineer's employer from great financial loss.

It is appropriate here to look into what the courts have said in the past about product safety, to provide at least a small measure of guidance to engineers in making their design decisions. There are no absolutely reliable guidelines; the courts have not always been consistent. One court may go one way, another court a different way. A case won at the trial court level may be reversed on appeal, and the law itself is changing as years pass. The purpose of this chapter is merely to introduce some of the basic concepts of product safety and to discuss some previous legal decisions. The chapter concludes with some advice to design engineers for ensuring product safety.

WARRANTIES

Express warranties are familiar to all of us. These are the pieces of paper that come to us at the time of sale and warrant that the product will perform in such-and-such a way for such-and-such a period of time. However, express warranties need not necessarily be in writing, provided that a court can be convinced at a later time that an oral warranty indeed was made. In such cases, some reasonable allowance for "puffery" is necessary. For example, in a Florida case, the court decided that no warranty regarding the sale of a ladder had been made when the salesperson said the ladder was "strong," would "last a lifetime," and would "never break." The ladder did break, but the court said that the statements, although exaggerated, did not constitute a warranty. In contrast, in an Oklahoma case involving the sale of a used car, the court held that the salesperson's statements *did* constitute a warranty. The salesperson had said, "This is a car we know — in A-1 shape." Because the statement presumably was based upon expert knowledge, the court said it was an express warranty.[2]

An express warranty is essentially a part of the contract of sale, but an *implied warranty* exists as a matter of legal duty, whether expressly stated or not. The Uniform Commercial Code, which has been adopted by most American states, says for goods to be merchantable they must pass without objection in the trade; be of fair, average quality; be fit for the ordinary purposes for which such goods are used; be adequately packaged and labelled; and conform to the statements made on the label.[3]

Ordinarily these rules would apply to sales made by merchants, not to casual sales between individuals; but courts are variable in their interpretations. The courts have been variable also in applying the rules to the sale of used goods. For our purpose here, it is enough to know that the rules exist.

The rules can apply to containers also. In an Oklahoma case, a person was opening a box bound with steel straps. One of the straps, when cut, flew up and injured the person's eye. The court said there was no liability, because one should expect such a thing to happen when a strap is cut. In a North Carolina case, however, a bottle of carbonated beverage exploded in a customer's hand as she was carrying it to the check-out counter in a grocery store. The customer won her suit, because one would not normally expect that to happen.[4]

STRICT LIABILITY

Most people have a general idea of what is meant by the term *negligence*: a certain standard of conduct is implied, the accused party did not conform to this standard, and the failure to conform caused injury to someone. But in the case of *strict liability*, no questions of negligence arise. The American Law Institute has published the following rules regarding *strict tort liability* (a "tort" is a wrongful civil act committed by one person against another, other than a breach of contract):

> (1) One who sells any product in a defective condition unreasonably dangerous to the user or consumer or to his property is subject to liability for physical harm thereby caused to the ultimate user or consumer, or to his property, if
>> (a) the seller is engaged in the business of selling such a product, and
>> (b) it is expected to and does reach the user or consumer without substantial change in the condition in which it is sold.
>
> (2) The rule stated in Subsection (1) applies although
>> (a) the seller has exercised all possible care in the preparation and sale of his product, and
>> (b) the user or consumer has not bought the product from or entered into any contractual relation with the seller.[5]

A number of things should be noted in the above. For one thing, it applies to *sellers*. But since manufacturers are necessarily sellers, it applies to manufacturers too. Note the use of the words "defective" and "unreasonably dangerous." These are difficult words to pin down in court. What seems to one person to be a defect may not appear so to another, and people also rarely agree on whether something is "reasonable" or "unreasonable." For example, knives are dangerous, but are they unreasonably so? A car moving at a legal speed on a freeway is certainly dangerous if it hits something, but is it unreasonably dangerous?

A number of other things should be noted in the above statement of strict liability. Rule (1)(b) says that the product must reach the consumer without substantial change. ("Substantial" is another word whose meaning must often be settled in court.) Rule (2)(a) says that the degree of care used by the seller (or manufacturer) is immaterial; in other words, negligence is not a necessary factor. Rule (2)(b) says that the user who is injured does not have to be the original buyer; there may have been many intervening owners. Obviously, in this last case, the product is not expected to remain safe for an infinite number of years: Wear and tear are obviously factors in a court's determination as to whether something is "reasonably" safe.

Unreasonable Danger

Any attempt to define the word "unreasonable" merely leads to the need for more definitions. For example, the American Law Institute attempts to define "unreasonably dangerous" as "dangerous to an extent beyond that which would be contemplated by the ordinary consumer ... with the ordinary knowledge common to the community."[6]

Now we are left with the job of finding out what "ordinary" means, instead of "unreasonable." But a judge in Massachusetts left no doubt as to what he thought "unreasonable" meant in what might be called "the fish chowder case." In this case, the plaintiff ate some fish chowder, and a bone became lodged in her throat. It took two operations to remove the bone. The plaintiff brought suit and lost. The court said that consumers "should be prepared to cope with hazards of fish bones, the occasional presence of which in chowders is to be anticipated." The court added that its opinion was based in part upon its unwillingness to overturn "age-old recipes."[7]

In the fish chowder case, we got a definition of what the "unreasonable" meant, at least with regard to fish bones in chowder. The reader is left with the uncomfortable feeling, however, that a different judge, perhaps with less respect for "age-old recipes," might have reached a different decision. Nevertheless, courts do tend to show a reluctance to overturn customs that have been long established. They are not likely to rule, for example, that all knives must be equipped with cumbersome safety guards or that all automobiles must be operated at speeds less than 30 kilometres per hour, even though such rules might cause many injuries and deaths to be avoided. In some instances, courts have even balanced safety issues with economic benefits, as will be seen later.

A couple of additional cases help to show where some courts have drawn the line between reasonable and unreasonable. In a Georgia case, a child was injured while riding after dark on a bicycle that was not equipped with a headlight or reflector. The child's father attempted to collect damages from the seller of the bicycle but lost. The court ruled that the father was aware of the danger and that the seller had no duty to protect against obvious, common dangers. On the other hand, in a South Carolina case, a child was injured by lawn mower blades, and the plaintiff did collect. The court agreed that the danger was obvious, but said that the seller of the lawn mower nevertheless had a duty to improve its safety. In this case, the court was swayed by the gravity of the danger and by the relative ease with which the danger could have been reduced, either by better design or through warnings. For design engineers, it is especially important to note that the viewpoint of the courts may be undergoing a significant change — away from judging cases on the basis of what an "ordinarily prudent person" might do and toward judging on the basis of what an "occasionally careless person" might do.[8]

Concealed Dangers

Courts are likely to be especially critical when it comes to concealed dangers. In a Florida case, the manufacturer of a folding aluminum lounge chair was held liable in a case in which a person lost a finger. If the chair was not fully unfolded, and if the user sat in it and simultaneously had a finger in the danger spot, the further unfolding of the chair under pressure would neatly amputate the finger.[9] In another case, a worker became entangled with a manufacturing robot, had difficulty reaching the on/off switch, and then died of a heart attack.[10] In a somewhat more complicated case, one person died and another was severely injured by accidental overdoses of radiation from a machine used to treat cancer. The problem here was in the software. The operator initially set the machine for too high an energy level. She recognized her error and entered the instructions to reset for a lower level, but she did this so quickly that the operating system for the machine was still engaged in setting itself up for the higher level. The result was that the machine ignored a part of her input, and the patient received 2½ times as much radiation as intended.[11] There was no reason why the operator should have been aware of such a possible outcome; this was an error of the software designer.

Another case involved a tractor that had a steering wheel made of rubber and fibre. (Other manufacturers used metal or wood.) The plaintiff, in using the tractor, occasionally supported himself by the wheel while turning. On one such occasion the wheel broke, and the driver fell under the tractor and was run over. The manufacturer was held liable because tests showed that the steering wheels would break under this kind of load, and the court said the manufacturer should reasonably have expected such things to occur.[12]

A somewhat similar case involved a tractor operator who slipped on a step while dismounting, injuring his back. It was shown that the operator could not see the step in dismounting, that mud had been thrown up by the tractor treads and had collected on the step, and that the step had no anti-skid material on it. The tractor manufacturer lost. An especially powerful message for design engineers in this case is that it was revealed during the trial that the tractor manufacturer had violated its own design guidelines, which required, among other things, that steps and ladders be designed to minimize the accumulation of mud and debris and that steps be provided with anti-skid material.[13]

Obvious Dangers

For the manufacturer of a knife, there is no duty to protect against the sharp edge, because the danger is obvious. However, just because a danger is obvious does not mean that the designer is relieved of responsibility. In a California case involving an earth-moving machine, a person standing behind the machine was run over and killed. The machine had a blind spot in the rear caused by the presence of a large engine box, and there were no rear-vision mirrors that gave a view of the blind spot. The manufacturer was held liable, the court saying that, even though the danger was obvious, it was unreasonable.[14]

In an Illinois case, a seven-year-old girl playing near a lawn mower slipped and fell as it approached her. There was a 20-cm gap under the mower, and she slid into it, losing her leg. The manufacturer in this case was *not* held liable, on the grounds that no defect existed and that the danger was obvious. However, this case has been heavily criticized in subsequent decisions, because it offers too much encouragement to manufacturers to make their products attractive on the basis of a low price.[15]

The manner in which the doctrine of product liability has evolved over the years becomes apparent as one reflects on what has happened with automobiles during recent decades. As recently as the 1960s, plaintiffs often lost cases involving injury during an auto accident. The doctrine in such cases essentially said that if a user was injured in an accident, the injury occurred because of an unintended use; the intended purpose of an automobile does not include its collision with other objects. Today, however, the doctrine has moved far beyond that. Any use of an automobile creates a certain risk of accidents, and manufacturers are expected to design them in such a way as to protect occupants from aggravated harm.[16] The word "aggravated" is another one that would have to be interpreted by a court, but some of the well-known results of this new doctrine are such things as collapsing steering columns, padded interiors, fuel tanks protected from rupture, and stronger roofs to protect during rollover.

FORESEEABILITY

It sometimes seems as if the designer of a product is expected to foresee everything and to detect every manner in which a product might be used or misused. As unfair as it may seem, this is approximately the case. Lawyers and courts may be allowed to use perfect 20/20 hindsight and pass judgement on what engineers did or did not do, but engineers have no such privilege. By the very nature of their calling, they have to look ahead and be right most of the time. One student of product liability has said:

> Many engineers and designers assume their products are safe if they meet all regulations and standards and if moving parts are protected with a guard when the product leaves the factory. In fact, a review of litigation resulting from product failure shows that accidents are caused less often by mechanical failure than by the designer's failure to consider how the product would be used.[17]

An interesting case that illustrates the point of foreseeability has to do with the packaging of doors for shipment. The doors, designed to contain glass panels, were packed in bundles without the glass in them. They were surrounded by cardboard, so the bundles were essentially large cavities, covered only with thin corrugated cardboard. A worker walked across one of these bundles as it lay in a warehouse, fell through the cardboard, and injured himself. At the trial court level, the worker won. The court said the situation was dangerous and that a prudent manufacturer would have protected against the danger by warnings or otherwise. On appeal, the decision was reversed. The court said the manufacturer was not obliged to protect against the danger unless it was aware of the practice of walking on packages of doors. On appeal to the U.S. Supreme Court, however, the decision was reversed again. The Supreme Court said that the dangerous condition was foreseeable and that it could have been corrected with little effort. [18]

Another case that involved foreseeability had to do with a coal-mining machine. The machine was 9.4 m long and travelled through the mine on crawler tracks with the operator moving alongside, on hands and knees if necessary. It was typical of such a machine that, if it encountered an irregularity in the mine floor, it might suddenly swerve to one side. In one case, a machine did swerve and crushed the operator against the mine wall, killing him. In subsequent investigations, it was not possible to prove that this is precisely what caused the accident, but it became apparent that the placement of the machine's controls contributed to the death of the worker. It was also shown that, in machines made by other manufacturers, two sets of controls were provided, so that the operator could choose which set would be safer to use. [19]

Another case involved a "printer-slotter" machine. It was frequently necessary to separate the machine into two free-standing halves with a 76-cm passage between them, to gain access to the inside of the machine for changing dies. When this occurred, one half of the machine was "dead," whereas the other half continued to be supplied with power so that an automatic roller-washing operation could continue while the dies were being changed. The object, of course, was to minimize change-over time; otherwise, the machine would have to be shut down completely, lengthening the time required for change-over. During such a change-over, a worker walked between the two halves of the machine. He was carrying a rag, and the rag was caught by the moving rollers on one half of the machine. His arm was drawn into the rollers and subsequently had to be amputated. He won his court case on the grounds that the machine should have been equipped with a safety switch (an "interlock" switch) that would cut off all power to *both* halves of the machines whenever it was opened. [20]

This seems like a simple case, merely involving the provision of an interlock switch — something with which engineers frequently deal. But some legal scholars have pointed out that it is not so simple as it seems. For example, given the pay incentive scheme being used by the machine operator's employer, there was a strong desire on the part of the operator to minimize change-over time. Even if an interlock had been provided, there would have been a strong incentive for the operator to disable the switch in order to cut down on change-over time. (Machine operators are notorious for disabling safety devices that are intended for their protection.) One might dismiss the case by saying, "Well, then that's the operator's own fault," but the fact remains that injury or death may occur, and these are not easily dismissed.

Lest it seem that courts are unfairly biased against manufacturers, one more case will be cited, in which a trade-off between safety and economics governed the outcome. In this case, the court was mindful of the fact that some products, although admittedly dangerous, still provide benefits that society wants. (It is again worthwhile to mention the automobile: cars kill 40 000 people a year in the United States, but the public is unwilling to do without them.)

The case in question involved serious injury to the plaintiff by a huge earth-moving machine. The operator of the machine saw the plaintiff standing in front of the machine but could not avoid the accident because the brakes were filled with mud and he could not stop quickly enough, nor could he swerve the machine fast enough. At the trial court level, the jury found for the plaintiff, but the case was reversed on appeal. The court said the manufacturer was "not required to expend exorbitant sums of money in research to devise a sophisticated braking system which would price its product completely out of the market." As for the steering system, the court said it "was reliable and durable. It was the standard steering system used in the heavy construction industry and no better turning device available was disclosed by the evidence."[21] Lest we place too much reliance on this opinion, it should be noted that there was a strong minority dissent in the case just cited, and a different court might disagree entirely.

ADVICE TO DESIGN ENGINEERS

There are many conflicting views regarding the state of affairs in product liability. Although some feel that the whole matter has gone too far, the prevailing view is that the current system serves to compensate victims who have suffered grievous harm and discourages bad design. But those who are concerned about excesses in the system observe that lawsuits most often are brought against those who have the capacity to pay large damage awards, those with "deep pockets." These are usually large manufacturers, and it is pointed out that it is not really the manufacturers who pay, but the public. The manufacturers obviously pass these costs on to the consumers if they can. If they cannot, then it is employees and stockholders who bear the burden. If the consequences are so great as to force the company out of business, it is not only the employees and stockholders who suffer, but the public at large, in the form of lost services, lost tax revenue, and increased welfare expenditures. To repeat an old bromide: *There is no free lunch.*[22]

Some corporate executives make no bones about it: the cost is too great. A manufacturer of small aircraft has stated that the cost of liability insurance has added $75 000 to the cost of each new plane. Another has declared that the current product liability system has essentially destroyed the piston aircraft industry in the United States. In 1979, 18 000 such aircraft per year were being built in the United States; by the end of the 1980s, that number had dropped to fewer than 1000 per year.[23] In a survey of a hundred executives from "*Fortune* 500" companies, 57 percent agreed with the statement "State-of-the-art products that could help the U.S. regain its competitive footing are not going forward for fear of liability suits." One of the executives said, "The current legal system forces companies to meet unrealistically high standards of safety. Nothing less than perfection is acceptable."[24]

But the courts have the last word. Besides, no one wants to cause injury or loss to anyone if it can be avoided. From the standpoint of the individual engineer, the following might represent a reasonable course of action.

- Be aware of, *and adhere to,* your company's own design standards. In court, the most damaging thing of all could be the admission that your company did not follow its own standards.

- Be aware of, *and adhere to,* any industry design standards. Among these might be such things as Underwriters' Laboratories procedures and ASME pressure vessel codes. Even if the standards are unwritten and informal, it is important to know about them and follow them.

- Make design choices that lean toward safety. Often these come at little or no cost penalty and merely require foresight.

- If there is a severe cost penalty associated with safety, make sure the issue is thoroughly understood and resolved at the highest levels in your organization.

It is tempting to adhere to the view that an unsafe product should never be placed on the market, but one should remember that even the word "unsafe" requires amplification and definition. Imagine, for example, that you work for an automobile manufacturer, and you are aware that cars kill 40 000 or more people a year. This means that cars are probably the most dangerous things with which we commonly come in contact. As an engineer bearing a great responsibility for public safety, must you demand of your employer that your cars be built like tanks in order to be safe? Then, recognizing that your tanklike cars will probably mangle quite a few pedestrians, does it now follow that you must demand that your employer cease manufacturing cars altogether?

On this cheerful note, we end this chapter. The obligation to protect the public from needless harm still exists. So does the obligation to provide the public with useful goods and services. There are indeed some products so dangerous that they should be banned altogether, although judgement must always play a part in reaching such decisions. If the issues become large enough, lawmaking bodies will make the final judgements, as they have with certain pesticides and chemicals. In the meantime, this chapter describes the environment in which engineers must honourably pursue their profession.

TOPICS FOR STUDY AND DISCUSSION

1. Examine newspapers and magazines — especially magazines like *IEEE Spectrum* and *Mechanical Engineering* — for articles describing product failures. If these cases have not already been decided in the courts, try to predict their likely outcomes, based upon what you now know about product liability.

2. Using the information gained from topic 1 above, work out design solutions that would have been better than those actually employed and that might have avoided the subsequent troubles.

3. In his book *Unsafe at Any Speed*, Ralph Nader said engineers "subordinate whatever initiatives might flow from professional dictates in favor of preserving their passive roles as engineer-employees."[25] Write a short essay on this statement, giving your own views on whether you think this statement is justified. In preparing your essay, it might be wise to obtain a copy of Nader's book from your library so that you can see the full scope of his arguments.

4. In the discussion of negligence in this chapter, it was pointed out that conforming to a standard of conduct is a critical issue. In establishing in court just what a particular standard might consist of, evidence regarding customary practices is often introduced. Think of some cases in which customary practices might not be acceptable to a court. (One

example: On almost every street and highway in North America, it is customary for a large fraction — maybe even a majority — of the motorists to exceed the speed limit. If you had an accident and were speeding at the time, do you believe a court would accept your argument that your speeding should not be a factor because it is "customary"?)

5. In one of the landmark cases establishing strict product liability, a combination power tool was being used as a lathe. A piece of wood being held in the lathe by set-screws came loose, flew up, and hit the operator in the head, inflicting serious injuries. Other product-liability cases have also involved set-screws that did not do their jobs. Examine the issue of employing set-screws as hold-down devices. (Some engineers believe that set-screws should never be used under any circumstances.) See if you can come up with some ideas for hold-down devices that would be safer and more reliable than set-screws but would not be excessively costly.

6. A case once occurred in which the plaintiff's shoes slipped on a wet laundromat floor, causing injury. The plaintiff brought suit against the seller of the shoes, alleging that they were dangerously inclined to slip. The plaintiff did not win this case, because it was shown that the shoes were no more slippery than any others and thus were not defective. Suppose you are a judge, and a case comes before you in which the shoes *are* more slippery than most. As the judge, what would you do? Since you are a good judge, you worry about how your ruling might stand up under further appeal, and you also worry about how any "slipperiness standard" you establish might be used for future guidance of shoe manufacturers. Since you know that some kinds of shoes are *supposed* to be slippery, such as dancing shoes, what would you do about all this?[26]

NOTES

1. D.L. Marston, *Law for Professional Engineers*, 2nd ed. (Toronto: McGraw-Hill Ryerson, 1985), 36.

2. D.W. Noel and J.J. Philips, *Products Liability*, 1st ed. (St. Paul, MN: West Publishing, 1974).

3. Noel and Philips, *Products Liability*, 1st ed., 16.

4. Noel and Philips, *Products Liability*, 1st ed., 19.

5. D.W. Noel and J.J. Philips, *Products Liability*, 2nd ed. (St. Paul, MN: West Publishing, 1981).

6. Noel and Philips, *Products Liability,* 1st ed., 116.

7. Noel and Philips, *Products Liability,* 1st ed., 116.

8. Noel and Philips, *Products Liability,* 1st ed., 121–22.

9. Matthews v. Lawnlite Co., 88 So. 2d 299 (Fla. S.C., 1956).

10. J.A. Horst, "Difficult Decisions for Engineering," IEEE *Potentials* (October 1986): 42–45.

11. "Faults and Failures," IEEE *Spectrum* (December 1987): 16.

12. Noel and Philips, *Products Liability,* 1st ed., 142.

13. Noel and Philips, *Products Liability,* 2nd ed., 138.

14. Noel and Philips, *Products Liability,* 1st ed., 149.

15. Noel and Philips, *Products Liability,* 1st ed., 151–52.

16. Noel and Philips, *Products Liability,* 1st ed., 155–57.

17. S. Gibson-Harris, "Looking for Trouble," *Mechanical Engineering* (June 1987): 36–38.

18. Noel and Philips, *Products Liability,* 1st ed., 169–71.

19. Gibson-Harris, "Looking for Trouble."

20. A.S. Weinstein et al., "Product Liability: An Interaction of Law and Technology," *Duquesne Law Review* 12, no. 3 (Spring 1974): 434–38.

21. Noel and Philips, *Products Liability,* 2nd ed., 150–51.

22. Weinstein et al., "Product Liability," 485.

23. P.H. Abelson, "Product Liability in a Litigious Society," *Science* (17 June 1988): 1589.

24. "Litigation Is Stifling Innovation," *Management Review* (June 1988): 8.

25. R.A. Nader, *Unsafe at Any Speed,* rev. ed. (New York: Bantam, 1973), 161.

26. Noel and Philips, *Products Liability,* 1st ed., 120–21.

CHAPTER 12

Disciplinary Powers and Procedures

The principal purpose of each provincial and territorial Association of Professional Engineers is to protect the public welfare by regulating the practice of professional engineering. To do so, each Association has been delegated the powers to prosecute persons who unlawfully practise professional engineering, and to discipline licensed engineers who are guilty of professional misconduct or incompetence.

The methods of dealing with these two types of infraction are completely different.

Prosecution for Unlawful Practice

A person who is not a member or licensee of a provincial or territorial Association but who nevertheless:

- practises professional engineering,

- uses the title "Professional Engineer,"

- uses a term or title to give the belief that the person is licensed, or

- uses a seal that leads to the belief that the person is licensed,

is guilty of an offence under the Act. The procedure for prosecution and the penalties vary slightly, depending on the territory or province. Each Association must initiate the action to prosecute offenders in the appropriate court, under the authority of the Act, and the judge of the court assesses the penalty, typically a fine proportional to the seriousness of the infraction. Professional engineers generally would not be involved in these proceedings, except perhaps as witnesses.

Discipline for Professional Misconduct

In the case of licensed members, disciplinary action for professional misconduct or incompetence is conducted within the Association by a discipline committee formed of members of the governing council and other professional engineers. Under the authority of the provincial Act, the committee has the power to discipline the member in several ways.

DEFINITION OF PROFESSIONAL MISCONDUCT

The various professional engineering Acts have slightly different definitions of what constitutes grounds for disciplinary action. These definitions are reproduced in Appendix A, which includes excerpts from all the provincial and territorial statutes. Although not identical, the definitions are very similar. In British Columbia, for example, "negligence, incompetence or unprofessional conduct" is grounds for disciplinary action.[1] In Ontario, the Act defines "professional misconduct" and "incompetence" as the basis for disciplinary action, although the regulations expand "misconduct" to include negligence.[2]

Typically, the provincial Acts identify six causes for disciplinary action: professional misconduct (or unprofessional conduct), incompetence, negligence, breaches of the code of ethics, physical or mental incapacity, and conviction of a serious offence. Each of these terms is discussed briefly in the following paragraphs.

Professional Misconduct

Professional misconduct (or unprofessional conduct, as it is called in some Acts) is the main source of complaints to provincial Associations. In about half of the Acts, the term is not defined, thus placing an additional burden of proof on the Association's legal counsel in any formal hearing, since alleged misconduct must be proven both to have been committed and to constitute professional misconduct.

However, Alberta, Newfoundland, and Prince Edward Island have much more general definitions. For example, the Alberta Act defines "any conduct ... detrimental to the best interests of the public" or that "harms or tends to harm the standing of the profession generally" as unprofessional conduct. While such clauses will stand the test of time because of their generality, they are not useful guides for individual conduct, and the codes of ethics must be consulted for more specific guidance.

At the other extreme, the definition of professional misconduct in Ontario (Regulation 538/84) includes some very specific acts, such as "signing or sealing a final drawing ... not actually prepared or checked by the practitioner."[3] The Ontario regulation is the most comprehensive definition of professional misconduct and may be of interest to readers, whether they live in Ontario or elsewhere (see Appendix A).

Incompetence

Incompetence is defined in several Acts as "a lack of knowledge, skill or judgement or disregard for the welfare of the public of a nature or to an extent that demonstrates the member ... is unfit to carry out the responsibilities of a professional engineer." This definition should be extended slightly. Depending on the Act, "undertaking work that the engineer is not competent to perform" may be considered either incompetence or professional misconduct. This rather subtle distinction covers the all-too-common occurrence of an engineer practising outside the area of his or her expertise, even though the engineer may be fully competent in his or her major area of practice.

Negligence

In most Acts, negligence means carelessness, or carrying out work that is below the accepted standard of care or performance. In many instances, it would mean the *omission* of an activity needed to ensure the proper care or safeguarding of life, health, and property. In fact, the omission of care or insufficient thoroughness in the performance of duties would probably be the most common complaint under this heading.

Breaches of the Code of Ethics

In four provinces (Alberta, New Brunswick, Newfoundland, and Nova Scotia) a breach of the code of ethics is specifically defined in the Act to be equivalent to professional misconduct. These codes therefore have the full force of the Act, in each case. In other provinces (British Columbia, Manitoba, Prince Edward Island, Quebec, and Saskatchewan) and the territories, where the term "professional misconduct" is undefined or defined in very general terms, it would be understood to include the code of ethics also, thus giving the code enforceability under the respective Act.

In Ontario, the code of ethics is not clearly enforceable under the Act. However, there is an extensive definition of professional misconduct in the regulations that contains most of the code of ethics, such as "failure to correct or report a situation that may endanger the safety or welfare of the public," failure to disclose a conflict of interest, and about sixteen additional clauses (see Appendix A). In other words, the definition of professional misconduct states in a *negative* way what the code of ethics states in a *positive* way. Therefore most of the Ontario code of ethics is also enforceable under the Act.

Physical or Mental Incapacity

Most Acts also include a "physical or mental condition" as a definition of incompetence, providing it is "of a nature and extent making it desirable in the interests of the public or the member ... that the member no longer be permitted to engage in the practice of professional engineering."

Conviction of an Offence

The provincial Acts also permit disciplinary action against a member who is guilty of an offence that is "relevant to suitability to practise." In other words, if a member should be found guilty of an offence under any other act, and the nature or circumstances of the offence affect the person's suitability to practise as a professional engineer, then the person can be found guilty of professional misconduct when proof of the conviction is provided to the discipline committee. This clause is used relatively rarely, since convictions for minor offences (traffic violations, local ordinance violations, and the like) do not affect one's suitability to practise engineering. However, convictions of serious offences such as fraud or embezzlement, which involve a betrayal of trust and questionable ethics, could be grounds for declaring a member to be unsuitable. This condition clearly imposes a standard of conduct upon professional engineers that is higher than that expected from the average member of the public.

THE DISCIPLINARY PROCESS

Disciplinary procedures are unpleasant; therefore they must be fair and they must be *seen* to be fair. When a complaint of negligence, incompetence, or professional misconduct is made against a licensed professional engineer, it sets in motion a three-stage process of gathering information, evaluating the complaint, and conducting a formal hearing that renders a judgement.

To ensure complete impartiality, the three stages of the disciplinary process are carried out by three different groups of people. No one who participates at an earlier stage is permitted to participate in the final hearing and judgement. The first stage is generally conducted by the Association staff. The second stage is conducted by a complaints committee or investigations committee (depending on the province) composed of members of the Association's governing council and other licensed engineers. The third stage is conducted by a discipline committee, which is composed of members of the governing council and persons who have not previously been involved with the case.

A description of the process as it is carried out in Ontario was recently published in *Engineering Dimensions* and is reprinted below. The procedure in other provinces and territories is very similar, although not precisely identical.

Any member of the public can make a complaint against a licensed engineer, although most complaints are brought by building officials, government inspectors or other engineers. Here's what happens:

Stage 1

- The complainant notifies the Association. A member of the Registrar's staff discusses the complaint, advising the complainant on the kind of evidence which will be necessary. Staff also assist on the wording of the complaint in relation to the Professional Engineers Act.
- Association staff do a preliminary investigation, hiring an expert witness if necessary.
- The complaint is reviewed by the Registrar, signed, and sent to the engineer in question, who has a period of time for response.
- The complainant is given the opportunity for rebuttal.

Stage 2

- All of this material is presented in confidence to the Complaints Committee, which may:
    1. refer the complaint in whole or in part to the Discipline Committee;
    2. not refer the complaint;
    3. send a letter of advice to the engineer without referring the case to the Discipline Committee;
    4. take such action as it considers appropriate under the circumstances; or
    5. direct staff to obtain more information.
  Reasons are given for whichever decision is taken.
- If the complainant is dissatisfied with the way a complaint has been handled, it can be reviewed by the Complaints Review Councillor, who reviews procedures only.

Stage 3

- If the case is referred to the Discipline Committee, a written notice of hearing is prepared by the Association's lawyer and served on the accused engineer, who usually hires legal counsel. A hearing date is set. A disclosure meeting is held between the respective lawyers, in which the Association makes its case known to the engineer's legal counsel.
- The hearing follows court procedure, with a court reporter present. The defendant can be represented by legal counsel. The Discipline Committee consists of five members, including a Lieutenant Governor-in-Council appointee. A written decision is given, with a copy to the complainant.
- Appeals are made through the civil courts.[4]

DISCIPLINARY POWERS

The penalties that can be meted out by the discipline committee are fairly general, including the payment of fines and costs but not, of course, imprisonment. The severity of the penalty would vary with the circumstances of the case. The disciplinary powers awarded under each provincial and territorial Act are listed in Appendix A. If a member or licensee should be found guilty, the discipline committee can:

- revoke the licence of the member;

- suspend the licence (usually for a period up to two years);

- impose restrictions on the licence, such as supervision or inspection of work;

- require the member to be reprimanded, admonished, or counselled and publish the details of the result, with or without names;

- require the member to pay the costs of the investigation and hearing;

- require the member to undertake a course of study or write examinations set by the Association; or

- impose a fine (up to $10 000 in Alberta; up to $5000 in Ontario; only hearing costs in Yukon).

The committee must publish the case, with names, if the decision involves suspension or revocation of a member's licence. In other situations, publishing details of the case is an option the discipline committee may choose to exercise.

In the above discussion and throughout this text, the terms "licensee" and "member" have been used interchangeably. The usage varies from province to province (to territory) across Canada. The disciplinary actions described in this chapter also apply to those practising with limited licences, temporary licences, and certificates of authorization, to permit holders, and to those designated as consulting engineers. That is, these forms of authorization may be revoked or suspended in the same manner as a member's licence.

▼ ▼ ▼

HISTORICAL STUDY 12.1—SUMMARY OF A DISCIPLINARY HEARING

This is a typical report of a disciplinary hearing conducted in Ontario. The report was published in the *Gazette*, the official publication of the Association of Professional Engineers of Ontario. Since the hearing resulted in an admonishment (a fairly light penalty) the engineer is not named.

Decision and Reasons Therefor

The Discipline Committee of the Association met in the offices of the Association to hear allegations of professional misconduct against a member (the engineer).

The Association was represented by legal counsel. The engineer represented himself.

The allegations of professional misconduct are set out in Appendix "A" of the Notice of Hearing filed as an exhibit and relate to the engineer's involvement as a structural engineer employed by a steel fabricator who was retained by a development company to provide the structural steel frame and roof joists for a 50 000-square-foot building located at a retail mall in Ontario. It was alleged that joist details and calculations bearing the engineer's seal were inaccurate, incomplete and failed to reflect acceptable engineering practice in that they failed to indicate appropriate member sizes for open web joists. The joist shop drawings bearing the engineer's seal, when analyzed, disclosed that there would be overstress in tension and compression in both top and bottom chords. His design assumption for obtaining the necessary composite action between the mezzanine floor joists and the concrete floor slab was incorrect. Additionally, the engineer certified that the structural steel for the shopping centre would support the load shown on the structural drawings notwithstanding the fact that no design brief had been prepared. Therefore, in making such a statement in the absence of a design brief, it was alleged that this constituted a failure to meet acceptable structural engineering design practice.

From the evidence given by two members of the local building department, the consulting structural engineer on the project and the engineer himself, the following scenario emerged.

1. In November of 1987 shop drawings prepared by the steel fabricator for the steel frame and roof joists were forwarded to the structural engineer for the project who rejected them as they were not stamped by a professional engineer. Despite further requests from the structural engineer, satisfactory shop drawings were not forthcoming, even though it appears that construction continued. After a site inspection report was forwarded to the owners in April 1988 by an engineering inspection company, a site meeting was held between the structural engineer, local building officials and the engineer. The structural engineer reiterated that he could not certify the project without stamped shop drawings and calculations being made available. This resulted in a letter addressed to the municipality from the steel fabricator signed and sealed by the engineer certifying in part that: "The structural steel (columns, beams, open web steel joists and connections) as supplied is capable of supporting the loads specified by the structural engineer on his drawing S9 dated August 1987."

   The structural engineer was not satisfied with this and again demanded stamped shop drawings. After the May meeting, the building department placed an Order to Comply on the project as it had discovered among other things, that the fabricating company was not certified as an erector nor was it certified by The Canadian Welding Bureau. The engineer was then directly engaged by the owners to prepare shop drawings as required and he stamped joist details and calculations on June 3, and 10, 1988 and submitted them to the structural engineer. These calculations were found to be in error. Remedial work was eventually designed by an independent professional engineer and carried out by a certified steel fabricator.

2. A consulting structural engineer gave expert testimony on behalf of the Association. He indicated that he had reviewed the engineer's calculations and drawings and in his view they contained errors, the most serious of which were, an analysis of four joists selected as typical samples disclosed, overstressing as follows: two bottom chords — 21% & 33%, three top chords — 14% to 20%, three web members in tension — 12% to 16%, nine web members in compression — 21% to 87%; a discrepancy in chord angle between the calculations and the shop drawings which resulted in a 12% overstress, and a failure to indicate properly the appropriate member sizes for open web steel joists.

3. With respect to the engineer's attempt to design the mezzanine floor joists to act compositively with the concrete floor slab, the APEO's engineering expert's view was that the design assumptions were incorrect in that the floor and joist cannot work together, therefore it was not acceptable. Further, one of the joists on the low roof was located in an area of significant snow accumulation, but the joist details did not indicate that snow accumulation was taken into account in the design.

The engineer gave evidence on his own behalf with respect to this project and two major items arose as a result of this.

- It was clear that this was a very difficult project and problems were encountered from day one. It is also clear that the engineer was not the only professional engineer involved in the project; however, he was the one who, by applying his stamp, assumed responsibility for the work.

- He did not produce any evidence which contradicted any of that given by the APEO's engineering expert.

After reviewing the evidence and exhibits and hearing arguments, the Committee found the engineer guilty of:

Section 86(2)(a) — Negligence in that he failed to maintain the standards that a reasonable and prudent practitioner would maintain in the circumstances in that he was carrying out work which he was not experienced enough to do. Testimony clearly indicated that the engineer lacked the qualifications and experience for the work he undertook on this project.

Section 86(2)(b) — Failure to make reasonable provision for safeguarding life, health or property of a person who may be affected by the work, in that this was a public place, an intended retail grocery store, the roof truss was under designed and expert testimony indicated that this could have resulted in a failure under design load.

Section 86(2)(d) — Failed to make responsible provision for complying with applicable statutes, regulations, codes, standards, by-laws and rules in connection with the work being undertaken, in that he failed to meet Building Code requirements and misread the composite standard steel deck manual produced by The Canadian Sheet Steel Building Institute.

Section 86(2)(j) — Conduct or an act relevant to the practice of professional engineering that, having regard to all the circumstances, would reasonably be regarded by the engineering profession as unprofessional. It is clear from the engineer's testimony that this matter was not handled professionally and he admitted that he was guilty of poor judgment in this matter. The Committee was not of the view that his conduct was disgraceful or dishonourable.

Turning to the matter of penalty, the Committee took into consideration the fact that the engineer admitted to errors in judgment and reasonably cooperated with the Association throughout this matter.

It noted that the engineer was only one professional engineer on a project which employed many other professional engineers and it is clear that he was not the only one involved in the problems which arose. On the other hand, it was clear to the Committee that the engineer was not competent to perform this work by virtue of his training and experience. Therefore the Committee felt that an effort should be made to educate the engineer as to his responsibilities from both the professional and the technical points of view.

By virtue of the power vested in it by Section 29 of the Professional Engineers Act, the Committee directs:

1. That the engineer be counselled as to his professional responsibilities by the chairman of the Discipline Committee, such counselling not to be recorded on the Register.

2. That the engineer sit and pass the Association's Professional Practice Examination and the Association's Examination CIV-B2 Advanced Structural Design, to be written at his own expense.

3. That the engineer provide a written undertaking to the Registrar of the APEO that he will not offer and provide engineering services to the public until such time as he successfully completes the above examinations.

4. The written Decision and Reasons of the Committee will be published in the official journal of the Association without names.

5. In the event that the engineer does not provide the above written undertaking within 30 days of the written decision of this Committee being handed down, then his Certificate of Authorization will be revoked, and the written decision and reasons of the Committee will be published in the official journal of the Association in full, with names.

6. There will be no order as to costs.

Dated at Toronto this 27th day of April, 1990.[5]

The engineer in question was served with the written decision and decided not to appeal. He provided the undertaking to the registrar and passed the technical examination in the spring of 1991, and his licence has been cleared.

TOPICS FOR STUDY AND DISCUSSION

1. Using Appendix A, compare the definitions of professional misconduct, negligence, and incompetence that form the basis for disciplinary action under each provincial or territorial Act. Which province or territory has the most specific definitions? Which has the most general definitions? Would you say that the Acts are generally in agreement on the definitions, or can you see serious inconsistencies between them?

2. Would an infraction of the code of ethics in your province or territory be clearly enforceable under your provincial Act? Should all codes always be fully enforceable, or should they be purely voluntary codes of personal behaviour? Regardless of your answer, check your provincial Act to see if it agrees with your viewpoint.

3. Using Appendix A, compare the disciplinary powers awarded under each provincial and territorial Act. Which Act provides the most severe

fines and penalties? Would you say that the Acts are generally in agreement, or are there serious inconsistencies between them?

4. Suppose, in your employment as an engineer, you discover that some of your engineering colleagues have been involved in kickback schemes with suppliers, which are in violation of the criminal law. What clause(s) in your provincial code of ethics have been broken by your colleagues? To what types of disciplinary action have they exposed themselves as a result? Suppose that you confront them and they promise that they will discontinue the kickback schemes, if you agree not to reveal them. Would this action be consistent with your provincial code of ethics? What disciplinary action (if any) could be brought against you, if you agreed?

NOTES

1. Engineers and Geoscientists Act, *Revised Statutes of British Columbia* 1979, c. 109, as amended August 1990.

2. Professional Engineers Act, 1984, *Statutes of Ontario* 1984, c. 13, as amended.

3. Ontario Regulation 538/84, s. 88, made under the Professional Engineers Act, 1984, *Statutes of Ontario* 1984, c. 13, as amended.

4. "Making a Complaint to APEO," *Engineering Dimensions* 2, no. 5 (September/October 1990): 46. Reproduced with permission.

5. "Decisions and Reasons Therefor of APEO Discipline Committee," *Gazette* (Association of Professional Engineers of Ontario) 10, no. 4 (July/August 1990): 1–2. Reproduced with permission.

Maintaining Engineering Competence

Keeping abreast of new technical methods and equipment is a serious problem for practising engineers, and with each new generation of computers, the rate of change seems to accelerate. Moreover, each engineer's interests and career aspirations are unique, and the needs for continuing education are similarly unique. The information required by practising engineers to keep current, therefore, differs widely depending on the discipline, is becoming more specialized as time passes, and could be limitless.

An intensive 1985 study of continuing education resulted in two important conclusions. First, engineers can work productively over a longer period if they have access to effective continuing education. Although business cycles can affect the demand for engineering work, engineers should always be considered a national resource. As such, they must be given the opportunity for continuing education, regardless of business cycles, if they are to remain on the frontiers of their profession.

Second, continuing education of engineers is essential to increasing national productivity. Technology is changing and interdisciplinary approaches to engineering are becoming more and more common. Thus, new concepts in science and mathematics must be regularly introduced to engineers. In addition, engineers continually need to develop non-technical skills that were not imparted by their formal training.[1]

Requirements for competence are embedded in some of the provincial and territorial Acts that regulate the engineering profession in Canada. When a licence is renewed, the implication is that the engineer's competence continues to be adequate. Although no provincial Association of Professional Engineers measures continuing competence, the issue has been discussed within the Association councils, and some requirement to show continuing competence may evolve in future years.

Maintaining engineering competence through some form of continuing study or experience is an important topic and likely to become more so. It is essential for individual engineers to seek methods for maintaining competence that are compatible with their individual needs and career aspirations. This chapter reviews the roles of the universities and engineering societies in providing continuing education. The purpose of engineering societies and the wide range of societies in existence are described in more detail in Chapter 14.

REQUIREMENTS OF RECENT ENGINEERING GRADUATES

Soon after graduation the feeling usually begins to grow in engineers that their education was lacking in certain respects. A Purdue University study shows that the perceived gap in education can be categorized by age groups.

- Those who have been out 5 years or less wish they had taken more courses of a practical nature.

- Those who have been out 5 to 15 years wish they had taken more mathematics and science.

- Those who have been out between 15 and 25 years wish they had taken more courses in business and management.

- Those who have been out more than 25 years wish they had taken more humanities and fine arts.[2]

The inference is obvious: a person's needs change throughout one's lifetime, and a four-year education completed between the ages of 18 and 22 cannot do everything for the entire 40-year period of a person's career. As a consequence, a strong demand exists for continuing education for engineers. Part of the demand stems from the rapid changes in technology, a factor that has led to the popular but inaccurate cliché that "the half-life of an engineering education is ten years." The implication is that half of what an engineer learns in school today will be obsolete in ten years. This is nonsense, provided that one's education emphasized *fundamentals*. Fundamentals do not decay at that rate, although other things may. One's own ability decays, unless kept alive by exercise; the demand for a special skill may decay; the level of competence for the entire profession may move upward, and this may cause a given individual to experience relative "decay" if nothing is done to keep up. In addition, a great deal of new scientific knowledge is continually being generated. The job of keeping up is a never-ending one, and engineers are coming more and more to accept the idea that a major portion of their time — throughout their entire careers — will be engaged in learning.

REQUIREMENTS OF OLDER ENGINEERS

Technical obsolescence is especially worrisome for older engineers. As long as the engineering profession was expanding rapidly, it tended to be made up of relatively young people, and the problem of obsolescence with age could be swept under the rug. But as the growth of the profession slowed, the age of the average engineer began to rise and the problem of obsolescence became more obvious. Research and development laboratories were especially worried. One extensive study of policies in seventeen such organizations showed that there was a general fear that organizational productivity would decline as the average age of their technical staff increased. All of them had become accustomed to perpetual growth, which automatically ensured that their staffs remained young. None of them seemed prepared to face steady state, with its implications of "corrective" layoffs in order to make way for younger people. University faculties faced identical problems. The only acceptable alternatives in view seemed to be financial encouragement toward early retirement or continuing education.[3]

However, there is little hard evidence that productivity truly does decline with age, even though the conventional folklore asserts that it does. In the study of R&D organizations just cited, some evidence emerged that scientific productivity may actually increase after age 50, although the productivity may be pulling together the ideas of one's lifework rather than major new ideas. The same study implied that engineers might actually improve with age if the work depended on experience and judgement and not so much on creativeness.

However, in another study, the investigators found definite evidence of declining performance with age, based upon evaluation of engineers by their managers. An especially significant finding in this study was that engineers with advanced degrees were considered productive for up to ten years longer than those with bachelor's degrees. Hence, the investigators made the recommendation that mid-career graduate work intensive enough to result in a degree might effectively prolong an engineer's productive life. To accomplish such a result would require company co-operation by means of released time to attend classes, participation in live TV educational systems designed to bring graduate courses in-house, or provision of sabbatical leaves for self-renewal.[4] Even though such programs would cost money, the engineer's employers would likely lose even more if their technical personnel were not kept productive.

The big advantage of a live TV course, such as those given by some technical societies and some universities, is that working engineers can walk a short distance to a classroom at their place of work, take a class, and be back at work immediately afterward. No time is lost in commuting to a university campus, yet the working engineer participates in a live classroom experience with full-time graduate students who are simultaneously sitting in a classroom on campus. In some systems, the engineer at the remote location can even ask questions during class by means of microwave links or leased telephone lines. Such systems have been very successful at many locations in Canada and the United States.[5]

SOURCES OF CONTINUING EDUCATION

There are three general categories of continuing education for engineers:

- specific and detailed courses on performing certain professional functions, for instance, computer-aided design and analysis

- courses in new technology, so that one can cope with a declining demand for current skills by learning some new ones

- general upgrading courses, which bring a person to a higher technical level

Engineers who take courses in the first two categories generally do so because of specific needs in their jobs, so they are not usually concerned about receiving graduate credit. Frequently, courses of this type are given in-house by employers; some may be given in the popular short-course format by universities, technical societies, and some industries. (In a short course, an overview of a subject, presented by leading authorities in the field, is packed into a course that runs full-time for a week or two weeks.) Those who pursue general upgrading courses usually expect their studies to lead to an advanced degree.

To satisfy the growing need for continuing education, the universities and engineering societies are responding.

The Role of the Universities

The engineering faculties of our universities have begun to offer more evening, part-time, and short courses to satisfy this need, and enrolment in postgraduate courses and in related courses presented by the universities is high; these courses are an excellent form of continuing education, discussed in more detail later in this chapter. However, this is not the only route, and it is not the preferred route for most practising engineers.

The Role of Engineering Societies

Alternative and growing sources of continuing education are the engineering societies, which, because of their specialized interests, are well equipped to keep practising engineers informed on specialized topics. Most of the technical societies exist, in fact, solely for the purpose of providing their members with regular publications, conferences, seminars, and courses, some of which are now being distributed through videocassettes and satellite television. It is this route that we must encourage for the vast majority of engineers. The engineering societies are, in the main, organized by discipline, highly specialized, and oriented toward obtaining useful results. See Chapter 14 for an extensive discussion of engineering societies.

THE TREND TOWARD GRADUATE STUDY

Historically, the length of higher education for the practising professional engineer has been four years in an undergraduate program. This is in sharp contrast with education in most of the other professions, such as medicine and law, where professional education usually begins *after* a bachelor's degree has been granted.

In the past, graduate education in engineering usually meant that one was preparing for a career in research or teaching. Full preparation for research or teaching meant going all the way to the doctorate, and the master's degree was merely a step in that direction.

However, this attitude has changed in recent years, and a master's degree is now recognized as a valuable professional qualification. For example, the U.S. report *Engineering Graduate Education and Research* made this statement in 1985:

> The master's degree in some branches of the engineering profession has assumed the role of a "capstone" degree — the highest educational level to be sought, with no intention of proceeding to a higher degree. This produces a situation quite

different from that prevailing in most fields of science, where full professional recognition by other scientists is usually accorded only to those with doctor's degrees.[6]

There have been many initiatives, in Canada and the United States, to make the master's degree the basic educational requirement for entry into the profession or, alternatively, to extend the bachelor's degree program into a five-year academic program (after university admission level). The reasons for proposing this increase are understandable; the computer concepts that now permeate every engineering course were virtually non-existent 25 or 30 years ago but must be included in the curriculum. University faculty are constantly faced with the dilemma of deleting courses and concepts that were considered essential, fundamental knowledge only a few years ago, to make room in the curriculum for new theories and methods, such as computer design, solid-state physics, and a burgeoning list of computer applications in every discipline.

Nevertheless, in spite of this constant problem of cramming new ideas into an already overburdened curriculum, it is extremely unlikely that a five-year requirement will ever be imposed. The reasons are matters of simple logistics. First, a large proportion of engineering graduates — some surveys say as many as 30 or 40 percent — go not into the areas of research, design, and development but into fields like manufacturing, sales engineering, operations, and contracting. For them, the bachelor-level engineering degree already provides an ideal background. Second, many engineering universities have recently adopted co-operative work/ study programs, which require engineering students to spend several (usually six) four-month "work terms" in industry. This work requirement already spreads the four-year program over a five-year timespan. Any move to further lengthen these programs would probably be resisted.

Furthermore, many employers fear that five-year bachelor's graduates would be more specialized than four-year graduates, and they find that the four-year graduates are just fine for their needs. Moreover, employers are not likely to pay more for five-year bachelor's graduates than for four-year graduates. Hence, students are likely to avoid the longer programs. If they select a five-year program, they probably want to be rewarded with a master's degree, not a bachelor's degree.

Given these objections, many people — both from industry and from education — have concluded that the best resolution to the problem may be the one we now have. Some 30 to 50 percent of current bachelor's graduates can gain entrance to graduate school if they want to. They are the ones most likely to profit from the greater mathematical rigour that is typical of graduate school, and if they sense the need for graduate work, they will seek it out. For industry at large, the broadly based, less specialized work that is typical of the undergraduate curriculum is ideal for many of their needs, and students who do not want and do not need graduate school will not be unnecessarily forced to go there.

Therefore, although pressure exists to lengthen the undergraduate program or to make the master's degree the basic educational requirement for licensing, this is unlikely to occur (at least in the near future). However, the need for further education exists, particularly for engineers planning to specialize in innovative design or research, and graduate study is an option that should be considered.

ADMISSION TO GRADUATE STUDY

Engineers who are thinking about graduate study should examine the annual university calendars or catalogues. Calendars are available in most public libraries, and copies may be obtained (usually free) by writing directly to the university. Admission requirements are clearly specified in the calendar. It is sometimes possible to make minor adjustments in the requirements for applicants who qualify as mature students, since they are usually more determined and more effective in their graduate studies.

Typical Admission Requirements

The requirements for admission to graduate study vary slightly from university to university. Moreover, admission requirements may be slightly different for master's programs that require a thesis (a "research" master's) and for those that require mainly courses (a "coursework" master's). Doctoral applicants usually must be familiar with research at the master's level in their area of study. It is important to become familiar with the research in progress at the university and to make personal contact with the professors in your area of interest.

To qualify for admission to study leading to a master's degree, an engineer from a Canadian accredited undergraduate program must usually have ranked in the upper half of the undergraduate class (B average or better). A master's degree usually requires a minimum of one academic year, although a year and a half or even two years may be required if the student must make up any deficiencies, or if the research project is particularly challenging or time-consuming.

Candidates for doctoral degrees must usually have ranked in the upper quarter of their undergraduate classes, and probably in the upper 5 or 10 percent. A minimum of three years beyond the bachelor's degree (or two years beyond the master's degree) is required for a doctoral degree, although the actual time is typically about a year longer than the minimum. One of the reasons for the longer time is that doctoral candidates usually work part-time as teaching assistants or research assistants. The usual engineering doctoral degree is the doctor of philosophy (PhD).

Some schools require a thesis for the master's degree, and some require courses in the place of the master's thesis, but for a doctoral degree a thesis is universally required. Since all doctoral candidates must write a thesis, admission preference is usually given to applicants who have completed a thesis at the master's level. The doctoral thesis is expected to represent an original contribution to the literature, but the master's thesis more generally is expected to represent "a contribution to the training of the candidate, rather than a contribution to knowledge."[7]

Although it is possible to be admitted directly into the doctoral program from the bachelor's degree in Canada, this is not common. The master's degree is usually required, although occasionally students who begin a master's degree and show exceptional ability are permitted to transfer to the doctoral program, thus achieving the same result.

Benefits and Sacrifices

Persons with graduate degrees start at higher salaries than do those with bachelor's degrees, of course. However, graduate school delays the time when those higher earnings begin. It may take five to ten years or more before the higher earnings make up for the lost earnings of the time spent in graduate school. In the long run, the higher degrees do pay off, although this will vary from discipline to discipline.

The greatest sacrifice is in the early years, when family time is limited and major financial purchases must be delayed; the greatest benefit is that one's professional life may be considerably extended, so that the high salaries will continue for many years longer than might otherwise be possible.

TOPICS FOR STUDY AND DISCUSSION

1. Sooner or later most engineers consider graduate school. For your own personal situation, write down the pros and cons of getting a graduate

degree. Consider such matters as full-time or part-time study and the effects that either of these might have on your earnings, both present and future, your family life, your career satisfaction, and any other factors that you feel are relevant. Prepare a summary on a single sheet, with advantages on the left side of the page and disadvantages on the right side. Does the summary show that you are following the proper path concerning graduate studies? If not, what action should you take?

2. Using the university catalogues in a local library, prepare a comparison of the graduate programs at three or four engineering universities of your choice. Prepare a summary of the comparison in chart form and rate the programs (and the universities) on at least six or eight characteristics, such as type of research in progress, graduate courses provided, size of laboratories, number of books in the library, number of students in graduate and postgraduate programs, tuition fees, etc. Using your results, rank the universities in terms of attractiveness to you as a potential postgraduate engineering student.

3. Many engineering graduates think about working toward the MBA (master of business administration) degree. Based on what you know about management and about the engineering profession, evaluate whether an MBA would be an appropriate degree for you. Whichever way you decide on this issue, write down your reasons for your conclusions.

4. As in topic 2 above, prepare a comparison of MBA programs, and rank the universities in terms of attractiveness to you as a potential MBA student.

5. If you are a recent university graduate, write an evaluation of your own engineering education. Did the program prepare you properly for work as an engineer? Was it adequate, better than average, or deficient in practical engineering subjects, mathematics, engineering science, management methods, and humanities? Prepare the evaluation in a brief letter and mail it to the chairperson of your former university department. Put a copy of the letter in a safe place and review it in five or ten years' time to see if your opinion has changed.

NOTES

1. *Continuing Education of Engineers* (M.A. Steinburg, Chairman) (Washington, DC: National Academy Press, 1985).

2. E.T. Cranch and G.M. Nordby, *Engineering at the Crossroads without a Compass*, paper presented at 53rd Annual Meeting of Accreditation

Board for Engineering and Technology, Phoenix, Arizona, October 15–18, 1985.

3. C.M. Van Atta, W.D. Decker, and T. Wilson, *Professional Personnel Policies and Practices of R&D Organizations* (Livermore, CA: Lawrence Livermore Laboratories, University of California, 1971).

4. C.W. Dalton and P.H. Thompson, "Accelerating Obsolescence of Older Engineers," *Harvard Business Review* (September–October 1971): 57–67.

5. H.H. Loomis, Jr. and H. Brandt, "Television as a Tool in Off-Campus Engineering Education," IEEE *Transactions on Education* (May 1973): 101–9.

6. *Engineering Graduate Education and Research* (J.D. Kemper, Chairman)(Washington, DC: National Academy Press, 1985).

7. *Manual of Graduate Study in Engineering* (Washington, DC: American Society for Engineering Education, 1952), 19.

Engineering Societies

As mentioned in Chapter 13, the problem of keeping abreast of new engineering theories, methods, and equipment is a serious issue for practising engineers. The continuous introduction of new computer techniques in engineering, such as computer-aided design and analysis, expert systems, and artificial intelligence, has put additional pressure on the professional engineer to remain up to date. Fortunately, engineering societies, because of their specialized interests, are well equipped to keep practising engineers current, through regular publications, conferences, seminars, and courses, some of which are now being distributed through videocassettes and satellite television. The societies also provide an avenue of communication among colleagues who have similar interests and a willingness to share information. Engineers should be aware of and should make use of this vast source of useful knowledge. In fact, most professional engineers consider participation in and promotion of engineering societies to be a normal professional responsibility, and they gain much personal satisfaction through advancing their profession.

THE PURPOSE OF ENGINEERING SOCIETIES

The major purpose of engineering societies, which has not changed in 150 years, is to encourage research into new theories or methods, to collect and classify this new information, and to disseminate it to members so that it can be put to good use. Engineering societies are the major publishers of new research results, in the form of conference proceedings and monographs, and are one of the leading groups in the development of new standards for design. Over the years, the libraries of the world have received many useful publications that resulted from the efforts of the engineering societies, and everyone has benefited from this free exchange of information. The impact on engineering practice is immense.

The purpose of the engineering societies is totally different from that of the provincial and territorial Associations, yet some engineers confuse them, perhaps because their duties sometimes overlap. For example, British societies do perform a sort of regulation through the awarding of "chartered engineer" status, and many Associations distribute technical information from time to time. Many American engineering societies publish codes of ethics, and infractions of such codes are grounds for expulsion from the societies; in Canada, codes of ethics are more commonly set and enforced by the provincial Associations.

THE EVOLUTION OF ENGINEERING SOCIETIES

The first technical society for engineers was the Institute of Civil Engineers, established in Britain in 1818, followed 30 years later by the Institution of Mechanical Engineers. Shortly thereafter, additional societies were established for naval architects and for gas, electrical, municipal, heating, and ventilating engineers.[1]

In the United States, the first engineering society was the American Society of Civil Engineers, founded in 1852. Many others were established in the 1800s, including the American Society of Mechanical Engineers (1880), the American Institute of Electrical Engineers (1884), and the American Society of Heating and Ventilating Engineers (1894), to mention only a few.

In Canada, the formation of societies began in 1885 with the Engineering Society of the University of Toronto; the "Society was, indeed, a 'learned society' and published and disseminated technical information ... in addition to looking after the University undergraduates in engineering."[2] The Engineering Institute of Canada was formed in 1887, followed by the Canadian Institute of Mining and Metallurgy in 1898. Many other engineering and technical societies were formed in the 1880s. However, some Canadian engineering societies have been established very recently. This resulted from the realization that one of the oldest and most prestigious societies, the Engineering Institute of Canada (EIC), could not maintain the diverse specialties of engineering within a single organization. Several "constituent" societies were established (the Canadian Geotechnical Society, the Canadian Society for Mechanical Engineering, the Canadian Society for Civil Engineering, and the Canadian Society for Electrical Engineering), and arrangements were made with others, such as the Canadian Society for Chemical Engineering. The Engineering Institute of Canada is now an executive or "umbrella" organization. Agreements signed with EIC and the Canadian Council of Professional Engineers (CCPE), which acts on behalf of the provincial Associations when requested, clearly state the roles and duties of the organizations: the provincial Associations are responsible for regulation of engineering, and the engineering societies are responsible for the traditional society role of collecting and disseminating technical information.[3] An engineer should be registered with a provincial Association (depending on the province of residence) and enrolled in an engineering society (depending on the branch of engineering).

Table 14-1 lists twelve of the most commonly encountered engineering societies in North America. The older, larger, better-established American societies have a greater storehouse of technical information and are usually able to offer a few more services to their members. The smaller, newer, Canadian societies are in the process of building up their reputation and membership. The names and addresses of these societies are listed below:

Addresses for Some Canadian Societies

- Head office for
  EIC (Engineering Institute of Canada)
  CSME (Canadian Society for Mechanical Engineering)
  CSCE (Canadian Society for Civil Engineering)
  CSEE (Canadian Society for Electrical Engineering):
  700 EIC Building
  2050 Mansfield Street
  Montreal, PQ H3A 1Z2

- CSChE (Canadian Society for Chemical Engineering):
  1785 Alta Vista Drive
  Ottawa, ON K1G 3Y6

- CGS (Canadian Geotechnical Society):
  170 Attwell Drive, Suite 602
  Rexdale, ON M9W 5Z5

- CIM (Canadian Institute of Mining and Metallurgy):
  400–1130 Sherbrooke Street West
  Montreal, PQ H3A 2M8

- CSAE (Canadian Society of Agricultural Engineering):
  151 Slater Street
  Ottawa, ON K1P 5H3

Address for Some U.S. Societies

- The five U.S. "founder societies" are so called because they founded the United Engineering Trustees, Inc., in 1904, which provides a central building and office space for more than

twenty U.S. engineering societies and related organizations. Head office for the five founder societies
ASCE (American Society of Civil Engineers)
AIME (American Institute of Mining, Metallurgical and Petroleum Engineers)
ASME (American Society of Mechanical Engineers)
IEEE (Institute of Electrical and Electronic Engineers)
AIChE (American Institute of Chemical Engineers):
345 East 47th Street
New York, NY USA 10017

CHOOSING A SOCIETY

The choice of which societies to join is influenced by one's engineering discipline, of course, and most major societies sponsor student chapters to acquaint undergraduate engineering students with their activities and to get them involved. However, most engineers will seek out the appropriate society by discussions with colleagues or senior engineers. A useful publication that summarizes the activities of about 450 societies throughout the world is the annual *Directory of Engineering Societies*, available in most libraries. This directory lists the purpose, membership, address, dues, and many other statistics for each society.[4]

In the rapidly evolving technical environment, the professional engineer has an obligation to remain well informed. Technical societies are one of the best sources of this technical information, and they are serving the same useful role today as they served during the Industrial Revolution. Each professional engineer should be a member of at least one society. Engineering society dues are deductible from personal income under Canadian tax laws.

Although the Canadian engineering societies are more effective in dealing with problems that are typically Canadian, they do not have the many years of publications and the continuing series of journals and transactions that the older American and British societies have. To get access to these publications, several "associate" memberships have been negotiated. The associate membership provides access to a foreign engineering society at a reduced membership fee. Agreements exist between the Canadian societies and most of the major American and British societies. It may be simpler, however, to join the foreign technical societies directly as well as the Canadian societies; for Canadians who want to support the development of Canadian societies yet retain links with foreign societies, this is probably the best answer.

Table 14-1

Comparison of Engineering Societies in the United States and Canada (1990)

	Civil			Mechanical		Electrical		Chemical		Mining	
	EIC	CGS (Geo-tech)	CSCE	ASCE	CSME	ASME	CSEE	IEEE	CSChE	AIChE	CIM	AIME
Founding Date:	1887	1969	1972	1852	1970	1880	1973	1884	1966	1908	1898	1871
No. of Staff:	12	1	4	160	2	325	5 (EIC)	550	1	90	27	4
Library Service:	No	No	No	Yes(ESL)	No	Yes(ESL)	No	Yes(ESL)	No	Yes(ESL)	No	Yes(ESL)
Local Sections:	32	10	9	80	12	198	7	267	8	103	65	—
Student Chapters:	Yes	None	27	211	27	270	4	578	20	145	59	—
Annual Budget (000):	$2000	—	$600	$18 500	$150	$30 000	See EIC	$83 000	$200	$11 000	$2900	$570
Annual Member Dues:	$85 to $125	$105	$125	$100	$100	$10 to $60	$85	$67	$95	$40 to $80	$70	—
No. of Individual Members:	12 000	1168	5000	91 853	2700	96 000	1084	243 919	1553	51 000	10 342	—
No. of Student Members:	4000	102	940	13 448	800	22 000	500	49 210	334	2000	1021	—
No. of Corporate Members:	90	None	None	None	None	None	None	None	None	None	219	4
Total Membership:	16 590	1270	5940	105 301	3500	118 000	1584	293 129	1887	53 000	11 582	—
Publications (Periodicals):	4	3	2	24 +	2	30 +	2	50 +	5	8	6 +	—
See Note	(1,3)	(2,3)	(2,3)	(3,4)	(2,3)	(3,4)	(2,3)	(3,4)	(3)	(3)	(3,4)	(3,4,5)

Notes:

1. The Engineering Institute of Canada (EIC) is an umbrella organization that consists of the four constituent societies: CGS, CSME, CSCE, and CSEE. The dues for the constituent societies include membership in EIC.

2. The staff and budget for CGS, CSME, CSCE, and CSEE are also included in the EIC totals.

3. Dollar amounts are in U.S. dollars for American organizations and Canadian dollars for Canadian organizations.

4. ESL — The Engineering Science Library, 345 East 47th Street, New York, NY 10017, was established in 1913 and is the official library of AIME, ASME, IEEE, ASCE, and AIChE. It contains 275 000 volumes in all branches of engineering and is open to the public.

5. The American Institute of Mining, Metallurgical and Petroleum Engineers (AIME) is a corporation owned by its four member societies: the Metallurgical Society, the Society of Mining Engineers, the Iron and Steel Society, and the Society of Petroleum Engineers.

Source: *Directory of Engineering Societies 1989.* Reproduced with permission of the American Association of Engineering Societies.

TOPICS FOR STUDY AND DISCUSSION

1. Visit a good engineering library (probably at a nearby university) and search through the card index or computer catalogue for periodicals in your area of engineering expertise. Make a list of the periodicals (including transactions, journals, and magazines) and note how many of them are published by engineering societies. Write to the engineering society that you encounter most frequently for membership information.

2. There is a debate as to whether additional Canadian engineering societies should be formed or whether Canadian engineers should belong to foreign-based societies that are already in existence and have a long history of transactions and an established membership base for economies of scale. Write a brief summary debating the pros and cons of these two alternatives. Does Canada need distinct engineering societies in every discipline and specialty? Are these societies truly non-political, or do national interests influence the content of journals and transactions? Are there uniquely Canadian conditions that would justify uniquely Canadian societies? Illustrate your summary with examples. If you believe that engineering societies should influence public policies, consider whether you should send a copy of your summary to your member of Parliament.

NOTES

1. L.C. Sentance, "History and Development of Technical and Professional Societies," *Engineering Digest* 18, no. 7 (July 1972): 73–74.

2. Sentance, "History and Development."

3. "Canadian Engineers Close the Ring," *Engineering Journal* 60, no. 1 (January 1977): 15–19.

4. *Directory of Engineering Societies* (New York: U.S. Engineers Joint Council, annual).

CHAPTER 15

Writing the Professional Practice and Ethics Examination

Most of the provincial Associations of Professional Engineers require applicants for membership to write a short examination on professional practice and ethics. The purpose of the examination is to ensure that the applicant is familiar with the provincial professional engineering Act and code of ethics. These topics are rarely covered in university courses but are essential basic knowledge for a professional engineer.

The format of the examination varies widely from province to province. Some provinces have a formal 1½-hour written examination, usually administered in a three-hour session with an engineering law examination. Other provinces, such as Manitoba, adopt a different approach; the examination is a rather lengthy homework assignment, which requires the applicant to review the provincial Act and code of ethics in minute detail. Both types of examination achieve the same goal: to determine whether the applicant is familiar with Canadian professional engineering practice and ethics.

This chapter gives some advice for readers preparing to write the professional practice and ethics examination and illustrates four types of examination format with questions taken from previous examinations. Readers who follow the advice in this chapter conscientiously will have little difficulty with the examination.

PREPARING FOR EXAMINATIONS

If you do not look forward to formal examinations, then you have company! Examinations cause some anxiety for most people, but they were originally devised, centuries ago, to prevent favouritism;

they ensure that people are admitted on knowledge and ability and not because of apple-polishing, bribery, or luck. There are no limits or quotas on the number of applicants who can pass; the examinations are merely an impartial gauge applied to see that everyone measures up.

Examinations are also a learning experience; in fact, the effort put into summarizing and organizing the subject matter in preparation for an examination is usually very efficient learning. However, even if you are well prepared, it is human nature to feel somewhat tense before an examination. Don't let it bother you; everyone else feels the same, even though others may not show it. The suggestions below may help you.

- Take a brisk walk before the examination. The mild exercise helps to combat anxiety and clear your mind. (A 15-km hike is *not* a brisk walk.)

- Arrive a little early, make sure you have an extra pen, and select a comfortable chair.

- *Read the examination paper!* It is amazing how many people waste time giving excellent answers to questions that were not asked.

- If you are faced with a really tough question, read it thoroughly, try to disengage your thoughts, and brainstorm for answers. If you still cannot respond, then go on to the next question. Your mind will work on it subconsciously, and when you come back to it, you may have the answer.

- Write clearly and arrange your answers in a logical order. This shows a methodical approach to problem solving. It frequently helps to jot down an outline before writing your response.

- Remember that the examination is a communication with the examiner; you may include any comments, references, or explanations that you would make verbally if you had the opportunity.

A STRATEGY FOR ANSWERING EXAMINATION QUESTIONS

When preparing to write the professional practice and ethics examination, it is important for applicants to recognize the purpose of the examination. Examiners are trying to determine whether the applicant is familiar with the provincial professional engineering Act and code of ethics, can make thoughtful decisions when a proposed course of action creates an ethical dilemma, and can explain a decision (or appropriate course of action) in a logical, convincing manner. This textbook will help applicants respond to all three of the above requirements.

Review the strategy for resolving complex ethical problems discussed in Chapter 6. The strategy can also be very useful in writing exams, although it was written as a guide for real people who are participants in a real ethical dilemma. The examination setting, by contrast, is an artificial situation, so the strategy should be modified slightly for this purpose.

For example, the first step in real problems is recognizing that the problem exists. Real problems usually develop slowly and unobtrusively; they are not presented in a numbered, typed format. Second, a key step in solving a real ethical problem is gathering the necessary information; in the examination setting, the information provided is all you get. Although it is important to read the questions thoroughly so that you don't miss anything, it is not possible to use other sources for new insight. Finally, the strategy described in Chapter 6 emphasizes the importance of generating alternative solutions or courses of action, and of striving for an optimum solution, rather than selecting from the first two alternatives that come to mind. This creative aspect is somewhat curtailed in the examination setting.

On the positive side, implementation of real solutions to ethical problems usually requires time, money, and (occasionally) personal confrontations. In an examination, solutions merely need to be written down to be "implemented."

This modified version of the strategy described in Chapter 6 will help readers about to sit professional practice and ethics exams.

1. *Read each question thoroughly.* Gather all the information that is available.

2. *Identify the ethical problem.* What courses of action are in conflict?

3. *Generate new courses of action.* As mentioned above, this possibility may be limited because of the artificial nature of the examination format, but you should still try to imagine whether alternative courses of action are possible.

4. *Analyze the possible courses of action.* Identify whether each course of action can be supported by, or is in contravention of, clauses in the professional engineering Act or code of ethics for your province or territory.

5. *Make a decision.* Occasionally, step 4 will show that one course of action is clearly superior. However, in many (if not most) cases,

step 4 results in two courses of action that seem equally undesirable, and you must make a choice. To resolve this deadlock, other considerations must be brought into the argument. For example, is one course of action *less* undesirable than the other, for some reason? Can you resort to applying the basic ethical theories (as well as the code of ethics) to obtain new insight? In the end, you must make a decision and give a reason for that decision.

6. *Write a summary of the decision.* Your answer for the examination paper is merely a brief summary of the thought processes in steps 2 to 5. However, it is usually required, when writing your answer, that you refer to the precise clauses in the Act or the code of ethics. It is not necessary to copy the clauses, but they must be identified by number. It is also important to write in a neat and legible style. The examiners will appreciate the courtesy.

QUESTIONS FROM PREVIOUS EXAMINATIONS

This section contains 60 examination questions selected from previous professional practice and ethics examinations in several provinces. The sources of the questions are not relevant, since similar ethical problems arise in every province and the answers will be essentially the same.[1] The basic principles of ethics are universal. The questions have been chosen to show the various formats that might be encountered: essay-type, short answers, multiple choice, and true-false. Readers are encouraged to attempt all questions. Solutions are suggested for a few of the questions, and an asterisk indicates where the specific clause number(s) from the appropriate code of ethics or Act should appear.

Essay-Type Examination Questions

In the examination, the applicant would probably be asked to answer only four or five questions and would be permitted about twenty minutes per question. The code of ethics is usually provided for reference during the examination.

1. Professional Engineer A takes a job with a manufacturing company and almost immediately thereafter is given responsibility for preparing the draft of a bid for replacement turbine runners for a power corporation. While working on the preparation of the bid for the manufacturing company, Engineer A, as president and shareholder of his own company, which he has reacti-

vated, writes to the power corporation requesting permission to submit a tender on the same project. A few days later, and while continuing work on this bid for the manufacturing company, he receives word from the power corporation that a bid from his company would be considered. The day after learning this, he resigns his position with the manufacturing company and proceeds to finalize and submit a bid on behalf of his own company.

Discuss Engineer A's actions from an ethical point of view.

Suggested Answer: Engineer A is clearly unethical in his actions. He is not being fair or loyal to his employer, as required by the code of ethics.* He has taken advantage of inside information, betrayed the trust of his employer, and yielded to a conflict of interest. If his reactivated company was unknown to his employer, then he has failed to disclose his conflict of interest as required by the code of ethics.* By his actions, he has failed to show the necessary devotion to professional integrity required by the code of ethics.

In his defence, it could be said that since he resigned before actually signing the contract, he did not compete with his employer, but this would be a technical point; the serious conflicts of interest occurred during the bid preparation stage. The only positive statement in his defence is that he provided an additional option for the power corporation in its selection of bids. Engineer A has exposed himself to the serious possibility of disciplinary action under the provincial or territorial Act.

2. You are a professional engineer with XYZ Consulting Engineers. You have become aware that your firm subcontracts nearly all the work associated with the set-up, printing, and publishing of reports, including artwork and editing. Your wife has some training along this line and, now that your children are at school, is considering going back to business. You decide to form a company to enter this line of business together with your neighbours, another couple. Your wife will be the president, using her birth name, and you and your neighbours will be directors.

Since you see opportunities for subcontract work from your company, you reason that there must be similar opportunities with other consulting firms. You are aware of the existing competition and their rates charged for services and see this as an attractive sideline business. Can you do this ethically and, if so, what steps must you take?

Suggested Answer: You *can* do this ethically, but there is a significant potential for a serious conflict of interest unless you scrupulously follow the code of ethics for your province or territory. You can undertake the sideline business providing it does not interfere with your regular employment and providing that your employer is fully informed, as required by the code of ethics.* Your wife, of course, is free to use any legal name in her business affairs; however, if the sole reason for using her birth name is to conceal your participation in the company's ownership and operation, then your co-operation could be considered unethical. If your employer is fully informed, your interest in the company should not create a problem for you, although it might worry other clients, since a company publishing reports would usually be in a position of trust not to reveal the contents of the reports for the advantage of others.* Therefore, you must be seen *not* to be involved in handling sensitive engineering information submitted by other clients for publishing.

3. Bill MacDonald, a professional engineer, is manager of a chemical plant in a northern Canadian town. Early this summer he noticed that the plant was creating slightly more water pollution for the lake into which its waste line drains than is legally permitted. If he contacts the provincial ministry of the environment and reveals the problem, the result will be a considerable amount of unfavourable publicity for the plant. The publicity will also hurt the lakeside town's resort business and may scare the community. Apart from that, solving the problem will cost his company well over $100 000. If he tells no one, it is unlikely that outsiders will discover the problem, because the violation poses no danger whatever to people. At the most, it will endanger a small number of fish.

   Should MacDonald reveal the problem despite the cost to his company, or should he consider the problem little more than a technicality and disregard it? Discuss the ethical considerations affecting his decision.

   Suggested Answer: MacDonald must, legally and ethically, take action to remedy this situation. He is obligated under the code of ethics to consider the public welfare as paramount.* The legal limit for pollution has been exceeded, and failure to take action could be considered professional misconduct under the Act.* If he has known about the excess for some time, he may already be considered negligent and therefore subject to disciplinary action under the Act.*

   MacDonald must abide by the ministry's regulations, which would probably require him to submit a complete, factual report to inform officials about the pollution. Before sending the report, he should discuss it fully with his employer. If the employer reacts adversely, MacDonald must, nevertheless, forward the report to the ministry, as required by law and the code of ethics.* If the employer attempts to dismiss him, MacDonald may find it useful to ask the provincial Association to mediate and to inform his employer of the requirements under the Act. Should MacDonald be dismissed while acting properly and in good faith, he would have grounds for a suit against the employer for wrongful dismissal, to recoup lost wages and costs. It would be advisable for him to consult a lawyer in that event.

The engineer's concern over adverse publicity and the cost to the company must not obscure the requirement to act within the law. If the situation is permitted to continue unabated, the long-term consequences will be much more serious. The pollution could ruin the neighbouring resort industry, and MacDonald could find himself subject to disciplinary action for negligence or professional misconduct.

4. You are a professional engineer employed by a consulting engineering firm. Your immediate superior is also a professional engineer. You have occasion to check into the details of a recent invoice for work done on a project for which your boss is the project manager, but on which both you and members of your staff have done work.

You are surprised to see how much of your time and the time of one of the senior engineers who reports to you are charged to the job. You decide to check further into this by reviewing the pertinent time sheets. The time sheets show that time charged to other work has been deliberately transferred to this job. You try to raise the subject with your boss but are rebuffed. You are quite sure something is wrong but are not sure where to turn. You turn to the code of ethics for direction.

What articles are relevant to this situation? What action must you take, according to the code of ethics?

Suggested Answer: According to the code of ethics, you must be loyal to the employer.* However, the code also states that you must be fair and loyal to clients.* This creates an ethical dilemma. The dilemma can be resolved by observing that the deliberate transfer of charges from one job or client to another could be a form of fraud or theft, which is illegal. Therefore, it is important to obtain a clear explanation or justification for this transfer. If your superior is completely unwilling to reassure you of the reasons for this action, you must expose this unprofessional, dishonest, or unethical conduct, in accordance with the code of ethics.* The information should be conveyed to the client who is being overcharged.

Should your superior threaten to dismiss you, consult the provincial Association and ask them to mediate or to explain the requirements placed upon you (and your superior) by the code of ethics.* If you are dismissed while following the requirements of the code of ethics in good faith, you should consult a lawyer about suing for wrongful dismissal.

5. A consulting engineering firm is preparing to submit a proposal to clean up an area contaminated by a chemical spill during a train derailment. From past experience, the engineers in the firm know the amount of work involved in doing the job properly. The experts will include people with training in ecology, water quality, groundwater, soils, air pollution, and other areas. The methodology that they feel must be followed will result in an expenditure of about $5 million. Before their proposal is submitted, however, the federal government, which is the potential client, issues a news release saying that it has budgeted only $1 million for this work.

    What can the consulting firm do? To reduce the level of work to one-fifth of what they think is necessary would infringe on their perceived ethical responsibilities to the environment.

6. Engineer A enters into a consulting contract with a client to provide design and construction supervision of road surfaces in a partially completed land development project. He has taken over from another consultant, who was discharged partway through the job. Before Engineer A can finish the project, his contract also is terminated. Shortly thereafter it becomes obvious that there are deficiencies in the work done under A's supervision. Investigation shows that hastily placed road surfaces, completed under adverse late-fall weather conditions, are not up to specifications. It seems that A is aware of this and intended to require remedial work by the contractor in the spring, but his termination occurred before that time. Engineer A did not advise his client that he was expecting to reinspect in the spring and to have deficiencies corrected, nor did he inform his client of the existing state of the roads after he was released from his contract.

    Did Engineer A act in an ethical way in his dealings with his client even though he may feel that he was unfairly terminated? Discuss the articles of the code of ethics that have a bearing on this case.

7. An engineer is employed by a large consulting engineering firm. Her work includes the designing and specifying of electrical equipment. She owns shares in a large, well-known electrical manufacturing company. Her shareholdings amount to only a very small fraction of one percent of all shares issued.

   Is it a violation of the code of ethics for this engineer to select and specify equipment made by this company in which she holds stock?

8. Engineer X, a civil engineer and an employee of ABC Consultants Ltd., signed the 1982 Ontario Application for Renewal of Certificate of Authorization for that company as the engineer taking responsibility to see that the Professional Engineers Act, its by-laws, and its regulations would be complied with.

   In 1982 ABC Consultants Ltd. prepared the electrical and mechanical designs for a multi-storey building and, although Engineer X had very little to do with this project, the drawings bore his seal. These designs were found to be deficient in a number of respects. Contrary to the Ontario Building Code, fire walls were omitted, fire dampers were not shown, and sprinklers were improperly connected, among other things. Upon investigation it was found that both the electrical work and the mechanical work were done by professional engineers.

   What is Engineer X's ethical position in this matter?

9. A building contractor engages a professional engineer to design and prepare drawings for the formwork and scaffolding for a reinforced concrete building, to meet the requirements of construction safety legislation. The engineer does this and affixes his seal and signature to the original tracings, which he turns over to the contractor. Is this acceptable professional practice? Later the engineer is asked to inspect the scaffolding as built and finds that in many significant parts his design has been ignored, and the contractor's superintendent has built it the way he thought it should be built.

   What should the engineer do? Discuss this situation, with particular emphasis on the engineer's professional responsibility and the safety of the workers.

10. After having been employed by Consulting Engineer B for several years, Engineer A terminates her work with B and starts her own practice of consulting engineering. Later B learns that some of his sub-professional employees are doing work for A on their own time. B is of the opinion that the outside work by his

sub-professional employees is so extensive that it diminishes their productivity.

Did A act unethically by employing the sub-professional employees of B under the conditions stated?

11. John Doe, an engineer employed by a testing laboratory, represents his firm on a standards committee for automobile products. All but two of the members of this ten-person committee are engineers. After much deliberation on one standard, the committee arrives at a consensus, but Mr. Doe is violently opposed to the result and registers his objection. After careful consideration of this objection, the committee passes the standard for formal publication. Subsequently the laboratory receives a contract to test automobile products to this standard, and Doe is assigned the job of supervising the tests, compiling the final report, which indicates that the samples meet the requirements of the standard, and signing the report on behalf of the firm. He objects because he considers that his signature on a report attesting to the conformance of a product with a standard indicates that he endorses the standard.

Is he correct in his assumption? What action should he take?

12. An engineer enters into a contract with a public body whereby he agrees to conduct such field investigations and studies as may be necessary to determine the most economical and proper method to design and construct a water supply system; he also agrees to prepare an engineering report, including an estimate of the cost of the project, and to estimate the amount of bond issue required. The contract provides that, if the bond issue passes, the engineer will be paid to prepare plans and specifications and supervise the construction, and he will be paid a fee for his preliminary services. If the bond issue should fail, the public body would not be obligated to pay for the preliminary work. The public body is prohibited by law from committing funds for the preliminary work until the bond issue is approved.

May an engineer ethically accept a contingent contract under these conditions?

13. An owner retains an architect to prepare plans and specifications for a building, using a standard contract form. The architect, in turn, retains a structural engineer for the structural portion of the plans and specifications. The building is erected. Both professionals complete their respective portions of the contract, except the execution of the required certificate of compliance. During the progress of the work, the owner makes

progress payments to the architect, and the architect pays the appropriate amount from his payments to the structural engineer. However, when the building is completed and ready for occupancy, the owner still owes and refuses to pay the architect a substantial sum due under the contract, and the architect accordingly owes the structural engineer a proportionate amount. The owner alleges that there have been several deficiencies in the work of the architect and refuses to pay him the balance due. The owner requests city officials to issue him an occupancy permit, and they request the architect, who in turn requests the structural engineer, to certify that the structural system has been completed in compliance with the applicable building code and regulations. Such a certification is required before the city may issue an occupancy permit to the owner. The structural engineer refuses to provide the certification until he has been paid for his services.

Is it unethical for the engineer to refuse to provide the certification that would enable the owner to secure the occupancy permit, on the grounds that he has not been paid for his services?

14. An engineer in private practice is retained by a client to design and supervise the construction of a warehouse. Some time later he is asked by another client to provide professional engineering services for a warehouse almost identical to that previously designed by him, except for those minor changes necessary to adapt the building to the site. This client suggests that the fee be lower than that charged for the original design services, because the engineer could use his same design with only minor changes.

For this reuse of his design, would it be ethical for the engineer to charge a fee substantially less than that recommended by the Association?

15. Your firm is asked by the City of Townsville to assess the effects of a tidal wave. Located at the end of a long, narrow inlet, Townsville is in an earthquake zone, although the last one occurred in 1950 when the city was really only a fishing port. To make sure they have an adequate picture of the disaster that could result, they ask your firm to examine the effects of the 200-year earthquake. Your findings are so horrendous that the city authorities are appalled, and they feel that if the public were to realize the extent of impending damage, mass hysteria would result. As well, because many of the authorities are elected officials and have been in their positions for many years, people could ask why such a study was not carried out years ago, and

why adequate planning by-laws were never formulated. So you are asked to keep the findings of the 200-year quake confidential and to undertake another study of the effects of the 100-year quake. The results are still frightening, and the city now asks you to study the 50-year quake.

Discuss this situation from an ethical point of view. What action will you take as a professional engineer? What advice will you give to the city council?

16. A Canadian professional engineer is working in a foreign country for a client building a power station. He is acting as technical adviser to the client. The client is directly supervising all construction labour. The client does not have any apparent safety procedures for his workers: no hard hats, no safety shoes, in some cases no shoes. Holes in floors do not have safety barricades. The conditions would be unacceptable in Canada. Even assuming the poor safety conditions will not affect the technical aspects of the power station, clearly they affect the safety of workers.

Would it be ethical for the Canadian engineer not to take any action? What kind of action could he take? Do you consider it likely that the poor safety practices could affect only the safety of workers and not have any relation to the technical aspects of the power station?

17. Consulting Firm A is preparing preliminary engineering and environmental impact studies for a client proposing an urban development project. The municipality has a planner on staff but has also engaged Consulting Firm B to assist with the review of the submissions of A.

Firm A has made several submissions to secure approval, but each time some aspects are not satisfactory and the requirements are redefined after each submission. Finally the engineer from B offers, in the presence of the municipal staff planner, to complete the assignment for A, since he knows what is required. In addition to paying the fees of his original consultant, A, the developer must also pay the costs of the municipality's review, including its consultant from B.

Is it ethical for the engineer from Firm B to offer to complete the assignment of Firm A? If you were A, what would your reaction be to this situation from an ethics point of view?

18. Engineer A is employed by an industrial corporation. Her immediate supervisor is Engineer B, who is chairman of a civic committee responsible for retaining an architect to design a civic

facility. When Engineer B receives the completed plans and specifications from the architect, he directs Engineer A to review them in order to gain knowledge, suggest improvements, and assure their compliance with the specified requirements.

Is the instruction of Engineer B to Engineer A consistent with the code of ethics? Is Engineer A ethically permitted to carry out the instructions given her by Engineer B? Explain.

19. Engineer E, a member of a city council, is chairman of its finance committee, which deals with and makes recommendations regarding appropriations for projects undertaken by the city. One such project is a pollution abatement project, for which funds have been allocated. Engineer E is one of the principals in a consulting engineering firm, EFG, which has established a good reputation in the pollution control field. EFG has submitted to the council a proposal to provide the engineering services required for the project under consideration.

    Under these circumstances, is it ethical for EFG to offer to undertake this engineering work? Explain.

20. Because of a tight competitive market for engineering employees, the engineering department of a large manufacturing company has adopted a policy of paying a bonus to any member of its engineering staff who is successful in having an engineer or engineers working with some other organizations recruited by the company. The theory is that the present engineering employee might know, or know of, other engineers who would consider employment with the company if approached by one of its engineering employees. The bonus offered is $100 per recruit.

    Is it ethical for the chief engineer to adopt this policy? Would it be ethical for the engineering employees of the company to participate in this recruitment program? Explain.

Short-Answer Examination Questions

21. Provide a definition of "ethics."

22. The code of ethics contains many clauses that describe the ethical responsibilities of the engineer with respect to professional life, relations with the public, relations with clients and employers, and relations with engineers. List at least half of these.

23. In a few sentences, describe what a "profession" is.

24. Is your province's code of ethics for engineers enforceable under your professional engineering Act? Explain.

25. Discuss a possible situation where an engineer's duty to his/her employer may be in conflict with his/her responsibility to the public.

26. What considerations and measures should an engineer take in the situation described in the previous question?

27. Explain what "conflict of interest" means.

28. Does your province's professional engineering Act explicitly restrict an engineer to practise in his or her branch of registration only? How does the code of ethics deal with the problem of practising outside of one's branch of registration?

29. a. The Association of Professional Engineers is the self-regulating organization responsible for the practice of engineering in your province. What is the principal objective of this organization?

    b. To become licensed to practise professional engineering in your province you must meet certain requirements. Discuss briefly the five most significant of these.

30. a. What is the difference between a limited licence and a temporary licence in the practice of professional engineering? [Does not apply in all provinces.]

    b. You are a practising professional engineer in a manufacturing company. Your division of the company has been transferred into Ontario from Manitoba. What must you do, if anything, to continue your engineering work under these circumstances?

Multiple-Choice Examination Questions

Some provinces administer the examination in a multiple-choice format, as illustrated in the next five questions. A typical examination is two hours long, consists of 100 multiple-choice questions, and is "closed-book" (no aids permitted). Usually, half the questions concern practice and ethics, and half concern engineering law.

31. According to the code of ethics, which of the following activities by a professional member would be considered *unethical*?

    a. Not charging a fee for presenting a speech.
    b. Signing plans prepared by an unknown person.

c. Reviewing the work of another member with that member's consent.

d. Providing professional services as a consultant.

Answer: b. It is unethical for professionals to sign plans not prepared by themselves or under their direct supervision.

32. Which of the following is the most common job activity of top-level managers?

a. Writing and reading corporate financial reports.
b. Developing and testing new products.
c. Designing and implementing production systems.
d. Directing and interacting with people.

Answer: d. Most top managers spend most of their time interacting with other people.

33. The professional's standard of care and skill establishes the point at which a professional:

a. may or may not charge a fee for services.
b. has the duty to apply "reasonable care."
c. may be judged negligent in the performance of services.
d. has met the minimum requirements for registration.

Answer: c. The standard of care is used to judge whether a professional has been negligent in the performance of services.

34. Which of the following is a minimum requirement for registration as a professional engineer?

a. Canadian citizenship.
b. Experience in engineering work.
c. Course work in engineering.
d. Residence in the province.

Answer: b. Of the items listed, engineering experience is the only requirement for registration that is absolutely essential. Each Act has provisions for persons lacking one or more of the other three.

35. To effectively reduce liability exposure, the professional geologist should:

a. pursue continuing educational opportunities.
b. work under the supervision of a senior geologist.
c. maintain professional standards of practice.
d. provide clients with frequent progress reports.

Answer: c. Maintaining professional standards of practice is the most effective way of reducing liability exposure.

True-False Examination Questions

The following 25 questions illustrate the format for a typical true-false examination required by one of the provincial Associations. The examination has 50 questions and is performed as a homework assignment. The applicant therefore has access to the code of ethics, provincial by-laws and regulations, and the provincial professional engineering Act. Each answer must be justified by citing the appropriate clause from the code, by-law, regulations, or Act. The questions apply to every province or territory, and readers are urged to attempt to answer them; they are an excellent review for every engineer, regardless of his or her province of residence.

36. A person may assume the title "Professional Engineer" before being registered with the Association if working under the direct supervision of a registered professional engineer.

    True: ___ False: ___ Reference: ___

37. If an employer knowingly engages a person for work that requires the services of a professional engineer, and that person is not registered or licensed with the Association, both the employer and the employee are in violation of the professional engineering Act.

    True: ___ False: ___ Reference: ___

38. A person convicted of a criminal offence under an act other than the professional engineering Act may be suspended from membership in the Association.

    True: ___ False: ___ Reference: ___

39. Members of the Armed Forces stationed in your province are subject to the provisions of the Professional Engineering Act.

    True: ___ False: ___ Reference: ___

40. A professional engineer must be aware of all the related facts before publicly expressing an opinion on an engineering subject.

    True: ___ False: ___ Reference: ___

41. A professional engineer must ensure that clients understand the full extent of his or her responsibilities.

    True: ___ False: ___ Reference: ___

42. It is voluntary, and not mandatory, for a professional engineer to strive to keep informed about new techniques in his or her field of endeavour.

    True: ___ False: ___ Reference: ___

43. A professional engineer may criticize the work of a fellow engineer publicly if he or she first advises the fellow engineer of the intent to do so.

    True: ___ False: ___ Reference: ___

44. If a person is working under the direct supervision of a professional engineer who assumes all responsibility, the subordinate is still required to be registered.

    True: ___ False: ___ Reference: ___

45. Unless a person is registered or licensed by the Association of Professional Engineers of any province, that person may not imply that he or she is entitled to engage in professional engineering.

    True: ___ False: ___ Reference: ___

46. As far as work is concerned, a professional engineer's first responsibility is to the employer.

    True: ___ False: ___ Reference: ___

47. A professional engineer may seal plans that have been prepared neither by himself/herself nor under his/her personal direction.

    True: ___ False: ___ Reference: ___

48. A professional engineer may be compensated by more than one interested party for the same service without the consent of all interested parties.

    True: ___ False: ___ Reference: ___

49. All specifications and reports must be sealed by the professional engineer who has done the work involved.

    True: ___ False: ___ Reference: ___

50. Council may ask witnesses to attend an inquiry on a discipline matter and has the power to ensure attendance.

    True: ___ False: ___ Reference: ___

51. If a member is found guilty of unprofessional conduct, the most severe penalty Council may mete out is a reprimand.

    True: ___ False: ___ Reference: ___

52. Council may initiate an inquiry where professional misconduct is suspected, even though no written complaint has been received.

    True: ___ False: ___ Reference: ___

53. A professional engineer, having first advised his or her fellow engineer of the intent to do so, may accept a commission to review the work of the fellow engineer.

    True: ___ False: ___ Reference: ___

54. It is not mandatory for a professional engineer to report a colleague he or she feels is engaged in unethical practice.

    True: ___ False: ___ Reference: ___

55. A professional engineer has no responsibility for the professional development of engineers in his or her employ.

    True: ___ False: ___ Reference: ___

56. If a professional engineer in charge of an assignment is overruled by his or her superior or client, the engineer should present clearly the consequences to be expected from the proposed deviations and then complete the assignments, provided that the ruling of the superior or client does not jeopardize public property, life, or the environment.

    True: ___ False: ___ Reference: ___

57. The objects of the Association are primarily to:

    a. ensure that the rights and interests of all engineers in the province are protected.

    True: ___ False: ___ Reference: ___

    b. ensure that the public interest is served and protected through the competent and ethical practice of engineering within the province.

    True: ___ False: ___ Reference: ___

58. Registration as a full member of the Association may be granted if the following education and experience requirements are met:

a. The applicant has an accredited engineering degree and has experience satisfactory to Council.

True: ___ False: ___ Reference: ___

b. The applicant has passed the examinations required by Council and has a minimum of six years of satisfactory engineering experience.

True: ___ False: ___ Reference: ___

59. The practice of engineering, as defined by the Act, covers a broad range of activities. However, the following persons are considered exempt from the provisions of the Act.

a. Those who were doing engineering work before the Act became law.

True: ___ False: ___ Reference: ___

b. Technicians working under the direct and personal supervision of professional engineers.

True: ___ False: ___ Reference: ___

c. Land surveyors, architects, electricians, and enginemen, provided they do not engage in the practice of engineering.

True: ___ False: ___ Reference: ___

d. Those who have ten or more years of good engineering experience and feel they are competent and have a basic right to work as an engineer.

True: ___ False: ___ Reference: ___

60. Mr. X, a registered member of another provincial Association, is transferred to Manitoba by his company and has taken up permanent residence in Winnipeg. His new title is chief design engineer for western Canada. For the past two months he has been the sole designer of a commercial building in Manitoba. He uses his title, and "P.Eng." after his name on his business card. He has not become a member of the Association. Assess the following statements:

a. Membership in the other provincial Association allows him to practise engineering in Manitoba; therefore, he does not have to become a member of the APEM.

True: ___ False: ___ Reference: ___

b. Mr. X should have applied for registration with APEM on arrival in Manitoba.

True: ___ False: ___ Reference: ___

c. Mr. X should immediately apply for a temporary licence to practise in Manitoba.

True: ___ False: ___ Reference: ___

d. Mr. X is in contravention of the Act since he is practising engineering and hence is liable for the penalty under the Act.

True: ___ False: ___ Reference: ___

e. Mr. X is in contravention of the Act for using the term "P.Eng." after his name.

True: ___ False: ___ Reference: ___

NOTE

1. The authors would like to express their appreciation to the Associations of Professional Engineers of Alberta, New Brunswick, Manitoba, Ontario, and Newfoundland for their assistance in obtaining questions and their permission to reprint these questions from previous examinations.

Excerpts from the Provincial and Territorial Engineering Acts and Regulations

This appendix consists of excerpts from the provincial and territorial Engineering Acts and Regulations that relate to practice and ethics. For the complete documents, please refer to the Act or Regulation cited. Although more recent Statutes and Regulations are written to be gender neutral, some of the older ones use the personal pronouns "he," "him," and "his" to refer to both men and women and have been reproduced here in this form.

ALBERTA

ENGINEERING, GEOLOGICAL AND GEOPHYSICAL PROFESSIONS ACT (*STATUTES OF ALBERTA* 1981, C. E-11.1, AS AMENDED)

1. Definition of Engineering (Section 1 of the Act)

"practice of engineering" means
(i) reporting on, advising on, evaluating, designing, preparing plans and specifications for or directing the construction, technical inspection, maintenance or operation of any structure, work or process

    (a) that is aimed at the discovery, development or utilization of matter, materials or energy or in any other way designed for the use and convenience of man, and

    (b) that requires in the reporting, advising, evaluating, designing, preparation or direction the professional application of the principles of mathematics, chemistry, physics or any related applied subject, or

(ii) teaching engineering at a university

"practice of geology" means
(i) reporting, advising, evaluating, interpreting, geological surveying, sampling or examining related to any activity

(a) that is aimed at the discovery or development of oil, natural gas, coal, metallic or non-metallic minerals, precious stones, other natural resources or water or that is aimed at the investigation of geological condition, and

(b) that requires in that reporting, advising, evaluating, interpreting, geological surveying, sampling or examining, the professional application of the principles of the geological sciences, or

(ii) teaching geology at a university

"practice of geophysics" means

(i) reporting on, advising on, acquiring, processing, evaluating or interpreting geophysical data, or geophysical surveying that relates to any activity

(a) that is aimed at the discovery or development of oil, natural gas, coal, metallic or non-metallic minerals or precious stones or other natural resources or water or that is aimed at the investigation of sub-surface conditions in the earth, and

(b) that requires in that reporting, advising, evaluating, interpreting, or geophysical surveying, the professional application of the principles of the geophysical sciences, or

(ii) teaching geophysics at a university

2. Membership Criteria (Section 21 of the Act and Section 13 of Alberta Regulation 244/81, as amended by Alberta Regulation 204/90, Section 3)

[Applications as professional members may be made by persons resident in Alberta who are Canadian Citizens or lawfully admitted to Canada as permanent residents, or as licensees if resident outside Alberta, or resident in Alberta but neither Canadian citizens nor lawfully admitted to Canada as permanent residents.]

Applicants must also meet 1 of the following qualifications:

(i) he is a graduate of a university program in engineering, geology or geophysics or has completed university qualifications in a related program acceptable to the Board of Examiners and has had, since graduation or completion, at least 2 years of experience in engineering, geological or geophysical work,

(ii) he has achieved an education satisfactory to the Board of Examiners consisting of

(a) the completion of at least 2 years of post secondary education in areas that relate to the science and technology of engineering, geology or geophysics, and

(b)   the receipt of credit, or the equivalent, in an adequate number of related fundamental subjects satisfactory to the Board of Examiners

and he has been engaged in work of an engineering, geological or geophysical nature for at least 3 years, or for 1 year following graduation from an engineering, geological or geophysical technology program recognized by the Board of Examiners, or

(iii)   he is registered as an engineer, geologist or geophysicist in a jurisdiction recognized by the Board of Examiners.

AR 244/81 s13; 204/90

3. Definition of Professional Misconduct (Section 43 of the Act)

43(1)   Any conduct of a professional member, licensee, permit holder, certificate holder or member-in-training that in the opinion of the Discipline Committee or the Council

(a)   is detrimental to the best interests of the public,

(b)   contravenes a code of ethics of the profession as established under the regulations,

(c)   harms or tends to harm the standing of the profession generally,

(d)   displays a lack of knowledge of or lack of skill or judgement in the practice of the profession, or

(e)   displays a lack of knowledge of or lack of skill or judgement in the carrying out of any duty or obligation undertaken in the practice of the profession,

whether or not that conduct is disgraceful or dishonourable, constitutes either unskilled practice of the profession or unprofessional conduct, whichever the Discipline Committee finds.

(2)   If an investigated person fails to comply with or contravenes this Act, the regulations or the by-laws, and the failure or contravention is, in the opinion of the Discipline Committee, of a serious nature, the failure or contravention may be found by the Discipline Committee to be unprofessional conduct whether or not it would be so found under subsection (1).

4. Disciplinary Powers (Sections 60, 61 of the Act)

60.   If the Discipline Committee finds that the conduct of the investigated person is unprofessional conduct or unskilled practice of the profession or both, the Discipline Committee may make any one or more of the following orders:

(a)   reprimand the investigated person;

(b)   suspend the registration of the investigated person for a specified period;

(c)   suspend the registration of the investigated person either generally or from any field of practice until

(i)   he has completed a specified course of studies or obtained supervised practical experience, or

(ii)   the Discipline Committee is satisfied as to the competence of the investigated person generally or in a specified field of practice;

(d)   accept in place of a suspension the investigated person's undertaking to limit his practice;

(e)   impose conditions on the investigated person's entitlement to engage in the practice of the profession generally or in any field of the practice, including the conditions that he

(i)   practise under supervision,

(ii)   not engage in sole practice,

(iii)   permit periodic inspections by a person authorized by the Discipline Committee, or

(iv)   report to the Discipline Committee on specific matters;

(f)   direct the investigated person to pass a particular course of study or satisfy the Discipline Committee as to his practical competence generally or in a field of practice;

(g)   direct the investigated person to satisfy the Discipline Committee that a disability or addiction can be or has been overcome, and suspend the person until the Discipline Committee is so satisfied;

(h)   require the investigated person to take counselling or to obtain any assistance that in the opinion of the Discipline Committee is appropriate;

(i)   direct the investigated person to waive, reduce or repay a fee for services rendered by the investigated person that, in the opinion of the Discipline Committee, were not rendered or were improperly rendered;

(j)   cancel the registration of the investigated person;

(k)   any other order that it considers appropriate in the circumstances.

61(1)   The Discipline Committee may, in addition to or instead of dealing with the investigated person in accordance with section 60, order that the investigated person pay

(a)   all or part of the costs of the hearing in accordance with the by-laws,

(b)   a fine not exceeding $10 000 to the Association, or

(c)   both the costs under clause (a) and a fine under clause (b), within the time fixed by the order.

(2) If the investigated person ordered to pay a fine, costs or both under subsection (1) fails to pay the fine, costs or both within the time ordered, the Discipline Committee may suspend the registration of that person until he has paid the fine, costs or both.

(3) A fine or costs ordered to be paid to the Association under this section is a debt due to the Association and may be recovered by the Association by civil action for debt.

1981 cE-11.1 s61; 1984 c17s19

5. Code of Ethics (Alberta Regulation 204/90, Schedule A, Established Pursuant to Section 18(1)(h) of the Act)

Preamble

Professional engineers, geologists and geophysicists shall recognize that professional ethics is founded upon integrity, competence and devotion to service and to the advancement of human welfare. This concept shall guide their conduct at all times. In this way each professional's actions will enhance the dignity and status of the professions.

Professional engineers, geologists and geophysicists, through their practice, are charged with extending public understanding of the professions and should serve in public affairs when their professional knowledge may be of benefit to the public.

Professional engineers, geologists and geophysicists will build their reputations on the basis of merit of the services performed or offered and shall not compete unfairly with others or compete primarily on the basis of fees without due consideration for other factors.

Professional engineers, geologists and geophysicists will maintain a special obligation to demonstrate understanding, professionalism and technical expertise to members-in-training under their supervision.

Rules of Conduct

1. Professional engineers, geologists and geophysicists shall have proper regard in all their work for the safety and welfare of all persons and for the physical environment affected by their work.

2. Professional engineers, geologists and geophysicists shall undertake only work that they are competent to perform by virtue of training and experience and shall express opinions on engineering, geological or geophysical matters only on the basis of adequate knowledge and honest conviction.

3. Professional engineers, geologists and geophysicists shall sign and seal only reports, plans or documents that they have prepared or that have been prepared under their direct supervision and control.

4. Professional engineers, geologists and geophysicists shall act for their clients or employers as faithful agents or trustees; always acting independently and with fairness and justice to all parties.

5. Professional engineers, geologists and geophysicists shall not engage in activities or accept remuneration for services rendered that may create a conflict of interest with their clients or employers, without the knowledge and consent of their clients or employers.

6. Professional engineers, geologists and geophysicists shall not disclose confidential information without the consent of their clients or employers, unless the withholding of the information is considered contrary to the safety of the public.

7. Professional engineers, geologists and geophysicists shall present clearly to their clients or employers the consequences to be expected if their professional judgement is overruled by other authorities in matters pertaining to work for which they are professionally responsible.

8. Professional engineers, geologists and geophysicists shall not offer or accept covert payment for the purpose of securing an engineering, geological or geophysical assignment.

9. Professional engineers, geologists and geophysicists shall represent their qualifications and competence, or advertise professional services offered, only through factual representation without exaggeration.

10. Professional engineers, geologists and geophysicists shall conduct themselves toward other professional engineers, geologists and geophysicists, and toward employees and others with fairness and good faith.

11. Professional engineers, geologists and geophysicists shall advise the Registrar of any practice by a member of the Association that they believe to be contrary to this Code of Ethics.

Under section 43 of the Act, a contravention of this Code of Ethics may constitute unprofessional conduct or unskilled practice which is subject to disciplinary action.

AR 244/81 Sched. A; 386/85; 204/90

Source: Engineering, Geological and Geophysical Professions Act, *Statutes of Alberta* 1981, c. E-11.1, as amended 1985. Reproduced with permission of the Queen's Printer, Alberta.

BRITISH COLUMBIA

ENGINEERS AND GEOSCIENTISTS ACT (*REVISED STATUTES OF BRITISH COLUMBIA* 1979, C. 109, AS AMENDED)

1. Definition of Engineering (Section 1 of the Act)

"practice of professional engineering" means the carrying on of chemical, civil, electrical, forest, geological, mechanical, metallurgical, mining or structural engineering, and other disciplines of engineering that may be designated by the council and for which university engineering programs have been accredited by the Canadian Engineering Accreditation Board or by a body which, in the opinion of the council, is its equivalent, including the reporting on, designing, or directing the construction of any works that require for their design, or the supervision of their construction, or the supervision of their maintenance, such experience and technical knowledge as are required by or under this Act for the admission by examination to membership in the association, and, without restricting the generality of the foregoing, shall include reporting on, designing or directing the construction of public utilities, industrial works, railways, bridges, highways, canals, harbour works, river improvements, lighthouses, wet docks, dry docks, floating docks, launch ways, marine ways, steam engines, turbines, pumps, internal combustion engines, airships and airplanes, electrical machinery and apparatus, chemical operations, machinery, and works for the development, transmission or application of power, light and heat, grain elevators, municipal works, irrigation works, sewage disposal works, drainage works, incinerators, hydraulic works, and all other engineering works, and all buildings necessary to the proper housing, installation and operation of the engineering works embraced in this paragraph; but the performance as a contractor of work designed by a professional engineer, the supervision of construction of work as foreman or superintendent or as an inspector, or as a roadmaster, trackmaster, bridge or building master, or superintendent of maintenance, shall not be deemed to be the practice of professional engineering within the meaning of this Act;

"practice of professional geoscience" means reporting, advising, acquiring, processing, evaluating, interpreting, surveying, sampling or examining related to any activity that
    (a) is directed toward the discovery or development of oil, natural gas, coal, metallic or non-metallic minerals, precious stones,

other natural resources or water or the investigation of surface or sub-surface geological conditions, and

(b) requires the professional application of the principles of geology, geophysics or geochemistry;

2. Membership Criteria (Section 10 of the Act and Section 11 of the By-laws, Established under Section 7 of the Act)

10 (1) The council shall admit an applicant to membership in the association who is a Canadian citizen or permanent resident of Canada, and who has submitted evidence satisfactory to the council

(a) that graduation in applied science, engineering or geoscience from an institute of learning approved by the council in a course approved by the council has been achieved,

(b) that examinations as established by the by-laws of the association or equivalent examinations of an association or institute approved by the council, requiring special knowledge in branches of learning specified by the council have been passed,

(c) that the experience in engineering or geoscience work established by the by-laws has been obtained,

(d) that the applicant is of good character and good repute, and

(e) that all examination and registration fees have been paid to the association.

(1.1) Notwithstanding subsection (1) or (4), the council may refuse registration or a licence to a person where the council has reasonable and probable grounds to believe that the person has been convicted in Canada or elsewhere of an offence that, if committed in British Columbia, would be an offence under an enactment of the Province or of Canada, and that the nature or circumstances of the offence render the person unsuitable for registration or licensing.

(2) A person desiring to become a member shall comply with the provisions of all by-laws relating to application for membership, and, if he is required to qualify by examination, shall also comply with section 12 (4).

(3) [Repealed.]

(4) Any nonresident of the Province whose qualifications are those required by paragraphs (a) to (d) of subsection (1), and who desires to engage temporarily in the practice of professional engineering or professional geoscience in the Province, shall first obtain a licence from the Council which will entitle him to engage in the practice of professional engineering or professional geoscience in respect of a particular work or for a temporary period, or both, as the council decides. On producing evidence satisfactory to the council of his qualifications and on payment of the prescribed fees, he shall be granted the licence.

(5) Neither corporations nor partnerships as such may become members of the association. Where professional engineers or professional geoscientists are employed by corporations or are members of partnerships, they individually shall assume the functions of and be held responsible as professional engineers or professional geoscientists.

Registered Members

11 (e) Registration as a full member of the Association may be granted when Council is satisfied that the applicant is of good character and repute and:

(1) Has graduated in applied science, engineering or geoscience from an institute of learning approved by the Council in a course approved by the Council and in addition has had two years' experience in engineering or geoscience satisfactory to the Council, or

(2) Has passed the examinations required by the Council or the equivalent examinations of an association or institute approved by the Council requiring special knowledge in branches of learning as may be specified by the Council and in addition has had five years' experience in engineering or geoscience satisfactory to the Council and has submitted as partial evidence of this experience an engineering or geoscience report or thesis satisfactory to the Council, or

(3) Has passed the examinations required by the Council or the equivalent examinations of an association or institute approved by the Council requiring special knowledge in branches of learning as may be specified by the Council and in addition has had eight years of experience in engineering or geoscience satisfactory to the Council.

3. Definition of Professional Misconduct

[Although the terms "incompetence," "negligence," and "unprofessional conduct" are used in the Act, section 24.5, these terms are not defined in the Act.]

4. Disciplinary Powers (Section 24.5 of the Act)

24.5 (1) The discipline committee may, after an inquiry under section 24.4, determine that the member or licensee

(a) has been convicted in Canada or elsewhere of an offence that, if committed in British Columbia, would be an offence under an enactment of the Province or of Canada, and that the nature or circumstances of the offence render the person unsuitable for registration or licensing.

(b) has contravened this Act or the by-laws or the code of ethics of the association, or

(c) has demonstrated incompetence, negligence or unprofessional conduct.

(2) Where the discipline committee makes a determination under subsection (1), it may, by order, do one or more of the following:

(a) reprimand;

(b) impose conditions on the membership or licence of;

(c) suspend the membership or licence of;

(d) revoke the membership or licence of the member or licensee.

(3) The discipline committee shall give written reasons for any action it takes under subsection (2).

(4) Where a member or a licensee is suspended from practice, the registration or licence shall be deemed cancelled during the term of the suspension and the suspended member or suspended licensee is not entitled to any of the rights or privileges of membership and shall not be considered a member while the suspension continues.

5. Code of Ethics (Section 14 of the By-laws, Established under Section 7 of the Act)

Preamble

14. The following is prescribed as the Code of Ethics of the Association, and the member is bound by its provisions just as he is bound by the provisions of the Engineers and Geoscientists Act, and by the By-laws of the Association.

The professional engineer or professional geoscientist shall act at all times with fairness, loyalty and courtesy to his associates, employers, employees and clients, and with fidelity to the public needs. He shall approach his work with devotion to high ideals, personal honour and integrity.

The purpose of the Code is two-fold:

(1) To give general statements of the principles of honourable conduct which, over the years, members of the professions of engineering and geoscience have come to accept as required of each member in order that he may fulfil his duty to the public, to the profession, and to his fellow members.

(2) To give some specifics in the sub-sections, both of required standards and prohibited actions, in order that they may act as a guide, to the intent of the general statements. These specifics, it is emphasized, are only some examples of the broad principles upon which members of this profession must appraise and govern their own conduct.

The following Code of Ethics is promulgated as a general guide and not as a denial of the existence of other duties equally imperative, but not specifically included.

Section 1
The Engineer or Geoscientist will be guided in all his professional relations by the highest standards of integrity.

(a) He will be realistic and honest in the preparation of all estimates, reports, statements and testimony.

(b) He will not distort or alter facts in an attempt to justify his decisions or avoid his responsibilities.

(c) He will advise his client or employer when he believes a project will not be successful or in the best interests of his client or his employer or the public.

(d) He will not engage in any work outside his salaried work to an extent prejudicial to his salaried position.

(e) In the interpretation of contract documents, he will maintain an attitude of scrupulous impartiality as between parties and will, as far as he can, ensure that each party to the contract will discharge the duties and enjoy the rights set down in the contract agreement.

(f) He will not use his professional position to secure special concessions or benefits which are detrimental to the public, his clients or his employer.

Section 2
The Engineer or Geoscientist will have proper regard for the safety, health and welfare of the public in the performance of his professional duties. He will regard his duty to the public safety and health as paramount.

(a) He will guard against conditions that are dangerous or threatening to life, limb, or property on work for which he is responsible, or if he is not responsible will properly call such conditions to the attention of those who are responsible.

(b) He will present clearly the consequences to be expected if his engineering judgement is overruled.

(c) He will seek opportunities to work for the advancement of the safety, health and welfare of his community.

(d) He will guard against conditions which are dangerous or threatening to the environment and he will seek to ensure that all standards required by law for environmental control are met.

Section 3

The Engineer or Geoscientist may promote and advertise his work or abilities provided that:

(a) The advertising preserves the public interest by reporting accurate and factual information which neither exaggerates nor misleads.

(b) The advertising does not impair the dignity of the profession.

(c) The Statements do not convey criticism of other engineers or geoscientists directly or indirectly.

Section 4

The Engineer or Geoscientist will endeavour to extend public knowledge and appreciation of engineering and geoscience and their achievements and will endeavour to protect the engineering and geoscience professions from misrepresentation and misunderstanding.

(a) He will not issue statements, criticisms, or arguments on engineering matters connected with public policy which are inspired or paid for by private interests, unless he indicates on whose behalf he is making the statement.

Section 5

The Engineer or Geoscientist may express an opinion on an engineering or geoscience subject only when founded on adequate knowledge and honest conviction.

(a) In reference to an engineering or geoscience project in a group discussion or public forum, he will strive for the use of pertinent facts, but if it becomes apparent to the member that such facts are being distorted or ignored, he should publicly disassociate himself from the group or forum.

Section 6

The Engineer or Geoscientist will undertake assignments for which he will be responsible only when qualified by training or experience; and he will engage, or advise engaging, experts and specialists whenever the client's or employer's interests are best served by such service.

(a)   He will not sign or seal plans, specifications, reports or parts thereof unless actually prepared by him or prepared under his supervision.

Section 7
The Engineer or Geoscientist will not disclose confidential information concerning the business affairs or technical processes of any present or former client or employer without his consent.

Section 8
The Engineer or Geoscientist will endeavour to avoid a conflict of interest with his employer or client, but when such conflict is unavoidable, he will fully disclose the circumstances to his employer or client.

(a)   He will inform his client or employer of any business connections, interests, or circumstances which may be deemed as influencing his judgement or the quality of his services to his client or employer.

(b)   He, while a member of any public body, will not act as a vendor of goods or services to that body.

Section 9
The Engineer or Geoscientist will uphold the principle of appropriate and adequate compensation for those engaged in engineering or geoscience work.

(a)   He will not normally undertake or agree to perform any professional service on a free basis, except for civic, charitable, religious, or nonprofit organizations when the professional services are advisory in nature.

(b)   He will not compete improperly by reducing his usual charges to underbid a fellow member after having been informed of that member's charge.

Section 10
The Engineer or Geoscientist will not accept compensation, financial or otherwise, from more than one interested party for the same service, or for services pertaining to the same work, unless there is full disclosure to and consent of all interested parties.

(a)   He will not accept financial or other considerations, including free professional services, from material or equipment suppliers as a reward for specifying their product.

(b)   He will not accept commissions or allowances, directly or indirectly, from contractors or other parties dealing with his clients or employer in connection with work for which he is responsible.

Section 11

The Engineer or Geoscientist will not compete unfairly with another engineer or geoscientist by attempting to obtain employment or advancement or professional engagements by taking advantage of a salaried position, or by criticizing other engineers or geoscientists or by other improper or questionable methods.

(a) He will not attempt to supplant another engineer or geoscientist in a particular employment after becoming aware that definite steps have been taken toward the other's employment.

(b) He will not offer to pay, or agree to pay either directly or indirectly, any commission, political contribution, gift, or other consideration in order to secure work.

(c) He will not solicit or accept an engineering or geoscience engagement on a contingent fee basis if payment depends on a finding of economic feasibility or other preconceived conclusion.

Section 12

The Engineer or Geoscientist will not attempt to injure maliciously or falsely, directly or indirectly, the professional reputation, prospects or practice of another person.

(a) He will not accept any engagement to review the work of a fellow engineer or geoscientist except with the knowledge of and after communication with such fellow engineer or geoscientist, where such communication is possible.

(b) He will refrain from expressing publicly an opinion on an engineering or geoscience subject unless he is informed as to the facts relating thereto.

(c) Unless he is convinced that his responsibility to the community requires him to do so, he will not express professional opinions which reflect on the ability or integrity of another person or organization.

(d) He will exercise due restraint in his comments on another engineer's or geoscientist's work.

(e) If he considers that an engineer or geoscientist is guilty of unethical, illegal or unfair practice, he will present the information to the Registrar of the Association.

(f) A member is entitled to make professional comparisons of the products offered by various suppliers.

Section 13

The Engineer or Geoscientist will not associate with or allow the use of his name by an enterprise of questionable character, or by one which is known to engage in unethical practice.

(a) He will not use association with a non-professional, a corporation, or partnership as a "cloak" for unethical acts, but must accept personal responsibility for his professional acts.

Section 14

The Engineer or Geoscientist will give credit for professional work to those to whom credit is due, and will recognize the proprietary interests of others.

(a) Whenever possible, he will name the person or persons who may be individually responsible for designs, inventions, writings, or other accomplishments.

(b) When a member uses designs supplied to him by a client or by a consultant, the designs remain the property of the client or consultant and should not be duplicated by the member for others without express permission.

(c) Before undertaking work for others in connection with which he may make improvements, plans, designs, inventions, or other records which may justify copyrights or patents, the engineer should enter into a positive agreement regarding the ownership of such copyrights and patents.

Section 15

The Engineer or Geoscientist will co-operate in extending the effectiveness of the profession by interchanging information and experience with other engineers, geoscientists and students, and will endeavour to provide opportunity for the professional development and advancement of engineers or geoscientists in his employ or under his supervision.

(a) He will encourage these employees in their efforts to improve their education.

(b) He will encourage these employees to attend and present papers at professional and technical society meetings.

(c) He will urge his qualified engineering or geoscience employees to become registered.

(d) He will assign a professional engineer or professional geoscientist duties of a nature to utilize his full training and experience, insofar as possible.

(e)   He will endeavour to provide a prospective engineering or geoscience employee with complete information on working conditions and his proposed status of employment, and after employment will keep him informed of any changes in them.

Section 16
The Engineer or Geoscientist will observe the rules of professional conduct which apply in the country in which he may practise. If there be no such rules, then he will observe those set out by this code.

Source: Engineers and Geoscientists Act, *Revised Statutes of British Columbia* 1979, c. 109, as amended. Reproduced with permission of the province of British Columbia, Queen's Printer.

MANITOBA

ENGINEERING PROFESSION ACT *(RE-ENACTED STATUTES OF MANITOBA* 1987, C. E120)

1. Definition of Engineering (Section 1 of the Act)

"practice of professional engineering" or "practice of engineering" means carrying on for hire, gain or hope of reward, either directly or indirectly, of one or more of the following branches of the science of engineering, namely:

(a) agricultural,
(b) biomedical,
(c) chemical,
(d) civil,
(e) electrical,
(f) forest,
(g) geological,
(h) industrial,
(i) mechanical,
(j) metallurgical,
(k) mining, or,
(l) structural,

or such other branch as hereafter may be recognized and adopted by by-law of the association as a branch of engineering and, without restricting the generality of the foregoing, includes the reporting on, advising on, valuing of, measuring for, laying out of, designing of, engineering inspection of (including the direction or supervision of any of the foregoing) or the construction, alteration, improvement or enlargement of, works or processes or any of them by reason of their requiring in connection with any of the operations above set forth, the skilled or professional application of the principles of mathematics, physics, mechanics, aeronautics, hydraulics, electricity, forestry, chemistry, geology, or metallurgy, but does not include the operation, execution or supervision of works as superintendent, foreman, inspector, road master, track master, bridge master, building master or contractor, where the works have been designed by and are constructed under the supervision of a professional engineer.

2. Membership Criteria (Section 15 of the Act)

15.   No person is entitled to be registered as a professional engineer or to become a member of the association unless he is of the full age of 18 years and
   (a)   submits evidence to the council showing that
      (i)   he is a graduate of a university, college or school in a program recognized by the council and has had such experience in engineering work as is satisfactory to the council, or
      (ii)   he has had at least six years actual experience in engineering work of a nature satisfactory to the council and submits to an examination or produces credentials in lieu thereof, as the council may decide, or
      (iii)   he is a resident of the province and is a duly registered member in good standing of an association of engineers in any other jurisdiction in Canada that is constituted similarly to the association and produces to the council a valid and subsisting certificate of membership in that association and otherwise complies with the requirements of council,
   and the council certifies in writing to the registrar, by minute or otherwise, that the evidence, examination or credentials are satisfactory to it;
   (b)   has paid such fees or dues as are prescribed by the by-laws;
   (c)   has subscribed to and agreed to abide by the code of ethics prescribed by the by-laws; and
   (d)   has complied with such other terms and conditions as the council, in accordance with this Act or the by-laws, may impose.

[NOTE: APEM By-Law No. 47 entitled "Practice of Engineering" states: "All programs accredited by the Canadian Engineering Accreditation Board of the Canadian Council of Professional Engineers shall be recognized as branches of Engineering pursuant to the Act."]

3. Definition of Professional Misconduct

[Although the Act uses the terms "misconduct" and "unprofessional conduct," the terms are not defined in the Act.]

4. Disciplinary Powers (Section 24 of the Act)

Complaint of misconduct, etc.
24(1) Subject to subsection (2), where a written complaint is made to the registrar that a member or a licensee has been
   (a) guilty of unprofessional conduct; or
   (b) guilty of conduct in the practice of engineering which is detrimental to the public interest; or
   (c) guilty of negligence in the practice of engineering; or
   (d) guilty of misconduct in the practice of engineering; or
   (e) convicted of a crime;
the council may hold a hearing into the complaint.

Decision of council
24(7) After completing a hearing into a complaint against a member or a licensee, if the council finds the member or licensee to have been
   (a) guilty of unprofessional conduct; or
   (b) guilty of conduct in the practice of engineering which is detrimental to the public interest; or
   (c) guilty of negligence in the practice of engineering; or
   (d) guilty of misconduct in the practice of engineering; or
   (e) convicted of a crime;
it may, subject to the by-laws, reprimand, censure, fine, suspend the registration or licence of, or cancel the registration or licence of, the member or licensee against whom the complaint was made and, it may order the member or licensee to pay all or any part of the costs and expenses incurred by the association in and for investigation of the complaint and the conduct of the hearing.

5. Code of Ethics (Established under Section 10 of the Act)

The code of ethics is a general guide to conduct and is not intended to deny the existence of other duties equally important though not specifically mentioned.

Council is empowered to enforce the rules herein established, but it is the privilege of any member to consult council as to the proper conduct to pursue in any specific case.

A breach of any of the following rules of conduct by any member of this association shall be considered inconsistent with honourable and dignified deportment in his professional practice, and such a member may be deemed guilty of unprofessional conduct, and thereby subject to discipline under section 24, subsection 7, of "The Engineering Profession Act."

1. Preamble

1.1 Honesty, justice and courtesy form a moral philosophy which, associated with mutual interest among men, constitute the foundation of ethics. The professional engineer should recognize such a standard, not in passive observance, but as a set of dynamic principles guiding his conduct and way of life. It is his duty to practise his profession according to this code of ethics.

1.2 As the keystone of professional conduct is integrity, the professional engineer will discharge his duties with fidelity to the public, his employers, and clients, and with fairness and impartiality to all. It is his duty to interest himself in public welfare, and to be ready to apply his special knowledge for the benefit of mankind. He should uphold the honour and dignity of his profession and also avoid association with any enterprise of questionable character. In his dealings with fellow engineers he should be fair and tolerant.

2. Duty to the state

2.1 The professional engineer owes a duty to the state, to maintain its integrity and its law.

2.2 He shall at all times act with candour and fairness when engaged as an expert witness and give, to the best of his knowledge and ability, an honest opinion based on adequate study of the matter in hand.

3. Duty to the public

3.1 The professional engineer shall regard the physical and economic well-being of the public as his first responsibility in all aspects of his work.

3.2 He shall advise on, design or supervise, only such projects as his training, ability and experience render him professionally competent to undertake.

3.3 He shall guard against conditions that are dangerous or threatening to health, life, limb or property on work for which he is responsible, or if he is not responsible, shall promptly call such conditions to the attention of those who are responsible.

3.4 He shall not associate himself with, or allow the use of his name by, an enterprise of doubtful character.

3.5 He shall not issue one-sided statements, criticism, or arguments on engineering matters which are initiated or paid for by parties with special interest, unless he indicates on whose behalf he is making the statement.

3.6 He shall refrain from expressing publicly an opinion on an engineering subject unless he is aware of all the related facts.

3.7 He shall not permit the publication of his reports, or parts of them in a manner calculated to mislead.

3.8 He shall on all occasions seal plans and specifications which legally require sealing and for which he is professionally responsible and ethically and legally entitled to seal, whether he acts in the capacity of a consultant or as an employee.

3.9 He shall sign or seal only those specifications and plans for which he is professionally responsible and which have been prepared by him or under his personal direction.

4. Duty to his client or employer

4.1 The professional engineer shall employ every resource of skill and knowledge that he commands to perform and satisfy the engineering needs of his client or employer in a truly worthy manner.

4.2 He shall act in professional matters for each client or employer as a faithful agent or trustee.

4.3 He shall ensure that the extent of his responsibility is fully understood by each client or employer before accepting a commission.

4.4 He shall not disclose any information concerning the business affairs or technical processes of clients or employers without their consent.

4.5 He shall engage, or advise each client or employer to engage, and shall co-operate with, other experts and specialists whenever the client's or employer's interests are best served by such service.

4.6 He shall present clearly the consequences to be expected from deviations proposed, if his engineering judgement is overruled by other authority, in cases where he is responsible for the technical adequacy of engineering work.

4.7 He shall inform his clients of any business connections, interest or circumstances which may be deemed as influencing his judgment or the quality of his services to his clients, before accepting a commission.

4.8 He shall not allow an interest in any business to adversely affect his decision regarding engineering work for which he is employed, or which he may be called upon to perform.

4.9 He shall not receive, directly or indirectly, any royalty, gratuity, or commission on any patented or protected article or process used in work upon which he is retained by his client, unless and until receipt of such royalty, gratuity or commission has been authorized in writing by his client.

4.10 He shall not accept compensation, financial or otherwise, from more than one interested party for the same service, or for services pertaining to the same work, without the consent of all interested parties.

4.11 He shall not be financially interested in the bids as or of a contractor on work for which he is employed as an engineer unless he has the written consent of his clients or employers.

4.12 He shall not accept commission, allowances, or fees, directly or indirectly, from contractors or other parties dealing with his client or employer in connection with work for which he is responsible, except proper engineering fees paid to him by the contractor for engineering work done prior to the award of the contract for a project for which the client subsequently appoints him consulting engineer, and then only if the client has been fully informed of the transaction prior to his appointment.

5. *Duty to the profession*

5.1 The professional engineer shall think highly of his profession and its members, its history and traditions and shall act in a manner worthy of its honour and dignity at all times.

5.2 He shall constantly strive to broaden his knowledge and experience by keeping abreast of new techniques and developments in his field of endeavour and to maintain his reputation for skill and integrity.

5.3 He shall participate in extending the effectiveness of the engineering profession by interchanging information and experience with other engineers and students, and by contributing to the work of the engineering societies, schools and scientific and engineering press.

5.4 He shall not advertise in an unprofessional manner by making misleading statements regarding his qualifications or experience.

5.5 He shall endeavour to extend public knowledge of engineering, shall discourage the spreading of unfair or exaggerated statements regarding engineering, and shall strive to protect the engineering profession collectively and individually from misrepresentation and misunderstanding.

5.6 He shall present appropriate information to the registrar of the association, if he considers that a professional colleague is engaging in unethical, illegal or unfair practice.

6. Duty to his colleagues

6.1 The professional engineer shall take care that credit for engineering work is given to those to whom credit is properly due.

6.2 He shall uphold the principle of appropriate compensation for those engaged in engineering work, including those in subordinate capacities, as being in the public interest by maintaining the standards of the profession.

6.3 He shall endeavour to provide opportunity for the development and advancement of engineers and technical people in his employ.

6.4 He shall not attempt to injure falsely or maliciously, directly or indirectly, the professional reputation, prospects or business of another engineer.

6.5 He shall not accept any commission to review the work of a fellow engineer except with the knowledge of, and after communication with, such fellow engineer, where such communication is possible.

6.6 He shall refrain from criticizing another engineer's work in public, recognizing the fact that the engineering societies and the engineering press provide the proper forum for technical discussions and criticisms.

6.7 He shall not attempt to supplant another engineer after definite steps have been taken toward the other's employment.

6.8 He shall not compete with another engineer by reducing his usual fees or salary after having been informed of the other's fees or salary.

6.9 [Repealed.]

6.10 He shall not use the advantages of a salaried position to compete unfairly with another engineer.

6.11 He shall always uphold the principle of a proper and separate fee being charged for engineering services for which he is responsible, whether acting as an independent consultant or as an employee of a firm supplying services in addition to those usually supplied by a consultant.

7. Duty to all contractual parties

7.1 The professional engineer shall act with fairness and honesty with his client or employer and any party who engages in a contractual agreement with them.

7.2 He shall co-operate with any parties under contract and make every reasonable effort to facilitate completion of the work in accordance with the terms of the contract.

7.3 He shall act in an impartial manner in dealing with disputes between the contractual parties.

I hereby subscribe to the above code of ethics
to which I set my seal and signature.

....P. Eng.

Adopted November 1st, 1921.
Rewritten and Adopted, February 28, 1968.

Source: Engineering Profession Act, *Re-enacted Statutes of Manitoba* 1987,
c. E120. Reproduced with permission of the province of Manitoba.

NEW BRUNSWICK

ENGINEERING PROFESSION ACT, 1986 (*STATUTES OF NEW BRUNSWICK* 1986, C. 88)

1. Definition of Engineering (Section 2(1) of the Act)

"engineering" means the application of scientific principles and
knowledge to practical ends such as the investigation, design, construction, or operation of works and systems for the benefit of man;

"practice of engineering" means the provision of services for another as an employee or by contract; and such services shall include
consultation, investigation, evaluation, planning, design, inspection, management, research and development of engineering works
and systems.

2. Membership Criteria (Section 10(1) of the Act)

10(1) Any applicant for registration who
  (a) is resident in New Brunswick;
  (b) is the age of legal majority;
  (c) is a graduate in engineering of an accredited university or
  other academic or technical institution recognized by the Council;
  (d) has fulfilled the requirements of approved engineering
  experience prescribed by the by-laws and satisfactory to the
  Council;
  (e) provides satisfactory evidence of good character; and
  (f) pays the fees prescribed by the by-laws;
upon approval of the Council, shall be entitled to become registered
as a member of the Association.

3. Definition of Professional Misconduct (Section 18 of the Act)

18(8)   A member, licensee, or the holder of a certificate of authorization may be found guilty of professional misconduct by the Discipline Committee if

(a)   the member, licensee or holder of a certificate of authorization has been found guilty of an offence which, in the opinion of the Committee, is relevant to suitability to practice engineering; or

(b)   the member, licensee, or holder of a certificate of authorization has been guilty, in the opinion of the Committee, of conduct relative to the practice of engineering which constitutes professional misconduct including, but not limited to, that defined in the by-laws.

18(9)   The Discipline Committee may find a member or licensee incompetent if in its opinion,

(a)   the member or licensee has displayed in his professional responsibility a lack of knowledge, skill, judgement, or disregard for the welfare of the public of a nature or to an extent that demonstrates the member or licensee is unfit to carry out the responsibilities of a professional engineer; or

(b)   the member or licensee is suffering from a physical or mental condition or disorder of a nature and extent making it desirable in the interests of the public, or the member or licensee, that he no longer be permitted to engage in the practice of professional engineering, or that his practice of professional engineering be restricted.

4. Disciplinary Powers (Section 18 of the Act)

18(10)   When the Discipline Committee finds a member, licensee, or the holder of a certificate of authorization guilty of professional misconduct or incompetence it may, by order, do any one or more of the following

(a)   revoke the right to practise engineering;

(b)   suspend the right to practise engineering for a stated period, not exceeding twenty-four months;

(c)   accept the undertaking of the member, licensee, or holder of a certificate of authorization to limit the professional work in the practice of engineering to the extent specified in the undertaking;

(d)   impose terms, conditions or limitations on the membership, licence, or certificate of authorization, including, but not limited to the successful completion of a particular course or courses of study, as specified by the Committee;

(e) impose specific restrictions on the membership, licence, or certificate of authorization, including but not limited to,

(i) requiring the member, licensee or holder of the certificate of authorization to engage in the practice of engineering only under the personal supervision and direction of a member,

(ii) requiring the member or licensee to not alone engage in the practice of engineering,

(iii) requiring the member, licensee, or the holder of the certificate of authorization to submit to periodic inspections by the Committee, or its delegate, of documents, records and work of the member or the holder in connection with his practice of engineering,

(iv) requiring the member, licensee, or the holder of the certificate of authorization to report to the Registrar or to such committee of the Council as the Committee may name on such matters with respect to the member's or holder's practice of engineering for such period and times, and in such form, as the Committee may specify;

(f) reprimand, admonish or counsel the member, licensee, or the holder of the certificate of authorization, and if considered warranted, direct that the fact of the reprimand, admonishment or counselling be recorded on the register for a stated or unlimited period of time;

(g) revoke or suspend for a stated period of time the designation of the member or licensee as a specialist, consulting engineer or otherwise;

(h) impose such fine as the Committee considers appropriate, to a maximum of five thousand dollars, to be paid by the member, licensee, or the holder of the certificate of authorization;

(i) subject to subsection (11) in respect of orders of revocation or suspension, direct that the finding and the order of the Committee be published in detail or in summary and either with or without including the name of the member, licensee or the holder of the certificate of authorization in the official publication of the Association and in such other manner or medium as the Committee considers appropriate in the particular case;

(j) fix and impose costs of any investigation or procedures by the Professional Conduct Committee or the Committee to be paid by the member, licensee or the holder of the certificate of authorization to the Association;

(k) direct that the imposition of a penalty or order be suspended
or postponed for such period, and upon such terms, or for such
purpose, including but not limited to,
  (i) the successful completion by the member or licensee of a
  particular course or courses of study,
  (ii) the production to the Committee of evidence satisfactory
  to it that any physical or mental handicap in respect of which
  the penalty was imposed has been overcome.

18(11) The Discipline Committee shall cause an order of the Committee revoking or suspending a membership, licence, or certificate of authorization to be published, with or without the reasons therefor, in the official publication of the Association together with the name of the member or holder of the revoked or suspended licence or certificate of authorization.

5. Code of Ethics (Section 2 of Part B of the Act)

1. Foreword

1 Honesty, justice and courtesy form a moral philosophy which, associated with mutual interest among people, constitute the foundation of ethics. Engineers should recognize such a standard, not in passive observance, but as a set of dynamic principles guiding their conduct and way of life. It is their duty to practise the profession according to the Act and the By-Laws including this Code of Ethics.

As the keystone of professional conduct is integrity, engineers shall discharge their duties with fidelity to the public, their employers and clients and with fairness and impartiality to all. It is their duty to interest themselves in public welfare and to be ready to apply their special knowledge for the benefit of humanity. They should uphold the honour and dignity of the profession and also avoid association with any enterprise of questionable character. In dealings with other engineers they should be fair and tolerant.

2. Professional Life

2.1 Engineers shall co-operate in extending the effectiveness of the engineering profession by interchanging information and experience with other engineers and students and by contributing to the work of engineering societies, schools and the scientific and engineering press.

2.2 Engineers shall encourage engineering employees to improve their knowledge and education.

2.3 Engineers shall strive to broaden their knowledge and experience by keeping abreast of new techniques and developments in their areas of endeavour.

2.4 Engineers shall report to the Association observed violations of the Engineering Profession Act or breaches of this Code of Ethics.

2.5 Engineers shall observe the rules of professional conduct which apply in the country in which they practise. If there are no such rules, they shall observe those established by this Code of Ethics.

2.6 Engineers shall not advertise their work or merit in a self-laudatory manner and will avoid all conduct or practice likely to discredit or do injury to the dignity and honour of the profession.

2.7 Engineers shall not advertise or represent themselves in an unprofessional manner by making misleading statements regarding their qualifications or experience.

3. Relations with the Public

3.1 Engineers shall endeavour to extend public knowledge of engineering and will discourage the spreading of untrue, unfair and exaggerated statements regarding engineering.

3.2 Engineers shall have due regard for the safety of life, health and welfare of the public and employees who may be affected by the work for which they are responsible.

3.3 Engineers, when giving testimony before a court, commission or other tribunal, shall express opinions only when they are founded on adequate knowledge and honest conviction.

3.4 Engineers shall not issue ex parte statements, criticism or arguments on matters connected with public policy which are inspired or paid for by private interests, unless it is indicated on whose behalf the arguments are made.

3.5 Engineers shall refrain from expressing publicly opinions on engineering subjects unless they are informed of the facts relating thereto.

4. Relations with Clients and Employers

4.1 Engineers shall act in professional matters for clients or employers as faithful agents or trustees.

4.2 Engineers shall act with fairness and justice between the client or employer and the contractor when dealing with contracts.

4.3 Engineers shall make their status clear to clients or employers before undertaking engagements if they are called upon to decide on the use of inventions, apparatus, etc. in which they may have a financial interest.

4.4 Engineers shall ensure that the extent of their responsibility is fully understood by each client before accepting a commission.

4.5 Engineers shall undertake only such work as they are competent to perform by virtue of their training and experience.

4.6 Engineers shall not sign or seal drawings, specifications, plans, reports or other documents pertaining to engineering works or systems unless actually prepared or verified by them or under their direct supervision.

4.7 Engineers shall guard against conditions that are dangerous or threatening to life, limb or property. On work for which they are not responsible, they shall promptly call such conditions to the attention of those who are responsible.

4.8 Engineers shall present clearly the consequences to be expected if their engineering judgement is overruled.

4.9 Engineers shall engage, or advise clients or employers to engage and shall co-operate with other experts and specialists whenever the clients' or employers' interests are best served by such service.

4.10 Engineers shall not disclose information concerning the business affairs or technical processes of clients or employers without their consent.

4.11 Engineers shall not accept compensation, financial or otherwise, from more than one interested party for the same service, or for services pertaining to the same work, without the consent of all interested parties.

4.12 Engineers shall not accept commissions or allowances, directly or indirectly, from contractors or other parties dealing with clients or employers in connection with work for which they are responsible.

4.13 Engineers shall not be financially interested in bids as contractors on work for which they are engaged as engineers unless they have the consent of the client or employer.

4.14 Engineers shall promptly disclose to clients or employers any interest in a business which may compete with or affect the business of the client or employer. They shall not allow an interest in any business to affect their decisions regarding engineering work for which they are employed, or which they may be called upon to perform.

4.15 Engineers serving as members of any public body shall not act as vendors of goods or services to that body without disclosure of their interest.

4.16 Engineers shall respect the right of employees to voice their professional concerns in an appropriate manner about engineering works which they believe to be dangerous or threatening to life, limb, or property.

5. *Relations with Engineers*

5.1 Engineers shall endeavour to protect the engineering profession collectively and individually from misrepresentation and misunderstanding.

5.2 Engineers shall take care that credit for engineering work is given to those to whom credit is properly due.

5.3 When an engineer uses a design supplied by a client or by a consultant, the design remains the property of the client or consultant and should not be duplicated by the engineer without the express permission of the client or consultant.

5.4 Engineers shall uphold the principles of appropriate and adequate compensation for those engaged in engineering work, including those in subordinate capacity, as being in the public interest and maintaining the standards of the profession.

5.5 Engineers shall not accept financial or other considerations, including free engineering designs, from material or equipment suppliers in return for specifying their product.

5.6 Engineers shall not solicit or accept an engineering engagement that requires the engineer to give a preconceived conclusion or opinion.

5.7 Engineers shall endeavour to provide opportunity for the professional development and advancement of engineers in their employ.

5.8 Engineers shall not directly or indirectly injure the professional reputation, prospects or practice of other engineers. However, if they consider that an engineer is guilty of unethical, illegal or unfair practice, they shall present the information to the proper authority for action.

5.9 The engineer shall exercise due restraint in criticizing another engineer's work in public, recognizing that the engineering societies and the engineering press provide the proper forum for technical discussions and criticism.

5.10 An engineer shall not try to supplant another engineer in a particular employment after becoming aware that definite steps have been taken toward the other's employment.

5.11 An engineer shall not compete with another engineer by reducing normal fees after having been informed of the charges named by the other.

5.12 An engineer shall not use the advantages of a salaried position to compete unfairly with another engineer.

5.13 Engineers shall not provide a commission, a gift or other consideration in order to secure work.

5.14 An engineer shall not associate with any engineering or non-engineering enterprise that does not conform to ethical practices.

Source: Engineering Profession Act, 1986, *Statutes of New Brunswick* 1986, c. 88. Reproduced with permission of the province of New Brunswick. Reprinted 11/89.

NEWFOUNDLAND

ENGINEERS AND GEOSCIENTISTS ACT *(STATUTES OF NEWFOUNDLAND* 1988, C. 48)

1. Definition of Engineering (Section 2 of the Act)

2. . . .

(j) "practice of engineering" means reporting on, advising on, evaluating, designing, preparing plans and specifications for or directing the construction, technical inspection, maintenance or operation of a structure, work or process

(i) that is aimed at the discovery, except by the practice of geoscience, development or utilization of matter, materials or energy or is designed for the use and convenience of human beings, and

(ii) that requires in the reporting, advising, evaluating, designing, preparation or direction the professional application of the principles of mathematics, chemistry, physics or a related applied subject,

and includes providing educational instruction on the matters contained in this paragraph to a student at an educational institution but excludes practising as a natural scientist;

(k) "practice of geoscience" means reporting on, advising on, evaluating, interpreting, processing, geological and geophysical surveying, exploring, classifying reserves or examining activities related to the earth sciences or engineering-geology

(i) that is aimed at the discovery or development of oil, natural gas, coal, metallic or non-metallic minerals or precious stones, water or other natural resources or that is aimed at the investigation of geoscientific conditions, and

(ii) that requires in the reporting, advising, evaluating, interpreting, processing, geoscientific surveying, exploring, reserve classifying, or examining the professional application of mathematics, chemistry or physics through the application of the principles of geoscience,

and includes providing educational instruction on the matters contained in this paragraph to a student at an educational institution;

2. Membership Criteria (Sections 20 to 22 of the Act and Section 5 of Newfoundland Regulation 209/89)

20. The Board of Examiners shall approve the registration as a professional engineer or geoscientist of a person who has applied to the Board and is eligible in accordance with this Act and the regulations to become a professional engineer or geoscientist.

21. The Board of Examiners shall approve the registration as a licensee of a person who has applied to the Board of Examiners and is eligible in accordance with this Act and the regulations to be registered to engage in the practice of engineering or of geoscience as a licensee.

22.

(1) The Council shall approve the registration as a permit holder of a person, a partnership or other association of persons, or of a corporation which has applied to the Council and is eligible under this section and the regulations to be registered to engage in the practice of engineering or of geoscience as a permit holder.

(2) A person, a partnership or other association of persons or a corporation that applies to the Council is eligible to be registered as a permit holder entitled to engage in the practice of engineering or of geoscience, or both, if it satisfies the Council that it complies with this Act and the regulations.

(3) The Council may grant a permit under one or more of the following classifications to:

Class A: a person, a partnership or other association of persons or a corporation, which is primarily engaged in offering and providing professional services to the public; and

Class B: a person, a partnership or other association of persons or a corporation, one of whose customary functions is to engage in the practice of engineering or the practice of geoscience, but whose principal activity is not the offering and providing of professional services to the public.

Regulation 5 (Registration as Professional Member)

5.

(1) In order to be eligible for registration as a professional member, an applicant shall, in addition to any other requirements of the act, the regulations and the by-laws;

(a) have knowledge of the Act, the regulations and by-laws, satisfactory to the Board of Examiners;

(b) have communication abilities in the English language satisfactory to the Board of Examiners or its Executive Committee as demonstrating the ability to competently practise engineering or geoscience in Newfoundland;

(c) have general knowledge of the practice of the professions demonstrated by successfully completing an examination in professional practice or by such other means as the Board of Examiners or its Executive Committee may require;

(d) be of good character and reputation; and

(e) satisfy all academic and practical experience requirements.

(2) In order to satisfy all academic and practical experience requirements an applicant shall have either:

(a) a Degree in Engineering or Geoscience from a university program approved by the Board of Examiners or its Executive Committee and at least two years of experience satisfactory to the Board of Examiners or its Executive Committee in the practice of engineering or geoscience subsequent to the conferral of the Degree; or

(b) academic standing equivalent to a Degree in Engineering or Geoscience demonstrated by successful completion of such confirmatory examinations as may be required by the Board of Examiners or its Executive Committee and at least two years of experience satisfactory to the Board of Examiners or its Executive Committee in the practice of engineering or geoscience subsequent to the attainment of such academic standing; or

(c) successfully completed such examinations as may be prescribed by the Board of Examiners or its Executive Committee and have a total of at least six years of experience satisfactory to the Board of Examiners or its Executive Committee in the practice of engineering or geoscience, one year of which must be obtained subsequent to successful completion of the prescribed examinations.

(3) In the event that an applicant for registration as a professional member seeks to transfer membership to this Association

and is a registered member in good standing of an association of professional engineers or geoscientists acceptable to the Board of Examiners or its Executive Committee, the Board of Examiners or its Executive Committee may waive any or all of the requirements for registration provided in subsection (1) and (2).

3. Definition of Professional Misconduct (Section 31 of the Act)

31.

(1) Any conduct of a professional member, licensee, permit holder or member-in-training whether in Canada or elsewhere that in the opinion of the Discipline Committee or the Council

(a) is detrimental to the best interests of the public;

(b) contravenes a code of ethics of the professions as established under the regulations;

(c) harms or tends to harm the standing of the professionals generally; or

(d) displays a lack of knowledge or skill or judgement in the practice of the profession or in the carrying out of a duty or obligation undertaken in the practice of the profession,

constitutes either unskilled practice of the profession or unprofessional conduct, whichever the Discipline Committee finds.

(2) If an investigated person fails to comply with or contravenes this Act, the regulations or the by-laws, and the failure or contravention is, in the opinion of the Discipline Committee, of a serious nature, the failure or contravention may be found by the Discipline Committee to be unprofessional conduct whether or not it would be so found under subsection (1).

4. Disciplinary Powers (Section 44 of the Act)

44. If the Discipline Committee finds that the conduct of the investigated person is unprofessional conduct or unskilled practice of the profession or both, the Discipline Committee may

(a) reprimand the investigated person;

(b) suspend the registration of the investigated person for a specified period;

(c) suspend the registration of the investigated person either generally or from any field of practice until

(i) the person has completed a specified course of studies or obtained supervised practical experience, or

(ii) the Discipline Committee is satisfied as to the competence of the investigated person generally or in a specified field of practice;

(d) accept in place of a suspension the investigated person's undertaking to limit his or her practice;

(e) impose conditions on the investigated person's practice of the profession generally or in a field of the practice, including the conditions that the person

(i) practise under supervision,

(ii) not engage in sole practice,

(iii) permit periodic inspections by a person authorized by the Discipline Committee, or

(iv) report to the Discipline Committee on specific matters;

(f) direct the investigated person to pass a course of study or satisfy the Discipline Committee of his or her practical competence;

(g) require the investigated person to take counselling or to obtain the assistance that in the opinion of the Discipline Committee is appropriate;

(h) direct the investigated person to waive, reduce or prepay a fee for services rendered by the investigated person that, in the opinion of the Discipline Committee were improperly rendered;

(i) cancel the registration of the investigated person; or

(j) make any other order that it considers appropriate in the circumstances.

5. Code of Ethics (Newfoundland Regulation 209/89, Schedule A, Established in Accordance with Section 17 of the Act)

1. A professional engineer or geoscientist shall recognize that professional ethics are founded upon integrity, competence and devotion to service and to the advancement of human welfare. This concept shall guide the conduct of the professional engineer or geoscientist at all times.

Duties of the Professional Engineer or Geoscientist to the Public
A professional engineer or geoscientist shall:

2. have proper regard in all his or her work for the safety, health and welfare of the public;

3. endeavour to extend public understanding of engineering and geoscience and their role in society;

4. where his or her professional knowledge may benefit the public, seek opportunities to serve in public affairs;

5. not be associated with enterprises contrary to the public interest;

6. undertake only such work as he or she is competent to perform by virtue of his or her education, training and experience;

7. sign and seal only such plans, documents or work as he or she has personally prepared or which have been prepared or carried out under his or her direct professional supervision;

8. express opinions on engineering or geoscientific matters only on the basis of adequate knowledge and honest conviction.

Duties of the Professional Engineer or Geoscientist to Client or Employer

A professional engineer or geoscientist shall:

9. act for his or her client or employer as a faithful agent or trustee;

10. not accept remuneration for services rendered other than from his or her client or employer;

11. not disclose confidential information without the consent of his or her client or employer;

12. not undertake any assignment which may create a conflict of interest with his or her client or employer without a full knowledge of the client or employer;

13. present clearly to his or her clients or employers the consequences to be expected if his or her professional judgement is overruled by other authorities in matters pertaining to work for which he or she is professionally responsible.

Duties of the Professional Engineer or Geoscientist to the Profession

A professional engineer or geoscientist shall:

14. endeavour at all times to improve the competence, dignity and reputation of his or her profession;

15. conduct himself or herself towards other professional engineers and geoscientists with fairness and good faith;

16. not advertise his or her professional services in self-laudatory language or in any other manner derogatory to the dignity of the profession;

17. not attempt to supplant another engineer or geoscientist in an engagement after definite steps have been taken toward the other's employment;

18. when in a salaried position, engage in a private practice and offer or provide professional services to the public only with the consent of his or her employer and in compliance with all requirements of such practice;

19. not exert undue influence or offer, solicit or accept compensation for the purpose of affecting negotiations for an engagement;
20. not invite or submit proposals under conditions that constitute only price competition for professional services;
21. advise the Council of any practice by another member of the profession which he or she believes to be contrary to this Code of Ethics.

Source: Engineers and Geoscientists Act, *Statutes of Newfoundland* 1988, c. 48. Reproduced with permission of the province of Newfoundland.

N O R T H W E S T   T E R R I T O R I E S

ENGINEERING, GEOLOGICAL AND GEOPHYSICAL PROFESSIONS ACT, (*STATUTES OF NORTHWEST TERRITORIES* 1988 (2), C. 7)

1. Definition of Engineering (Section 1 of the Act)

"professional engineer" means a member or licensee qualified to practise professional engineering;
"professional engineering" means
    (a) the application of scientific principles and knowledge to practical ends as in the investigation, inspection, design, construction or operation of works, systems, structures or processes for the benefit of humans, and without restricting the generality of paragraph (a), includes
    (b) the provision or performance of services including consultation, investigation, evaluation, reporting, planning, design, technical inspection, preparation of plans and specifications for, surveying for, supervision, management, research, co-ordination of design or construction, or both, and directing the construction, technical inspection, maintenance or operation of works, systems, structures or processes, but does not include
    (c) the execution or supervision of the construction, technical inspection, maintenance or operation of works, systems, structures, or processes in the capacity of contractor, superintendent, work supervisor or inspector or in a similar capacity, when the works, systems, structures or processes have been designed by and the execution or supervision is being carried out under the direct supervision of a professional engineer, or

(d) any of the services mentioned in paragraph (b) when they are carried out by a technician, technologist or engineer-in-training under the direct supervision of a professional engineer;

"professional geologist" means a member or licensee qualified to practise professional geology;

"professional geology" means reporting, advising, evaluating, interpreting, geological surveying, sampling or examining related to any activity

(a) that is aimed at the discovery or development of oil, natural gas, coal, metallic or non-metallic minerals, precious stones or other natural resources or water, or that is aimed at the investigation of geological conditions, and

(b) that requires the professional application of the principles of the geological sciences or any related subject including mineralogy, paleontology, economic geology, structural geology, stratigraphy, sedimentation, petrology, geomorphology, photogeology and similar fields,

but does not include any of the activities mentioned in paragraphs (a) and (b) that are normally associated with the business of prospecting when carried on by a prospector or any of the activities mentioned in paragraphs (a) and (b) carried on by a technician, technologist or geologist-in-training under the direct supervision of a professional geologist;

"professional geophysicist" means a member or licensee qualified to practise professional geophysics;

"professional geophysics" means reporting, advising, evaluating, interpreting or geophysical surveying related to any activity

(a) that is aimed at the discovery or development of oil, natural gas, coal, metallic or non-metallic minerals, precious stones or other natural resources or water, or that is aimed at the investigation and measurement of the physical properties of the earth, and

(b) that requires the professional application of the principles of one or more of the subjects of physics, mathematics or any related subject including elastic wave propagation, gravitational, magnetic and electrical fields, natural radioactivity, and similar fields, but does not include the routine maintenance or operation of geophysical instruments, or any of the activities mentioned in paragraphs (a) and (b) that are normally associated with the business of prospecting when carried on by a prospector or by a technician, technologist or geophysicist-in-training under the direct supervision of a professional geophysicist;

2. Membership Criteria (Sections 11 and 13 of the Act)

11.

(1) Subject to this section, an applicant shall, before being approved for registration,

(a) be a graduate of a university program in engineering, geology or geophysics that is approved by the Board of Examiners; and

(b) have at least two years experience satisfactory to the Board, subsequent to university graduation, in the practise of engineering, geology or geophysics.

(2) Where an applicant for registration is a graduate of a university program in engineering, geology or geophysics that is not approved by the Board of Examiners, the applicant shall, before being approved for registration.

(a) pass confirmatory examinations set by the Board; and

(b) have at least two years experience satisfactory to the Board, subsequent to university graduation, in the practise of engineering, geology or geophysics.

(3) Where an applicant for registration has not graduated from a university program in engineering, geology or geophysics, the applicant shall, before being approved for registration,

(a) pass examinations set by the Board of Examiners; and

(b) have at least six years experience satisfactory to the Board in the practise of engineering, geology or geophysics.

(4) This section does not apply to a person referred to in clause 13(1)(c)(iii)(B) or 13(2)(c)(ii)(B).

13.

(1) The council shall register as a member every person, other than a licensee, who

(a) applies in accordance with the by-laws;

(b) pays the required fees; and

(c) satisfies the council that he or she

(i) is a resident of the Territories,

(ii) is a Canadian citizen, a permanent resident or is otherwise lawfully permitted to work in Canada, and

(iii) either

(A) satisfies the requirements set out in section 11, or

(B) is a member of an association or corporation in any other jurisdiction having requirements for registration considered by the council to be equivalent to those of the Association.

(2) The council shall register as a licensee every person, other than a member, who

(a) applies in accordance with the by-laws;

(b) pays the required fees; and

(c) satisfies the council that he or she

(i) is a Canadian citizen, a permanent resident or is otherwise lawfully permitted to work in Canada, and

(ii) either

(A) satisfies the requirements set out in section 11, or

(B) is a member or a licensee of an association or corporation in any other jurisdiction having requirements for registration considered by the council to be equivalent to those of the Association.

(3) Notwithstanding anything in this Act, the council may require an applicant for registration to write such professional practice examinations as the council considers necessary, and the council may refuse to register as a member or licensee any person who fails such examinations.

(4) Where an application for registration is rejected, the council shall furnish the unsuccessful applicant with a written notice of that fact stating the reason for the rejection of the application.

(5) The Board of Examiners shall determine whether a successful applicant is to be designated as a professional engineer, a professional geologist or a professional geophysicist or any two or all of these, and on registration as a member or a licensee he or she shall be designated accordingly.

3. Definition of Professional Misconduct (Section 25 of the Act)

25.

(1) The question of whether a person is guilty of conduct unbecoming a registrant or permit holder shall be determined by the council or, on appeal, by the Supreme Court.

(2) For the purposes of this Act, conduct that, in the judgement of the council, or the Supreme Court on appeal, constitutes professional misconduct, gross negligence, incompetence or misrepresentation or that is contrary to the best interests of the public or the profession of engineering, geology or geophysics shall be deemed to be conduct unbecoming a registrant or permit holder.

4. Disciplinary Powers (Sections 35, 36 of the Act)

35.

(1) Where on completion of a hearing, the council forms the opinion that the conduct under investigation is not conduct un-

becoming a registrant of the relevant classification or a permit holder, the council shall

(a) dismiss the complaint or take no further action on the matter; and

(b) notify the complainant, if any, and the person whose conduct has been the subject-matter of the hearing.

(2) Where, on completion of a hearing, the council

(a) forms the opinion that the conduct under investigation is conduct unbecoming a registrant of the relevant classification or a permit holder, and

(b) considers that the conduct is not of such gravity or importance as to warrant suspension of the registrant or permit, the striking of the person's name from the register or the revocation of the permit,

the council may reprimand the registrant or permit holder.

(3) Where, on completion of a hearing, the council

(a) forms the opinion that the conduct under investigation is conduct unbecoming a registrant of the relevant classification, or permit holder, and

(b) considers the conduct to be sufficiently grave to merit suspension of the registrant or permit, the striking of the person's name from the register, or the revocation of the permit,

the council may order that

(c) the name of a member or licensee be struck from the register of the Association;

(d) a member or licensee be suspended from practising professional engineering, professional geology or professional geophysics for such period as the council considers proper;

(e) the permit of a permit holder be suspended for such period as the council considers proper or revoked; or

(f) the complaint or matter, if it relates to a person-in-training or student, be disposed of in a manner set out in the by-laws.

(4) The council may order that a person whose name is to be struck from the register or whose permit is to be revoked under this section shall

(a) pass examinations set by the Board of Examiners, and

(b) pass a particular course of study or obtain experience generally or in a field of practice satisfactory to the Board of Examiners,

before the council shall reinstate that person as a member, licensee or permit holder.

(5) Notwithstanding anything in this Act, the council shall not register as a member or licensee, nor grant a permit to, any person

whose name has been struck from the register or whose permit has been revoked under this section, unless the council is satisfied that the person has complied with any order made under subsection (4).

36.

The council, in addition to a reprimand, or in addition to or in the place of an order under subsection 35(3), may order

(a) the registrant or permit holder to pay a fine not exceeding $5000 to the Association within the time fixed by the order;

(b) the registrant or permit holder to pay to the Association the costs of the hearing in an amount and within a time fixed by the council; and

(c) that the registrant or the permit be suspended in default of payment of a fine or costs ordered to be paid until the fine or costs are paid.

5. Code of Ethics (Part II of the By-Laws, Established under Section 5 of the Act)

Preamble

Professional Engineers, Geologists, and Geophysicists shall recognize that professional ethics are founded upon integrity, competence, devotion to service, and to advancement of human welfare. Their concepts shall guide their conduct at all times. In this way, each professional's actions will enhance the dignity and status of the professions.

Professional Engineers, Geologists, and Geophysicists, through their practice, are charged with extending public understanding of the professions and should serve in public affairs when their professional knowledge may be of benefit to the public.

Professional Engineers, Geologists, and Geophysicists will build their reputations on the basis of merit of their services, and shall not compete unfairly with others or compete primarily on the basis of fees without due consideration of other factors.

Professional Engineers, Geologists, and Geophysicists will maintain a special obligation to demonstrate understanding, professionalism, and technical expertise to members-in-training under their supervision.

Rules of Conduct

Professional Engineers, Geologists and Geophysicists:

1. shall have proper regard in all their work for the safety and welfare of all persons and for the physical environment affected by such work.

2. shall undertake only such work as they are competent to perform by virtue of training and expertise, and shall express opinions on engineering, geological and geophysical matters only on the basis of adequate knowledge and honest conviction.

3. shall sign and seal only reports, plans or documents which they have prepared or which have been prepared under their direct supervision and control.

4. shall act for their clients or employers as a faithful agent or trustee; always acting independently and with fairness and justice to all parties.

5. shall not engage in activities nor accept remuneration for services rendered, which may create a conflict of interest with their clients or employers, without the knowledge and consent of their clients or employers.

6. shall not disclose confidential information without the consent of their clients or employers, unless the withholding of such information is deemed contrary to the safety of the public.

7. shall present clearly to their clients or employers the consequences to be expected if their professional judgement is overruled by other authorities in matters pertaining to work for which they are professionally responsible.

8. shall not offer or accept covert payment for the purpose of securing an engineering, geological, or geophysical assignment.

9. shall represent their qualifications and competence, or advertise professional services offered, only through factual representation without exaggeration.

10. shall conduct themselves toward other professional engineers, geologists, geophysicists, employees and others with fairness and good faith.

11. shall advise the Executive Director of any practice by another member of the Association, which they believe to be contrary to this code of ethics.

Source: Engineering, Geological and Geophysical Professions Act, *Statutes of Northwest Territories* 1988(2), c. 7. Reproduced with permission of the Northwest Territories.

NOVA SCOTIA

ENGINEERING PROFESSION ACT *(REVISED STATUTES OF NOVA SCOTIA* 1989, C. 148)

1. Definition of Engineering (Section 2 of the Act)

2.

(g)

"Engineering" means the science and art of designing, investigating, supervising the construction, maintenance or operation of, making specifications, inventories or appraisals of, and consultations or reports on machinery, structure, works, plants, mines, mineral deposits, processes, transportation systems, transmission systems and communication systems or any other part thereof.

2. Membership Criteria (Section 7 of the Act)

7.

1. Any person shall be entitled to be registered as a member of the Association upon filing with the Registrar satisfactory proof that such person is a resident of the Province, has tendered the fees and dues prescribed by the By-laws, and

(a) has obtained a degree in engineering from a school, college or university, which degree is approved by the Council, and has had two years experience in engineering;

(b) has obtained a degree in science, other than engineering, from a school, college or university, which degree is approved by the Council, and has had four years experience in engineering;

(c) is a registered member of an association of engineers, which association in the opinion of the Council is similarly constituted and has similar membership requirements to this Association, and furnishes the Registrar with a certificate of membership in good standing in such other Association;

(d) has passed the examinations prescribed by the Council and has had sufficient number of years of experience in engineering to qualify such person in the opinion of the Council to practise professional engineering; or

(e) has had in the opinion of the Council outstanding experience in engineering.

(2) Every person, who in the opinion of the Council, expressed by a resolution thereof, has complied with subsection (1), shall be registered as a member.

3. Definition of Professional Misconduct (Section 24 of the By-Laws)

24. Members, persons licensed to practise and engineers-in-training shall conduct themselves in accordance with the Code of Ethics appended hereto, and without restricting the meaning of unprofessional conduct, any breach of the Code of Ethics shall be deemed to be a form of unprofessional conduct.

4. Disciplinary Powers (Section 17 of the Act)

17(1) The Council may, in the manner provided by the by-laws, reprimand and censure any member, person licensed to practise or engineer-in-training, or suspend or cancel the certificate of registration of any member or the license to practise of any person or the enrolment of any engineer-in-training, who is guilty of unprofessional conduct, negligence or misconduct in the execution of the duties of his office, or of any breach of this Act or of the by-laws, or who has been convicted of a criminal offence by any court of competent jurisdiction.

5. Code of Ethics (Appendix to the By-Laws)

General
1. A Professional Engineer shall recognize that professional ethics are founded upon integrity, competence and devotion to service and to the advancement of public welfare. This concept shall guide his conduct at all times.

Relations with The Public
A Professional Engineer:
2. shall regard his duty to public welfare as paramount.
3. shall endeavour to enhance the public regard for his profession by extending the public knowledge thereof.
4. shall undertake only such work as he is competent to perform by virtue of his training and experience.
5. shall sign and seal only such plans, documents or work as he himself has prepared or carried out or as have been prepared or carried out under his direct professional supervision.
6. shall express opinions on engineering matters only on the basis of adequate knowledge, competence and honest conviction.

7. shall express opinions or make statements on engineering projects of public interest that are inspired or paid for by private interest only if he clearly discloses on whose behalf he is giving the opinion or making the statements.

8. shall not be associated with enterprises contrary to public interest or sponsored by persons of questionable integrity.

Relations with Clients and Employers

A Professional Engineer:

9. shall act for his client or employer as a faithful agent or trustee and shall act with fairness and justice between his client or employer and the contractor when contracts are involved.

10. shall not accept compensation, financial or otherwise, from more than one interested party for the same service, or for service pertaining to the same work, without the consent of all interested parties.

11. shall not disclose confidential information without the consent of his client or employer.

12. shall not be financially interested in bids on competitive work for which he is employed as an engineer unless he has the consent of his client or employer.

13. shall not undertake any assignment which may create a conflict of interest with his client or employer without the full knowledge of the client or employer.

14. shall present clearly to his clients or employers the consequences to be expected if his professional judgement is overruled by other authorities in matters pertaining to work for which he is professionally responsible.

15. shall refrain from unprofessional conduct or from actions which he considers to be contrary to the public good, even if expected or directed by his employer or client, to act in such a manner.

16. shall not expect or direct an employee or subordinate to act in a manner that he or the employee or subordinate considers to be unprofessional or contrary to the public good.

17. shall guard against conditions that are dangerous or threatening to life, limb or property on work for which he is responsible, or if he is not responsible, will promptly call such conditions to the attention of those who are responsible.

Relations with The Profession

A Professional Engineer:

18. shall co-operate in extending the effectiveness of the engineering profession by interchanging information and experience with other engineers and students and by contributing to the work of engineering societies, schools and the scientific and engineering press.

19. shall endeavour at all times to improve the competence, and thus the dignity and prestige of his profession.

20. shall not advertise his work or merit in a self-laudatory manner and shall avoid all conduct or practice likely to discredit or do injury to the dignity and honor of his profession.

21. shall not attempt to supplant another engineer in an engagement after a definite commitment has been made toward the other's employment.

22. shall not exert undue influence or offer, solicit or accept compensation for the purpose of affecting negotiations for an engagement.

23. shall not compete with another engineer on the basis of charges for work by underbidding, through reducing his normal fees after having been informed of the charges named by the other.

24. shall not use the advantages of a salaried position to compete unfairly with another engineer.

25. shall advise the Discipline Committee of any practice by another member of his profession which he believes to be contrary to this Code of Ethics.

26. shall take care that credit for engineering work is given to those to whom credit is properly due.

27. shall uphold the principle of appropriate and adequate compensation for those engaged in engineering work including those in subordinate capacities as being in the public interest maintaining the standards of the profession.

28. shall endeavour to provide opportunity for the professional development and advancement of engineers in his employ.

Source: Engineering Profession Act, *Revised Statutes of Nova Scotia* 1989, c. 148. Reproduced with permission of the Government of Nova Scotia.

ONTARIO

PROFESSIONAL ENGINEERS ACT, 1984, *(STATUTES OF ONTARIO*, C. 13, AS AMENDED)

1. Definition of Engineering (Section 1 of the Act)

1.

(m) "practice of professional engineering" means any act of designing, composing, evaluating, advising, reporting, directing or supervising wherein the safeguarding of life, health, property or the public welfare is concerned and that requires the application of engineering principles, but does not include practising as a natural scientist; "professional engineer" means a person who holds a licence or a temporary licence;

2. Membership Criteria (Section 14 of the Act)

14.

(1) The Registrar shall issue a licence to a natural person who applies therefor in accordance with the regulations and,

(a) is a citizen of Canada or has the status of a permanent resident of Canada;

(b) is not less than eighteen years of age;

(c) has complied with the academic requirements specified in the regulations for the issuance of the licence and has passed such examinations as the Council has set or approved in accordance with the regulations or is exempted therefrom by the Council;

(d) has complied with the experience requirements specified in the regulations for the issuance of the licence; and

(e) is of good character.

(2) The Registrar may refuse to issue a licence to an applicant where the Registrar is of the opinion, upon reasonable and probable grounds, that the past conduct of the applicant affords grounds for belief that the applicant will not engage in the practice of professional engineering in accordance with the law and with honesty and integrity.

(3) The Registrar, on his own initiative, may refer and on the request of an applicant shall refer the application of the applicant for the issuance of a licence,

(a) to the Academic Requirements Committee for a determination as to whether or not the applicant has met the academic requirements prescribed by the regulations for the issuance of the licence;

(b) to the Experience Requirements Committee for a determination as to whether or not the applicant has met the experience requirements prescribed by the regulations for the issuance of the licence; or

(c) first to the Academic Requirements Committee and then to the Experience Requirements Committee for determinations under clauses (a) and (b).

(4) A determination by a committee under subsection (3) is final and is binding on the Registrar and on the Applicant.

(5) A committee shall receive written representations from an applicant but is not required to hold or to afford to any person a hearing or an opportunity to make oral submissions before making a determination under subsection (3).

(6) The Registrar shall give notice to the applicant of a determination by a committee under subsection (3) and, if the applicant is rejected, the notice shall detail the specific requirements that the applicant must meet.

3. Definition of Professional Misconduct (Section 86 of Ontario Regulation 538/84)

86.

(1) In this section, "negligence" means an act or an omission in the carrying out of the work of a practitioner that constitutes a failure to maintain the standards that a reasonable and prudent practitioner would maintain in the circumstances.

(2) For the purposes of the Act and this Regulation, "professional misconduct" means,

(a) negligence;

(b) failure to make reasonable provision for the safeguarding of life, health or property of a person who may be affected by the work for which the practitioner is responsible;

(c) failure to act to correct or report a situation that the practitioner believes may endanger the safety or the welfare of the public;

(d) failure to make responsible provision for complying with applicable statutes, regulations, standards, codes, by-laws and rules in connection with work being undertaken by or under the responsibility of the practitioner;

(e) signing or sealing a final drawing, specification, plan, report or other document not actually prepared or checked by the practitioner;

(f) failure of a practitioner to present clearly to his employer the consequences to be expected from a deviation proposed in work, if the professional engineering judgement of the practitioner is overruled by non-technical authority in cases where the practitioner is responsible for the technical adequacy of professional engineering work;

(g) breach of the Act or regulations, other than an action that is solely a breach of the code of ethics;

(h) undertaking work the practitioner is not competent to perform by virtue of his training and experience;

(i) failure to make prompt, voluntary and complete disclosure of an interest, direct or indirect, that might in any way be, or be construed as, prejudicial to the professional judgement of the practitioner in rendering service to the public, to an employer or to a client, and in particular without limiting the generality of the foregoing, carrying out any of the following acts without making such a prior disclosure:

1. Accepting compensation in any form for a particular service from more than one party.

2. Submitting a tender or acting as a contractor in respect of work upon which the practitioner may be performing as a professional engineer.

3. Participating in the supply of material or equipment to be used by the employer or client of the practitioner.

4. Contracting in the practitioner's own right to perform professional engineering services for other than the practitioner's employer.

5. Expressing opinions or making statements concerning matters within the practice of professional engineering of public interest where the opinions or statements are inspired or paid for by other interests;

(j) conduct or an act relevant to the practice of professional engineering that, having regard to all the circumstances, would reasonably be regarded by the engineering profession as disgraceful, dishonourable or unprofessional;

(k) failure by a practitioner to abide by the terms, conditions or limitations of the practitioner's licence, limited licence, temporary licence or certificate;

(l) failure to supply documents or information requested by an investigator acting under section 34 of the Act;

(m) permitting, counselling or assisting a person who is not a practitioner to engage in the practice of professional engineering except as provided for in the Act or the regulations.

O. Reg. 538/84, s. 86.

4. Disciplinary Powers (Section 29 of the Act)

29.

(1) The Discipline Committee shall,

(a) when so directed by the Council, the Executive Committee or the Complaints Committee, hear and determine allegations of professional misconduct or incompetence against a member of the Association or a holder of a certificate of authorization, a temporary licence or a limited licence;

(b) hear and determine matters referred to it under section 25, 28 or 38; and

(c) perform such other duties as are assigned to it by the Council.

(2) A member of the Association or a holder of a certificate of authorization, a temporary licence or a limited licence may be found guilty of professional misconduct by the Committee if,

(a) the member or holder has been found guilty of an offence relevant to suitability to practise, upon proof of such conviction;

(b) the member or holder has been guilty in the opinion of the Discipline Committee of professional misconduct as defined in the regulations.

(3) The Discipline Committee may find a member of the Association or a holder of a temporary licence or a limited licence to be incompetent if in its opinion,

(a) the member or holder has displayed in his professional responsibilities a lack of knowledge, skill or judgement or disregard for the welfare of the public of a nature or to an extent that demonstrates the member or holder is unfit to carry out the responsibilities of a professional engineer; or

(b) the member or holder is suffering from a physical or mental condition or disorder of a nature and extent making it desirable in the interests of the public or the member or holder that the member or holder no longer be permitted to engage in the practice of professional engineering or that his practice of professional engineering be restricted.

(4) Where the Discipline Committee finds a member of the Association or a holder of a certificate of authorization, a temporary licence or a limited licence guilty of professional misconduct or to be incompetent it may, by order,

(a) revoke the licence of the member or the certificate of authorization, temporary licence or limited licence of the holder;

(b) suspend the licence of the member or the certificate of authorization, temporary licence or limited licence of the holder for a stated period, not exceeding twenty-four months;

(c) accept the undertaking of the member or holder to limit the professional work of the member or holder in the practice of professional engineering to the extent specified in the undertaking;

(d) impose terms, conditions or limitations on the licence or certificate of authorization, temporary licence or limited licence, of the member or holder, including but not limited to the successful completion of a particular course or courses of study, as are specified by the Discipline Committee;

(e) impose specific restrictions on the licence or certificate of authorization, temporary licence or limited licence, including but not limited to,

(i) requiring the member or the holder of the certificate of authorization, temporary licence or limited licence to engage in the practice of professional engineering only under the personal supervision and direction of a member,

(ii) requiring the member to not alone engage in the practice of professional engineering,

(iii) requiring the member or the holder of the certificate of authorization, temporary licence or limited licence to accept periodic inspections by the Committee or its delegate of documents and records in the possession or under the control of the member or the holder in connection with the practice of professional engineering,

(iv) requiring the member or the holder of the certificate of authorization, temporary licence or limited licence to report to the Registrar or to such committee of the Council as the Discipline Committee may specify on such matters in respect of the member's or holder's practice for such period of time, at such times and in such form, as the Discipline Committee may specify;

(f) require that the member or the holder of the certificate of authorization, temporary licence or limited licence be reprimanded, admonished or counselled and, if considered warranted, direct that the fact of the reprimand, admonishment or counselling be recorded on the register for a stated or unlimited period of time;

(g) revoke or suspend for a stated period of time the designation of the member or holder by the Association as a specialist, consulting engineer or otherwise;

(h) impose such fine as the Discipline Committee considers appropriate, to a maximum of $5000, to be paid by the member of the Association or the holder of the certificate of authorization, temporary licence or limited licence to the Treasurer of Ontario for payment into the Consolidated Revenue Fund;

(i) subject to subsection (5) in respect of orders of revocation or suspension, direct that the finding and the order of the Discipline Committee be published in detail or in summary and either with or without including the name of the member or holder in the official publication of the Association and in such other manner or medium as the Discipline Committee considers appropriate in the particular case;

(j) fix and impose costs to be paid by the member or the holder to the Association;

(k) direct that the imposition of a penalty be suspended or postponed for such period and upon such terms or for such purpose, including but not limited to,

(i) the successful completion by the member or the holder of the temporary licence or the limited licence of a particular course or courses of study,

(ii) the production to the Discipline Committee of evidence satisfactory to it that any physical or mental handicap in respect of which the penalty was imposed has been overcome,

or any combination of them.

(5) The Discipline Committee shall cause an order of the Committee revoking or suspending a licence or certificate of authorization, temporary licence or limited licence to be published, with or without the reasons therefor, in the official publication of the Association together with the name of the member or holder of the revoked or suspended licence or certificate of authorization, temporary licence or limited licence.

5. Code of Ethics (Section 91, Ontario Regulation 538/84, Established under Section 7 of the Act)

91. The following is the Code of Ethics of the Association:

(1) It is the duty of a practitioner to the public, to his employer, to his clients, to other members of his profession, and to himself to act at all times with,

(i) fairness and loyalty to his associates, employers, clients, subordinates and employees,

(ii) fidelity to public needs, and

(iii) devotion to high ideals of personal honour and professional integrity.

(2) A practitioner shall,

(i) regard his duty to public welfare as paramount,

(ii) endeavour at all times to enhance the public regard for his profession by extending the public knowledge thereof and discouraging untrue, unfair or exaggerated statements with respect to professional engineering,

(iii) not express publicly, or while he is serving as a witness before a court, commission or other tribunal, opinions on professional engineering matters that are not founded on adequate knowledge and honest conviction,

(iv)   endeavour to keep his licence, temporary licence, limited licence or certificate of authorization, as the case may be, permanently displayed in his place of business.

(3)   A practitioner shall act in professional engineering matters for each employer as a faithful agent or trustee and shall regard as confidential information obtained by him as to the business affairs, technical methods or processes of an employer and avoid or disclose a conflict of interest that might influence his actions or judgement.

(4)   A practitioner must disclose immediately to his client any interest, direct or indirect, that might be construed as prejudicial in any way to the professional judgement of the practitioner in rendering service to the client.

(5)   A practitioner who is an employee-engineer and is contracting in his own name to perform professional engineering work for other than his employer, must provide his client with a written statement of the nature of his status as an employee and the attendant limitations on his services to the client, must satisfy himself that the work will not conflict with his duty to his employer, and must inform his employer of the work.

(6)   A practitioner must co-operate in working with other professionals engaged on a project.

(7)   A practitioner shall,

(i)   conduct himself toward other practitioners with courtesy and good faith,

(ii)   not accept an engagement to review the work of another practitioner for the same employer except with the knowledge of the other practitioner or except where the connection of the other practitioner with the work has been terminated,

(iii)   not maliciously injure the reputation or business of another practitioner,

(iv)   not attempt to gain an advantage over other practitioners by paying or accepting a commission in securing professional engineering work, and

(v)   give proper credit for engineering work, uphold the principle of adequate compensation for engineering work, provide opportunity for professional development and advancement of his associates and subordinates, and extend the effectiveness of the profession through the interchange of engineering information and experience.

(8)   A practitioner shall maintain the honour and integrity of his profession and without fear or favour expose before the proper

tribunals unprofessional, dishonest or unethical conduct by any other practitioner.

O. Reg. 538/84, s. 91.

Source: Professional Engineers Act, 1984, *Statutes of Ontario* 1984, c. 13, as amended. © Reproduced with permission from the Queen's Printer for Ontario.

PRINCE EDWARD ISLAND

ENGINEERING PROFESSION ACT *(STATUTES OF PRINCE EDWARD ISLAND* 1990, C. 12)

1. Definition of Engineering (Section 1 of the Act)

"engineer" means a person who is skilled, through specialized education, training and experience, in the principles and practice of professional engineering

"professional engineer" means a member or an engineer having a licence to practise under the provisions of this Act

"professional engineering" or the "practice of engineering" means the provision of services for another as an employee or by contract, and such services shall include consultation, investigation, instruction, evaluation, planning, design, inspection, management, research, development and implementation of engineering works and systems

"engineering works and systems" includes

(i) transportation systems and components related to air, water, land or outer space, movement of goods or people,

(ii) works related to the location, mapping, improvement, control and utilization of natural resources,

(iii) works and components of an electrical, mechanical, hydraulic, aeronautical, electronic, thermic, nuclear, metallurgical, geological, mining or industrial character and others dependent on the utilization or the application of chemical or physical principles,

(iv) works related to the protection, control and improvement of the environment including those of pollution control, abatement and treatment,

(v)   the structural, electrical, mechanical, communications, transportation and other utility aspects of building components and systems,

(vi)   structures and enclosures accessory to engineering works and intended to support or house them, and

(vii)   systems relating to surveying and mapping

2. Membership Criteria (Section 5 of the Act)

5.

(1)   Every person who engages in the practice of engineering in the Province of Prince Edward Island must have a valid certificate of registration, licence to practise or certificate of engineer-in-training in accordance with this Act and by-laws.

(2)   Any applicant for a certificate of registration who satisfies Council that he

(a)   is a resident or is coming to reside in Prince Edward Island;

(b)   is a graduate in engineering or applied science of an academic or technical institution recognized by the Council;

(c)   has fulfilled the requirements of approved engineering experience as prescribed in the by-laws;

(d)   has successfully completed any examinations that may be prescribed by Council;

(e)   has provided evidence of good character; and

(f)   has paid the fees as prescribed in the by-laws,

shall be entitled to become registered as a member of the Association.

...

(11)   The Council may refuse to issue a licence to practise to an applicant where the Council is of the opinion, upon reasonable and probable grounds, that the past conduct of the applicant affords grounds for belief that the applicant will not engage in the practice of professional engineering in accordance with the law and in a manner consistent with the provision of good service to the public.

3. Definition of Professional Misconduct (Section 13 and Section 18 of the Act)

13.   Members, persons licensed to practise, and engineers-in-training shall conduct themselves in accordance with the Code of Ethics

for Engineers, and without restricting the meaning of professional misconduct, any breach of the Code of Ethics shall be deemed to be a form of professional misconduct.

18.

(1) A member, licensee, engineer-in-training or holder of a certificate of authorization may be found guilty of professional misconduct by the Discipline Committee if

(a) the member, licensee, engineer-in-training or holder of a certificate of authorization has been found guilty of an offence which, in the opinion of the Committee, is relevant to suitability to engage in the practice of engineering; or

(b) the member, licensee, engineer-in-training or holder of a certificate of authorization has been guilty, in the opinion of the Committee, of conduct that is not in the best interest of the public or tends to harm the standing of the Association.

(2) The Discipline Committee may find a member, licensee, or engineer-in-training incompetent if, in its opinion

(a) the member, licensee, or engineer-in-training has displayed in his professional activities a lack of knowledge, skill or judgement, or disregard for the welfare of the public of a nature or to an extent that demonstrates the member or licensee is unfit to carry out the responsibilities of a professional engineer; or

(b) the member, licensee or engineer-in-training is suffering from a physical or mental condition or disorder of a nature and extent making it desirable in the interests of the public, the member, licensee, or engineer-in-training that he no longer be permitted to engage in the practice of professional engineering, or that his practice of professional engineering be restricted.

4. Disciplinary Powers (Section 20 of the Act)

20.

(1) All findings of the Discipline Committee shall be based exclusively on evidence submitted to it.

(2) Upon completion of the hearing, the Discipline Committee may pass a resolution dismissing the complaint or, if the Discipline Committee finds a member, licensee, engineer-in-training or the holder of a certificate of authorization guilty of professional misconduct or incompetence, or in breach of any of the requirements of this Act or any bylaws made hereunder, the Committee may, by order, do any one or more of the following:

(a)   revoke the right to practise professional engineering for a stated period of time after which time the person or holder of certificate of authorization may reapply for membership, license to practise, enrolment as an engineer-in-training or certificate of authorization;

(b)   suspend the right to practise professional engineering for a stated period, not exceeding twenty-four months;

(c)   accept the undertaking of the member, licensee, engineer-in-training or holder of a certificate of authorization to limit the professional work in the practice of engineering to the extent specified in the undertaking;

(d)   impose terms, conditions or limitations on the member, licensee or engineer-in-training including, but not limited to the successful completion of a particular course of study, as specified by the Committee;

(e)   impose specific restrictions on the member, licensee or engineer-in-training or holder of a certificate of authorization including

(i)   requiring the member, licensee, or engineer-in-training to engage in the practice of engineering only under the personal supervision and direction of a member,

(ii)   requiring the member, licensee, or engineer-in-training to not alone engage in the practice of engineering,

(iii)   requiring the member, licensee, engineer-in-training or the holder of the certificate of authorization to submit to periodic inspections by the Committee, or its designate, of documents, records and work of the member, licensee, engineer-in-training or the holder of a certificate of authorization in connection with his practice of engineering,

(iv)   requiring the member, licensee, engineer-in-training or the holder of the certificate of authorization to report to the Discipline Committee or its designate on such matters with respect to the member's, licensee's, engineer-in-training or holder's practice of engineering for such period and times, and in such form, as the Committee may specify;

(f)   reprimand, admonish or counsel the member, licensee, engineer-in-training or the holder of certificate of authorization, and if considered warranted, direct that the fact of the reprimand, admonishment or counselling be recorded on the register for a stated or unlimited period of time;

(g)   direct that the imposition of a penalty or order by suspended or postponed for such period, and upon such terms, or for such purpose, including

(i) the successful completion by the member, licensee, or engineer-in-training of a particular course of study,

(ii) the production to the Committee or its designate of evidence satisfactory to it that any physical or mental handicap in respect of which the penalty was imposed has been overcome.

5. Code of Ethics (Section 14 of the By-laws)

14.1 Foreword

Honesty, justice, and courtesy form a moral philosophy which, associated with mutual interest among people, constitute the foundation of ethics. Engineers should recognize such a standard, not in passive observance, but as a set of dynamic principles guiding their conduct and way of life. It is their duty to practise the profession according to this Code of Ethics.

As the keystone of professional conduct is integrity, engineers will discharge their duties with fidelity to the public, their employers, and clients, and with fairness and impartiality to all. It is their duty to interest themselves in public welfare, and to be ready to apply their special knowledge for the benefit of mankind. They should uphold the honour and dignity of the profession and also avoid association with any enterprise of questionable character. In dealings with other fellow engineers they should be fair and tolerant.

14.2 Professional Life

14.2.1 Engineers will co-operate in extending the effectiveness of the engineering profession by interchanging information and experience with other engineers and students and by contributing to the work of engineering societies, schools, and the scientific and engineering press.

14.2.2 Engineers will not advertise their work or merit in a self-laudatory manner, and will avoid all conduct or practice likely to discredit or do injury to the dignity and honour of the profession.

14.3 Relations with the Public

14.3.1 Engineers will endeavour to extend public knowledge of engineering.

14.3.2 Engineers will have due regard for the safety of life and health of the public and employees who may be affected by the work for which they are responsible.

14.3.3 Engineers will not issue ex parte statements, criticisms, or arguments on matters connected with public policy which are inspired or paid for by private interests, unless it is indicated on whose behalf the statements are made.

14.3.4 Engineers will refrain from expressing publicly opinions on engineering subjects unless they are informed as to the facts relating thereto.

14.4 Relations with Clients and Employers

14.4.1 Engineers will act in professional matters for clients or employers as faithful agents or trustees.

14.4.2 Engineers will act with fairness and justice between the client or employer and the contractor when dealing with contracts.

14.4.3 Engineers will make their status clear to clients or employers before undertaking engagements if they may be called upon to decide on the use of inventions, apparatus, or any other thing in which they may have a financial interest.

14.4.4 Engineers will guard against conditions that are dangerous to life, limb, or property on work for which they are responsible, or if they are not responsible, will promptly call such conditions to the attention of those who are responsible.

14.4.5 Engineers will present clearly the consequences to be expected from deviations proposed if their engineering judgement is overruled by non-technical authority in cases where they are responsible for the technical adequacy of engineering work.

14.4.6 Engineers will engage, or advise clients or employers to engage, and will co-operate with, other experts and specialists whenever the clients' or employers' interests are best served by such service.

14.4.7 Engineers will not accept compensation, financial or otherwise, from more than one interested party for the same service, or for services pertaining to the same work, without the consent of all interested parties.

14.4.8 Engineers will not accept commissions or allowances, directly or indirectly, from contractors or other parties dealing with clients or employers in connection with work for which they are responsible.

14.4.9 Engineers will not be financially interested in bids as or of contractors on competitive work for which they are employed as engineers unless they have the consent of the client or employer.

14.4.10   Engineers will promptly disclose to clients or employers any interest in a business which may compete with or affect the business of the client or employer. They will not allow an interest in any business to affect their decisions regarding engineering work for which they are employed, or which they may be called upon to perform.

14.5   Relations with Engineers

14.5.1   Engineers will endeavour to protect the engineering profession collectively and individually from misrepresentation and misunderstanding.

14.5.2   Engineers will take care that credit for engineering work is given to those to whom credit is properly due.

14.5.3   Engineers will uphold the principle of appropriate and adequate compensation for those engaged in engineering work, including those in subordinate capacities, as being in the public interest and maintaining the standards of the profession.

14.5.4   Engineers will endeavour to provide opportunity for the professional development and advancement of engineers in their employ.

14.5.5   Engineers will not directly or indirectly injure the professional reputation, prospects, or practice of other engineers. However, if they consider that an engineer is guilty of unethical, illegal, or improper practice, they will present the information to the proper authority for action.

14.5.6   An engineer will not compete with another engineer on the basis of charges for work by underbidding, through reducing normal fees after having been informed of the charges named by the other.

14.5.7   An engineer will not use the advantages of a position to compete unfairly with another engineer.

14.5.8   An engineer will not become associated in responsibility for work with engineers who do not conform to ethical practices.

Source: Engineering Profession Act, *Statutes of Prince Edward Island* 1990, c. 12. Reproduced with permission of the province of Prince Edward Island.

QUEBEC

ENGINEERS ACT (*REVISED STATUTES OF QUEBEC 1986, C. I-9*)

1. Definition of Engineering (Sections 1, 2, and 3)

1. "Engineer": a member of the Order.

2. Works of the kinds hereinafter described constitute the field of practice of an engineer:

(a) railways, public roads, airports, bridges, viaducts, tunnels and the installations connected with a transport system the cost of which exceeds three thousand dollars;

(b) dams, canals, harbours, lighthouses and all works relating to the improvement, control or utilization of waters;

(c) works of an electrical, mechanical, hydraulic, aeronautical, electronic, thermic, nuclear, metallurgical, geological or mining character and those intended for the utilization of the processes of applied chemistry of physics;

(d) waterworks, sewer, filtration, purification works to dispose of refuse, and other works in the field of municipal engineering, the cost of which exceeds one thousand dollars;

(e) the foundations, framework and electrical and mechanical systems of buildings the cost of which exceeds one hundred thousand dollars and of public buildings within the meaning of the Public Buildings Safety Act;

(f) structures accessory to engineering works and intended to house them;

(g) temporary framework and other temporary works used during the carrying out of works of civil engineering;

(h) soil engineering necessary to elaborate engineering works;

(i) industrial work or equipment involving public or employee safety.

3. The practice of the engineering profession consists in performing for another any of the following acts, when they relate to the works mentioned in section 2:

(a) the giving of consultations and opinions;

(b) the making of measurements, of layouts, the preparation of reports, computations, designs, drawings, plans, specifications;

(c) the inspection or supervision of the works.

2. Membership Criteria (Sections 15 to 17)

15.

(1) The Bureau shall admit as a member of the Order, subject to its regulations, any Canadian citizen domiciled in Québec and any candidate who fulfils the conditions prescribed by section 44 of the Professional Code, who holds a diploma recognized by the Gouvernement as leading to a permit to practise the profession of engineer, or holds a diploma considered equivalent by the Bureau.

(2) The Bureau shall also, subject to its regulations, admit as a member of the Order any Canadian citizen and any candidate who fulfils the conditions prescribed by section 44 of the Professional Code who establishes:

(a) he is domiciled in Québec;

(b) he has passed an examination before the committee of examiners on the theory and practice of engineering and especially in one of the following branches at his option: civil, mechanical, electrical, agricultural, geological, industrial, mining, metallurgical or chemical engineering or, at the discretion of the committee of examiners, in any combination or subdivision thereof; and

(c) he has paid the required fees fixed by regulation of the Bureau.

16. The Bureau, however, in all cases and notwithstanding the method of admission provided, may refuse admission to any candidate who cannot provide evidence of good character to the Bureau's satisfaction.

17. The Bureau, upon a written report by the committee of examiners to the effect that the candidate possesses the required knowledge and qualifications, may admit as a member of the Order any Canadian citizen domiciled in Québec, or domiciled in an adjacent province and practising his profession continuously and exclusively in Québec, provided that such candidate:

(a) holds a diploma in engineering or the degree of bachelor of applied sciences, or an equivalent diploma from a school or university recognized by the Gouvernement, or is a member of an engineering society recognized by the bureau;

(b) pays the requisite fee for admission to practice.

3. Definition of Professional Misconduct

[Although the Act refers to "professional competence," the term is not defined. Conviction in a Canadian court of an indictable offence (or in a foreign court, of an offence of equal seriousness) is considered equivalent to an offence against the Act.]

4. Disciplinary Powers (Sections 156 and 188 of the Professional Code, R.S.Q. c. C-26)

156. The committee on discipline shall impose on a professional convicted of an offence against this Code, the act constituting the corporation of which he is a member or the regulations made under this Code or the said act, one or more of the following penalties in respect of each count contained in the complaint:

(a) reprimand;

(b) temporary or permanent striking off the roll, even if he has not been entered thereon from the date of the offence;

(c) a fine of at least $500 for each offence;

(d) the obligation to remit to any person entitled to it a sum of money the professional is holding for him;

(e) revocation of his permit;

(f) revocation of his specialist's certificate;

(g) restriction or suspension of his right to engage in professional activities.

For the purpose of subparagraph (c) of the first paragraph, when an offence is continuous, its continuity shall constitute a separate offence, day by day.

The committee on discipline may decide on the terms and conditions of the penalties it imposes.

188. Every person who contravenes a provision of this Code or the act or letters patent constituting a corporation is guilty of an offence and is liable on summary proceeding to a fine of not less than $500 nor more than $5000.

5. Code of Ethics (R.S.Q., c. I-9, r. 3, as revised in 1983)

Division I — General Provisions
1.01. This Regulation is made pursuant to section 87 of the Professional Code (R.S.Q., c. C-26).

1.02. In this Regulation, unless the context indicates otherwise, the word "client" means a person to whom an engineer provides professional services, including an employer.

1.03. The Interpretation Act (R.S.Q., c. I-16), with present and future amendments, applies to this Regulation.

Division II — Duties and Obligations toward the Public
2.01. In all aspects of his work, the engineer must respect his obligations toward man and take into account the consequences of

the performance of his work on the environment and on the life, health and property of every person.

2.02. The engineer must support every measure likely to improve the quality and availability of his professional services.

2.03. Whenever an engineer considers that certain works are a danger to public safety, he must notify the Ordre des ingénieurs du Québec (Order) or the persons responsible for such work.

2.04. The engineer shall express his opinion on matters dealing with engineering only if such opinion is based on sufficient knowledge and honest convictions.

2.05. The engineer must promote educational and information measures in the field in which he practises.

Division III — Duties and Obligations toward Clients

§ 1. General Provisions

3.01.01. Before accepting a mandate, an engineer must bear in mind the extent of his proficiency and aptitudes and also the means at his disposal to carry out the mandate.

3.01.02. An engineer must at all times acknowledge his client's right to consult another engineer. If it is in the client's interest, the engineer shall retain the services of experts after having informed his client thereof, or he shall advise the latter to do so.

3.01.03. An engineer must refrain from practising under conditions or in circumstances which could impair the quality of his services.

§ 2. Integrity

3.02.01. An engineer must fulfil his professional obligations with integrity.

3.02.02. An engineer must avoid any misrepresentation with respect to his level of competence or the efficiency of his own services and of those generally provided by the members of his profession.

3.02.03. An engineer must, as soon as possible, inform his client of the extent and the terms and conditions of the mandate entrusted to him by the latter and obtain his agreement in that respect.

3.02.04. An engineer must refrain from expressing or giving contradictory or incomplete opinions or advice, and from presenting or using plans, specifications and other documents which he knows to be ambiguous or which are not sufficiently explicit.

3.02.05. An engineer must inform his client as early as possible of any error that might cause the latter prejudice and which cannot be easily rectified, made by him in the carrying out of his mandate.

3.02.06. An engineer must take reasonable care of the property entrusted to his care by a client and he may not lend or use it for purposes other than those for which it has been entrusted to him.

3.02.07. Where an engineer is responsible for the technical quality of engineering work, and his opinion is ignored, the engineer must clearly indicate to his client, in writing, the consequences which may result therefrom.

3.02.08. The engineer shall not resort to dishonest or doubtful practices in the performance of his professional activities.

3.02.09. An engineer shall not pay or undertake to pay, directly or indirectly, any benefit, rebate or commission in order to obtain a contract or upon the carrying out of engineering work.

3.02.10. An engineer must be impartial in his relations between his client and the contractors, suppliers and other persons doing business with his client.

§ 3. Availability and Diligence

3.03.01. An engineer must show reasonable availability and diligence in the practice of his profession.

3.03.02. In addition to opinion and counsel, the engineer must furnish his client with any explanations necessary to the understanding and appreciation of the services he is providing him.

3.03.03. An engineer must give an accounting to his client when so requested by the latter.

3.03.04. An engineer may not cease to act for the account of a client unless he has just and reasonable grounds for so doing. The following shall, in particular, constitute just and reasonable grounds:

    (a) the fact that the engineer is placed in a situation of conflict of interest or in a circumstance whereby his professional independence could be called in question;

    (b) inducement by the client to illegal, unfair or fraudulent acts;

    (c) the fact that the client ignores the engineer's advice.

3.03.05. Before ceasing to exercise his functions for the account of a client, the engineer must give advance notice of withdrawal within a reasonable time.

§ 4. Responsibility

3.04.01. An engineer must affix his seal and signature on the original and the copies of every plan, specification, technical report, survey, contract specification and other engineering documents prepared by himself or prepared under his immediate control and supervision by persons who are not members of the Order.

An engineer may also affix his seal and signature on the original and the copies of documents mentioned in this section which have been prepared, signed and sealed by another engineer.

An engineer must not affix his seal and signature except in the cases provided for in this section.

§ 5. Independence and Impartiality

3.05.01.   An engineer must, in the practice of his profession, subordinate his personal interest to that of his client.

3.05.02.   An engineer must ignore any intervention by a third party which could influence the performance of his professional duties to the detriment of his client.

Without restricting the generality of the foregoing, an engineer shall not accept, directly or indirectly, any benefit or rebate in money or otherwise from a supplier of goods or services relative to engineering work which he performs for the account of a client.

3.05.03.   An engineer must safeguard his professional independence at all times and avoid any situation which would put him in conflict of interest.

3.05.04.   As soon as he ascertains that he is in a situation of conflict of interest, the engineer must notify his client thereof and ask his authorization to continue his mandate.

3.05.05.   An engineer shall share his fees only with a colleague and to the extent where such sharing corresponds to a distribution of services and responsibilities.

3.05.06.   In carrying out a mandate, the engineer shall generally act only for one of the parties concerned, namely, his client. However, where his professional duties require that he act otherwise, the engineer must notify his client thereof. He shall accept the payment of his fees only from his client or the latter's representative.

§ 6. Professional Secrecy

3.06.01   An engineer must respect the secrecy of all confidential information obtained in the practice of his profession.

3.06.02.   An engineer shall be released from professional secrecy only with the authorization of his client or whenever so ordered by law.

3.06.03.   An engineer shall not make use of confidential information to the prejudice of a client or with a view to deriving, directly or indirectly, an advantage for himself or for another person.

3.06.04.   An engineer shall not accept a mandate which entails or may entail the disclosure or use of confidential information or documents obtained from another client without the latter's consent.

§ 7. Accessibility of Records

3.07.01   An engineer must respect the right of his client to take cognizance of and to obtain copies of the documents that concern the latter in any record which the engineer has made regarding that client.

§ 8. Determination and Payment of Fees

3.08.01. An engineer must charge and accept fair and reasonable fees.

3.08.02. Fees are considered fair and reasonable when they are justified by the circumstances and correspond to the services rendered. In determining his fees, the engineer must, in particular, take the following factors into account:

(a) the time devoted to the carrying out of the mandate;

(b) the difficulty and magnitude of the mandate;

(c) the performance of unusual services or services requiring exceptional competence or speed:

(d) the responsibility assumed.

3.08.03. An engineer must inform his client of the approximate cost of his services and of the terms and conditions of payment. He must refrain from demanding advance payment of his fees; he may, however, demand payment on account.

3.08.04 An engineer must give his client all the necessary explanations for the understanding of his statement of fees and the terms and conditions of its payment.

Division IV — Duties and Obligations toward the Profession

§ 1. Derogatory Acts

4.01.01. In addition to those referred to in sections 57 and 58 of the Professional Code, the following acts are derogatory to the dignity of the profession:

(a) participating or contributing to the illegal practice of the profession;

(b) pressing or repeated inducement to make use of his professional services;

(c) communicating with the person who lodged a complaint, without the prior written permission of the syndic or his assistant, whenever he is informed of an inquiry into his professional conduct or competence or whenever a complaint has been laid against him;

(d) refusing to comply with the procedures for the conciliation and arbitration of accounts and with the arbitrators' award;

(e) taking legal action against a colleague on a matter relative to the practice of the profession before applying for conciliation to the president of the Order;

(f) refusing or failing to present himself at the office of the syndic, of one of his assistants or of a corresponding syndic, upon request to that effect by one of those persons;

(g) not notifying the syndic without delay if he believes that an engineer infringes this Regulation.

§ 2. Relations with the Order and Colleagues

4.02.01. An engineer whose participation in a council for the arbitration of accounts, a committee on discipline or a professional inspection committee is requested by the Order, must accept this duty unless he has exceptional grounds for refusing.

4.02.02. An engineer must, within the shortest delay, answer all correspondence addressed to him by the syndic of the Order, the assistant syndic or a corresponding syndic, investigators or members of the professional inspection committee or the secretary of the said committee.

4.02.03. An engineer shall not abuse a colleague's good faith, be guilty of breach of trust or be disloyal towards him or willfully damage his reputation. Without restricting the generality of the foregoing, the engineer shall not, in particular:

(a) take upon himself the credit for engineering work which belongs to a colleague;

(b) take advantage of his capacity of employer or executive to limit in any way whatsoever the professional autonomy of an engineer employed by him or under his responsibility, in particular with respect to the use of the title of engineer or the obligation of every engineer to be true to his professional responsibility.

4.02.04. Where a client requests an engineer to examine or review engineering work that he has not performed himself, the latter must notify the engineer concerned thereof and, where applicable, ensure that the mandate of his colleague has terminated.

4.02.05. Where an engineer replaces a colleague in engineering work, he must notify that colleague thereof and make sure that the latter's mandate has terminated.

4.02.06. An engineer who is called upon to collaborate with a colleague must retain his professional independence. If a task is entrusted to him and such task goes against his conscience or his principles, he may ask to be excused from doing it.

§ 3. Contribution to the Advancement of the Profession

4.03.01. An engineer must, as far as he is able, contribute to the development of his profession by sharing his knowledge and experience with his colleagues and students, and by his participation as professor or tutor in continuing training periods and refresher training courses.

Source: Engineers Act, *Revised Statutes of Quebec* 1986, c. I-9. Reproduced with permission of Publications Quebec.

SASKATCHEWAN

ENGINEERING PROFESSION ACT (*REVISED STATUTES OF SASKATCHEWAN* 1979, C. E-10, AS AMENDED)

1. Definition of Engineering (Section 2 and Schedule A of the Act)

(h) "Professional engineering" or "the practice of professional engineering" means reporting on, advising on, valuing, measuring for, laying out, designing, directing, constructing or inspecting any of the works or processes set forth in schedule A,* or such works or processes omitted therefrom as are similar to those set forth therein by reason of their requiring the skilled application of the principles of mathematics, physics, mechanics, aeronautics, hydraulics, electricity, chemistry or geology in their development and attainment; and includes such reporting, advising, valuing, measuring for, laying out, designing, directing, constructing or inspecting by any person under the general supervision of a professional engineer; but does not include the execution or supervision of works as contractor, foreman, superintendent, inspector, road master, superintendent of maintenance, technical assistant, student or engineer in training where the work has been designed by and is done under the responsible supervision of a professional engineer.

[*Note: Schedule A, mentioned above, is an extensive list of engineering works, structures, and activities. As the above definition indicates, Schedule A nevertheless does not include all of the works or activities that are included in the definition.]

2. Membership Criteria (Section 5 of the Act)

5.

(1) The council shall admit an applicant to membership in the association if he pays the proper fees and submits evidence satisfactory to the council:

(a) that he resides in Saskatchewan;

(b) that he is of good character; and

(c)   that he:

(i)   is a graduate in engineering of The University of Saskatchewan, The University of Regina or of an institution of learning recognized by The University of Saskatchewan with respect to its program in applied science or engineering and has had not less than two years' postgraduate experience in engineering work satisfactory to the council; or

(ii)   has passed the examinations required under section 8 and has been engaged for not less than eight years in some branch of engineering recognized and approved by the council; or

(iii)   is a registered member in good standing of an association recognized by the council as being comparable to The Association of Professional Engineers of Saskatchewan and complies with such other terms and conditions as the council may impose.

(2)   The council may admit an applicant to membership in the association if he pays the proper fees and submits evidence satisfactory to the council:

(a)   that he resides in Saskatchewan;

(b)   that he is of good character; and

(c)   that he is a graduate with a degree in an honours course, or in a course of which the content is equivalent to an honours course, in a science related to engineering, from The University of Saskatchewan, The University of Regina or an institution with respect to its program in such science and has had not less than three years' postgraduate experience in engineering work satisfactory to the council.

3. Definition of Professional Misconduct (Section 35 of the Act)

4. Disciplinary Powers (Section 35 of the Act)

35.

(1)   The council may in its discretion reprimand, censure, fine, suspend or expel any member or licensee who:

(a)   has been convicted in Canada or elsewhere of any offence that, if committed in Canada, would be punishable under the *Criminal Code* with imprisonment for two years or more;

(b)   is shown to have been guilty, after registration, in Canada or elsewhere, of any professional misconduct or of negligence or misconduct in the execution of the duties of his office, or of any breach of this Act or the bylaws.

(2) If the fine imposed on a member or licensee is not paid, the council may suspend the member or suspend the licence of the licensee until the fine has been paid.

(3) Any matter, conduct or thing that is not in the best interest of the public or tends to harm the standing of the association is professional misconduct within the meaning of this section.

R.S.S. 1965, c. 309, s. 36; 1974-75, c. 14, s. 11.

5. Code of Ethics (Section 37 of the By-laws Established under Section 13(b) of the Act)

37. For the governance of the conduct of the members and licences of the Association, the following Code of Ethics is hereby established;

Preamble

Honesty, justice, and courtesy form a moral philosophy, which associated with mutual interest among men, constitute the foundation of ethics. The Professional Engineer should recognize such a standard, not in passive observance but as a set of dynamic principles guiding his conduct and way of life. It is his duty to practise his profession according to this Code of Ethics.

General

1. A professional engineer owes certain duties to the public, his employers, other members of his profession and to himself and shall act at all times with,

(a) fidelity to public needs;

(b) fairness and loyalty to his associates, employers, subordinates and employees; and

(c) devotion to high ideals of personal honour and professional integrity.

Duty of Professional Engineer to the Public

2. A professional engineer shall,

(a) regard his duty to the public as paramount;

(b) endeavour to maintain public regard for his profession by discouraging untrue, unfair or exaggerated statements with respect to professional engineering;

(c) not give opinions or make statements on professional engineering projects of public interest that are inspired or paid for by private interests unless he clearly discloses on whose behalf he is giving the opinions or making the statements;

(d)   not express publicly or while he is serving as a witness before a court, commission or other tribunal, opinions on professional engineering matters that are not founded on adequate knowledge and honest conviction;

(e)   make effective provisions for the safety of life and health of a person who may be affected by the work for which he is responsible; and shall act to correct or report any situation which he feels may endanger the public.

(f)   not knowingly associate with, or allow the use of his name by, an enterprise of doubtful character, nor shall he sanction the use of his reports, in part or in whole, in a manner calculated to mislead, and if it comes to his knowledge they have been so used, shall take immediate steps to correct any false impression given by them;

(g)   on all occasions sign or seal reports, plans and specifications which legally require sealing and for which he is professionally responsible;

(h)   not offer his services for a fee without first notifying the Council of the Association of his intent to do so and of the area of speciality in which he proposes to practise, and receiving from the Council of the Association permission to do so.

Duty of Professional Engineer to Employer

3.   A professional engineer shall,

(a)   act for his employer as a faithful agent or trustee and shall regard as confidential any information obtained by him as to the business affairs, technical methods or processes of his employer, and avoid or disclose any conflict of interest which might influence his actions or judgement;

(b)   present clearly to his employers the consequences to be expected from any deviations proposed in the work if his professional engineering judgement is overruled in cases where he is responsible for the technical adequacy of professional engineering work;

(c)   advise his employer to engage experts and specialists whenever the employer's interests are best served by so doing;

(d)   have no interest, direct or indirect in any materials, supplies or equipment used by his employer or in any persons or firms receiving contracts from his employer unless he informs his employer in advance of the nature of the interest;

(e)   not act as consulting engineer in respect of any work upon which he may be the contractor unless he first advises his employer; and

(f)   not accept compensation, financial or otherwise, for a particular service, from more than one person except with the full knowledge of all interested parties.

Duty of Professional Engineer to Other Professional Engineers
4.   A professional engineer shall,

(a)   not attempt to supplant another engineer after definite steps have been taken toward the other's employment;

(b)   not accept employment by a client, knowing that a claim for compensation or damages, or both, of a fellow engineer previously employed by the same client, and whose employment has been terminated, remains unsatisfied, or until such claim has been referred to arbitration or issue has been joined at law, or unless the engineer previously employed has neglected to press his claim legally, or the Council of the Association gives its consent;

(c)   not accept any engagement to review the work of another professional engineer for the same employer except with the knowledge of that engineer, or except where the connection of that engineer with the work has been terminated;

(d)   not maliciously injure the reputation or business of another professional engineer;

(e)   not attempt to gain an advantage over other members of his profession by paying or accepting a commission in securing professional engineering work, or by reducing his fees below the approved minimums;

(f)   not advertise in a misleading manner or in a manner injurious to the dignity of his profession.

(g)   give proper credit for engineering work;

(h)   uphold the principle of adequate compensation for engineering work;

(i)   provide opportunity for professional development and advancement of his professional colleagues;

(j)   extend the effectiveness of the profession through the interchange of engineering information and experience.

Duty of Professional Engineer to Himself
5.   A professional engineer shall,

(a)   maintain the honour and integrity of his profession and without fear or favour expose before the proper tribunals unprofessional or dishonest conduct by any other member of the profession;

(b) undertake only such work as he is competent to perform by virtue of his training and experience; and

(c) constantly strive to broaden his knowledge and experience by keeping abreast of new techniques and developments in his field of endeavour.

Source: Engineering Profession Act, *Revised Statutes of Saskatchewan* 1979, c. E-10. Reproduced with permission of the Saskatchewan Queen's Printer.

YUKON TERRITORY

ENGINEERING PROFESSION ORDINANCE *(REVISED ORDINANCES OF YUKON TERRITORY 1958, C. 36, AS AMENDED)*

1. Definition of Engineering (Section 2 of the Ordinance)

"practice of professional engineering" means the carrying on of any branch of chemical, civil, electrical, forestry, mechanical, mining, geological, metallurgical, structural or any other form of engineering, any professional service or creative work requiring engineering education, training and experience, or the application of special knowledge of any of the mathematical or physical sciences to such professional services or creative work as consultation, investigation, evaluation, planning, designing and engineering supervision of construction or operations in connection with any public or private utilities, structures, machines, equipment, processes, works or projects;

"professional engineer" means a person who is registered or duly licensed under this Ordinance;

2. Membership Criteria (Section 12 of the Ordinance)

12.

(1) The Council shall admit a person to membership in the Association who

(a) applies for membership in the Association in the form prescribed by the Council;

(b) has attained the age of 23 years;

(c) has produced evidence to the Council that he is of good character and repute;

(d) establishes to the satisfaction of the Council

(i) that he is a duly registered member in good standing of an association or corporation of professional engineers of any province of Canada, or

(ii) that he is fully qualified for admission to membership in one of the associations or corporations referred to in sub-paragraph (i) in accordance with the relevant laws governing admission to such membership;

(e) has had at least two years actual experience in engineering work of a nature satisfactory to the Council; and

(f) pays all fees prescribed by the Council.

(2) The Council may, subject to such terms and conditions as it may impose, issue a temporary licence to engage in the practice of professional engineering in the Territory to any person who

(a) is qualified for membership in the Association pursuant to subsection (1),

(b) applies for a temporary licence in the form prescribed by the Council, and

(c) pays all fees prescribed by the Council.

(3) A temporary licence shall specify

(a) the purposes for which it is issued; and

(b) the period during which it shall remain in force.

(4) No corporation or partnership shall

(a) be admitted as a member in the Association, or

(b) be issued a temporary licence.

(5) Where professional engineers are employed by corporations or are members of partnerships, they individually shall assume the functions of and be held responsible as professional engineers.

R. O. 1958, c. 36, s. 12; 1961 (1st) c. 8, s. 3(1), (2); 1965 (1st) c. 2, s. 1.

3. Definition of Professional Misconduct

[Although the terms "unprofessional conduct" and "misconduct" are used in sections 26 and 27 of the ordinance, these terms are not defined in the ordinance.]

4. Disciplinary Powers (Sections 26, 27 of the Ordinance)

26.

(1) Notwithstanding anything contained in this Ordinance, no person who has been convicted in Canada of an indictable offence shall be entitled to be registered, and the Council may remove from the register the name of any member of the Association who has been convicted in Canada of an indictable offence; but the Council may, if it sees fit, permit a person who has been so

convicted to become or remain a member of the Association, or may restore to the register the name of any person whose name has been removed under this section; and the registration of a person shall not be refused and the name of a person shall not be removed on account of a conviction for an offence which ought not, in the opinion of the Council, either from the nature of the offence or from the circumstances under which it was committed, to disqualify a person from practising under this Ordinance.

(2)   The Council may cancel the temporary licence of any person who has been convicted in Canada of an indictable offence.

R. O. 1958, c. 36, s. 25; 1961 (1st) c. 8, s. 11.

27.

(1)   The Council, after giving written notice to any person affected, may, and upon application of any three members of the Association shall, cause inquiry to be made into matters respecting any fraudulent or incorrect entry in the register, unprofessional conduct, negligence or misconduct of or relating to any member or a person licensed under this Ordinance, or any violation of the Ordinance or the by-laws by any such member or such licensee.

(2)   Any person to whom notice is given is entitled to be heard and to submit evidence at the inquiry.

(3)   After the inquiry the Council may in its discretion order the removal or correction of any entry in the register or roll or the cancellation of any licence, and may reprimand, censure, suspend or expel from the Association any person found guilty.

(4)   Where a member of the Association is suspended from practice, the registration of such member shall be deemed to be cancelled during the term of his suspension and he shall not be deemed to be a member of the Association or entitled to any of the rights or privileges thereof so long as the suspension continues.

5. Code of Ethics (Section 16 of the By-laws Established under Section 9 of the Act)

(a) General

A professional engineer owes certain duties to the public, to his employers, to his clients, to other members of his profession and to himself and shall act at all times with:

(1)   fairness and loyalty to his associates, employers, clients, subordinates and employees;

(2)   fidelity to public needs and

(3)   devotion to high ideals of personal honour and professional integrity.

(b) Duty of Professional Engineer to the Public

A professional engineer shall:

(1)   regard his duty to the public welfare as paramount;

(2)   endeavour at all times to enhance the public regard for his profession by extending the public knowledge thereof and discouraging untrue, unfair or exaggerated statements with respect to professional engineering;

(3)   not give opinions or make statements, on professional engineering projects of public interest, that are inspired or paid for by private interests unless he clearly discloses on whose behalf he is giving the opinions or making the statements;

(4)   not express publicly, or while he is serving as a witness before a court, commission or other tribunal, opinions on professional engineering matters that are not founded on adequate knowledge and honest conviction;

(5)   make effective provisions for the safety of life and health of a person who may be affected by the work for which he is responsible; and at all times shall act to correct or report any situation which he feels may endanger the safety or welfare of the public;

(6)   make effective provisions for meeting lawful standards, rules, or regulations relating to environmental control and protection in connection with any work being undertaken by him or under his responsibility;

(7)   sign or seal only those plans, specifications and reports made by him or under his personal supervision and direction or those which have been thoroughly reviewed by him as if they were his own work, and found to be satisfactory and

(8)   refrain from associating himself with or allowing the use of his name by an enterprise of questionable character.

(c) Duty of Professional Engineer to Employer

A professional engineer shall:

(1)   act in professional engineering matters for each employer as a faithful agent or trustee and shall regard as confidential any information obtained by him as to the business affairs, technical methods or processes of an employer and avoid or disclose any conflict of interest which might influence his actions or judgement;

(2)   present clearly to his employers the consequences to be expected from any deviations proposed in the work if he is informed that his professional engineering judgement is overruled

by nontechnical authority in cases where he is responsible for the technical adequacy of professional engineering work;

(3)   have no interest, direct or indirect, in any materials, supplies or equipment used by his employer or in any persons or firms receiving contracts from his employer unless he informs his employer in advance of the nature of the interest;

(4)   not tender on competitive work upon which he may be acting as a professional engineer unless he first advises his employer;

(5)   not act as consulting engineer in respect of any work upon which he may be the contractor unless he first advises his employer and

(6)   not accept compensation, financial or otherwise, for a particular service from more than one person except with the full knowledge of all interested parties.

(d)   Duty of Professional Engineer in Independent Practice to Client
A professional engineer in private practice, in addition to all other sections, shall:

(1)   disclose immediately any interest, direct or indirect, which may in any way be constituted as prejudicial to his professional judgement in rendering service to his client;

(2)   if he is an employee-engineer and is contracting in his own name to perform professional engineering work for other than his employer, clearly advise his client as to the nature of his status as an employee and the attendant limitations on his services to the client. In addition he shall ensure that such work will not conflict with his duty to his employer;

(3)   carry out his work in accordance with applicable statutes, regulations, standards, codes, and by-laws and

(4)   co-operate as necessary in working with such other professionals as may be engaged on a project.

(e)   Duty of Professional Engineer to Other Professional Engineers
A professional engineer shall:

(1)   conduct himself toward other professional engineers with courtesy and good faith;

(2)   not accept any engagement to review the work of another professional engineer for the same employer or client except with the knowledge of that engineer, or except where the connection of that engineer with the work has been terminated;

(3)   not maliciously injure the reputation or business of another professional engineer;

(4)   not attempt to gain an advantage over other members of his profession by paying or accepting a commission in securing professional engineering work;

(5) not advertise in a misleading manner or in a manner injurious to the dignity of his profession, but shall seek to advertise by establishing a well-merited reputation for personal capability; and

(6) give proper credit for engineering work, uphold the principle of adequate compensation for engineering work, provide opportunity for professional development and advancement of his associates and subordinates; and extend the effectiveness of the profession through the interchange of engineering information and experience.

(f) Duty of Professional Engineer to Himself

A professional engineer shall:

(1) maintain the honour and integrity of his profession and without fear or favour expose before the proper tribunals unprofessional or dishonest conduct by any other members of the profession; and

(2) undertake only such work as he is competent to perform by virtue of his training and experience, and shall, where advisable, retain and co-operate with other professional engineers or specialists.

Source: Engineering Profession Ordinance, *Revised Ordinances of Yukon Territory* 1958, c. 36, as amended. Reprinted with permission.

Addresses for the Provincial and Territorial Engineering Associations

CONSTITUENT MEMBERS OF THE CANADIAN COUNCIL OF PROFESSIONAL ENGINEERS (CCPE)

Canadian Council of
Professional Engineers
116 Albert Street, Suite 401
Ottawa, Ontario K1P 5G3
Assistant Director,
Educational Affairs:
Tel. (613) 232-2474
Fax (613) 230-5759

Association of Professional
Engineers, Geologists and
Geophysicists of Alberta
#1500 Scotia Place, Tower One
10060 Jasper Avenue
Edmonton, Alberta T5J 4A2
Director of Registration:
Tel. (403) 426-3990
Fax (403) 426-1877

Association of Professional
Engineers and Geoscientists
of British Columbia
2210 West 12th Avenue
Vancouver, British Columbia
V6K 2N6
Director, Registration:
Tel. (604) 736-9808
Fax (604) 736-2984

Association of Professional
Engineers of Manitoba
530 – 330 St. Mary Avenue
Winnipeg, Manitoba R3C 3Z5
Director of Admissions:
Tel. (204) 942-6481
Fax (204) 942-3718

Association of Professional
Engineers of New Brunswick
123 York Street
Fredericton, New Brunswick
E3B 3N6
Executive Director
and Registrar:
Tel. (506) 458-8083
Fax (506) 458-2617

Association of Professional
Engineers and Geoscientists
of Newfoundland
P.O. Box 9715, Postal Station B
St. John's, Newfoundland
A1A 4J6
Registrar:
Tel. (709) 737-8934
Fax (709) 753-6131

**Association of Professional
Engineers, Geologists and
Geophysicists of the
Northwest Territories**
P.O. Box 1962
Northwest Tower, 8th Floor
Yellowknife, NWT
 X1A 2P5
Executive Director:
Tel. (403) 920-4055
Fax (403) 873-5872

**Association of Professional
Engineers of Nova Scotia**
P.O. Box 129
1355 Barrington Street
Halifax, Nova Scotia B3J 2M4
Executive Director:
Tel. (902) 429-2250
Fax (902) 423-9769

**Association of Professional
Engineers of Ontario**
101 – 1155 Yonge Street
Toronto, Ontario M4T 2Y5
Director of Admissions:
Tel. (416) 961-1100
Fax (416) 961-1499

**Association of Professional
Engineers of Prince
Edward Island**
549 North River Road
Charlottetown, PEI
C1E 1J6
Executive Director:
Tel. (902) 566-1268
Fax (902) 566-5551

**Ordre des ingénieurs
du Québec**
2020 rue University, 14e étage
Montréal, Québec H3A 2A5
Secrétaire et Directeur général:
Tel. (514) 845-6141
Fax (514) 845-1833

**Association of Professional
Engineers of Saskatchewan**
2255 Thirteenth Avenue
Regina, Saskatchewan S4P 0V6
General Manager and
Registrar:
Tel. (306) 525-9547
Fax (306) 525-0851

**Association of Professional
Engineers of the
Yukon Territory**
P.O. Box 4125
Whitehorse, Yukon Territory
Y1A 3S9
Secretary-Treasurer:
Tel. (403) 667-6727

The Ritual of the Calling of an Engineer

THE IRON RING

While most engineers in Canada wear the Iron Ring and have solemnly obligated themselves to an ethical and diligent professional career through the Ritual of the Calling of an Engineer, many may benefit from a review of the history and purposes of the Corporation of the Seven Wardens started in 1922 when a group of prominent engineers met in Montreal to discuss a concern for the general guidance and solidarity of the profession, and to develop a proposal that seven of Canada's most prominent engineers form the nucleus of an organization whose object would be to bind all members of the engineering profession in Canada more closely together, and to imbue them with their responsibility towards society.

These seven men enlisted the services of the late Rudyard Kipling who developed an appropriate Ritual and the symbolic Iron Ring. The purpose was outlined by Rudyard Kipling in the following words:

"The Ritual of the Calling of an Engineer has been instituted with the simple end of directing the young engineer towards a consciousness of his[/her] profession and its significance, and indicating to the older engineer his[/her] responsibilities in receiving, welcoming and supporting the young engineers in their beginnings."

The Ritual has been copyrighted in Canada and the United States, and the Iron Ring has been registered. The Corporation of the Seven Wardens is entrusted with the responsibility of administering and maintaining the Ritual, which it does through a system of separate groups, called Camps, across Canada. There are presently 20 such Camps.

The Corporation of Seven Wardens is not a "secret society." Its rules of governance, however, do not permit any publicity about its activities and they specify that Ceremonies are not to be held in the presence of the general public.

The original seven senior engineers who met in Montreal in 1922 were, as it happens, all past presidents of the Engineering Institute of Canada. There is, however, no direct connection between the

Engineering Institute of Canada and the Corporation of the Seven Wardens.

The wearing of the Iron Ring, or the taking of the obligation, does not imply that an individual has gained legal acceptance or qualification as an engineer. This can only be granted by the provincial bodies so appointed and, as a result, it should also be mentioned that the Corporation of the Seven Wardens has no direct connection with any provincial association or order.

The obligation ceremonies for graduating students are held in cities where Camps are located, and for convenience, in some cases, on the university campus itself. Such ceremonies must not be misconstrued as being an extension of the engineering curriculum. The Iron Ring does not replace the diploma granted by the University or the School of Engineering nor is it an overt sign of having successfully passed the institution's examinations.

The purpose of the Corporation of the Seven Wardens and the Ritual is to provide an opportunity for men and women to obligate themselves to the standard of ethics and diligent practice required by those in our profession. This opportunity is available to any who wish to avail themselves to it, whether they be new graduates or senior engineers. The Ritual of the Calling of an Engineer is, of course, attended by all those who wish to be obligated, along with invited senior engineers and, when space permits, immediate family members. A complete explanation of the Ritual, its obligations and history is given to every man and woman before the ceremony so that they may decide in advance whether or not they wish to take part in the spirit intended. A few people, for one reason or another, have chosen to refrain from being obligated, and so cannot rightfully wear the Iron Ring. The Corporation of the Seven Wardens feels that this in no way detracts from their right to practise in the profession and further feels that the obligation should continue to be a matter of personal choice, taken only by those who wish to take part in the serious and sincere manner intended.

Source: J.B. Carruthers, P.Eng. Reprinted with permission from *Project Magazine: The National Magazine for Engineering Students* (April 1985): 19.

Professional Engineering Admission Requirements in the United States

GETTING THE LICENCE: KNOWING WHAT TO EXPECT CAN MAKE IT EASIER TO APPLY FOR THE P.E. LICENCE AND TAKE THE EXAMS

Applying for a professional engineer's licence is not a cut-and-dried procedure. Various combinations of educational and professional experience can fulfil the qualification criteria, and many applicants are unsure about how to document and evaluate their record to best advantage.

There are seven basic requirements, but these may vary slightly from state to state. It is therefore advisable to check with the state board for the latest rules. State board addresses can be obtained from the National Council of Engineering Examiners, Box 1686, Clemson, South Carolina 29633-1686; [Telephone:] (803) 654-6824. The seven requirements are concerned with:

- Age: The minimum age for most states is 25 for a full licence, and 21 for an engineer-in-training licence. In New York State, the minimum age to apply for a full licence is 18.

- Citizenship: Most states do not require U.S. citizenship. However, the boards recognize that inadequate proficiency in English can pose a risk to the safety and health of the public. Accordingly, they insist that a foreign applicant demonstrate proficiency in English.

- Graduation: The applicant must have a certificate of graduation from an accredited high school or the approved equivalent.

- Degree: An engineering degree is necessary from an engineering school approved by the Accreditation Board for Engineering and Technology (ABET), or the equivalent in approved practical engineering experience. Graduates of nonaccredited institutions must submit transcripts to the PE board of record. They must also have an additional number of years of board-approved experience. The board of registration will determine whether or not an applicant's experience is equivalent to an engineering degree. Copies of "Accredited Programs Leading to Degrees in Engineering" are available from ABET, 345 E. 47th Street, New York, NY 10017.

- Experience: The applicant must supply documented evidence of sufficient qualifying engineering experience. If experience has been acquired overseas, the applicant must list the names and addresses of people who can attest to that experience.

- Character: References from licensed PEs personally acquainted with the applicant attesting to his or her moral character and integrity are required.

- Examination: The candidate is required to pass both parts of the written examination administered by the state board through the National Council of Engineering Examiners (NCEE). Waivers are seldom granted.

Experience

Appropriate experience is the most important requirement for obtaining a licence. The NCEE defines qualifying experience as

> the legal minimum number of years of creative engineering work requiring the application of the engineering sciences to the investigation, planning, design, and construction of major engineering works. It is not merely the laying out of the details of design, nor the mere performance of engineering calculations, writing of specifications, or making tests. It is rather a combination of these things, plus the exercise of sound judgement, taking into account economic and social factors in arriving at decisions and giving advice to the client or employer, the soundness of which has been demonstrated in actual practice.

Professional Experience – Although it is not always easy to determine whether or not specific activities are professional, some guidelines do exist. These include:

- design, specification, and/or supervision of the construction of major equipment; preparing plant layouts; performing economic balances;

- developing processes and pilot plants;

- performing research;

- preparing technical reports, manuals, and the like;

- taking charge of broader fields of engineering;

- consulting, appraising, evaluating, and working on patent laws;

- operating major plants; product testing; technical service; technical sales;

- teaching full time at the college level or at an ABET-accredited engineering school; editing and writing technical materials.

There are in addition some specific abilities that can be considered professional and that apply to all branches of engineering. These include:

- selecting technical procedures for use in problem solving and developing new approaches and methods when necessary;

- analysing physical events in mathematical terms so as to determine the physical behaviour of materials and structures;

- converting designs into products and evaluating needs in terms of equipment and facilities;

- using the basic tools of engineering (mathematics, chemistry, physics, fluid mechanics, dynamics, thermodynamics, heat transfer, materials mechanics, and basic electricity) in the everyday performance of one's duties.

Subprofessional Experience – This type of experience usually includes:

- constructing and installing major equipment, plants, piping, and pumping systems;

- working as a shift operator in manufacturing plants or pilot plants, or as a troubleshooter;

- drafting flowsheet layouts, instrument making, and servicing;

- selling standard equipment that does not involve the use and application of engineering knowledge;

- teaching as an assistant, without full responsibilities, in an accredited school or college, or teaching nonengineering subjects in an engineering college or elsewhere;

- completing correspondence school courses in engineering; taking in-house, non-credit courses sponsored by a company; continuing-education activities;

- performing routine analyses and computations, routine tests of equipment or apparatus, or routine tests of materials;

- working in nonengineering jobs in connection with engineering projects;

- finishing work projects before completing high school or reaching age 18; working in a co-operative college course or between terms of a college course;

- performing military service involving routine duties (no research, development, or design).

When the duties of the applicant involve both engineering and nonengineering assignments, the general practice is to grant partial credit. In describing his[/her] experience, the applicant should indicate the amount of time spent on the duties performed.

Borderline Experience – Included in an engineer's daily work are certain tasks that are not considered professional in themselves but which, when performed in combination with other tasks, may constitute professional experience. There borderline cases include:

- performing calculations concerned with heat transfer, fluid flow, fluid transport, drying, etc.;

- preparing flowsheets and logic diagrams;

- designing machinery components (tanks, pumps, dryers, etc.) and systems (noise, dust, and fume control);

- installing large-scale control, production, or environmental systems and specifying plant layouts, taking into consideration economics, from raw material to finished product.

Documenting Experience – A state board's evaluation of an applicant's experience is conducted solely on the basis of his record and the testimony of references. One of the most common mistakes made in describing work experience is to resort to generalities. For example, an applicant might write, "My duties consisted of designing mechanical plants, including economic evaluations of the sites and original investment costs." This is merely a paraphrase of the definition of engineering in the statutes. Without a description of specific duties and responsibilities, the board cannot tell whether the applicant was a draftsman, designer, or print co-ordinator, or if he[/she] performed all or none of those functions. At the other extreme, an applicant may claim that he[/she] "had full responsibility for the following projects." Without amplification, this statement is meaningless, since it can apply to many upper-level administrators who have no knowledge of engineering.

Approved Experience – For an applicant's experience to be considered satisfactory by the board of registration, it must demonstrate an increasing level of quality and responsibility, and must not have been obtained in violation of the state registration law. Ideally, it should have been gained under the direct supervision of a licensed PE. It should be in the branch of engineering in which the applicant claims proficiency, and it should not have been gained in jobs of short duration with various companies.

In addition to the major disciplines of chemical, civil/sanitary/structural, electrical, and mechanical engineering, examinations are now available in agricultural, ceramic, industrial, manufacturing, nuclear, petroleum, fire protection, mining/mineral, and metallurgical engineering. Examinations in the four major disciplines are offered twice a year; information regarding the others can be obtained from NCEE.

For sales experience to be creditable, it must be demonstrated that engineering principles and knowledge were actually employed.

Responsibility – The basic criterion that the boards use to evaluate professional experience is that the applicant be "in responsible charge" of people or work. This implies a degree of competence and accountability sufficient for him[/her] to supervise or independently pursue engineering work. It is not enough for the applicant to be assigned work by a supervisor who is a licensed professional engineer. An engineer who is assigned work, but who requires a supervisor's continued attention, is not considered to be in responsible charge. The engineering graduate who started out at the drafting board must show that he[/she] has progressed to the point where he[/she] can independently apply basic principles to everyday work.

An applicant meeting the board's standard of responsibility makes decisions that could affect the health, safety, and welfare of the public. It is not sufficient to merely review the decisions made by subordinates. The applicant must be able to judge the qualifications of technical specialists and the validity and applicability of their recommendations, before those recommendations are incorporated into the work or design. Decisions made by an engineer in charge are generally at the project level or higher. These kinds of decisions include selecting the engineering alternative to be investigated and comparing those alternatives; selecting or developing design standards, methods, and materials; and developing and controlling operating and maintenance procedures.

It is not necessary for the applicant to defend decisions he[/she] has made, but only to demonstrate that he[/she] made them and possessed sufficient knowledge of the project to do so.

Evaluating Experience – A job title is not necessarily a good indicator of professional experience. An engineer engaged in flowsheet layout or flow diagrams may be doing high-grade work but, if the work is routine, he[/she] is not working at a professional level. Many engineers and draftsmen become highly proficient in the use of handbooks, standard procedures, computers, and other tools for accelerating the design process, without ever attempting to understand the principles on which those tools are based.

Essentially, the board's evaluation of an applicant's experience is based on what he[/she] actually does. Each case is evaluated on its own merits, and the emphasis is placed on the total engineering effort involved in planning, organizing, scheduling, and controlling projects. It may be helpful to keep a journal of job assignments and to file away each completed project or assignment description chronologically for future reference.

Examinations

The NCEE's uniform examinations are divided into two sections: Fundamentals of Engineering (Part A) and Principles and Practice of Engineering (Part B). Each part consists of two four-hour sessions. All states offer these 16-hour written examinations.

The Principles and Practice of Engineering examinations in all disciplines are now based on a matrix that lists clusters of tasks conducted by significant numbers of licensed engineers in each discipline, plotted against specialized technical areas in which those engineers work. The number of questions in each subject is intended to conform with the various grids in the matrix. Basing its test specifications on this matrix, NCEE has developed examinations that emphasize those areas in which licensed engineers are most active. NCEE also gives due weight to those areas in which beginning engineers need to be knowledgeable, based on the responses to a task-analysis survey of licensed engineers conducted by the council in 1981.

Fundamentals of Engineering – The morning section of this part of the examination consists of 140 multiple-choice questions graded by machine; there are five possible responses to each question, only one of which is correct. The questions are intended to establish the candidate's retention of knowledge and ability to apply that knowledge to fundamental problems. Abstruse concepts, and those that are rarely applied, are not included. The examination is offered in both SI and non-SI units. Part A is an open-book exam. Candidates may use textbooks, handbooks, bound reference books and materials, and battery-operated silent calculators. No writing tablets or unbound notes are permitted in the examination room. Sufficient paper is provided in the test books for scratchwork, and candidates are not permitted to exchange reference materials or aids during the examination.

The afternoon section of the exam is also graded by machine and consists of sets of multiple-choice problems for which there are five choices each. Of 50 questions, 15 are in engineering mechanics, 15 in mathematics, 10 in electrical circuits, and 10 in engineering economics. In addition, there are 20 questions in two other subjects, chosen by the applicant from among computer programming, electronics and electrical machinery, fluid mechanics, mechanics of materials, and thermodynamics/heat transfer.

Both the morning and the afternoon sections of the examination must be taken to receive a score. Scores are computed from the number of questions answered correctly; there is no penalty for incorrect answers. Each section carries equal weight, and scores are on a scale from zero to 100.

Principles and Practice – This part of the examination consists of a four-hour morning and a four-hour afternoon section. It was developed by practising engineers and is graded by hand by professional engineers. Its purpose is to determine whether the candidate is prepared to take charge of engineering projects. Textbook questions, proofs, derivations, and abstruse problems are avoided. Like Part A, this is an open-book exam, and the same rules apply regarding materials that can be brought into the examination room.

There are four problems in each section, and only the most general principles of engineering are required to solve them. Of primary importance is the application of good judgement to the selection and evaluation of pertinent information, and the ability to make reasonable assumptions. Merely routine numerical solutions do not justify a passing grade. Careful definition of the problem and the method of its solution are as important as the numerical answers themselves. Partial credit is given when the correct principles have been applied, even if the solution is incomplete or the final answer incorrect. For example, an applicant will receive partial credit if he[/she] ran out of time but still managed to fill in the terms of the equation with the numerical values and to indicate the unit and dimension of the final answer.

In 1983, NCEE adopted new test specifications for Part B in mechanical engineering, based on the task analysis of licensed engineers. There are now approximately eight problems in mechanical design, one in management, six in energy systems, one in control systems, three in thermal and fluid processes, and one in engineering economics. The problem in engineering economics is common to all disciplines.

Local boards of registration do not make past exams available to applicants. However, typical exams and study aids are available from NCEE headquarters.

Source: John D. Constance, P.E. (Consulting Engineer, Cliffside Park, New Jersey), *Mechanical Engineering* (December 1986): 67–69. Reproduced with permission.

Codes of Ethics for Some Engineering Societies

THE INSTITUTE OF ELECTRICAL AND ELECTRONICS ENGINEERS CODE OF ETHICS

We, the members of the IEEE, in recognition of the importance of our technologies in affecting the quality of life throughout the world, and in accepting a personal obligation to our profession, its members and the communities we serve, do hereby commit ourselves to the highest ethical and professional conduct and agree:

1. to accept responsibility in making engineering decisions consistent with the safety, health, and welfare of the public, and to disclose promptly factors that might endanger the public or the environment;

2. to avoid real or perceived conflicts of interest whenever possible, and to disclose them to affected parties when they do exist;

3. to be honest and realistic in stating claims or estimates based on available data;

4. to reject bribery in all its forms;

5. to improve the understanding of technology, its appropriate application, and potential consequences;

6. to maintain and improve our technical competence and to undertake technological tasks for others only if qualified by training or experience, or after full disclosure of pertinent limitations;

7. to seek, accept, and offer honest criticism of technical work, to acknowledge and correct errors, and to credit properly the contributions of others;

8. to treat fairly all persons regardless of such factors as race, religion, gender, disability, age, or national origin;

9. to avoid injuring others, their property, reputation, or employment by false or malicious action;

10. to assist colleagues and co-workers in their professional development and to support them in following this code of ethics.

Source: © 1990 IEEE. Reprinted with permission from The Institute of Electrical and Electronics Engineers.

AMERICAN SOCIETY OF MECHANICAL ENGINEERS CODE OF ETHICS

The Fundamental Principles

Engineers uphold and advance the integrity, honour, and dignity of the Engineering profession by:

I using their knowledge and skill for the enhancement of human welfare;

II being honest and impartial, and serving with fidelity the public, their employers, and clients, and

III striving to increase the competence of the engineering profession.

The Fundamental Canons

1. Engineers shall hold paramount the safety, health and welfare of the public in the performance of their professional duties.

2. Engineers shall perform services only in the areas of their competence.

3. Engineers shall continue their professional development throughout their careers and shall provide opportunities for the professional development of those engineers under their supervision.

4. Engineers shall act in professional matters for each employer or client as faithful agents or trustees, and shall avoid conflict of interest.

5. Engineers shall build their professional reputation on the merit of their services and shall not compete unfairly with others.

6. Engineers shall associate only with reputable persons or organizations.

7. Engineers shall issue public statements only in an objective and truthful manner.

Source: American Society of Mechanical Engineers. Reproduced with permission.

NATIONAL SOCIETY OF PROFESSIONAL ENGINEERS CODE OF ETHICS

Preamble

Engineering is an important and learned profession. The members of the profession recognize that their work has a direct and vital impact on the quality of life for all people. Accordingly, the services provided by engineers require honesty, impartiality, fairness and equity, and must be dedicated to the protection of the public health, safety and welfare. In the practice of their profession, engineers must perform under a standard of professional behaviour which requires adherence to the highest principles of ethical conduct on behalf of the public, clients, employers and the profession.

I. Fundamental Canons

Engineers, in the fulfilment of their professional duties, shall:

1. Hold paramount the safety, health and welfare of the public in the performance of their professional duties.

2. Perform services only in areas of their competence.

3. Issue public statements only in an objective and truthful manner.

4. Act in professional matters for each employer or client as faithful agents or trustees.

5. Avoid deceptive acts in the solicitation of professional employment.

II. Rules of Practice

1. Engineers shall hold paramount the safety, health and welfare of the public in the performance of their professional duties.
   a. Engineers shall at all times recognize that their primary obligation is to protect the safety, health, property and welfare of the public. If their professional judgement is overruled under circumstances where the safety, health, property or welfare of the public are endangered, they shall notify their employer or client and such other authority as may be appropriate.

    b. Engineers shall approve only those engineering documents which are safe for public health, property and welfare in conformity with accepted standards.

    c. Engineers shall not reveal facts, data or information obtained in a professional capacity without the prior consent of the client or employer except as authorized or required by law or this Code.

    d. Engineers shall not permit the use of their name or firm name nor associate in business ventures with any person or firm which they have reason to believe is engaging in fraudulent or dishonest business or professional practices.

    e. Engineers having knowledge of any alleged violation of this Code shall co-operate with the proper authorities in furnishing such information or assistance as may be required.

2. Engineers shall perform services only in the areas of their competence.

    a. Engineers shall undertake assignments only when qualified by education or experience in the specific fields involved.

    b. Engineers shall not affix their signatures to any plans or documents dealing with subject matter in which they lack competence, nor to any plan or document not prepared under their direction and control.

    c. Engineers may accept assignments and assume responsibility for co-ordination of an entire project and sign and seal the engineering documents for the entire project, provided that each technical segment is signed and sealed only by the qualified engineers who prepared the segment.

3. Engineers shall issue public statements only in an objective and truthful manner.

    a. Engineers shall be objective and truthful in professional reports, statements or testimony. They shall include all relevant and pertinent information in such reports, statements or testimony.

    b. Engineers may express publicly a professional opinion on technical subjects only when that opinion is founded upon adequate knowledge of the facts and competence in the subject matter.

    c. Engineers shall issue no statements, criticisms or arguments on technical matters which are inspired or paid for by interested parties, unless they have prefaced their comments by explicitly identifying the interested parties on whose behalf they are speaking, and by revealing the existence of any interest the engineers may have in the matters.

4. Engineers shall act in professional matters for each employer or client as faithful agents or trustees.

   a. Engineers shall disclose all known or potential conflicts of interest to their employers or clients by promptly informing them of any business association, interest, or other circumstances which could influence or appear to influence their judgement or the quality of their services.

   b. Engineers shall not accept compensation, financial or otherwise, from more than one party for services on the same project, or for services pertaining to the same project, unless the circumstances are fully disclosed to, and agreed to by, all interested parties.

   c. Engineers shall not solicit or accept financial or other valuable consideration, directly or indirectly, from contractors, their agents, or other parties in connection with work for employers or clients for which they are responsible.

   d. Engineers in public service as members, advisors or employees of a governmental body or department shall not participate in decisions with respect to professional services solicited or provided by them or their organizations in private or public engineering practice.

   e. Engineers shall not solicit or accept a professional contract from a governmental body on which a principal or officer of their organization serves as a member.

5. Engineers shall avoid deceptive acts in the solicitation of professional employment.

   a. Engineers shall not falsify or permit misrepresentation of their, or their associates', academic or professional qualifications. They shall not misrepresent or exaggerate their degree of responsibility in or for the subject matter of prior assignments. Brochures or other presentations incident to the solicitation of employment shall not misrepresent pertinent facts concerning employers, employees, associates, joint ventures or past accomplishments with the intent and purpose of enhancing their qualifications and their work.

   b. Engineers shall not offer, give, solicit or receive, either directly or indirectly, any political contribution in an amount intended to influence the award of a contract by public authority, or which may be reasonably construed by the public of having the effect or intent to influence the award of a contract. They shall not offer any gift or other valuable consideration in order to secure work. They shall not pay a commission, percentage or brokerage fee in order to secure

work except to a bona fide employee or bona fide established commercial or marketing agencies retained by them.

III. Professional Obligations

1. Engineers shall be guided in all their professional relations by
    the highest standards of integrity.
    a. Engineers shall admit and accept their own errors when
        proven wrong and refrain from distorting or altering the
        facts in an attempt to justify their decisions.
    b. Engineers shall advise their clients or employers when they
        believe a project will not be successful.
    c. Engineers shall not accept outside employment to the detri-
        ment of their regular work or interest. Before accepting any
        outside employment, they will notify their employers.
    d. Engineers shall not attempt to attract an engineer from
        another employer by false or misleading pretences.
    e. Engineers shall not actively participate in strikes, picket
        lines, or other collective coercive action.
    f. Engineers shall avoid any act tending to promote their own
        interest at the expense of the dignity and integrity of the
        profession.

2. Engineers shall at all times strive to serve the public interest.
    a. Engineers shall seek opportunities to be of constructive
        service in civic affairs and work for the advancement of the
        safety, health and well-being of their community.
    b. Engineers shall not complete, sign, or seal plans and/or
        specifications that are not of a design safe to the public
        health and welfare and in conformity with accepted engi-
        neering standards. If the client or employer insists on such
        unprofessional conduct, they shall notify the proper
        authorities and withdraw from further service on the
        project.
    c. Engineers shall endeavour to extend public knowledge and
        appreciation of engineering and its achievements and to
        protect the engineering profession from misrepresentation
        and misunderstanding.

3. Engineers shall avoid all conduct or practice which is likely to
    discredit the profession or deceive the public.
    a. Engineers shall avoid the use of statements containing a
        material misrepresentation of fact or omitting a material fact
        necessary to keep statements from being misleading or in-
        tended or likely to create an unjustified expectation; state-

ments containing prediction of future success; statements containing an opinion as to the quality of the Engineers' services; or statements intended or likely to attract clients by the use of showmanship, puffery, or self-laudation, including the use of slogans, jingles, or sensational language or format.

b. Consistent with the foregoing, Engineers may advertise for recruitment of personnel.

c. Consistent with the foregoing, Engineers may prepare articles for the lay or technical press, but such articles shall not imply credit to the author for work performed by others.

4. Engineers shall not disclose confidential information concerning the business affairs or technical processes of any present or former client or employer without his[/her] consent.

a. Engineers in the employ of others shall not without the consent of all interested parties enter promotional efforts or negotiations for work or make arrangements for other employment as a principal or to practise in connection with a specific project for which the Engineer has gained particular and specialized knowledge.

b. Engineers shall not, without the consent of all interested parties, participate in or represent an adversary interest in connection with a specific project or proceeding in which the Engineer has gained particular specialized knowledge on behalf of a former client or employer.

5. Engineers shall not be influenced in their professional duties by conflicting interests.

a. Engineers shall not accept financial or other considerations, including free engineering designs, from material or equipment suppliers for specifying their product.

b. Engineers shall not accept commissions or allowances, directly or indirectly, from contractors or other parties dealing with clients or employers of the Engineer in connection with work for which the Engineer is responsible.

6. Engineers shall uphold the principle of appropriate and adequate compensation for those engaged in engineering work.

a. Engineers shall not accept remuneration from either an employee or employment agency for giving employment.

b. Engineers, when employing other engineers, shall offer a salary according to professional qualifications.

7. Engineers shall not attempt to obtain employment or advancement or professional engagements by untruthfully criticizing other engineers, or by other improper or questionable methods.

    a. Engineers shall not request, propose, or accept a professional commission on a contingent basis under circumstances in which their professional judgement may be compromised.

    b. Engineers in salaried positions shall accept part-time engineering work only to the extent consistent with policies of the employer and in accordance with ethical consideration.

    c. Engineers shall not use equipment, supplies, laboratory, or office facilities of an employer to carry on outside private practice without consent.

8. Engineers shall not attempt to injure, maliciously or falsely, directly or indirectly, the professional reputation, prospects, practice or employment of other engineers, nor untruthfully criticize other engineers' work. Engineers who believe others are guilty of unethical or illegal practice shall present such information to the proper authority for action.

    a. Engineers in private practice shall not review the work of another engineer for the same client, except with the knowledge of such engineer, or unless the connection of such engineer with the work has been terminated.

    b. Engineers in governmental, industrial or educational employ are entitled to review and evaluate the work of other engineers when so required by their employment duties.

    c. Engineers in sales or industrial employ are entitled to make engineering comparisons of represented products with products of other suppliers.

9. Engineers shall accept responsibility for their professional activities; provided, however, that Engineers may seek indemnification for professional services arising out of their practice for other than gross negligence, where the Engineer's interests cannot otherwise be protected.

    a. Engineers shall conform with state registration laws in the practice of engineering.

    b. Engineers shall not use associations with a nonengineer, a corporation, or partnership, as a "cloak" for unethical acts, but must accept personal responsibility for all professional acts.

10. Engineers shall give credit for engineering work to those to whom credit is due, and will recognize the proprietary interests of others.

    a. Engineers shall, whenever possible, name the person or persons who may be individually responsible for designs, inventions, writings, or other accomplishments.

    b. Engineers using designs supplied by a client recognize that the designs remain the property of the client and may not be duplicated by the Engineer for others without express permission.

    c. Engineers, before undertaking work for others in connection with which the Engineer may make improvements, plans, designs, inventions, or other records which may justify copyrights or patents, should enter into a positive agreement regarding ownership.

    d. Engineers' designs, data, records, and notes referring exclusively to an employer's work are the employer's property.

11. Engineers shall co-operate in extending the effectiveness of the profession by interchanging information and experience with other engineers and students, and will endeavour to provide opportunity for the professional development and advancement of engineers under their supervision.

    a. Engineers shall encourage engineering employees' efforts to improve their education.

    b. Engineers shall encourage engineering employees to attend and present papers at professional and technical society meetings.

    c. Engineers shall urge engineering employees to become registered at the earliest possible date.

    d. Engineers shall assign a professional engineer duties of a nature to utilize full training and experience, insofar as possible, and delegate lesser functions to subprofessionals or to technicians.

    e. Engineers shall provide a prospective engineering employee with complete information on working conditions and proposed status of employment, and after employment will keep employees informed of any changes.

"By order of the United States District Court for the District of Columbia, former Section 11(0) of the NSPE Code of Ethics prohibiting competitive bidding, and all policy statements, opinions, rulings or other guidelines interpreting its scope, have been rescinded as unlawfully interfering with the legal rights of engineers, protected under the antitrust laws, to provide price information to prospective clients; accordingly, nothing contained in the NSPE Code of Ethics, policy statements, opinions, rulings or other guidelines prohibits the submission of price quotations or competitive bids for engineering services at any time or in any amount."

Statements of NSPE Executive Committee

In order to correct misunderstandings which have been indicated in some instances since the Issuance of the Supreme Court decision and the entry of the Final Judgement, it is noted that in its decision of April 25, 1978, the Supreme Court of the United States declared: "The Sherman Act does not require competitive bidding."

It is further noted that as made clear in the Supreme Court decision:

1. Engineers and firms may individually refuse to bid for engineering services.

2. Clients are not required to seek bids for engineering services.

3. Federal, state, and local laws governing procedures to procure engineering services are not affected, and remain in full force and effect.

4. State societies and local chapters are free to actively and aggressively seek legislation for professional selection and negotiation procedures by public agencies.

5. State registration board rules of professional conduct, including rules prohibiting competitive bidding for engineering services, are not affected and remain in full force and effect. State registration boards with authority to adopt rules of professional conduct may adopt rules governing procedures to obtain engineering services.

6. As noted by the Supreme Court, "nothing in the judgement prevents NSPE and its members from attempting to influence governmental action. ..."

Notes – In regard to the question of application of the Code to corporations vis-à-vis real persons, business forms or type should not negate nor influence conformance of individuals to the Code. The Code deals with professional services, which services must be performed by real persons. Real persons in turn establish and implement policies within business structures. The Code is clearly written to apply to the Engineer and it is incumbent on a member of NSPE to endeavour to live up to its provisions. This applies to all pertinent sections of the Code.

Source: NSPE Publication No. 1102, as revised January 1990. Reproduced with permission.

National Society of Professional Engineers (NSPE)

Guidelines to Professional Employment for Engineers and Scientists

Supported and Endorsed By:

American Association of Cost Engineers
American Association of Engineering Societies
American Council of Independent Laboratories
American Institute of Chemical Engineers
American Institute of Chemists
American Institute of Plant Engineers
American Microscopical Society
American Nuclear Society
American Society of Agricultural Engineers
American Society of Civil Engineers
American Society of Mechanical Engineers
American Society of Naval Engineers
Board of Certified Safety Professionals
Engineering Society of Detroit
Institute of Electrical and Electronics Engineers
Institute of Industrial Engineers
Institute of Transportation Engineers
Instrument Society of America
The Minerals, Metals & Materials Society
Mycological Society of America
National Council of Teachers of Mathematics
National Institute of Ceramic Engineers
National Society of Professional Engineers
Policy Studies Organization
Sigma Xi, The Scientific Research Society
Society for the Advancement of Material and Process Engineering

Society for Economic Botany
Society for Experimental Mechanics
Society of Fire Protection Engineers
Society of Packaging Professionals
Society of Women Engineers
System Safety Society
U.S. Metric Association

FOREWORD

The following Guidelines were developed for use by employers in evaluating their own practices, by professional employees in evaluating their own responsibilities and those of their employers, and by new graduates and other employment seekers in evaluating their prospective employment posture. They are intended to promote a satisfactory employer-employee working relationship.

Because of variations in individual circumstances and organization practices, it is inappropriate to consider evaluations on the basis of any single policy or benefit or on the basis of certain policies or benefits. Rather, attention should be focussed on evaluating the entire employment "package," including compensation (salary and other benefits) and such factors as opportunities for advancement, participation in profits, job location, and local cost of living.

These Guidelines should continue to be viewed as general goals rather than a set of minimum standards. Where practices do not fully measure up to the spirit of these Guidelines, it is recommended that employers initiate action for improvement; employers and employees should discuss situations and work together to minimize personnel problems, reduce misunderstandings, and generate greater mutual respect. Taking a constructive and flexible approach is essential to deal with individual circumstances and varying organization practices.

The Guidelines reflect the combined experience and judgement of many employers and professional employees. This Third Edition includes changes and additions incorporated to improve clarity and to reflect current practice trends and legal implications.

Questions regarding interpretation of these Guidelines should be referred to the headquarters office of any of the endorsing societies.

OBJECTIVES

The endorsing societies, with their avowed purpose to serve the public and the professions they represent, recognize that professional employees and employers must establish a climate conducive to the proper discharge of their mutual responsibilities and obligations. Prerequisites for establishing such a climate include:

1. Developing a sound relationship between the professional employee and the employer, based on ethical practices, co-operation, mutual respect, and fair treatment.

2. Recognizing employers' and employees' responsibility to safeguard the public's health, safety, and welfare.

3. Encouraging employee professionalism and creativity to support the employer's objectives.

4. Providing employees the opportunity for professional growth, based on employee initiative and employer support.

5. Recognizing that discrimination based on age, race, religion, political affiliation, or sex must not enter the professional employee-employer relationship. Employers and employees should jointly accept the concepts reflected in the "Equal Employment Opportunity" regulations.

6. Recognizing that local conditions may result in differences in the interpretation of, and deviations from, details of these Guidelines. Such differences should be discussed to gain a mutual understanding that meets the spirit of the Guidelines.

I. RECRUITMENT

Hiring should be based on a professional's competence and ability to meet specific job requirements. Employee qualifications and employment opportunities should be represented in a factual and forthright manner. An employer's employment offer and a prospective employee's acceptance of the offer should be in writing. Agreements between employers or between an employer and a professional employee that limit the opportunity for professional employees to seek other employment or, subsequent to separation, establish independent enterprises, are contrary to the spirit of these Guidelines.

Professional Employee

1. Prospective employees (applicants) should attend interviews and accept reimbursement only for those job opportunities in which they have a sincere interest. Applicants should charge the prospective employer(s) for no more than the expenses incurred for the interview(s).

2. Applicants should carefully evaluate past, present, and future confidentiality obligations regarding trade secrets and proprietary information connected with potential employment. They should not seek or accept employment on the basis of using or divulging any trade secrets or proprietary information. All applicants should be aware of their legal rights and obligations in this regard.

3. Having accepted an employment offer, applicants are ethically obligated to honour the commitment unless they are formally released after giving adequate notice of intent.

4. Applicants should not use a current employer's funds or time to seek new employment unless approved by the current employer.

Employer

1. Employers should make clear their policy on paying expenses incurred by the applicant for attending an arranged interview prior to the interview. Potential employers should reimburse all legitimate expenses incurred by an applicant when the employer requests the interview.

2. Applicants should be interviewed by the prospective employer and, if possible, by the prospective supervisor, so the applicant will understand clearly the technical and business nature of the job opportunity.

3. Ethically, prospective employers should be responsible for all representations regarding the conditions of employment.

4. Employment applications should be kept confidential. Prospective employers should seek the expressed consent from applicants before contacting a current employer.

5. Employers should minimize hiring during periods of major reductions of personnel.

6. Hiring professional employees should be planned, wherever possible, to provide satisfying careers.

7. An employer's written offer of employment should state all relevant terms, including salary, relocation assistance, expected type and duration of employment, and patent obligations. Prospective employees should be informed of any documents requiring signature.

8. Having accepted an applicant, an employer who finds it necessary to rescind an offer of employment should make equitable compensation to the applicant for any resulting monetary loss.

II. EMPLOYMENT

Terms of employment should be in accordance with applicable laws and be consistent with generally accepted ethical and professional practices. These terms should be based on mutual respect between employer and employee.

Professional Employee

1. Professional employees should accept only those assignments for which they are qualified; should diligently, competently, and honestly complete assignments; and should contribute creative, resourceful ideas to the employer while making a positive contribution toward establishing a stimulating work atmosphere and maintaining a safe working environment.

2. Professional employees should have due regard for the health, safety, and welfare of the public and fellow employees in all work for which they assume responsibility. When the technical adequacy of a process or product is unsatisfactory, professional employees should withhold approval of the plans and should state the reasons for such action. If an employee's professional judgement is ignored or overruled under circumstances where public safety, health, property or welfare is endangered, the employee should first formally notify the employer and then, if necessary, notify such other authority as may be appropriate.

3. Professional employees should sign or seal only plans or specifications they prepared, or personally reviewed and satisfactorily checked, or those prepared by employees under their direct supervision.

4. Professional employees are responsible for the effective use of time in the employer's interest and the proper care of the employer's facilities.

5. Professional employees should avoid conflicts of interest with their employers, and should immediately disclose any actual or potential conflicts.

6. Professional employees should co-operate fully with their employers in obtaining patent protection for inventions.

7. Professional employees should not divulge proprietary information.

8. Professional employees should not accept any payments or gifts of significant value, directly or indirectly, from parties dealing with a client or employer.

9. Professional employees should act in a manner consistent with their profession's code of ethics.

Employer

1. Employers should keep professional employees informed of the organization's objectives, policies, and programs.

2. Employers should provide professional employees with salary and other benefits commensurate with a professional's contribution, taking into account the employee's abilities, professional status, responsibilities, education, experience, and the potential value of the work to be performed.

3. Employers should establish a salary policy that takes into account current salary surveys for professional employees. The salary established should be commensurate with those for other professional and nonprofessional employees within the organization. The salary structure should be reviewed periodically with respect to the current economy.

4. Each individual position should be properly classified in the overall salary structure. The evaluation of each position should consider such factors as skills required for acceptable performance, the original thinking required for solving problems involved, and the accountability for actions and their consequences.

5. Duties, levels of responsibility, and the relationship of positions within the organization should be defined.

6. Employers should restrict use of titles denoting professional engineering or scientific status to those employees qualified by graduation from an appropriate baccalaureate program, or by professional licensure. [Professional licence is essential in Canada.] Appropriate titles and career patterns not denoting professional status should be developed for other categories of employees such as those holding associate degrees in engineering technology.

7. Economic advancement should be based on merit. Provision should be made for accelerated promotion or extra compensation for superior performance or special accomplishments, including generation of significant proprietary information, patents, or inventions. Compensation should be evaluated at least annually.

8. Employers should encourage [a] continuing dialogue with professional employees emphasizing the relationship between current activities and potential future activities in support of organizational goals. This may be accomplished through regular performance evaluations. Professional employees should be informed when their performance is unsatisfactory and should be advised of steps required for improvement. This information should be documented and a copy should be provided to the employee.

9. Employers should consider an equivalent ladder for compensation and advancement of professional employees whose aptitudes and interests are technical rather than managerial.

10. It is inappropriate for professional employees to use a time clock to record arrival and departure.

11. If the work demanded of professional employees regularly exceeds the normal working hours for extended periods, the employer should provide extra compensation for this continuing extra effort according to the employer's clearly stated policy.

12. Employers should also provide such benefits as pensions, life insurance, health insurance (including coverage of catastrophic illness and long-term disability), sick leave, vacations, holidays, and savings or profit-sharing plans consistent with current industrial practices. To the extent such benefits are not provided, equivalent additional compensation should be provided.

13. Employers should provide a pension plan for employees who meet minimum participation standards. Based on a full career, the minimum employer-sponsored pension benefit at retirement should be no less than 50 percent of the average best five years' salary. Employer-sponsored pension plans should provide for early participation and vesting, full portability, and survivor benefits. Consideration should be given to periodic increases in pension benefits relating to increases in the cost of living. Pension benefits should not be integrated with Social Security. The fund that supports the plan should not be terminated until all obligations to vested employees and retirees have

been met. Tax-sheltered savings plans should be available to provide incentives for individual investment for retirement.

14. Employers should provide support staff and physical facilities that promote the maximum personal effectiveness, health, and safety of their professional employees.

15. Employers should not require professional employees to accept responsibility for work not performed or supervised by those employees.

16. Employers should have established policies for reviewing all items that involve public safety, health, property, and welfare that are brought to their attention by a professional employee. The results of this review should be reported to the employee in a timely manner and opportunity should be given for further input by the employee. Employers should not penalize employees for invoking these policies.

17. Employers should defend any suits and indemnify claims against present or former individual professional employees in connection with their authorized activities on behalf of the employer.

18. There should be no employer policy that requires or forbids a professional employee to join a labour organization as a condition of continued employment.

19. Employers should clearly identify proprietary information and should release employees' inventions and other information that is not useful to the employer.

20. Employers should not discriminate on the basis of national origin, ethnicity, age, race, religion, political affiliation, or sex, with regard to compensation, job assignment, promotion, or other matters.

21. In the event of transfer, employers should allow adequate time for transferring employees to settle personal matters before moving. All normal moving costs of transfers should be paid by the employer, including household moving expenses, realtor fess, travel expenses to the new location to search for housing, and reasonable living expenses for the families until permanent housing is found. Unusual moving expense reimbursement should be settled in a discussion between the employee and employer.

III. PROFESSIONAL DEVELOPMENT

Both professional employees and their employers have responsibilities for professional development—the employee to establish goals and take the initiative to reach them and the employer to provide a supportive environment and appropriately challenging job assignments.

Professional Employee

1. Professional employees should maintain technical competence through continuing education programs and by broadening experience.

2. Professional employees should belong to, and participate in, the activities of appropriate professional societies in order to obtain additional knowledge and experience. Such participation should include preparing professional and technical papers for publication and presentation.

3. Professional employees should achieve appropriate registration and/or certification as soon as they are eligible.

4. Professional employees should participate in public service activities, including civic and political activities of a technical and nontechnical nature. If such participation interferes with the timely execution of work, employees should seek the agreement of their employers.

Employer

1. Employers should encourage their employees to maintain technical competence and broaden experience, for example, through appropriate work assignments of a rotational nature, and support of continuing education by self-improvement, courses in-house and at institutions of higher learning, and meetings and seminars on appropriate subjects. They should also encourage and support employees' membership and participation in professional society activities.

2. Employers should consider compensated leaves of absence for professional studies that will improve competence and knowledge.

3. Consistent with employer objectives, employees should be given every opportunity to publish work promptly and to present findings at technical society meetings.

4. Employers should encourage and assist professional employees to achieve registration and/or certification in their respective fields.

IV. TERMINATION

Adequate notice of termination of employment should be given by the employee or employer as appropriate.

Professional Employee

1. When professional employees decide to terminate employment, they should provide sufficient notice to enable the employer to maintain a continuity of function. When termination is initiated by the employee, no severance pay is due.

2. Upon termination, professional employees should maintain all proprietary information as confidential.

Employer

1. Employers should inform employees in a personal interview of the specific reasons for termination.

2. Additional notice of termination, or compensation in lieu thereof, should be provided by employers in consideration of responsibilities and length of service. Employees should receive notice or equivalent compensation equal to one month, plus at least one week per year of service. In the event that the employer elects notice in place of severance compensation, then the employer should allow the employee reasonable time and facilities to seek new employment.

3. Employers should make every effort to relocate terminated professional employees either within their own organizations or elsewhere. Provision should be made to continue major employee protection plans for a reasonable period following termination, and to reinstate them fully in the event of subsequent reemployment.

4. If employers seek to encourage employees to retire, employers should do so without using coercion, and solely by means of offering an adequate financial incentive.

5. Employers should seek agreement with employees on the amount of compensation to be paid for the employees' assistance in obtaining patent protection or in patent litigation on behalf of the employer.

Source: Third edition, October 31, 1989. Reproduced with permission.

Index

To the Owner of this Book:

We are interested in your reaction to *Canadian Professional Engineering Practice and Ethics* by Gordon C. Andrews and John D. Kemper. With your comments, we can improve this book in future editions. Please help us by completing this questionnaire.

1. What was your reason for using this book?
   _____preparation for professional practice examination
   _____university course
   _____college course
   _____continuing education course
   _____personal interest
   _____other (specify)

2. If you used this text for a course, what was the name of that course?

3. If you are a student, which university or college do you attend?

4. Approximately how much of the book did you use?
   _____all   _____3/4   _____1/2   _____1/4

5. Which chapters or sections were omitted from your course?

6. What is the best aspect of this book?

7. Is there anything that should be added?

8. Please add any comments or suggestions.

- -

(fold here)